BENDING HISTORY

BROOKINGS FOCUS BOOKS

Brooking Focus Books feature concise, accessible, and timely
assessment of pressing policy issues of interest to a broad audience.
Each book includes recommendations for action on the issue discussed.

Also in this series:

Fast Forward: Ethics and Politics in the Age of Global Warming
by William Antholis and Strobe Talbott

Brain Gain: Rethinking U.S. Immigration Policy
by Darrell M. West

*The Next Wave: Using Digital Technology
to Further Social and Political Innovation*
by Darrell M. West

The Pursuit of Happiness: An Economy of Well-Being
by Carol Graham

A BROOKINGS FOCUS BOOK

BENDING HISTORY

BARACK OBAMA'S FOREIGN POLICY

Martin S. Indyk
Kenneth G. Lieberthal
Michael E. O'Hanlon

BROOKINGS INSTITUTION PRESS
Washington, D.C.

Copyright © 2012
THE BROOKINGS INSTITUTION
1775 Massachusetts Avenue, N.W., Washington, D.C. 20036
www.brookings.edu

Library of Congress Cataloging-in-Publication data
Indyk, Martin.
Bending history : Barack Obama's foreign policy / Martin S. Indyk, Kenneth G. Lieberthal, Michael E. O'Hanlon.
   p.   cm. — (Brookings focus book)
Includes bibliographical references and index.
Summary: "Examines first years of the Obama presidency and effects on American foreign policy, including the U.S. relationships with China and Pakistan, war in Afghanistan and withdrawal from Iraq, movement toward Middle East peace, response to the Arab Spring, agendas involving energy, climate, and weak states, and approaches to rogue states"—Provided by publisher.
ISBN 978-0-8157-2182-6 (hardcover : alk. paper)
1. United States—Foreign relations—2009– I. Lieberthal, Kenneth.
II. O'Hanlon, Michael E. III. Title.
E907.I53 2012
973.932—dc23   2012001924

9 8 7 6 5 4 3 2 1

Printed on acid-free paper

Typeset in Sabon

Composition by Cynthia Stock
Silver Spring, Maryland

Printed by R. R. Donnelley
Harrisonburg, Virginia

CONTENTS

PREFACE

ON ANY PARTICULAR MORNING IN the last three years, Americans have awoken to a world in turmoil. Whether it is wars in the greater Middle East, a global economic crisis, natural disasters in Haiti and Japan, revolution in the Arab World, or the rise of China and India, one can feel the tectonic plates of the international order shifting.

Barack Obama was thrust into the maelstrom from his first day in office. Confronting a deep economic recession, two wars, and emerging powers demanding greater attention to their interests, Obama was determined to improve the world and, in doing so, attempt to bend history's arc in a better direction.

This is the story of what happened when a new president, representing a new generation, took his vision of a new world order and attempted to apply it in a complicated world resistant to his will.

In attempting to tell this story and analyze Obama's successes and failures, we are deeply conscious of the fact that it can only be an interim assessment. Three years into his presidency, much of Obama's foreign policy effort remains a work in progress. And whether he will have a chance to finish what he managed to start will depend on whether he wins a second term. Nevertheless, as a new presidential campaign begins, we thought it important to undertake this effort.

We wanted to give Americans our sense of how well Obama has done in protecting the nation and promoting its interests and provide a succinct framing of the foreign policy challenges facing the country and the next president, whoever he may be, at this momentous time in world affairs. We also wanted to give non-Americans our analysis of what Obama's purpose is in foreign policy, for the intentions and objectives of an American president are often difficult to discern and easily misunderstood from afar.

This book is a collaborative effort among three scholars with different areas of foreign policy expertise and experience—an expert on war-fighting and defense policy, an expert on peacemaking and the Middle East, and an expert on China and Asia. None of us worked in the Obama administration, but all of us have advised the Obama team on some aspect of its foreign policy, either formally or informally. We believe this combination of expertise and insight enables us to attempt a comprehensive analysis and assessment of Barack Obama's foreign policy.

We are grateful to many colleagues at Brookings for their advice and comments on the manuscript, notably Jeff Bader, Richard Bush, Kevin Casas-Zamora, Carol Graham, Robert Kagan, Ted Piccone, Steven Pifer, Jonathan Pollack, Evans Revere, Bruce Riedel, Strobe Talbott, and last but by no means least, Justin Vaisse. Tony Gambino provided important advice, too. Ella Chou, Ian Livingston, Dimitrios Koutsoukos, Robert O'Brien, and Mary Fox provided invaluable research and administrative support.

Numerous members of the Obama administration provided us with their insights into the often obscure workings and calculations of a complex foreign policy decisionmaking process. We promised them anonymity, but our gratitude needs to be openly acknowledged.

Special thanks go to the wonderful, energetic, and enthusiastic team at the Brookings Press under Robert Faherty's leadership, especially Starr Belsky and Diane Hammond, as well as Janet Walker, Susan Woollen, and others, and to our colleagues Gail

Chalef, Chris Kelaher, and Melissa McConnell for helping in this book's promotion.

Finally, we are very grateful to Herb Allen, David Rubenstein, and John Thornton, and the members of the Brookings Foreign Policy Program Leadership Committee for all the support that they give to our endeavors.

Despite the excellent advice we received, we of course assume full responsibility for any remaining weaknesses or mistakes.

Washington DC
February 1, 2012

CHAPTER ONE

INTRODUCTION

ON JANUARY 20, 2009, Barack Hussein Obama was sworn into office as the first black American president of the world's most powerful country. He bore the name of his Muslim father from Kenya, but his white mother and her parents—who hailed from Kansas—had raised him in Indonesia and Hawaii. He was already a historic figure on the day that he entered the Oval Office, and history has weighed heavily on his shoulders ever since. Elected president at a time when the U.S. economy was plummeting into the Great Recession, awarded the Nobel Peace Prize at the end of his first year in office while the United States was still engaged in two wars in the greater Middle East, he had ample reason to feel that his destiny was to make history. And from his first days in office, Barack Obama was intent on doing more than just being there, undertaking a breathtaking array of domestic initiatives in his first year as president.

When it came to foreign policy, he had already developed an activist vision of his role in history: he intended to refurbish America's image abroad, especially in the Muslim world; end its involvement in two wars; offer an outstretched hand to Iran; reset relations with Russia as a step toward ridding the world of nuclear weapons; develop significant cooperation with China on both regional and

1

global issues; and make peace in the Middle East. By his own account, the forty-fourth president of the United States sought nothing less than to bend history's arc in the direction of justice, and a more peaceful, stable global order.[1]

This vision manifested itself early in Obama's bid for the presidency. It appeared at first to be a campaign tactic designed to differentiate his candidacy from the record of the George W. Bush administration as well as the policies advocated by his main primary rival, Hillary Rodham Clinton. But it would subsequently become clear that Obama's vision was thought through as both good politics and ambitious foreign policy. Its leitmotif was uplifting rhetoric—"Change we can believe in," "Yes, we can," "Our time has come"—notable more for its inspirational and emotional character than policy specifics. He borrowed a phrase from early Obama supporter and former presidential candidate Bill Bradley, as he developed the idea of a "new American story."[2] And while his primary focus was on the home front, his messages about foreign policy, America's role in the world, and the demands of the twenty-first century across the globe were also central to his vision for what he would do if the American people chose him as their president.

When it came to specifics, there was a clear "anything but Bush" flavor to many of his stances, beginning with opposition to the Iraq war, a willingness to engage pragmatically with dictators, and an emphasis on enhancing the roles of diplomacy and multilateralism in American foreign policy. These three aspects of Obama's strategy—and his role in implementing it—were interwoven into what became a seamless and appealing message from a candidate whom the American people would soon vault into the White House.

For most other candidates, foreign policy amounted to a set of policy positions. For Obama, by contrast, his foreign policy vision became part of the atmosphere and attitudes that his campaign evoked. For example, in his "Yes, we can" speech given on January 8, 2008—after *losing* the New Hampshire primary to Hillary

Clinton that same evening—he wrapped his global vision into his broader message of hope: "Yes, we can, to justice and equality. Yes, we can, to opportunity and prosperity. Yes, we can heal this nation. Yes, we can repair this world. Yes, we can."[3]

Healing the nation and repairing the world were two sides of Obama's coin—a message of change, hope, and audacity unified his domestic and overseas agendas under a common banner. And his particular "American story" spoke to many around the world as well.[4] Indeed, a BBC poll taken in September 2008 in twenty-two foreign countries showed a four-to-one advantage for Obama over his general election opponent Senator John McCain.[5]

Obama sought to define himself as a progressive candidate who had consistently opposed what had become an unpopular war in Iraq. This enabled him to appeal to the party's left at the same time as he distinguished himself from those candidates, notably Hillary Clinton, who had voted for the war.[6] Among the primary contestants, he was not the most hurried in his plan to get out of Iraq; Governor Bill Richardson, Representative Dennis Kucinich, and Senator John Edwards were to his left on that point. But he was hardly the model of caution, either. His initial proposal in early 2007 would have redeployed all U.S. combat forces out of Iraq by March 2008—within fourteen months, before Obama could even become president and before the troop surge ordered by President Bush could be given a chance to work.

In a July 14, 2008, *New York Times* op-ed published just before he left for Iraq on a battlefield tour, he reiterated what had become his plan for rapidly downsizing forces there should he be elected president. While emphasizing the need to be "as careful getting out of Iraq as we were careless getting in," he spoke of redeploying the combat brigades in sixteen months—before the summer of 2010.[7]

Another signature Obama idea from the campaign emphasized his willingness to negotiate with rogue state leaders in places such as Iran and North Korea. He was careful not to sound apologetic for these countries' actions or optimistic that talks would themselves quickly produce breakthroughs. But he opened himself to the charge, amplified by Senator McCain, that he was too willing to negotiate personally with such leaders. Obama retorted that he would choose the time and place of any such meeting in a manner consistent with American interests.[8] While this did not satisfy critics who thought he was demeaning the office of the presidency and displaying naïveté about what it would take to convince the likes of Mahmoud Ahmadinejad and Hugo Chavez to change their hostile policies toward the United States, Obama was willing to run that risk. He was happy to appear the anti-Bush candidate on the matter, but it also fit his pragmatic approach. In situations of conflict in his own life, he had always sought to bridge differences through dialogue, and he believed that dealing with foreign leaders—for which he had almost no experience—should be no different.

This approach offered a pathway toward better relations with allies and neutral countries—who often perceived the Bush administration as unilateralist and too quick to use force—if not necessarily with the extremists themselves. By returning to diplomacy and countering the perception of America as prone to knee-jerk military interventionism, Obama hoped to find a way to restore U.S. standing, especially in the Arab and Muslim worlds. As he put it in a speech at the Woodrow Wilson Center in Washington in the summer of 2007:

> The lesson of the Bush years is that not talking does not work. Go down the list of countries we've ignored and see how successful that strategy has been. . . . It's time to turn the page on the diplomacy of tough talk and no action. It's time to turn the page on Washington's conventional wisdom that agreement must be reached before you meet, that talking to other countries is some kind of reward, and that Presidents can only meet with people who will tell them what they want to hear.[9]

Going beyond what he saw as repairing the damage of his predecessor's mistakes, Obama also emphasized a more fundamental reorientation of American foreign policy. In substance, Obama argued, it needed to pay more attention to the "global commons" that were threatened by terrorism, nuclear proliferation, climate change, and pandemic disease. In style, American leadership required a new spirit of humility, "of quiet confidence and sober intelligence, a spirit of care and renewed competence."[10] But there was nothing humble about his objectives, as he outlined them in his July 2008 speech in Berlin: a planet saved from famine, rising oceans, and carbon emissions; a world without nuclear weapons; and the redemption of those left behind by globalization through providing them with dignity, opportunity, and "simple justice."[11]

Clearly Obama knew that he would not end global hunger, abolish nuclear weapons, and end the threat of global warming within a four-year or even an eight-year presidency. Taking all of his goals so literally would be unrealistic and unfair. But it would be equally incorrect to dismiss his focus on such high-minded objectives as simply cynical campaign politics. While he would be quick to acknowledge that the road would be long and arduous, he nevertheless believed that he could make meaningful progress on all or most of these historic challenges on his watch—and he certainly recognized the degree to which laying out such ambitious visions could motivate followers and electrify the world at the prospect of his presidency.

Not all of Obama's words were peacelike. In addition to his toughness on Afghanistan— promising to deploy at least two more brigades there—the candidate was also firm in his statements about how to handle terrorists and insurgents who resided in Pakistan's tribal areas. In the same summer 2007 speech notable for its promise to return to diplomacy, even with extremist states, Obama declared, "If we have actionable intelligence about high-value terrorist targets [in Pakistan] and President Musharraf won't act, we will."[12]

At the time, both Senators McCain and Clinton lambasted Obama for showing his inexperience by suggesting that he would ignore Pakistani sovereignty when pursuing terrorists.[13] Commentators saw it—together with his promise to step up the war in Afghanistan—as an attempt by Obama to cover his flanks from Republican charges that he was weak on defense as he advanced his progressive foreign policy agenda. But as the killing of Osama bin Laden on May 2, 2011, in Abbottabad, Pakistan, would demonstrate, the candidate was deadly serious.

Above all, Obama was promising a major break with the past and historic change for the future. This image of a new domestic agenda, a new global architecture, and a transformed world was crucial to his ultimate success as a candidate. Just how well it would set him up to assume the reins of power once elected was, however, a different matter. There was inevitable tension between his soaring rhetoric and desire to depart fundamentally from the policies of the Bush administration, on the one hand, and his instinct for governing pragmatically, on the other. He may have recognized the tension all along, but certainly not all of his followers did. Nor did many of those in Congress and foreign capitals with whom he would have to work in pursuing his vision.

In seeking to resolve that tension, Obama's foreign policy has repeatedly manifested a combination of the realist's pragmatic approach to the world as it is and the idealist's progressive approach to a new world order that he seeks to shape. He is, in that sense, a hybrid president: a progressive pragmatist. He is progressive in his earnest efforts to promote the big-picture goals of reducing nuclear dangers, the risks of climate change, poverty, and conflict—bending history in the direction of justice, as Martin Luther King inspired him to do. At times this stance has served him well, but at other times it has generated a yawning gap between his declared objectives and the means he is prepared to use to achieve them. Obama has proven to be progressive where possible but pragmatic when necessary. Given the harsh, tumultuous reality of international politics in the twenty-first century, that necessity has won out most of the time.

FROM REMAKING THE WORLD TO REPAIRING IT

Obama's pragmatic side manifested itself early in his presidency, as the state of the U.S. economy required immediate and sustained attention. Even as Obama's victory was making history, developments of historic proportions were occurring in the nation's financial sector. For Obama, this became issue number one, not only for domestic policy but foreign policy, too, as the president-elect began to build his team and prepared to assume office.

The magnitude of the economic crisis that President Obama inherited was profound. Just before the rescue of Fannie Mae and Freddie Mac, the collapse of Lehman Brothers, and the bailout of AIG in September of 2008, the Congressional Budget Office issued a semiannual projection of the country's future economic prospects. Among its prognostications were deficits for the following three fiscal years of $438 billion, $431 billion, and $325 billion. GDP growth rates for 2008 and 2009 were expected to be low but positive—1.5 percent and 1.1 percent, respectively. That was then.

In practice, the situation deteriorated rapidly and drastically. Deficits skyrocketed, a result of the crisis and ensuing slowdown in the economy (meaning reduced tax revenues and increased countercyclical costs for programs like unemployment insurance) as well as the costs of the financial bailout and subsequent Obama stimulus package. A 4.1 percent reduction in GDP made this the steepest peak-to-trough recession in the post–World War II era. Actual deficits exceeded $1 trillion in 2009, 2010, and 2011.[14] Warren Buffett described the situation as an economic Pearl Harbor, the equivalent of a wartime situation—phrases that he had never used before in his career.[15] Real estate values declined by 10 percent before the recession even began, and then by more than 20 percent additionally before beginning an anemic and only piecemeal recovery. Household wealth fell by more than 20 percent across the nation over the course of the recession.[16] Unemployment grew to 10 percent and declined from those heights only very slowly, even well after the recession technically ended. Obama and his team—Michael Froman and Larry Summers at the White House, Timothy Geithner at Treasury, together with the Federal Reserve's Ben Bernanke and others—worked furiously to arrest the mushrooming crisis.

Arguably the most difficult steps to avert catastrophe were taken late in the Bush presidency, with the Troubled Assets Relief Program, passed by Congress early in October, as well as associated actions by the Treasury and Federal Reserve designed to bail out or otherwise sustain key financial institutions. But Obama still had to play a major role in determining which institutions to rescue (like General Motors) and taking other steps to arrest the economy's free fall and attempt to stimulate growth.

The economic collapse and threat of worse things to come had profound implications for Obama's foreign policy. The crisis, though largely—if not primarily—American made, quickly became global in its economic effects. For example, in the last quarter of 2008, global GDP declined at a 6 percent annual rate.[17] If a global collapse were to be avoided, quick collective action with other powerful economies would be essential.

The Obama administration did this, first informally and then more formally, by working with a broader group of countries than the traditional G-8 of the world's larger economies. The formal membership of that group excluded countries such as China, India, and Brazil, whose economies were still experiencing rapid growth and could help most in staving off collapse. As a result, Obama turned to the larger but nascent G-20, in which all the emerging economic powers were represented. At the April 2009 G-20 summit in London, Obama succeeded in persuading most key countries to pass major stimulus packages, with the combined effects of new policies and existing countercyclical tools totaling upwards of $5 trillion in aggregate demand.[18]

The London summit provided additional resources to the International Monetary Fund so that it could help countries in particular need with rescue packages, and undertook a coordinated tightening of rules regulating financial institutions.[19] The danger of each country acting to protect its own economy at the expense of others was largely avoided, demonstrating a surprising degree of collaborative common sense about shared interests.

Even achieving these limited goals required a great deal of effort during the administration's early months. The president personally, along with Secretary Geithner and much of the administration's foreign policy and economic teams, was frequently involved in promoting and coordinating the international bailout packages. In the early weeks, many of Obama's initial calls to foreign leaders focused on the crisis, as did his first meeting with a foreign head of government (the Japanese prime minister, in February), his first trip abroad (to Canada), and his first major overseas trip (to Europe).[20]

Despite these generally successful efforts at triage, America's role in precipitating the global crisis through the popularization of dubious financial instruments had severely tarnished the "Washington consensus" of free markets, reduced government deficits, deregulation, and trade liberalization (among other things) as the model that the rest of the world should adopt. Instead of promoting growth and global economic development through these measures, the United States was now seen by much of the rest of the world as having been responsible for precipitating a profound economic crisis, precisely because of the harm done by its purposely deregulated financial markets. This reputation posed a daunting challenge for Obama as he sought to lead the world out of a crisis that was largely American made.

It should be recognized that Obama's considerable efforts to reach out to global audiences, both on the campaign trail and once in the White House, probably softened the world's anger at the United States. A different sort of U.S. president, at that moment in history, might have become a lightning rod for the international community's frustrations. Obama deserves more credit than he commonly receives for avoiding such an atmosphere and for his imperfect but still significant steps to coordinate a global response to the financial meltdown and recession. Hardly an apologist for America's mistakes, as sometimes alleged, he was nonetheless able to strike a balanced tone. He employed a sense of humility and a consultative style to go along with his supreme self-confidence and his recognition that despite it all, America must still lead.

Nonetheless, the crisis catapulted China into the forefront of economic powers as Beijing adopted the world's largest stimulus package and helped fuel the global economic recovery. The perception of China's accelerated rise, and of America's relative decline, would complicate U.S.-China relations during the Obama presidency. And indeed, it poses a central dilemma still for American foreign policy, an issue treated in the pages that follow and in the book's concluding chapter.

With its economy in crisis, its armies stretched thin in Iraq and Afghanistan, its traditional allies seemingly in decline, emerging powers in Asia and Latin America demanding their due, and challenges to a Western-led international order being mounted by rogue leaders in Iran, Venezuela, and North Korea, the United States that Obama inherited was no longer the "überpower." America's reputation had been tarnished by the wars and the financial crisis, its hard power strained, and its pursuit of democracy and free markets abroad seriously discredited.

Barack Obama therefore had to find a way to adjust his ambitions and the expectations that he had ignited in the United States and across the globe to the grim realities of world conditions. The progressive instincts of a newly elected Democratic president—to shape the world according to an American liberal's perspective—would have to be tempered. Looking back after Obama's first year in office, observers noted how those realities had elicited pragmatism from the new president—some argued that he had been "mugged by reality." But in fact, the pragmatism had been present long before Obama's quest for the presidency.

Obama is a deeply intelligent and deliberative individual. His experience with community organizing in Chicago seems to have bred in him a belief in human progress achieved in small but determined steps. In his Nobel Peace Prize speech at the end of his first year, Obama cited President Kennedy's call to focus on "a more practical, more attainable peace, based not on a sudden revolution in human nature, but on a gradual evolution in human institutions." His task, as he defined it, was not to seek transformational change abroad but to pursue a more modest effort to "bend history in the direction of justice."

This balancing act pleased few and provided fodder for Obama's critics. His compromises were interpreted as signs of weakness, and his inability to produce clean outcomes in short order was taken as an indication of incompetence. His efforts to engage competing powers seemed to come at the cost of ignoring traditional allies. His initial reluctance to unfurl the banner of human rights and democracy in Iran, the Arab world, and China was labeled as an abandonment of values-based diplomacy. Above all, his approach caused some to question whether he had any strategy beyond responding to the situation he inherited by making pragmatic adjustments to manage adversaries and competitors abroad—so that he could focus on pressing domestic priorities.

This composite narrative on Obama's foreign policy, however, misses a significant subtext in the president's approach to the world, which is now emerging in sharper focus as it takes on greater form and substance. Put simply, Obama is more than just a reactive realist pursuing a "counterpunch" grand strategy. The forty-fourth president of the United States has it clearly in mind to pursue his higher vision: to shape a new, multilateral global order with America still in the lead, especially in matters of hard power, but sharing more responsibilities and more burdens with others where possible or necessary.

USHERING IN THE EMERGING NEW GLOBAL ORDER

The first pillar of this new order was a changed relationship with the large rising powers in Asia. This meant, Obama believed, treating China with the respect it deserved as an emerging global power while encouraging it to assume the responsibilities that went with such status. It also required an even greater focus on India as a rapidly growing economic power in China's neighborhood than under Bush and Clinton, one whose potential could, over time, rival that of China. It took a while for the president to arrange a visit to India, but his announcement there that the United States would support a permanent seat for India in the UN Security Council— however far-fetched in current circumstances—underscored the enhanced role he hoped India would play in the new global order.

This did not quite add up to a fundamental remaking of the international system for the twenty-first century; indeed, with its focus on "Russia reset" and occasional reference to the diplomatic style of the first President Bush, Obama's worldview on multilateralism was quite realist in its calculations: India would not only receive a seat at the high table, its rise could also help to balance China's power. Securing Russian cooperation would also serve the purpose of containing Iran's ambitions.

But this was intended, in other ways, as a fundamental break from the behavior of the second President Bush, especially during the latter's first term. Under President Obama, the United States would no longer attempt to dictate to others or act unilaterally, on the easy assumption that other states would simply fall in line. In making more room for other powers, Obama would also seek to recast American power. There would be a greater focus on diplomacy and engagement, including with rogue states such as Iran and North Korea; an attempt to recapture moral leadership by ending the war in Iraq and solving the Israeli-Palestinian conflict; and a necessary emphasis on rebuilding America's strength at home, the better to continue America's role abroad as the key global power.

In particular, President Obama sought Chinese and Indian partnerships in managing the "global commons" through dealing with climate change and promoting trade and development. In this context, Obama's decision to elevate the role of the G-20 over the G-8 in his first days in office was more than just a pragmatic response to urgent circumstances; it fit within his broader purpose of encouraging India and China to assume their responsibilities for the wellbeing of the planet.

Understandably, the Europeans feared being left behind by Obama's focus on emerging powers, a fear underscored by their absence from the room in Copenhagen when Obama negotiated the Copenhagen Climate Accord with the Indian, Chinese, Brazilian, and South African leaders late in 2009. Nevertheless, there was a role for them, too, in Obama's global vision. Because the Europeans shared common values and interests with the United States, Obama sought a stronger and more united Europe to serve as a like-minded partner for global action and to secure "a century that is more peaceful, more prosperous, and more just."[21] But if the United States would have to accept a diminished role as "first among equals," so too would Europe have to adjust by making room for the emerging powers to take their seats at the table, whether it be in the G-20, the International Monetary Fund, or an eventually enlarged UN Security Council.

A second pillar of Obama's framework for the emerging global order was nuclear disarmament and nonproliferation, "to seek the peace and security of a world without nuclear weapons," as the president put it in his April 2009 Prague speech.[22] Russia was a critical partner in this effort, which is why Obama sought the "reset" in relations to remove the frictions generated by Bill Clinton's and George W. Bush's efforts to expand NATO's writ to Russia's borders and by the latter's determination to deploy an antimissile defense system in Poland and the Czech Republic. The New Strategic Arms Reduction Treaty (New START) signed with Russian president Medvedev in March 2010, with its reductions in U.S. and Russian nuclear arsenals, was a manifestation of this new partnership, designed to set an example to the rest of the world. Obama also sought to promote a rules-based system in which the "world must stand together to prevent the spread of these weapons"—hence the April 2010 Nuclear Security Summit's effort to promote greater international control of nuclear material, and the 2010 Nuclear Posture Review. The latter enunciated a new doctrine covering America's nuclear arsenal: the United States declared a "no first use" nuclear commitment toward those states that would foreswear nuclear weapons.

In this new U.S.-shaped order, Obama wanted to ensure that those who broke the rules would face consequences—sanctions that "exact a real price." Hence the passage of a UN Security Council resolution in June 2010, with Russia and China voting in favor, that mandated tougher sanctions against Iran for its violations of the Non-Proliferation Treaty.

A third pillar of Obama's framework involved turning Bush's combative relations with the Muslim world into a positive partnership. This goal was particularly important to Obama's vision, in part because the United States was engaged in two wars in the Muslim world, and having public opinion there support America could help the effort. But improved relations were also needed to advance the broader effort of combating terrorism and pressuring Muslim Iran to curb its nuclear program. Obama also believed that resolving the Israeli-Palestinian conflict by establishing a Palestinian state living in peace alongside Israel would be helpful to solidifying this U.S.-Muslim rapprochement. Middle East peacemaking therefore became his priority, too.

Although Obama's vision included combating terrorism as part and parcel of this global agenda—"a common cause on behalf of our common security"—he did not embrace Bush's concept of a "global war on terror." Instead, his strategy for combating terrorism entailed a very specific focus on defeating al Qaeda in Afghanistan and Pakistan (as well as in Yemen and Somalia) and removing it as a threat to the United States and the emerging global order that Obama sought to shape.

Promoting democracy abroad also was not part of Obama's vision, evidently reflecting his strong conviction that George W. Bush's foreign policy was an unmitigated disaster for the United States. The war in Iraq, which Obama considered unjustified from the start, was ultimately justified by Bush as a way to spread democracy to the Arab world. That goal, together with Bush's insistence on elections as the vehicle for achieving it, had led to the election of Hamas in the Palestinian territories. Obama preferred supporting the more abstract notion of "universal human rights"—freedom of speech and assembly, equal rights for women, rule of law, and accountable government—rather than free elections that would end authoritarianism in the Middle East. In Cairo in June 2009, he declared that "there is no straight line to realize this promise" and that without those rights, "elections alone do not make true democracy."[23]

At the outset Obama had two more concrete foreign policy goals: preventing a global economic meltdown while also protecting America from immediate threats. Beyond that, establishing workable relations with states such as China and Russia, controlling nuclear dangers, and improving the U.S. relationship with the Muslim world were his top priorities. There were other important foreign policy goals, such as mitigating climate change, but promotion of democracy or human rights received less emphasis since Obama recognized that shaping a new global order would inevitably require partnerships with countries that did not meet democratic standards. Only a revolution in the Arab world—one that Obama did not anticipate, let alone promote—would provide him with the opportunity to allow his progressive instincts to take flight by elevating democracy promotion as a foreign policy priority. But as we shall see, such instincts were still tempered by the pragmatist's caution in places where America's interests trumped progressive values.

BUILDING THE FOREIGN POLICY TEAM

While Obama had a clear vision, he had no experience in making or executing foreign policy. To implement his grand design, the new president would have to surround himself with a talented and experienced national security team. His choice of defense secretary would be critical to his ability to end America's involvement in two wars while at the same time defeating al Qaeda and denying his political opponents the opportunity to paint him as weak on defense. His choice of secretary of state would be critical to his ability to pursue "tough diplomacy" that included engaging rogue dictators, recasting relations with established and emerging powers, and resolving conflicts in South Asia and the Middle East. Since his instincts were pragmatic, he chose nonideological, practical people to help him. And since he modeled himself on Abraham Lincoln and was hardly lacking in self-confidence, he was intrigued by the idea of putting together a "team of rivals"— strong personalities from across the political aisle and from among his Democratic primary competitors who could give him political cover even as they might offer him hard-nosed and sometimes contradictory advice.

Viewed in this context, Obama's decision to ask Robert Gates to remain as secretary of defense seems natural, even obvious. But it was unprecedented: no other secretary of defense has served two consecutive presidents from different parties, especially not after a president controversial for his global activities was succeeded by someone who had consistently and stridently criticized his predecessor for that very foreign policy.[24]

On one level, the Gates selection made sense: the nation was at war; a young, inexperienced senator from a party often criticized for its national security performance had been elected president; so why not maintain continuity with an experienced leader who was widely viewed as nonpartisan, serious, and effective? Yet Gates was a Republican, and there were highly qualified Democrats available to do the job who had been loyal to their party and to Obama.[25]

The decision by Obama was thus clearly about more than politics. Obama chose Gates on merit for his pragmatism, seriousness, focus, and good judgment, as well as his ability to help the young progressive president overcome the skepticism of the military.[26]

Gates provided a sure and steady hand during the Iraq and Afghanistan strategy reviews that occupied much of 2009 for the president. He also provided wise counsel on national security matters such as the challenge of Iran and the rise of China. And he was vocal about favoring a boost in the State Department's capabilities so that diplomacy could play a bigger and more effective role. Gates would joke that there were more people in the bands and orchestras of the U.S. armed forces than in the entire U.S. diplomatic corps. That was music to Obama's ears.

Gates also provided continuity on key matters such as defense strategy and the defense budget.[27] He focused defense resources even more intently on the wars the nation was involved in and canceled several futuristic weapons systems he did not think the nation could afford.[28] And within a couple of years, when huge deficits contributed to the rise of the Tea Party, the Republican takeover of the House in the fall 2010 elections, and growing anxiety about the country's economic future and national security fundamentals, Gates became a credible voice pushing for modest but real reductions in defense spending.[29]

Obama's choice of Hillary Rodham Clinton as secretary of state was based on a more political calculation. Obama liked her toughness, intellect, work habits, diligence, and, of course, pragmatism. But her popularity within the Democratic Party also gave this choice a powerful political logic. In one stroke it removed the divisions of a hard-fought and drawn-out primary campaign. It tamed Bill Clinton and removed Hillary from the Senate, thereby displacing from the arena two high-profile and credible potential critics.

When this advantage was combined with her natural attributes, Hillary Clinton became an obvious choice.[30]

Over time, Obama's relations with Gates and Clinton differed significantly. Gates worried little about being on precisely the same page as the president—after all, what could Obama do? Firing Gates, or even criticizing him, would undermine the cover that Gates provided. On the other hand, in the first year at least, Clinton showed a serious desire to prevent any daylight from showing between herself and the president, presumably out of concern that she would be accused of disloyalty. When the president had made up his mind, his secretary of state tended to amplify his policy in public; when he was still deliberating, she avoided staking out a public position.

By about the second year, with her popularity soaring and Obama's plummeting, the balance of dependency shifted as talk of putting her on the ticket for Obama's reelection bid emerged. Nevertheless, on the one occasion that she inadvertently showed independence—over whether Egypt's Hosni Mubarak should stay or go—the White House backgrounders pounced with alacrity, and she took care not to let it happen again, expressing her frustration instead by making clear that she intended to resign her post at the end of Obama's first term. However, as Obama entered his fourth year, his necessary preoccupation with reelection left Clinton with greater room to take the lead in foreign affairs, staking out a stronger position than Obama had expressed on democratic transitions in the Arab world and nurturing the effort to counter China in Asia.

With strong and experienced personalities at the helm at the Pentagon and State Department and a vice president with deep experience in foreign policy, Obama felt he needed a particular type of person to head up his National Security Council. He decided against selecting among his closest foreign policy advisers during the campaign—Susan Rice, Greg Craig, and James B. Steinberg. Rice and Craig had clashed too openly with the Clinton campaign for either of them to assume the job of coordinating the activities of the new secretary of state. Dispatching Rice to the UN proved to be a good solution since her combination of idealism and toughness would help greatly in generating support for Obama's global agenda. Taking Craig on as White House counsel proved less efficacious because his efforts to fulfill the president's commitment to close Guantanamo ran afoul of domestic politics. Teaming Steinberg with Clinton as deputy secretary of state generated its own complications.

Steinberg was well suited to the task of national security adviser, having served as deputy national security adviser during Bill Clinton's second term and developed a keen ability to balance strategy and politics in his development of policy options for the president. His contributions were numerous, perhaps most of all on China policy, and his departure from the State Department after two years was a loss for Obama.

The net effect, however, was that in selecting his national security team, Obama chose to sideline or subordinate those campaign advisers who might have reinforced his progressive instincts in favor of outsiders or adversaries who would promote his more pragmatic side. The choice of General James Jones as national security adviser again reflected a presidential desire to balance his own appearance of idealism, youth, and inexperience with a team of seasoned, older defense and foreign policy experts. Jones certainly had the defense credentials as a former Marine commandant and NATO supreme allied commander. But he barely knew Obama and had no exposure to his worldview; indeed, he had a closer relationship with Obama's rival for the presidency, John McCain. Jones could coordinate a complex foreign policy apparatus, but he was not known as a global strategist.

Whatever the justification, Obama's choice suggested that he wanted a coordinator, rather than a strategic thinker in the mold of Henry Kissinger or Zbigniew Brzezinski, as the person who would be the president's closest adviser on national security issues. This penchant for selecting a coordinator as national security adviser continued with Obama's choice of Tom Donilon to succeed Jones after the latter had spent only two years in the position. As Jones's deputy, Donilon had demonstrated both considerable skill at coordination and finely tuned political antennae. But his previous foreign policy experience had been limited to two years as Secretary of State Warren Christopher's chief of staff, another coordinating position; Donilon was not a likely candidate to develop the integrated strategy that would help Obama fulfill his grand design.

Obama's motive in making these two appointments only emerged over time, as it became increasingly clear that the young and inexperienced president intended to be his own overall national security strategist. Beyond Jones and Donilon, he depended on two National Security Council staffers who had worked closely with him during the campaign—Denis McDonough and Ben Rhodes; as of 2012 both are serving as Donilon's deputies. However, they had no previous foreign policy experience in the executive branch; their task was to articulate the president's foreign policy rather than design and conceptualize it.

Obama's interest in presenting to the world a team of experienced people—but not depending on them for designing overall strategy—also manifested itself in his appointment of two highfliers as special envoys for Afghanistan-Pakistan and Middle East peace. Richard Holbrooke had successfully negotiated the Dayton Accords that ended the war in Bosnia; George Mitchell had successfully negotiated the Belfast Agreement that ended the conflict in Northern Ireland. Both were well suited to deal with the most complicated diplomatic challenges on Obama's agenda. But over time it would become clear that Obama did not intend that they would actually fly high. Instead, the White House clipped their wings and denied them the backing they needed to play effective roles. Holbrooke died in office; Mitchell left quietly after two years of fruitless effort. Neither of them fulfilled his mandate.

Obama nevertheless believed strongly in a deliberative process in which he wanted to know the views of all the NSC principals and would focus their presentations by asking them penetrating questions. He would listen attentively and then retire to take his own counsel and make his decisions. Often, especially in the case of his decision to send additional troops to Afghanistan, he would take his time, leaving his lieutenants uncertain about his policy preferences for long periods. On other occasions he would take matters into his own hands when it would have been better to leave them to his principals to implement.

In these ways, Obama deliberately put a huge burden on himself for the conceptualization, articulation, and sometimes even implementation of his foreign policy. Brilliant, self-confident, ambitious, and aloof, he intended to remake the world in his own manner, developing the strategy for doing so essentially by himself, leaving to his aides the maintenance work.

AN INCOMPLETE AGENDA

Along the way, Obama the candidate with a vision became Obama the president with a pragmatic approach to implementing it. Seemingly intractable circumstances turned him from the would-be architect of a new global order into a leader focused more on repairing relationships and reacting to crises—most notably the global economic crisis. Yet it is still possible to discern him trying to shape the emerging order in the process. That is a central story of Obama's foreign policy in the first three years of his presidency. Judged by the standard of protecting American interests, it has so far worked out reasonably well; judged by the standard of fulfilling his vision of a new global order, it unsurprisingly remains very much a work in progress.

As we detail in these pages, there have been some notable foreign policy successes: rebuilding America's standing in much of the world, resetting the relationship with Russia, effectively managing relations with China, achieving a UN Security Council resolution imposing harsh sanctions on Iran, overdue but welcome free trade accords, a ratified New START treaty, the elimination of Osama bin Laden and significant weakening of al Qaeda, the withdrawal of troops from Iraq, and the beginning of downsizing U.S. troops in Afghanistan.

However, there also have been some notable setbacks: no progress on resolving the Israeli-Palestinian conflict, Iran still bent on acquiring the means to produce and deliver nuclear weapons, North Korea still developing its nuclear arsenal, deepening frictions in U.S.-Pakistan relations, Mexico awash in drugs and violence, America's standing in the Muslim world as low as in Bush's time, and major setbacks on combating climate change.

Still, along the way, one can discern some promising signs of change in the global order: some G-20 coordinated action to deal with the global economic crisis; UN Security Council Resolution 1973, which mandated the use of all necessary means to protect the people of Libya; and Russian and Chinese support for sanctions on Iran.

Part of this mixed record can be attributed to the degree of difficulty involved in reordering the world in the aftermath of a global economic crisis widely viewed as "made in America," compounded by a deeply polarized political environment in Washington that diverted the president's attention and constrained some high-priority foreign policy initiatives, such as that on climate change. Part of it can be attributed to the steep learning curve experienced by any new president, especially one so determined to keep foreign policy initiatives in his own inexperienced hands. And part of it is a function of the hand he has been dealt, where developments beyond Obama's control have rendered some of his best laid plans inoperable.

Now Obama confronts unanticipated revolutions across the Arab world that have compelled him to elevate promotion of democratic change as a priority, even as they jeopardize long-standing American diplomatic and security positions in the vital Middle East. While these crises potentially create new opportunities for Barack Obama to bend the arc of history, his presidency to date highlights both the tumultuous forces of change now coursing through the global system and the equally daunting obstacles to bending those changes to Obama's will and vision.

We have wrestled collectively with the key question of discerning an overall foreign policy strategy out of the individual elements of Obama's incrementalist approach to world affairs. The fact that other foreign policy experts have offered so many competing versions of Obama's supposed doctrine demonstrates how hard it is to pin him down. Our central thesis begins with the assessment that Obama is a competent pragmatist. He has protected American interests well given the circumstances and, whatever his mistakes along the way, prevented an economic disaster that might have been much worse. But he has not yet put his indelible stamp on foreign affairs or bent the arc of human history in the positive transformational way to which he aspires. And indeed, he has lost some of his ability to explain his bigger vision—to connect the day-to-day management of global affairs with his ambition to lead the country and world in a better direction.

To some extent his challenges in conducting foreign policy have resulted from the magnitude of the global economic crisis, as well as the domestic political difficulties of trying to lead a badly divided country at home. That said, presidents must confront the world as it is and play the hand they are dealt. Obama is not the first chief executive to face far different challenges than he expected when deciding to run for the highest office in the land and most powerful position in the world. Regardless of whether he becomes a one-term or two-term president, ultimately Obama's legacy will be shaped largely by how he is able to help the United States regain its economic strength, confidence, and international appeal. He wanted to heal a nation badly divided in partisan terms, and it appears unlikely that he will succeed anytime soon with that task. But he may still have the chance to do something even bigger and more fundamental: get the wounded nation that he leads back on its feet and able to sustain the leadership role that, even in these changing times, the world still needs it to play.

CHAPTER TWO

EMERGING POWER: CHINA

ONE OF THE KEY CHARACTERISTICS of the current international system is the increasing importance of the emerging powers. This trend, under way for several decades, has arguably become more significant in the wake of the global financial crisis. China's development has been the most consequential for the international system to date, and since January 2009, Beijing has posed the full array of issues for President Obama that the emergence of new major players entails. While Obama's handling of China has had many features unique to the particulars of the U.S.-China relationship, it also reflects his broader goal of reshaping the world order to encourage greater constructive participation in regional and global issues by the large emerging powers.

CHINA: OBAMA'S THEORY OF THE CASE

Barack Obama began his presidential political campaign with no discernible background on China. But developing a policy toward China would draw together almost all of the major issues he confronted other than actual war fighting. Not surprisingly, this policy evolved over time in terms of both expectations and implementation. During the Obama presidency, moreover, China has achieved the undisputed status of having the world's second-largest economy and second most rapidly advancing military capabilities.[1] Furthermore, China has become the world's largest consumer of energy and emitter of greenhouse gases.[2] In short, China is a central factor in major global developments, and this context has deeply affected the Obama administration's China policy. Throughout his time in office, the president has found that major international issues generally require China's active cooperation or at least neutrality if they are to be addressed effectively.

Even before his election, Obama decided that having the United States treat China as a country of consequence—not only on bilateral and regional but also on global issues—would encourage more active Chinese participation in line with the goals and basic rules of the existing global regimes (or what Robert Zoellick in 2005 dubbed as being "a responsible global stakeholder").[3] This approach assumed that China, having long chafed at what it perceived as American condescension, would welcome being invited to the high table on global issues. The elevation of China to the status of major power would, therefore, not only accurately reflect its greater impact as the global financial crisis deepened but also appeal to the country's leaders and public and elicit more cooperative behavior from Beijing.

Candidate Obama also determined that the United States should become far more engaged in Asia overall than it had been under President Bush, whose administration had, in Obama's view, maintained relatively good relations with China and Japan (at least during the Koizumi era) but neglected Asia as a whole. This was reflected in top administration officials' infrequent visits to the region and in Bush's rhetoric when in Asia, which highlighted the importance of Asia's role in the global war on terror rather than focusing on regional issues of concern to his audiences.[4]

Candidate Obama recognized that America's future would be inextricably tied up with Asia, the most important region in the world for American prosperity over the long run. He therefore determined to shore up U.S. alliances and partnerships, help develop and participate in regional institutions, and create a relationship with China that would be constructive, avoid zero-sum thinking on both sides, and deal directly and firmly with problematic Chinese behavior.[5]

THE CHINA CONTEXT

The Chinese leadership, it should be noted, saw many of these issues differently. While it never said so officially, Beijing clearly appreciated the benefits China derived from having the United States consumed by an unpopular war in the Middle East and not focused on China's immediate neighborhood.[6] The Chinese also felt very comfortable with President George W. Bush, who saw the world in hard power terms, had a record of backing his words with actions, and was determined to maintain good relations with the People's Republic of China (PRC).[7] In this connection, Beijing regarded Bush's relative neglect of Asian regional issues as all to the good, especially if American war policies and related diplomacy decreased Washington's capacity in general to impose its will around the globe.

President Obama, moreover, entered office during a period of dramatic change in China's views of the United States. China had experienced a very troubled history since the late 1800s, and the desire to get onto a steady path toward wealth and power has long been a key facet of the country's national psyche and politics. It is only in the most recent decades that China's leaders and public had begun to feel confident that they had put themselves on the necessary trajectory.[8]

Within this context the United States casts a long shadow. As a superpower America could either facilitate or enormously frustrate China's efforts to become a part of the global system while rapidly building its own economic capabilities. In the security realm, American power is the key fact of life in Asia and has particular relevance for Beijing's aspiration to bring Taiwan under its wing. In virtually every major global effort, from counterterrorism to organizing the global response to the financial crisis to combating climate change, among many other issues, America's presence has loomed large.

In addition, China looked to the United States for better understanding of how a truly modern economy functions. There was no thought of completely emulating the American economic model, especially since the South Korean and other models in Asia provided approaches far more compatible with the Chinese mindset.[9] But China closely studied and admired key aspects of the American system and moved its own reforms in directions deeply influenced by the American example. Nowhere was this truer than in the financial sector.[10]

The financial crisis that mushroomed in late 2008 and the first half of 2009 significantly affected this view of the United States. Where previously many key officials in China's financial sector and related think tanks felt that America had mastered the financial wizardry key to a modern economy, now those who had been skeptical of America's supercharged financial services surged to the fore with biting critiques of the disastrous policies underlying America's seeming success. They argued that the financial and related economic crises in the advanced industrial countries validated China's state capitalist approach to economic development.[11]

More fundamentally, the enormous cost of the crisis to the U.S. economy reduced very significantly America's power and prospects. The ensuing protracted and uncertain nature of America's economic recovery was seen as an indicator that the global leadership that the United States enjoyed in the wake of the cold war was rapidly coming to a close, to be replaced with questions about the country's future capabilities. These perceptions reflected China's awareness of Washington's seeming inability to come to grips with its own fiscal problems and the fact that those fiscal constraints would very likely ultimately force reductions in investments in the major pillars that support national power: education, science, infrastructure, new energy sources, and the military.

For China, moreover, the global financial crisis was a trade crisis, not an overall financial crisis. Exports dropped precipitously during the winter of 2008–09, reportedly costing twenty million jobs.[12] But China's banks had shied away from the risky financial instruments and entanglements that got so many others into deep trouble, and the national government called on both its treasury and the major state-owned commercial banks to flood the country with liquidity to sustain rapid growth.[13] This is a strategy that as of 2011–12 is posing serious problems to the economy, but it produced robust GDP growth from the second half of 2009 onward.[14]

Chinese like to think in terms of "comprehensive national power," which is a loose measure of economic, military, and soft power combined.[15] They had expected as of 2007 that their comprehensive national power would grow rapidly, potentially to the point that by about 2013 they might be increasingly considered a major global power. They had no doubt that the United States would maintain its dominant position in comprehensive national power for many decades to come, but discussion in the country had already begun about China's obligations and opportunities once it achieved global power status.[16]

The global financial crisis, seen in China as "made in America," profoundly altered this set of assumptions. By 2010 it had become popular conventional wisdom in China that the gap between America's and China's comprehensive national power had diminished greatly, with the momentum now clearly in China's favor.[17] In addition, by 2009 China suddenly found itself regarded across the globe as a major player of key importance to issues from economic recovery to climate change to nuclear proliferation and counterterrorism.

These very rapid shifts posed nettlesome issues for Beijing's leaders. With some elites and most ordinary Chinese believing that China was on the cusp of eclipsing the United States, the leadership experienced increasing popular pressure to assert more forcefully China's positions on issues of U.S. foreign policy. In addition, China suddenly had to confront global expectations that Beijing would assume more of the responsibilities of a major power, for example, in addressing the global economic crisis. But in Beijing there was no consensus as to how the PRC should handle such issues.

A fundamental factor shaping Beijing's responses has been deep distrust of America's overall intentions. Put simply, China is convinced that America, as the most powerful country in the world, must be working actively to slow down or disrupt China's own rise. At both popular and elite levels, this underlying perception leads the Chinese to believe that every American action is in some way part of a strategic, disciplined, highly coordinated set of initiatives to entangle China in responsibilities that will distract it from its development tasks, exacerbate its relations with its neighbors, and increase the chances of instability, which America will then seize upon to effect the collapse of the Chinese Communist Party. Numerous factors encourage the Chinese to believe in this narrative, such as the alacrity with which America supported the demonstrators in Tiananmen Square in 1989, Washington's global democracy promotion agenda, U.S. arms sales to Taiwan and maintenance of its alliance system in Asia nearly two decades after the collapse of the U.S.S.R, and a *real politik* assumption that no hegemonic power will tolerate the rise of a new major power without a fight. [18]

In this context, the Obama administration assumed office with a theory on how to elevate relations with China that in important particulars did not actually resonate well in Beijing. The global financial crisis shifted the ground during this period in dramatic ways that to an extent made the new Obama administration's overall approach even more challenging and less compelling for the cautious leadership in Beijing to embrace. In addition, some impending deadlines, especially the Copenhagen Conference scheduled for December 2009, amplified the underlying tensions in the relationship, given the difference between the new U.S. administration's perspective on China's global role and the very different views in Beijing.

Over time, the administration's policy changed. During 2010 and most of 2011, it became more active in responding to problematic actions by China in Asia, often at the entreaty of American friends and allies in the region. By the end of 2011, the administration highlighted an integrated, multipronged strategy across the region, from India to Australia to Japan, to make clear that America would play a leadership role in Asia for decades to come. Some in the administration, especially in the State Department, viewed this policy primarily in terms of constraining Chinese threats to the region. The president, however, while becoming increasingly frustrated over China's lack of responsiveness on economic and trade issues that he considered vital, nevertheless did not adopt a broader belief in an inevitable fundamental Chinese threat. He viewed a successful overall regional strategy as vital for U.S. national interests and remained convinced of the feasibility and importance of seeking win-win cooperation with China to the extent possible over the long run.

A PROMISING START

The Obama administration brought in experienced managers of U.S.-China relations, in particular Jeffrey Bader as senior director for East Asian affairs at the National Security Council and James B. Steinberg as deputy secretary of state. These individuals understood full well the classic pattern of U.S.-China relations when a new administration assumed office: an initial one to three years of serious difficulties as the new administration would seek to correct for its predecessor's seemingly overly indulgent treatment of China, followed by an improvement in ties as the new administration came to appreciate the value of earlier policies and the costs of leaving them behind. After a rocky period, each administration (except, ironically, that of the most China-friendly president, George H. W. Bush, because of the Tiananmen tragedy of 1989) moved U.S.-China relations forward beyond the bounds of its predecessor.

The Obama administration was determined not to repeat this syndrome, especially given the global economic crisis and the importance of working constructively with China to address it. Rather, the administration viewed the first year in office primarily as a time to articulate its general themes, begin to build personal ties between key officials on each side, and start to develop a transactional record on substantive issues that would provide insights into how best to manage the relationship in the future.

Three issues—recovery from the financial crisis and restructuring of the related global architecture, addressing climate change, and constraining nuclear proliferation—highlighted the potential and limitations of U.S.-China cooperation on global issues during this first year.

Managing the Financial Crisis

The financial crisis underpinned a decisive shift from the G-7 to the G-20 in addressing global financial and economic issues. The G-20 was founded in 1999 as part of the response to the Asian financial crisis.[19] It also reflected the changing global distribution of economic power, as the countries of the G-7 no longer dominated the world's economy. The Obama administration fully embraced the G-20 as part of its approach to managing the global financial crisis. G-20 summits, which normally occur annually, were held in London and Pittsburgh in 2009, in Toronto and Seoul in 2010, and in Cannes in 2011.

The Obama administration worked assiduously with the Chinese in 2009 to have the G-20 support strong national stimulus programs as a necessary tool for dealing with the financial crisis. This posture had run into serious trouble in Europe, especially in Germany.[20] Chinese support proved very welcome, and as noted above, Beijing adopted the world's largest stimulus program during 2009–10.[21] But U.S.-China cooperation at the G-20 began to fade as the world economy moved into recovery, so that by the Seoul summit in 2010, America focused its attention on China's role in producing global imbalances, and Beijing pushed back hard on America's own monetary and fiscal policies.[22] At the 2011 G-20 summit, the European debt crisis became a major focus.

President Obama made a state visit to Beijing in November 2009 to consolidate the gains made to date and lay a strong basis for future cooperation. This summit produced a joint statement in which the U.S. side recognized the concept of core interests (which China had used to highlight the inviolability of its positions on Taiwan, Tibet, and Xinjiang) and regarded China as a major power to be treated with appropriate respect. This same joint statement affirmed that "China welcomes the United States as an Asia-Pacific nation that contributes to peace, stability and prosperity in the region" and raised an issue that both sides knew to be important: the failure, after thirty years of diplomatic relations, to resolve the issue of mutual distrust over each other's long-term intentions.[23] Presidents Obama and Hu Jintao pledged to address this issue directly. Finally, both sides felt that they had established a basis for a viable agreement at Copenhagen, although the specifics of that understanding have not been made public.

The November 2009 summit was largely panned in the American media, unfairly so.[24] It sought in fact to cement the principles that would guide U.S.-China relations in the future and to calibrate those on the basis of China's more important position in the world. Given that this came toward the end of the first year of a new administration and while the world was still reeling from the perturbations of the global financial crisis, it highlighted the effectiveness of the Obama administration's early strategy toward China. But as things moved forward, this comity was not destined to last for long. .

Addressing Climate Change

One of President Obama's signature issues—climate change—moved front and center in U.S.-China relations following the president's Beijing visit. Because this issue exemplifies the mix of domestic and international considerations and the underlying element of distrust that have affected U.S.-China cooperation in many spheres, it warrants a more detailed review.

The George W. Bush administration had come into office with the president articulating support for efforts to limit carbon emissions, but it soon abandoned this posture with a vengeance as it viewed such measures as potentially harmful to U.S. economic growth. In 2001 President Bush formally withdrew from the Kyoto Protocol, which the Clinton administration had signed but not ratified. From that point on, the Bush administration shifted between grudging accommodation and outright hostility to international efforts to control greenhouse gas emissions.[25]

President Obama voiced strong support for efforts to combat climate change, and he appointed a team of officials well versed in this issue and committed to reversing the Bush administration's approach to it. In terms of working with China on the issue, the appointment of Nobel Prize winner Steven Chu, a Chinese American, as secretary of energy held out particular promise. Secretary Chu enjoyed nearly rock star celebrity in China.

By 2009 China and the United States were by far the world's two largest emitters of greenhouse gases, with many scientists arguing that Chinese emissions had surpassed those of the United States in 2008. But China had a longstanding position on climate change that it would not change easily. That position stipulated that the Kyoto Protocol's division of countries into Annex I (industrialized countries that had largely accounted for the greenhouse gas problem to date and should take the lead in reducing emissions) and Annex II (developing countries that had no such formal obligations) remains valid, and China properly should retain its position as an Annex II country. China might decide to shift from its historic business-as-usual policy and make strenuous domestic efforts to reduce greenhouse gas emissions, but it would not agree to international rules that obligated it to do so.[26]

This stance conforms to China's broader international efforts to maintain its identity as a "developing country" despite the size of its GDP, a posture that it sees as conferring both symbolic and substantive dividends. If accepted by the international community, Annex II status allows China to take significant domestic steps to develop and deploy clean energy technologies without being under international obligation to do so, thereby preserving its flexibility to change its targets or otherwise modify its actions without violating international obligations or suffering potentially embarrassing international inspections.

For President Obama, getting the Chinese to play a constructive role at Copenhagen was important to passing a U.S. domestic cap-and-trade system to limit future greenhouse gas emissions. Opponents to cap and trade argued that China would fail to adopt measures to put a price on its own carbon emissions, resulting in a comparative advantage for China in global manufacturing and increased emissions from China that would offset U.S. reductions as American firms shifted production to the PRC to reap the regulatory advantages there. The bottom line: without comparable Chinese measures, a cap-and-trade system in the United States would cost American jobs and not reduce overall global greenhouse gas emissions. President Obama wanted Chinese cooperation on this vital issue, and Special Envoy for Climate Change Todd Stern worked hard to get it.[27]

In the months leading up to the Copenhagen summit, Beijing, among other concerns, lacked confidence that the Obama energy legislation would pass the Senate. Within China those opposed to assuming international obligations at Copenhagen argued, inter alia, that the Obama administration's pressure was simply a ruse in order to trick Beijing into accepting such obligations. The Obama administration, they argued, would then back out of its own obligations, pleading inability to get the necessary legislation through the Senate. The net result would be to put China at a competitive disadvantage and retard its economic rise. President Obama's fixation on health care reform provided grist for this line of thinking in that this made it less likely that the president would expend sufficient political capital to have cap-and-trade legislation adopted by the Senate.

These two narratives effectively meant that both countries had to move together or neither would be able to take on substantial obligations at Copenhagen. We will never know what China would have done had the U.S. Senate supported cap-and-trade legislation. Given its history on the greenhouse gas emissions issue, there is every possibility that Beijing would have remained opposed to changes in the Kyoto Protocol even if the Obama administration proved successful in its energy legislation effort. And the Chinese had reason to doubt the latter: each time Xie Zhenhua, the key official in China on this issue, visited Washington, he heard very encouraging statements from the administration but then went to Capitol Hill and left convinced that the Senate would not adopt the necessary legislation.[28] His pessimism eventually proved warranted, and Xie ultimately became a key architect of wide-ranging energy policies in China that promoted non-fossil fuels and improved energy efficiency but also opposed any substantive changes to the structure of the Kyoto Protocol and China's position under it.

Thus at Copenhagen in December 2009, China assumed a position vigorously in line with its traditional position on Kyoto, a stand that the Obama administration could not possibly accept and hope to retain any possibility of passing its own cap-and-trade legislation.[29] Going into Copenhagen, the Obama administration itself had to thread a needle: it needed some indication that China would internationalize its obligations on greenhouse gas emissions but could not itself sign onto a global treaty because the Senate almost certainly would not ratify such a presidential fait accompli.[30]

In this context, the informal meeting of the leaders of China, India, South Africa, Brazil, and the United States on the final evening of the Copenhagen conference produced exactly what President Obama needed. As this meeting convened, it appeared to

Beijing that the entire conference would collapse in failure, and China would be blamed in large measure for the collapse. Beijing therefore moved somewhat away from its firm stance, and Premier Wen Jiabao agreed to language in a negotiated compromise, subsequently dubbed the Copenhagen Accord, that stopped short of assuming formal global obligations but did commit China to register its domestic targets in an international document and take some related measures that marked at least a welcome change in body language.[31] President Obama won a tactical victory here but fell far short of his initial goals regarding climate change in 2009.

Constraining Proliferation

Nuclear nonproliferation as a U.S.-China issue at the beginning of the Obama administration focused primarily on managing the threat of proliferation from the North Korean nuclear program. Although the Obama administration regarded North Korea as very important in terms of the global nuclear proliferation issue, it determined that North Korea would not be a major driver of the administration's Asian policy.

Despite a generally fraught U.S.–North Korea relationship under President Bush, an October 2007 six-party agreement created a process for North Korea to disable its plutonium program and mandated the North's full disclosure of its nuclear history.[32] The Obama administration wanted to build on this progress toward complete removal of North Korea's nuclear capabilities so that they could not be restarted or easily reconstituted. But given the history of North Korean violations of past agreements (including that of October 2007), the Obama administration was determined not to provide inducements for North Korea to return to the Six-Party Talks or to accept North Korean violations that had occurred since the October 2007 agreement. The United States sought China's cooperation in this effort.

A major problem was the Bush administration's mixed legacy. Although it had achieved the 2007 agreement, it had proved willing to engage with North Korea only after North Korea had tested a nuclear weapon. The lesson Pyongyang drew from this sequence was that demonstrating progress in its nuclear program was the key to moving the U.S. position forward. In addition, North Korea concluded that it was now fully a nuclear state and that this was a reality that the United States and all other nations needed to recognize.[33] These lessons put North Korea squarely on a different path from the one the Obama administration pursued upon assuming office.

These issues came to a head when North Korea first tested a long-range missile on April 5, 2009, and then conducted its second nuclear test on May 25, 2009.[34] The missile test succeeded in its first two stages and failed in its third—but it put North Korea closer to a capacity to strike the United States than it had ever been before. The nuclear test also showed progress and made clear that North Korea had no intention of completely giving up its nuclear weapons program.[35] The two developments together were a game changer in the Obama administration's approach to the North Korean nuclear issue.

James Steinberg and Jeffrey Bader traveled to Beijing on June 5, 2009, to discuss cooperation in responding to the North Korean tests. They first went to Japan and South Korea to develop a coordinated response. In Beijing they made clear that the Obama administration considered the North Korean nuclear test to be an inflection point in the nonproliferation issue.

Beijing was initially very critical of the North's nuclear test, and it cooperated in the development and adoption of a strong, new sanctions resolution at the UN.[36] But over the course of the summer, China began backing away from implementation of the UN sanctions, especially its financial provisions. By September 2009, Beijing apparently had decided to increase its engagement with Pyongyang. Kim Jung-il's health was uncertain due to a serious stroke he suffered in the summer of 2008, and Beijing evidently sought to improve its understanding of the politics and institutional interests there. It seems likely that the North Korean succession, already under way, contributed to this decision. During October 4–6 Premier Wen Jiabao traveled to North Korea (the highest level Chinese delegation since 2005) and brought mostly economic officials with him.[37] Defense Minister Liang Guanglie followed up with a military delegation on November 22. China clearly signaled that it sought improved ties with North Korea.[38]

North Korea's nuclear program works against China's interests on various levels. It increases tensions in Northeast Asia, produces capabilities that China does not want to see on the Korean peninsula, and renders ineffective the multilateral negotiation that China's leadership is most associated with—the Six-Party Talks. But the events in 2009 demonstrated that China is not prepared to get tough enough with North Korea to help bring that program to a halt. This, in turn, means that North Korea is and will remain a source of tension in U.S.-China relations. It also exemplifies how China limits its responsibilities on global issues (nonproliferation) in order to satisfy its immediate national concerns (maintaining North Korea's viability as a buffer state).[39]

In sum, U.S.-China relations went well during most of the Obama administration's first year, despite underlying problems; by contrast, during 2010 U.S.-China relations proved difficult despite underlying commonalities of interest.

AFTER THE HONEYMOON

It is difficult to gauge with confidence the views of China's leaders as of the end of the first year regarding the president's skills, toughness, and goals. On a trip to Beijing in late 2009, one of the authors queried ministerial level officials about the top Chinese leadership's assessment of President Obama and received responses that were surprisingly consistent: President Obama is smart and eloquent, but he places too much faith in the capacity of ideas to bend history, whereas the Chinese understand the greater importance of *real politik*. Top U.S. administration officials argue that those assessments were ill informed, as the actual dynamics of President Obama's meetings could not have left President Hu with the impression that Obama was either an idealist or someone who could be pushed around.[40] In either case, American positions in the ensuing months demonstrated both toughness and, in Chinese eyes, clear strategic intent.

This played out especially in security matters. In the realms of economics and trade, both countries remained keenly aware of their deep interdependence. Even as tensions rose over specific issues, neither side was prepared to push things too far, and both sides remained in constant, detailed communication. But in the security arena, tensions rose in the South China Sea, East China Sea, Yellow Sea, and in China's exclusive economic zone (EEZ). On global issues, China proved generally unwilling to do anything that might slow down the development of its domestic economy. It focused instead on expanding the PRC's access to energy and other natural resources and on maintaining its ability to increase exports.[41]

Further complicating things, the American political calendar is strewn with minefields for U.S.-China relations. For example, every six months the Treasury Department must announce whether it regards China (or any other country) as a currency manipulator.[42] In addition, each year the Department of Defense is obligated to publish its analysis of China's military development. Every recent president has met with the Dalai Lama in the residential quarters or public ceremonial rooms outside of the West Wing of the White House, and failure to do so would therefore be regarded as a significant concession to Beijing. And periodically pressure grows for an announcement of additional military capabilities that Taiwan will be permitted to buy.[43] Each of these issues, among others, is highly neuralgic in Beijing and requires new Chinese judgments as to how to calibrate their displeasure.

After the relative honeymoon of the first eleven months, this underlying political calendar moved to the fore. The administration through 2009 postponed action on these traditionally rancorous issues in U.S.-China bilateral relations so as to provide a period of calm during which to put the relationship firmly on track. But such measures could not remain off the docket for 2010. Indeed, the administration informed the Chinese in late 2009 that it would, in the early part of 2010, both allow Taiwan to make additional arms purchases and permit the Dalai Lama to pay a visit to the White House.[44] Beijing voiced its objections, but in the view of the American officials involved, those objections were pro forma.

As noted above, the global economic crisis affected both China's relative position in the world and its national psychology. It is not surprising that under these new circumstances, Beijing would at a minimum vent its disagreement—especially on those issues where China had long felt frustrated by U.S. actions—in a more robust way.

The U.S. initiatives in early 2010 fed the narrative in China that America was on the decline but determined to take forceful action to demonstrate its ongoing strength and to weaken China by stirring up domestic tensions there. The Obama administration's one-two punch of a Taiwan arms sale announcement in January and a presidential meeting with the Dalai Lama at the White House on February 18 elicited reactions from China that, especially on the arms sale, impressed American policymakers with their apparent stridency.[45] The Americans thought they had given Beijing fair warning, but China reacted with assertions that these steps had violated the letter and spirit of the November joint statement and that such actions were no longer acceptable, given the new basis for U.S.-China relations (translation: given America's new weakness and China's new strength).[46]

Beijing's intense reaction was exacerbated by other issues, such as Google's announcement that it would withdraw from China rather than continue to submit to China's censorship of the Google search engine.[47] U.S.-China relations took a downward spiral that quickly reached the point where Chinese leader Hu Jintao refused either to commit to participate in a nuclear summit that President

Obama announced for April or to set a date for his own summit visit to the United States in 2010 (which had been agreed to in principle during the November Beijing summit). Hu clearly felt that he could not attend the April nuclear summit as long as there was a possibility that the U.S. Treasury would declare China to be a currency manipulator—the announcement was due shortly before the summit convened.[48]

In response, the administration orchestrated a diplomatic minuet with Beijing that resulted in a press conference by Deputy Secretary of State James Steinberg in which he reiterated America's "one China" policy and welcomed China's support for the UN sanctions resolution on Iran.[49] Eleven days before the nuclear summit President Hu announced that he would attend.[50] Failure to do so would have been particularly egregious. China would have spurned a key meeting on the global nuclear proliferation issue because of pique over purely bilateral issues, thereby spotlighting Beijing's narrowly nationalist approach to the responsibilities of a major global power. This choice would have been especially apparent because Hu Jintao had already agreed to travel to Latin America directly after the April nuclear summit.

Hu's participation in the nuclear summit marked a limited turnaround in China's policies toward the United States, with some muting of the drumbeat of criticism over the Taiwan arms sale announcement and the Dalai Lama's visit. In turn, after the Chinese president left, the Treasury Department issued its semiannual report and did not cite China as a currency manipulator.[51]

SECURITY

Issues in the Asian region posed problems for U.S.-China relations throughout 2010. In both countries a confluence of events engendered growing consternation and distrust. Both leaderships wanted to keep the bilateral relationship stable and calm, but the interplay on broader issues stoked distrust and created additional ammunition for the more skeptical players on both sides. As of

2010 America's Asia policy was neither China centered nor fully integrated, but the China factor loomed increasingly large. Concerted efforts by both national leaderships put things on a more even keel at the end of 2010, but the new equilibrium differed significantly from that at the conclusion of President Obama's Beijing summit in November 2009, and by the end of 2011 it would lead to a more integrated, basically China-centered American strategy across Asia.

The United States became increasingly concerned with what it perceived to be far more assertive Chinese behavior, especially involving the People's Liberation Army (PLA). The particulars varied across the region, and in some instances local dynamics complicated matters. But the net effect was that the United States became drawn into a larger and more robust engagement throughout Asia, with many countries asking the United States to provide a counterweight that would prevent Beijing from leveraging its increased confidence and its growing regional economic strength for diplomatic and security advantage. In turn China felt it faced more assertive challenges from around the region, with the United States both instigating and supporting those changes.[52]

The reality probably lies somewhere in between. As countries in the region voiced alarm to Washington (which they did directly and at very high levels), U.S. diplomats sought to provide reassurance. Even before entering the Oval Office, Obama had determined in any case that he should increase the American presence in Asia as he reduced U.S. commitments in Iraq (and eventually Afghanistan). This included more frequent personal trips to the region by ranking U.S. officials, more robust relationships with friends and allies, more engagement in Asian regional organizations, and more attention to regional issues. The cries for greater support emanating from the region thus amounted to pushing on an open door. Moreover, in some instances, certain U.S. officials appear to have stoked fears of China in order to draw Asian countries closer to the United States.[53] They also may have promoted a more robust and integrated set of U.S. responses, but that was not the overall American policy.

Tensions between China and other major countries in Asia increased throughout 2010 and 2011. Specific issues in each locality complicated and shaped American actions. With Japan the United States was struggling to shift attitudes within the Democratic Party of Japan (DPJ) government toward a more pro-American and pro-alliance position. In South Korea, American actions were driven partly by the need to stand by an alliance partner as North Korea carried out attacks more lethal than any since the 1980s and continued to create major nuclear proliferation dilemmas. In the South China Sea, Vietnam and the Philippines increasingly tried to draw the United States into support for their maritime territorial claims, even as they themselves became very active in asserting those positions. The bottom line is that for various reasons the United States found itself bolstering ties with regional governments—even including Australia and India—that were worried about Chinese activities.[54]

Beijing, in turn, saw in these various efforts confirmation of its belief that the United States, as the number one global power, would inevitably actively seek to stifle the rise of China to protect its own privileged position. China's suspicions, rhetoric, and activities in turn have increasingly convinced key American policymakers that China's ambitions in Asia are growing, its military is playing a more central role in shaping Beijing's foreign policy, and therefore the United States must demonstrate convincingly that it is prepared to push back in order to maintain its position in the region. These views found particularly strong expression in the State Department's policy deliberations. A closed loop reinforcing strategic distrust on both sides increasingly took hold.

In addition, China revealed an impressive selective capacity to complicate the U.S. military's unfettered access to maritime areas in the Western Pacific, where American forces had long enjoyed relative freedom of movement. This unfolding reality has implications for cross–Taiwan Strait relations and Beijing's eventual ability to shape thinking in Taiwan to favor a unification agreement. It also has inspired the U.S. military to work hard to create capabilities—including a new "air-sea battle concept"—to overcome any "area denial" effort China makes.[55] Where China sees its legitimate security needs at stake, America sees potential challenges to its vital interests. Again, each side is adopting fundamental postures that inadvertently stoke the other's fears and lead to reciprocal actions that further exacerbate the concerns.

Three additional factors encouraged Beijing to adopt a more muscular regional posture. First, China's media, reflecting sentiment that the gap between China and the United States had significantly narrowed, increased pressure on the government not to back down when its longstanding positions were challenged.[56] Second, over time the ongoing tensions in U.S.-China relations strengthened the influence of hardliners in Beijing, in both domestic and foreign policy. Finally, there was the growing role of the PLA, which had increasing capabilities and deployable assets.[57]

North Korea

North Korean misbehavior during 2010 drove a wedge between Beijing and Seoul and strengthened the alliance between the United States and the Republic of Korea (ROK)—neither outcome being to Beijing's liking. Three incidents dominated the year: the March 26 sinking of the South Korean naval vessel *Cheonan,* with the loss of 46 lives; the North Korean artillery barrage on Yeonpyeong Island on November 23, which caused two civilian and two military fatalities; and North Korea's revelation that it was operating a uranium enrichment program in direct violation of its previous assurances and obligations.[58] South Korea set up an international inquiry to examine the evidence once the *Cheonan* had been salvaged from the bottom of the sea, and that investigation concluded that the ship had been sunk by a North Korean torpedo.[59] This marked the largest loss of life in any North-South military incident since the 1953 armistice. But China steadfastly refused to acknowledge North Korea's culpability, and it protected North Korea as the UN Security Council debated a response. In the final analysis, China would permit only a "presidential statement" from the UN, the mildest form of action, and even that statement, while condemning the attack and noting the results of the investigation, stopped short of explicitly ascribing blame clearly to North Korea.[60]

The *Cheonan* incident put China in a very difficult position. North Korea denied responsibility, and Beijing did not want to directly contradict Pyongyang on such a major issue. But the provocation was so egregious that it caused consternation in South Korea, and the United States took a position very strongly supportive of its ROK ally (while also quietly trying to keep Seoul from engaging in a response that might lead to military escalation). The net result was that Chinese relations with South Korea plummeted, while the United States was deeply concerned by Beijing's unwillingness to condemn the North's actions even in this uniquely horrendous situation.[61] The situation was further exacerbated when the United States and the ROK decided to hold joint military exercises in the Korean West Sea (Yellow Sea) to demonstrate their resolve, and Beijing objected that these posed a "threat to China," even though they clearly would not occur in Chinese waters or its EEZ.[62]

The November 23 artillery barrage on Yeonpyeong Island raised outrage in South Korea to a new level, especially among the younger generation. Again, China refused to condemn the North, instead calling for both sides to exercise restraint and prevent escalation without assigning blame.[63] In terms of relations among the United States, China, and the ROK, this shelling incident reinforced the trends already under way from the March attack on the *Cheonan*. Although China privately lamented to Americans that it had no control over North Korea and that it was seeking to nurture better behavior there, Beijing's bottom line amounted to running international interference for deadly provocations committed by the North.

At the same time, China was also cementing its support for the dynastic succession under way in Pyongyang, where Kim Jong-il was putting his son Kim Jong-un in place to succeed him. Such dynastic succession is unprecedented in communist countries outside North Korea, but China decided on balance to signal its support and to host the elder Kim on repeated visits to the PRC.[64] When Kim Jong-il died suddenly in December 2011, Beijing moved with alacrity to declare its support for the legitimacy of Kim Jong-un's accession.[65]

In sum, China persisted in its strategy of increasing its contacts with and international protection of North Korea, despite the problems that created for the PRC's own foreign policy. This changed only at the end of 2010—and then perhaps only temporarily—as it appears that Beijing very forcefully warned Pyongyang against committing any more provocations before Hu Jintao's January summit visit to Washington.

Japan

The accession of the DPJ to power put U.S.-Japan relations under tremendous strain, as the new government called for reviewing the U.S.-Japan alliance and indicated a desire to turn more toward Asia in general and China in particular.[66] Longstanding problems in relocating U.S. Marine Corps Air Station Futenma on Okinawa added to the tensions.[67] But by the end of 2010, the alliance was in far firmer shape, in substantial part because of Tokyo's rising concerns about Chinese actions.[68]

In the wake of the DPJ ouster of the Liberal Democratic Party, China initially sought out opportunities to improve Sino-Japanese ties and to nurture the notion of an East Asian community that the new Japanese leadership had suggested.[69] But throughout 2010 there were low-level problems in the Japan-China relationship. Some of these concerned the long-standing disagreements about development of a gas field in the East China Sea that overlaps the EEZs of both countries.[70] In late June 2010, Japan warned China not to conduct marine research in Japan's 200-nautical-mile EEZ off the northeastern Tohoku region. A Chinese marine research vessel had apparently explored Japan's EEZ without obtaining Tokyo's consent.[71]

But two key incidents especially raised the temperature in Tokyo. First, in both March and early April 2010, China sent flotillas through the Miyako Strait. Tokyo had never before confirmed such a large number of Chinese vessels near Japan, and when it dispatched ships to conduct surveillance on the second flotilla, the People's Liberation Army Navy reportedly provocatively buzzed the Japanese destroyer *Suzunami* with a Chinese Ka-28 ASW helicopter, which came within ninety meters of the Japanese warship.[72] And then in September 2010, an apparently drunk captain of a Chinese fishing vessel rammed Japanese boats sent to chase him out of waters claimed by Japan. When Japanese authorities brought the crew to shore and held the captain for trial, Beijing reacted with fury, eventually reportedly cutting off its exports of rare earth metals to Japan. Given the importance of such metals for Japanese manufacturing in electronics and clean technologies, this was viewed as a startlingly hostile move.[73] The net result of these various tensions was a further consolidation of the U.S.-Japan alliance and public opinion polls in Japan showing overwhelmingly negative views of China.[74]

South China Sea

A UN deadline of May 13, 2009, for various claimants to set out the full case for their territorial claims in the South China Sea inevitably sharpened disagreements in that region.[75] China has had long-standing, specific claims to the Spratly and Paracel Islands. In addition, the PRC has pursued claims based on the "nine-dashed line," first asserted by the Nationalist Chinese government before the 1949 revolution. This line places more than 80 percent of the entire South China Sea within China's territorial limits. While Beijing has affirmed this very extensive territorial claim, it has not sought to detail it with reference to specific land features in most of the southern half of the South China Sea.[76]

There are numerous, protracted territorial disputes regarding islands in the South China Sea, with China, Brunei, Vietnam, the Philippines, Taiwan, and Malaysia all parties to interwoven disagreements over territorial demarcations and EEZs. The sharpest conflicts are between China and Vietnam, but the Philippines and others have also seen tensions with China rise.[77] China's nine-dashed line claim has all countries in the region on edge, especially given the increased presence of the People's Liberation Army Navy and other Chinese maritime assets in the region.

The South China Sea territorial disputes embroil U.S.-China relations in several ways. The United States takes no position on the various parties' claims, but America wants such disputes to be handled without resort to the threat or use of force. It also wants the region to remain open to international commerce and, especially, to protect freedom of navigation within the South China Sea.

The first major U.S.-China clash regarding the South China Sea occurred at the Association of Southeast Asian Nations (ASEAN) Regional Forum (ARF) meeting in Hanoi on July 23, 2010.[78] Chinese foreign minister Yang Jiechi heard a chorus of complaints from members of ASEAN. Secretary of State Clinton's own brief speech made key points that were predictably very unwelcome to Chinese ears: all parties should engage in a multilateral negotiation to develop a formal code of conduct in the South China Sea, and the United States would be willing to help facilitate such a negotiation; the territorial disputes should likewise be resolved through a collaborative process; the United States supports peaceful resolution of these disputes; all maritime claims must be based on valid land-based territorial claims; and the United States has a very strong national interest in preserving freedom of navigation throughout the South China Sea.[79]

The United States failed to clarify to the Chinese that the use of the term "collaborative" to describe the process to resolve territorial disputes was not intended to mean "multilateral." The administration in fact had carefully differentiated between its support for a multilateral process to reach a code of conduct (with U.S. facilitation, if requested) and its position that it has no direct role in the settlement of territorial disputes. "Collaborative" simply conveyed that Washington felt the territorial disputes should be approached in a positive fashion by the parties concerned. Beijing, however, interpreted "collaborative" to mean "multilateral," and in that context reacted very negatively. As Beijing understood them, these positions ran counter to China's preference to avoid a formal code of conduct and to resolve territorial disputes on the basis of bilateral negotiations, with the United States playing no role in any of this.

Foreign Minister Yang Jiechi therefore reacted very harshly to Secretary Clinton's remarks, especially as it became clear that the United States had discussed its proposed positions in advance with all of the Southeast Asian countries but not with China.[80] His biting response reflected Beijing's deep chagrin that the United States was injecting itself directly into the politics of the South China Sea. His response at the ARF meeting castigated the ASEAN countries that had made points parallel to those of Secretary Clinton.[81] This exchange put the South China Sea clearly and contentiously on the U.S.-China agenda.

The fact that China's capabilities dwarf those of other claimants and its nine-dashed line territorial claim is so extensive are legitimate causes of concern. Beijing has repeatedly called for joint development of undersea resources in localities that are disputed, but the nine-dashed line claim amounts to declaring that extraordinarily large sections of the South China Sea fall into that "disputed" category.[82] Since the 2010 ARF meeting in Hanoi, the Philippines and Vietnam have worked especially hard to line up the United States in direct support of their claims.[83] Over time, though, they have also sought to reduce the tensions with China through mutual declarations of intent to resolve disputes through negotiations and to avoid incidents.[84]

The perception among key American policymakers as of 2012 is that the Chinese have become especially aggressive in the South China Sea. This has had the effect of increasing America's role in protecting the security interests of relevant friends and allies. But China views this quite differently, accusing Washington of using the continuing disputes in the South China Sea to increase anti-China sentiment in the region and provide an excuse for greater American military involvement there. The most carefully drawn analysis of developments in this region based on public sources concludes that "Chinese behavior . . . reflects the combined influence of increasing capabilities in support of long-held national objectives and responses to actions regarded [by China] as provocative or unprecedented."[85]

China's Exclusive Economic Zone

The United States and China have different interpretations of actions permitted in a country's Exclusive Economic Zone (EEZ). Beijing argues that all foreign military activities, including those involving the study of undersea currents, surveys, and intelligence gathering within an EEZ, require the consent of the littoral state.[86] It therefore insists that foreign military vessels provide prior notification before entering an EEZ. America (and most other states) has a far more permissive interpretation of activities allowed in an EEZ under the United Nations Convention on the Law of the Sea. This disagreement has produced some dangerous encounters, most notably with the U.S. ship *Impeccable* in 2009.[87] While there have been no comparably dangerous incidents since then, there is also no significant agreement on rules of the road regarding activities in EEZs, and the situation continues to cause mutual recriminations and pose the danger of a serious incident.[88]

Cybersecurity

Among the security issues affected by the growing distrust of strategic intent, cybersecurity has emerged as an additional concern of rapidly growing importance.[89] Cyberspace is a particularly difficult realm in which to make sound judgments. The attribution problem remains largely unsolved, as it is rarely possible to identify with complete certainty the ultimate source of a cyber attack.[90] The nature of the digital universe also means that cyber activity raises espionage (economic, diplomatic, and military) to an entirely new level. For example, a cyber intrusion extracted virtually the entire design information for the F-35 fighter before the first plane was built—a total of four terabytes of classified data.[91] The Indian government in 2009 discovered a massive, successful invasion of its computer system apparently from China and the loss of enormous amounts of sensitive data.[92] The International Monetary Fund reportedly has also suffered an intrusion that potentially extracted terabytes of data about confidential financial conditions and its negotiations involving many countries around the world.[93] A very substantial array of attacks on American targets are launched from servers in China, and the types of information extracted add to the suspicion that Chinese entities are responsible for many of these attacks.[94] China, in turn, feels especially vulnerable to cyber attack due to its poor defense systems in this realm and the very widespread use of pirated software, even among government agencies.[95]

The United States and China have begun to engage on the cyber issue but are far from a mature dialogue on how to move forward. In the meantime, specialists on both sides are becoming more alarmed by the supposed activities of the other, with the result that mutual strategic distrust is growing.[96]

ECONOMICS AND TRADE

China now has the second-largest economy in the world, is the largest holder of foreign exchange reserves, is the largest trading partner of almost every country in Asia, is rapidly increasing its overseas foreign direct investment, and runs a trade balance that reached as high as 9 percent of GDP in 2007 and through 2010 still remained at above 4 percent of GDP.[97] Its continued rapid

economic growth through the global downturn in 2009–10 was
key for global demand growth. With what is widely regarded as
an undervalued currency and a highly interventionist approach to
trade and investment, China presents uniquely large issues for the
global trade and investment systems.

China also is the largest foreign holder of U.S. sovereign and
agency debt as well as the largest source of American imports.[98]
American firms are major investors in the PRC, and China is
fully integrated into the supply chains of many U.S. corporations.
Indeed, the vast majority of America's 500 largest multinationals
have significant presence in the PRC. In short, China both plays
a major role in global economics and trade and is a critical trade
and investment partner of the United States and of every American
friend and ally in Asia.

The Obama administration's focal points in economic and trade
relations with China have evolved to reflect changes in both countries' economies and the world's economic situation. Overall, in
part because of the leadership of Treasury Secretary Timothy Geithner (who brought to the job substantial expertise on dealing with
China), U.S. policy has been highly engaged, pragmatic, and sensitive to China's legitimate concerns as well as to American priorities.

Bilaterally, the initial focus was on China's undervalued currency, which inhibited growth in American exports to the PRC
and arguably amounted to a de facto subsidy for Chinese exports
into the U.S. market. The currency issue has a long pedigree on
Capitol Hill, where for years members of Congress have blamed it
for America's growing trade deficit with China.[99]

During the course of 2010–11, other issues also moved to the
fore. The United States worried increasingly about the methods
China began to employ to build up its own capacity for innovation
through investments, subsidies, and leveraging technologies out
of foreign firms. These partly entailed Chinese government procurement restrictions on products that did not contain "Chinese"
innovation—a major protectionist measure.[100] China's system for

protecting intellectual property continued to look good on paper but in reality fell far short, with the judicial system providing scant protection in most instances.[101] And, increasingly, China leveraged its rapid growth and controls over access to its large domestic market to force foreign companies to trade their intellectual property for access.[102] These measures in combination made American firms increasingly pessimistic about their long-term prospects in the PRC, despite their unprecedented profits on current investments there.[103] As a consequence, U.S.-based multinational corporations—traditionally among the strongest advocates of good U.S.-China relations—gradually became more critical of Chinese practices.[104]

China had its own concerns, in particular worries about the value of the U.S. dollar (in which, arguably, China had overinvested), perceived obstacles to Chinese direct investment in the United States, continued restrictions on U.S. technology transfers to China, and the potential growth of American protectionism.[105]

None of the aforementioned issues is close to resolution, but each side has shown sensitivity to the concerns of the other. Beijing gradually began to raise the value of its currency vis-à-vis the U.S. dollar in mid-2010. At the Joint Committee on Commerce and Trade meeting in late 2010, China pledged to improve intellectual property rights protections.[106] And during his January 2011 summit meeting in Washington, President Hu Jintao promised to drop the requirements for "indigenous innovation" in Chinese government procurement policies. The United States committed to review its technology restrictions with a view to loosening them where possible, indicated its openness to Chinese overseas foreign direct investment, and reassured the Chinese overall about the seriousness with which America regarded its own fiscal problems.[107]

THE WASHINGTON SUMMIT

Both the Obama administration and China's leaders became alarmed at the overall deterioration in relations by the latter part of 2010. Once President Hu committed to a summit in Washington in mid-January 2011, both countries made a strong effort to put the relationship back on track and to lay the foundation that would hopefully provide overall stability to U.S.-China relations through 2012, when both countries would decide on their national leaders for the ensuing four to five years.

The lead-up to the summit saw important initiatives to establish the right framework for the meeting itself. The Chinese side agreed to reinstate the military-to-military relations that it had suspended at the time of the January 2010 U.S. arms sales to Taiwan, and Defense Secretary Robert Gates visited Beijing shortly before the summit itself.[108] As noted above, the Joint Committee on Commerce and Trade meeting in late 2010 went well, as did the U.S.-China Defense Consultative Talks in December.[109] Significantly, Dai Bingguo, the Chinese official most responsible for overall management of foreign policy, published a major article in early December 2010 that called for China to readjust its foreign policy away from the more muscular approach that had been so evident during most of the year.[110]

At the summit itself, both presidents articulated a practical, nononsense approach to U.S.-China relations. Both stressed the consensus that although the two countries will continue to disagree on many issues because of differences in histories, political systems, cultures, and interests, both sides should take care not to allow these specific disagreements to overwhelm the entire relationship. The spirit of the summit was very much one of establishing a pragmatic framework to maintain overall stability and manage underlying tensions.[111]

President Obama personally took great pains to ensure the success of the summit and to avoid mistakes that had marred Hu Jintao's last official visit to Washington in 2006.[112] The elaborate state dinner he hosted and his very careful attention to protocol left President Hu delighted with the results of this engagement.

The third annual U.S.-China Strategic and Economic Dialogue then convened in May 2011 and further solidified the major themes of the summit. It produced two documents, one strategic and one economic, that highlighted the areas of agreement on policies and intentions.[113] The two sides also convened a related Strategic Security Dialogue that for the first time brought uniformed military representatives into the discussions held by civilian officials. The United States had pressed for this additional forum, believing that strictly separating military and civilian talks inhibits understanding and progress on many of the politico-military issues that increasingly are at the center of U.S.-China relations. The Security Dialogue, which took up such sensitive issues as cybersecurity, is slated to be a regular feature of future Strategic and Economic Dialogue meetings.[114]

The Strategic and Economic Dialogue mechanism—led by Secretaries Clinton and Geithner on the U.S. side and by Vice Premier Wang Qishan and State Councilor Dai Bingguo on the Chinese side—exemplifies two other key aspects of relationship management in the Obama administration: a focus on developing strong personal relations among the key officials on both sides, in the hope of enhancing mutual understanding and reducing strategic distrust; and a conscious practice of holding very high level meetings several times each year because such meetings create strong incentives in both governments to move issues forward and thus increase the likelihood of a successful encounter.

As of early 2012, President Obama had met with Hu Jintao on ten occasions, in addition to talking with him frequently on the phone. Obama has also met repeatedly with Premier Wen Jiabao. In August 2011 Vice President Biden made an official trip to China to consult with Vice President Xi Jinping, who is expected to become the head of the Chinese Communist Party in the fall of 2012, and to become China's next president the following spring.[115] This trip also laid the groundwork for a return visit by Xi in early 2012, when he and his staff should have an opportunity to begin to build personal ties with President Obama and top members of the administration.

In these private meetings, the spirit has been one of explaining each side's positions in language beyond formal talking points in order to gain mutual understanding and increase mutual trust. The starting point has been mutual respect and recognition of the deep interconnected interests between China and the United States. Such closed-door discussions are intended to lessen the chances of unnecessary Sino-U.S. hostility. This quiet dimension of bilateral diplomacy seeks to manage U.S.-China tensions going forward and to set the tone and agenda for the many regular meetings between the two governments throughout the course of any given year.

THE PIVOT TO ASIA

During 2010 and 2011, the Obama administration responded concretely to various Chinese initiatives that were seen as potentially leveraging China's economic power to achieve diplomatic and security gains in the region. These responses were combined with very active bilateral U.S.-China diplomacy to keep the relationship on track and to manage expectations on both sides. The successful state visit of President Hu Jintao in Washington in January 2011 showed that this combination of firmness on defined issues and active bilateral diplomacy had left the U.S.-China relationship on reasonably solid footing.

This approach, however, concealed a more fundamental dynamic within the administration's China policy. As noted above, China policy from its earliest days was shaped especially by the close cooperation between Deputy Secretary of State James B. Steinberg and National Security Council Senior Director for East Asia Jeffrey Bader. They were the first two top officials assigned to deal with China policy in 2009, and their cooperation was very effective in maintaining the leadership of the White House not only with regard to China but concerning related, broader Asian policies.

From late 2009 onward, however, a different strand of thinking developed in the State Department, supported by some in the Pentagon, that sought a tougher stance toward China and favored warning others in the region to be wary of China's growing capabilities and to unite to constrain PRC initiatives. These two streams of policy were not in sharp conflict, but each side sought to shape overall American policy and often proffered different tactical advice as various issues arose.

While all pertinent players agreed on the overall importance of enhancing U.S. activities in Asia, strengthening American alliances there, and affirming the ongoing vital role America will play in Asia, those who advocated a tougher stance tried to cement the American position in Asia in ways that would pose a more obvious challenge to China. They placed more emphasis on democracy and human rights in the region; were more prepared to cultivate closer security ties with China's nemeses, such as Vietnam; were more willing to encourage Asian counterparts to view China's actions as posing a serious threat; and argued more strenuously that the PLA's role in shaping Chinese foreign policy was growing ominously and would, within a few years, predominate.[116]

Steinberg and Bader left the government in the spring of 2011.[117] Their departures left no China specialist at the level of bureau chief or higher in the State Department, National Security Council, or Pentagon. It appears that over the remainder of 2011, American policy toward China shifted toward the tougher line that Bader and Steinberg had convinced the president to keep in check while they were still in office.

Other factors also may have affected American policy during this time. The presidential campaign got under way in earnest, and Mitt Romney's focus on getting tough with China likely encouraged the president and his political advisors to tilt more in that direction, at least on economic and trade issues.[118] With prospective large cuts in the Pentagon budget looming, some military hawks may have seen an assertion of American leadership in Asia to counter China as a good way to help protect defense dollars.

In any case, President Obama's November 2011 trip to Honolulu, Australia, and Indonesia showcased an integrated diplomatic, military, and economic strategy that stretched from the Indian subcontinent through Northeast Asia. Such an integrated strategy is unprecedented in modern American history, and its very sweep is intended to maximize the message that America intends to play a leadership role in Asia for decades to come. The White House press backgrounder for the trip termed this a new "pivot" toward Asia, terminology that Secretary Clinton echoed repeatedly in her November travels to the region.[119]

Major Elements of the Pivot

The president's November 2011 Asia trip highlighted that U.S. policy has now taken a significant step forward in four areas.

Multilateral Organizations. Over the past decade, China invested substantial effort in the Association of Southeast Asian Nations (ASEAN), the ASEAN +3 (ASEAN, plus China, Japan, and South Korea), and the ASEAN Regional Forum (ARF). Beijing negotiated a free trade agreement with ASEAN that provided for generous "early harvest" measures in the mid-2000s; the full agreement came into effect in 2010.[120] This agreement, of course, excluded the United States. Beijing also supported the ARF as the key regional security forum, possibly because the ARF had demonstrated over many years that it would operate wholly by consensus and would not take up difficult specific issues.

Against this background, President Obama in November 2011 brought to fruition his decisions to support decisively two different multilateral organizations. On the economic and trade side, the president declared that the United States hopes to see the Trans-Pacific Partnership (TPP), still being negotiated, become a high-quality trade and investment platform that would include the major economies of the Asia-Pacific. TPP is being structured around principles America champions: transparency, protection of intellectual property, labor rights, environmental protection, and so forth (these could be considered to be "WTO plus"). President Obama noted that all who accept its principles will be welcome to join.[121] However, the TPP principles differ greatly from those that guide most Chinese actions in the economic and trade arena.[122] China is not among the initial group of countries negotiating to establish the TPP.

On the security side, the United States formally joined the East Asia Summit, and President Obama used his inaugural participation to steer this new body toward focusing on difficult, concrete security issues in the region, especially maritime security. This was not at all to Beijing's liking, but most summit participants supported the overall American approach.[123]

In short, President Obama moved boldly to shift the center of gravity among the key multilateral organizations in Asia, favoring those that include the United States and leading them to take approaches favored by Washington but neuralgic for Beijing.

Economics and Trade. The Obama administration had a disappointing record on trade issues during its first two-and-a-half years in office. But in early November 2011, it finally achieved ratification of the free trade agreement with South Korea, and it then, as noted above, turned its focus to developing the TPP as a new trade and investment platform in the Asia-Pacific.[124] This pair of initiatives has thrust Asia back into the center of U.S. economic and trade initiatives, in line with President Obama's oft-repeated assertion that there is no region as vital as Asia to America's future economic prosperity.[125] All of this came amid rising economic and trade tensions with China—tensions that are unlikely to subside during 2012, a year of electoral politics in Washington and succession politics in Beijing.[126]

Security. President Obama asserted on this trip that he will protect America's Asian security investments from any future cutbacks in overall American military spending. In Australia, moreover, he signed an agreement to allow rotational deployments of up to 2,500 marines in Darwin, the point in Australia closest to the South China

Sea.[127] Following a trip by Defense Secretary Leon Panetta to the region a few weeks earlier, the president left no doubt that the American military and overall security focus was now shifting from Iraq and Afghanistan to Asia and that this would be a long-term posture that would remain at the top of America's security priorities.[128]

Democracy. A global democracy agenda had not been a prominent part of President Obama's tenure, but this changed significantly with the 2011 Arab Spring. During his November 2011 trip, the president made clear that America will lead in Asia in promoting democracy and human rights, declaring in Australia that "other models have been tried and they have failed—fascism and communism, rule by one man and rule by committee. And they failed for the same simple reason: They ignore the ultimate source of power and legitimacy—the will of the people."[129] At his final stop, President Obama announced that Secretary Clinton would visit Burma (Myanmar) in early December—the first U.S. secretary of state in fifty years to do so—to take the temperature of new reformist stirrings there and encourage progress toward more democratic governance.[130]

The new comprehensive strategy, in short, elevated the democratic component of American diplomacy in Asia. This strikes indirectly at Hu Jintao's position that authoritarian governments can best manage the transition to modernity. In the case of Burma, moreover, Beijing had invested heavily in ensuring that China would be the dominant outside power in the country.[131] And all of this played to the Chinese concern that the ultimate goal of the United States is to bring about the collapse of the Chinese Communist Party.

Most of the specific initiatives unveiled on the president's November 2011 trip had their antecedents before 2011.[132] But since the end of 2009, the United States had only selectively pushed back when it objected to Chinese actions and focused great attention on managing the overall U.S.-China relationship. The November 2011 trip marked a significant shift. Washington remained very much focused on sustaining a constructive U.S.-China relationship.

But in late 2011, it seized the initiative in a comprehensive, strategically integrated fashion to bring the rest of its Asia policies together into a mutually reinforcing whole that explicitly seeks to affirm and sustain American leadership throughout Asia for the foreseeable future, with potentially major consequences for China.

China's Response

By all accounts China was surprised at the scope and detail of the American initiatives in November. Its initial reaction was mild, possibly in part because of private assurances received during meetings between the top leaders and also in part because of the political succession this coming year in Beijing.[133] The Hu Jintao leadership very likely wants to avoid any serious deterioration in U.S.-China relations and does not want to generate a major internal review of U.S.-China relations during this very sensitive political year.

But China, not surprisingly, is worried about these new developments. In many ways they reinforce Beijing's abiding suspicions about the United States. From the Chinese perspective, America has always been concerned primarily with protecting its own global dominance—which perforce means doing everything it can to retard or disrupt China's rise. That America lost its stride during the global financial crisis and weak recovery while China became the world's second-largest economy in 2010 has only increased Beijing's concerns about American determination to postpone the day when China will inevitably surpass the United States to become the world's most powerful country.

China's leaders retain enough respect for American strength and capabilities that President Obama's self-assured declaration of America's ongoing leadership role in Asia—backed by ample evidence of comprehensive U.S. strategic thinking and diplomacy—has at least raised the unwelcome possibility of a significantly different context for China's own regional strategy. At the same time, China's leaders do not want to fall seriously behind popular nationalist sentiment if it turns hostile over perceived American efforts to prevent a rising China from assuming its rightful place in Asia.[134] The fact that the U.S. initiatives apparently received warm vocal support from nearly all major countries at the East Asia Summit reinforced these concerns.[135]

GOING FORWARD

The Obama administration does not seek to confront China across the board. Rather, it has adopted a two-pronged approach: to reaffirm and strengthen cooperative ties with China, and to establish a strong and credible American presence across Asia, both to encourage constructive Chinese behavior and to reassure other countries in the region that they need not yield to potential Chinese regional hegemony. A key issue going forward is American credibility.

American Credibility

The new tougher line may in fact produce more constructive Chinese behavior if it convinces Beijing that America retains the capacity to lead in Asia over the long run but also is willing to encourage China's ongoing development so long as that does not produce behavior that challenges America's overall position or vital interests in the region. China's leaders are, on balance, very pragmatic. They are unlikely to "take on" the United States if America has adopted a strategically coherent Asia strategy that is widely respected and viewed as credible in the region. Credibility is crucial to achieve this outcome, and credibility requires demonstrably having the resources and capabilities to implement the overall strategy over the long run.

In this context, it is striking that on their November 2011 trips, both President Obama and Secretary Clinton talked as if Asians did not view the global financial crisis as "made in America," as if the American system of democracy has recently been performing splendidly, and as if the American military had all the resources necessary to sustain any type of deployment Washington wishes across the vast Pacific region. But it is clear to all Asians that none of this is true.

The biggest question in Asia is whether America will bounce back from its fiscal crisis and soon get onto a path to fiscal health and future strength. The political meltdown over raising the debt ceiling in August 2011 did enormous damage to America's standing in Asia because it generated such a strong negative signal on exactly this issue.[136] As the president laid out his strategy toward Asia in November, the congressional "select committee" was failing to reach even a minimal agreement to present to Congress as a whole—a failure that was announced within days of the president's return to Washington.[137]

Thus there may have been more than a little wishful thinking in the president's rhetoric during his Asia trip. While the president indicated that all countries would be welcome to join in Asian prosperity if they accepted the high standards being developed for the TPP, the reality is that at present it is China and not the United States that is the largest trade partner for every major economy in the region, and China does not operate according to these standards.[138] No Asian country appears willing to do anything to jeopardize its economic ties with the rapidly growing Chinese economy, especially at a time of weak American growth and a very uncertain economic future for Europe.

The U.S. military, moreover, faces potential total budget reductions of over a trillion dollars during the coming ten years. Most Asian governments wonder whether this will, despite current protestations, adversely affect American military capabilities—and the United States' willingness to use them—in Asia. China's military, far weaker than that of the United States, appears set to enjoy double-digit annual budget increases for years to come.[139]

In short, a tremendously important factor shaping the future American role in Asia will be how well the United States does in repairing its domestic economy and in demonstrating that, as has happened so often in U.S. history, the American system can bounce back from severe domestic problems stronger than ever thanks to the changes the crisis has forced America to adopt.

China's Trajectory

There is also the matter of China's own prospects. Whenever Beijing's international role is discussed, there is an impression that China's growth momentum is unstoppable and that its system is on very firm ground domestically. But in fact, both of these impressions are subject to question. Beijing has already made clear that it must change its development model, since the model that has proven so successful in the past few decades has run its course and is now increasingly generating outcomes that are economically unsustainable and socially destabilizing.[140] But there is sparse evidence to indicate that the very tough political decisions required to effect this change—decisions that will challenge vested interests in the corporate world and among some powerful local leaders—actually will be made during this time of succession politics in Beijing.

Indeed, the protracted nature of the succession warrants pessimism about substantial domestic reforms before about 2014, if then. Yet China's political stability cannot be ensured without the types of changes in the political system that have become very difficult—perhaps too difficult—to make. Should China experience major political unrest or a sharp disruption in its growth momentum, perceptions throughout the Asia-Pacific region will shift in ways that can easily affect attitudes toward China's role and the U.S.-China balance in the region.

CONCLUSION

The Obama administration entered office with an agenda that included returning America to a far more active engagement with Asia, improving U.S. ties with its friends and allies in the region, and moving U.S.-China relations toward greater cooperation on both traditional bilateral and regional issues and also on the major global issues, where China's impact was increasingly evident. The new administration fully accepted that China's relative importance in the world was growing rapidly and that the United States could no longer exercise the degree of global dominance that it had enjoyed for many years.

The preceding narrative cannot fully capture the range of issues and efforts included in the Obama administration's approach to managing U.S.-China relations. As China's rise has become one of the most important factors affecting global balances in many spheres, a vast array of American policies and initiatives have had to consider the role of China. Generally, the Obama administration has been appropriately attentive to this China factor across the board.

Despite enormous attention, the administration's efforts to develop more wide-ranging, cooperative relations with the PRC have yielded mixed results. To be sure, a major deterioration in relations has been avoided, but that outcome may reflect the underlying maturity of U.S.-China relations, even before President Obama took office, and the desire of the Chinese as well as the American leadership to keep disagreements within bounds. High-level meetings, such as the two summits and the annual Strategic and Economic Dialogue, created strong incentives for both countries to stabilize relations and articulate areas of cooperation in order to produce successful events. But subsequent implementation of the intentions expressed at these key meetings has typically fallen short.

The greatest overall challenge to U.S.-China relations stems from the repercussions of the global financial and economic crisis of 2008–09. This combined crisis was viewed in China as "made in America," and it did great damage to China's respect for American sagacity, even as it increased China's global stature and dimmed America's own prospects. Underlying disagreements about the real extent of these changes, moreover, created added uncertainties and tensions between the United States and China.

A major goal of the Obama administration has been to have China become a responsible player in the current global system, one that accepts the system's major goals and rules and contributes to their overall success. However, the administration learned during its first three years that China's transition to the status of global power perhaps occurred too quickly for Beijing to fully keep up. China as of 2012 may exert a global impact, but there is little to suggest that it has become a global player—one that is ready to assume the responsibilities of a major power on global issues. Rather, no consensus on what those responsibilities would entail is as yet in evidence in Beijing. Indeed, China still views itself as a developing country, whose obligation is first of all to grow its economy to the point where it can rightly call itself a middle-class society.[141]

This underlying disagreement over how much responsibility China should now be prepared to assume has in subtle but important ways increased U.S.-China tensions and distrust, as neither side feels confident that it understands the other's "real" goals and motives as both sides engage on the global playing field. Indeed, perhaps the greatest policy failure for each country has been the inability to mitigate mutual strategic distrust. Almost every American policy is seen by many in China as part of a wide-ranging, sophisticated U.S. conspiracy to complicate and retard China's rise and thus to prevent the PRC from further closing the gap in comprehensive national power with the United States.[142]

This underlying distrust played out during the Arab Spring, when China's domestic reaction was stronger than most Americans had anticipated. The leadership significantly increased internal surveillance and repression and took many measures to protect the PRC from possible contagion.[143] Beijing also watched the Obama administration's policy toward the Arab world evolve and concluded that America would quickly turn against even long-time authoritarian allies as soon as they were challenged by seemingly democratic dissidents.[144] Chinese suspicions were stoked further when someone in the United States posted messages calling on Chinese citizens to gather in public places at fixed times to show their dissatisfaction with the government, and subsequently U.S.

ambassador Jon Huntsman appeared near one of the designated spots (a MacDonald's in central Beijing) at the appointed time.[145] All this seemed to affirm China's concern that the United States ultimately seeks to overthrow the Chinese government. Furthermore, Beijing's reactive increase in domestic repression underscored the sharp differences in values that make it more difficult to establish mutual trust.

In addition, Washington has increasingly seen Beijing as a bully in Asia that seeks to use its growing military capabilities and economic position to cow its neighbors into accepting Chinese domination of the region. Washington is well aware that although almost every country in Asia wants the United States to help counterbalance the growing Chinese pressures, no country in Asia wants to have to make a stark choice between siding with either the United States or Beijing.

In this context, President Obama's bold strategic pivot to Asia, announced in November 2011, clearly sought to generate confidence in America's future leadership in this region and respect for Washington's capacity to orchestrate this very impressive diplomatic tour de force. Many in Asia have been worrying about American decline. President Obama projected American optimism, principles, determination, and leadership.

This strategy has substantial potential benefits, but its full implementation is not nearly as certain as the president and Secretary of State Clinton made it sound. Most important, the United States will not have the resources and capacity to fully meet the president's promises unless it addresses its domestic fiscal and related political problems far more effectively than recent history indicates. In addition, the Chinese may respond to this initiative in increasingly challenging ways, especially as their domestic politics intrude on international policy.

Most countries in Asia, moreover, are determined to continue to expand their economic and trade relations with China even as they worry that Beijing will leverage its growing economic clout for diplomatic and security advantage. Though they want the United States to prevent China from successfully taking advantage of others in the region, no country wants to see a tension-filled U.S.-China relationship that creates pressure for everyone else to choose sides. They would prefer to maintain equally effective relations with China and the United States and to derive benefit from both the cooperation and the competition between the two giants in the region. The notion that the United States will shape the major outcomes in the region because countries there will welcome clear American leadership ignores these more complex calculations within the region.

The United States responded to entreaties from its friends and allies in the region by taking actions primarily on the diplomatic and security side until well into 2011. This ran the immediate risk that some countries, such as Vietnam and the Philippines, might succeed in dragging the United States into their own territorial disputes with China, a situation that Washington had wisely taken care to avoid in the past. More fundamentally, this whole approach ran the longer-term risk that Asia would increasingly become a cost center for the United States (providing security is expensive) while the region would continue to serve as a growing profit center for China (due to its vast economic engagement). Given America's fiscal plight, that is not a comforting or possibly even a sustainable trajectory.

The Obama administration's rebalancing toward Asia prospectively establishes a more balanced economic, diplomatic, and security approach. The recent ratification of the U.S.-Korea Free Trade Agreement and efforts to create the TPP are very important steps in this direction. But this new integrated Asia strategy has its own risks: overreach (or at least oversell) by creating expectations that Washington will not be able to meet, feeding Chinese suspicions that may lead to a far more irascible U.S.-China relationship, and making assumptions about the goals of other Asian countries that fail to account for more complex perceptions of American prospects and strategies in the region.

It is therefore very important for American officials to keep tight control of their rhetoric as they seek to flesh out the details of the shift toward Asia to avoid unnecessary distrust and tension. The United States must also understand the critical importance of putting America's domestic house in order as a necessary condition for the success of the new Asia strategy.

And while significant progress in U.S.-China relations is unlikely during the coming year because of the succession or election taking place in each country, the United States should not neglect the need to enhance the relationship with Beijing as part of any successful regional and global strategy. No amount of success with the other countries of Asia will alone produce the regional results that President Obama seeks.

Indeed, both the United States and China must keep in mind that they are best served by adopting positions that engender a healthy respect in the other capital concerning capabilities and goals so that neither acts rashly and both have strong incentives to cooperate where possible. As of now, it is too soon to tell whether the Obama administration's November trip has laid the basis for a truly more balanced, sustainable strategy in Asia.

CHAPTER THREE

WAR, COUNTERTERRORISM, AND HOMELAND PROTECTION

DESPITE HIS DESIRE TO BEND history on a global scale, upon assuming office Barack Obama quickly realized that two critical obligations would necessarily occupy much of his time and resources: to repair the nation's economy and to manage the nation's wars. Even with a crowded domestic and foreign policy agenda, the hard-power issues of counterterrorism, Iraq, Afghanistan, and Pakistan have been particular focus points. And the hallmark of Obama's approach quickly became a blend of pragmatism and patience, especially toward Iraq and Guantanamo Bay, combined with resoluteness, especially toward Afghanistan and Pakistan.

There have been elements of ambivalence in the president's approach, as in his June 2011 decision to accelerate the drawdown of U.S. forces in Afghanistan faster than commanders in the field—or his own previous campaign plan—counseled. The ambivalence probably had its roots partly in the president's own nuanced worldview, as expressed for example in *The Audacity of Hope,* in which he states flatly about America's foreign policy history that "our record is mixed," decrying previous doctrines like manifest destiny as well as much of the cold war logic that led to, among other things, the tragedy of Vietnam. He clearly brought to office a wariness about American interventionism, reinforced by his desire to devote more resources to nation building at home. He also saw the challenges of the present era as largely revolving around failed and weak states and related problems such as terrorism. He campaigned on an agenda of focusing more on the Afghanistan conflict while ending what he viewed as the ill-advised Iraq war. And as president he has viewed Afghanistan and Pakistan as crucial countries for global security but has found it frustrating to address their problems, given the difficulty in producing irrefutable progress in either country.

As President Obama completes his third year in office and begins his reelection run, his legacy from the wars remains fundamentally uncertain. The killing of Osama bin Laden by U.S. Special Operations Forces on May 2, 2011, is his signature accomplishment, the product of a bold operation that Obama specifically ordered. That decision took considerable courage, given the risks involved and the huge political cost to him personally if the operation had failed. There were also huge risks in not authorizing the raid, or in bombing rather than sending in commandos. Bombing, for example, might have missed its target or failed to provide conclusive proof of bin Laden's death. That said, Obama managed the whole operation efficiently and competently, maintaining the necessary secrecy to keep the U.S. media and the Pakistanis unaware. The decision was both resolute and wise.

The raid plus many other successful strikes that Obama has ordered, most of them by drones in the tribal areas of Pakistan, have decimated al Qaeda's top leadership. President Obama asserts that, generally working with Pakistan, the United States had taken out more than half of al Qaeda's leadership by June 2011.[1] Secretary of Defense Leon Panetta claimed in July 2011 that the United States and its allies were "within reach of strategically defeating al Qaeda."[2] Independent terrorism experts like Peter Bergen concur with this judgment.[3] And the U.S. drone strike in Yemen that killed Anwar al-Awlaki on September 30, 2011, took out arguably the most dangerous global terrorist left alive after bin Laden was killed.

The American homeland has also been spared from another attack. To some extent this has involved luck—the Christmas Day 2009 "underwear bomber" on the flight over Detroit, the May 2010 Times Square bomber, and the 2010 printer-cartridge plot to bring down airliners over the United States all could have worked, as none was prevented by U.S. intelligence or homeland security officials. But Obama's concentrated attention on counterterrorism has been considerable, and his administration has not shied away from taking muscular steps overseas to pursue extremists rigorously and even ruthlessly.

Beyond the direct strikes against al Qaeda leaders, Obama's war-fighting policy record is more complex, with fewer clean wins and losses. Conditions in Afghanistan and Pakistan remain unsettled as of this writing, with unpredictable situations in both countries as American forces begin their drawdown from Afghanistan. U.S.-Pakistan relations are probably worse than they have ever been in the post-9/11 era, and Pakistan's internal cohesion remains problematic. The country with the world's fastest-growing nuclear arsenal could be one of the countries most threatened by internal strife and terrorism.

Even if al Qaeda is on the ropes globally, moreover, it would be unwise to consider it to be no longer a threat. There have been frequent reminders of the dangers from transnational terrorism during the Obama presidency—the Fort Hood army shootings in November 2009 and, as noted, the Christmas Day attempted airliner bombing the next month, to say nothing of plots against the New York City subway by al Qaeda associates and the attempted Times Square bombing by Pakistani Taliban affiliates during 2009–10. Indeed, even after the bin Laden raid, John Brennan, the president's assistant for homeland security and counterterrorism, called attention to threats posed by al Qaeda and associates to the U.S. homeland, including from homegrown or domestic-based terrorists.[4]

Iraq also remains in flux. President Obama's decision to withdraw all U.S. military units by the end of 2011 suggests that he was unable to persuade Iraqis of the need for a sustained partnership with the United States—though it is also possible that the president did not really want American forces to stay in substantial numbers and actually welcomed the Iraqi decision to deny U.S. troops the legal immunities that would have rightly been required for them to stay. The total withdrawal of American troops risks reinforcing a dynamic that could generate a renewal of sectarian warfare. That said, Obama is largely implementing George Bush's plan for withdrawing forces: he did double the duration of the gradual withdrawal relative to his initial campaign promises, and there is a limit to how hard Washington can productively pressure the government in Baghdad on such a politically sensitive issue.

At least Obama has limited the downsides of the wars for the country. There has been no new major attack on the United States—though there were some smaller acts of terrorist violence. There has been no debacle in Afghanistan, and it appears unlikely that it will be Obama's Vietnam, either—though victory per se may prove an unattainable concept. There has been gradual progress in Pakistan's internal war against its own insurgents, and no new Mumbai-like terror attack has occurred to take Pakistan and India to the brink of war, though the overall U.S.-Pakistan relationship remains deeply troubled. Extralegal detentions are down, and no Abu Ghraib–like travesties have occurred; yet Guantanamo is still open. Given the nature of the struggle, Obama's record, though incomplete, is solid.

IRAQ

Obama began his presidential campaign in 2007 on an anti–Iraq war platform. Unlike most of the other Democrats running for the highest office in the land, he had not been part of the Senate back when George W. Bush asked the country to go to war in 2002 and 2003. As such he had never voted for—or against—the war. In this sense he was lucky. He was also young enough to be able to pick his moment on when to run for president, and his views aligned very nicely as of 2007 with the temperament and worldview of much of the Democratic Party base.

But he also knew his own mind on the subject. There was little reason to doubt his contention that he was always against the invasion. In October 2002 in Chicago for example, before announcing his candidacy for the Senate, Obama declared in a speech that the invasion of Iraq would be "a dumb war . . . a rash war." He and his inner circle would continue to point to that position, and that speech, as proof of his conviction, sincerity, and good judgment.[5]

For the typical Democratic primary voter at least, other candidates seemed more opportunistic, and less sincere, when making the antiwar case. Obama's promise to get all U.S. combat forces out of Iraq fast—either within sixteen months of inauguration or at the somewhat faster pace of one to two brigades a month, depending on when and where he spoke—was not unusual within the party. Indeed, Governor Bill Richardson, Senator John Edwards, and Representative Dennis Kucinich were all to his left on this issue. But he was bolder than Senator Hillary Clinton on the matter—and he conveyed a level of conviction that probably exceeded hers in the eyes of the antiwar and anti-Bush faithful.

Then Obama truly did get lucky. Just as he had to make the transition from winning a nomination to winning a general election, the military situation in Iraq improved dramatically, and he was able to make his pivot without opening himself up to the Republican charge of weakness on this preeminent national security issue. During the period of the Democratic primaries, one could debate whether the surge was working; one could hardly debate it by the spring of 2008. That might have seemed to be a reason the issue would favor Senator John McCain. But Iraq improved so much and so fast that talk of rapid withdrawal no longer appeared irresponsible by the summer of 2008. In fact, Iraq's own leader, the Shiite prime minister Nouri al-Maliki, suggested a timeline for U.S. downsizing that was not radically different from Obama's own plan.[6] The early months of the surge cut violence rates nationwide by about three-fourths by the end of 2007. Then the battles of Basra and in the Sadr City section of Baghdad, which the Iraqi prime minister initiated and the Iraqi army led, occurred in the spring of 2008.[7] Iraq's levels of violence dropped further as a result. Not only did that improve the situation on the ground, it also improved Maliki's standing among Iraqi nationalists, who wanted a strong state, and among Sunnis and Kurds, who had previously doubted his willingness to stand up against Shia extremists.[8]

Nobody could have foreseen this sequence of events. But it happened, almost on cue. All of a sudden, Obama's long-standing calls to devote more forces to Afghanistan and fewer to Iraq seemed not the rant of "the most liberal member of the Senate," as some had designated him, but the prescient prescriptions of someone who was leading the country to a new conventional wisdom about how to fight the nation's antiterrorism wars.

Once he became president, Obama dispensed with ideology and partisanship and became simply pragmatic. Inheriting a war effort with fifteen brigades in Iraq, his promises would have implied a departure of all but small numbers of trainers and logisticians within roughly twelve to sixteen months of inauguration. (Again, he had sometimes spoken of getting one or two brigades a month out of the country, which would have taken fewer than sixteen months to accomplish.) Instead, he decided to take nineteen months to draw down to 50,000 U.S. troops, configured into roughly six brigades. He then left those forces in Iraq for another year before beginning the next phase of the drawdown, culminating in the complete departure of all major American military units from Iraq by the end of 2011. This was not a random or minor tweaking of the numbers. It was a major modification of what Obama had originally proposed, and for that reason, when announced in late February of 2009, it caused considerable dissension within the Democratic Party.[9] And while remaining forces were reconfigured into "advise and assist brigades," so that the president could claim to have honored the spirit of his promise to remove all combat troops in short order, in fact those new brigades had 80–90 percent the same structure—and same weapons—as the old ones, a point lost on few within Iraq itself (even if often overlooked in the U.S. debate).[10]

The decision to keep 50,000 troops into 2011 was based on guidance from General Raymond Odierno, who commanded American forces in Iraq, from General David Petraeus, who had led the surge until September 2008, when he returned home to run U.S. Central Command, and from Secretary of Defense Robert Gates. It also built on the accord negotiated by Bush and Maliki in late 2008 that directed U.S. forces to leave Iraq's cities by June 2009 and leave the country altogether by December 2011.

Obama was lucky to have Petraeus and Odierno as his Iraq generals. He had wisely kept Gates at a time when conventional politics would surely have counseled choosing a new secretary of defense. With such a strong team leading the war effort, it became straightforward for Obama to modify his campaign promise. After all, nineteen months could be portrayed as not that different from sixteen, and 50,000 residual troops in Iraq, while many more than had been expected or implied during the campaign, was still far less than the 135,000 Obama inherited on January 20, 2009. Most of all, who could criticize Obama for listening to his Pentagon advisers when they were so well regarded and in such lockstep on the issue?

By modifying the plans in this way, Obama could avoid any big drawdowns of U.S. troops in Iraq in the unsettled year of 2009—when Iraqis would be taking his measure, and when American troops would be pulling out of Iraqi cities and thereby conferring far more responsibility on the Iraqi army and police. This was too fraught a time to test the stability of Iraq by launching into a predetermined exodus. With Obama's new plan, U.S. troop numbers could stay robust through the crucial Iraqi elections of March 2010—the second real election in that young democracy, a delicate moment in any country that has recently thrown off the yoke of dictatorship and adopted representative government.

These Obama decisions were prudent and pragmatic, not historic or transformative. Delaying the bulk of America's departure from Iraq a few months, and the rest of the exit another year or year and a half, hardly incurred huge risks or costs for the new president. This may have added some $100 billion to the war's total price tag, relative to what his plan from the campaign implied. But in the context of a trillion-dollar war and trillion-dollar annual federal budget deficits, that number was hardly a game changer. To be sure, American casualties would continue during the drawdown too—but they were already much reduced relative to earlier levels, having dropped to 314 fatalities in 2008, after averaging 800–900 annually in 2004 through 2007. The totals thereafter were 149 in 2009, 60 in 2010, and about the same in 2011. Those latter losses were tragic and deeply distressing to be sure, but there was hardly any guarantee that they would have been less had the United States rushed for the exits—and indeed there was a real chance they would have been greater.[11] So even if Obama's decisions were not Churchillian, they were thoughtful, careful, and effective.

Obama's smart moves did not end there. At an Oval Office meeting in early 2009, Gates and Secretary of State Clinton were discussing the numerous challenges that Iraq faced and what to do about them. Obama quickly realized there was no natural lead agency for the challenges ahead. The military still had huge numbers of troops in Iraq, to be sure. That argued for giving the Pentagon the lead. But combat in Iraq was beginning to wind down. It appeared that the country's future would be determined primarily by the ability of its leaders to work across sectarian lines, despite bitter personal rivalries and animosities, many dating back to the Saddam era. In other words, Iraq policy was increasingly about influencing Iraqi politics, which meant that it was a task primarily for the State Department. But because Secretary Clinton had lots on her plate already, the president turned to Biden and said, "Joe, you take this one." That was it. Decision made. No previous consultation with the vice president, no asking for his blessing of the idea, no effort to assuage any offended egos at the Pentagon or Foggy Bottom. "No-drama Obama" had made a call, and everyone supported it.

This decision was in some contrast, incidentally, to the selection of Christopher Hill to be the administration's first ambassador to Iraq. Hill, a capable career foreign service officer with considerable experience in East Asia, and a close associate of Richard Holbrooke among others, was controversial in light of Hill's lack of Arabic language skills and regional experience.[12] Hill's successor, Jim Jeffrey, was more experienced in the region and less controversial.

Biden had a background on Iraq from his Senate days. In 2002 he had held important hearings on how to stabilize post-Saddam Iraq, hearings that the Bush administration would have done well to heed. Biden subsequently called for a more federated Iraq (what some call "soft partition") when in 2005 and 2006 it seemed the war was being lost. Although soft partition was controversial, it was initially a reasonable proposal for a member of the loyal opposition in the Senate to advance at a time when Plan A was clearly failing.[13]

This new challenge to Biden was wholly different: he was being asked as the incumbent vice president—authorized by the president and working primarily behind the scenes—to make the existing Iraq policy succeed. That required endless and mostly quiet diplomacy. Traveling to Iraq every few months (he made at least his eighth visit as vice president late in 2011), hosting Iraqis of all political persuasions in Washington, mastering the issues, initiating the calls and follow-up calls, playing the role of adviser and at times even mentor while respecting Iraqi sensitivities, Biden thrived.[14] Throughout, he generally avoided the limelight both in the United States and in Iraq. Knowing that the United States remained politically unpopular in Iraq, he avoided saddling any Iraqi politician with his endorsement or open support. Knowing also that Iraqis wanted to solve their own problems, he resisted advising them on whether to form a grand coalition government, or on whether to avoid contact with Iran, or on when they should address key issues like the territorial disputes among Arabs, Kurds, and Turkomen in the country's north.[15]

And the vice president succeeded, at least to a degree. It is rare to hear Iraqi politicians complain about too much pressure from Washington. Polling in the summer of 2010 showed that Iraqi citizens were wary about the accelerating U.S. troop drawdown, implying that the United States was not seen as overbearing. If anything, it has been too hurried in leaving, in the eyes of most major Iraqi political figures except the Sadrists, a sentiment that intensified with the somewhat surprising announcement by the White House in October 2011 that all U.S. military units would leave Iraq by year's end.[16] Meanwhile, Iraq has made tangible progress. It has continued to improve security, despite the occasional high-profile attack that suggests otherwise. It also finally created a new government after the nine-month delay that followed the March 2010 elections.

During the winter of 2010, Prime Minister Maliki seemed intent on exploiting gray areas—and even some not so gray areas—in Iraqi election law to ensure he would hold onto power.[17] Biden did much to get him to desist from further electoral shenanigans.[18] Partial recounts in districts where other parties besides Maliki's had done well were, it was agreed, not a good idea. Banning former members of Saddam's Baathist Party from holding office after they had won seats was without legal foundation. To drive home such points, the vice president could count on his boss's backing when necessary. As Biden put it to one of us, "When I need the big man to make a phone call to an Iraqi politician to make a point, he's happy to do so too." Obama had delegated, but he hadn't stood aside or forgotten the issue.[19] The progress that the surge, the Sunni awakening, the Basra and Sadr City offensives, and related developments produced in the latter Bush years has been solidified during Obama's years in the White House. The Iraqi civil war as such is over (at least for now). Violence is down more than 90 percent relative to 2006 and early 2007 levels. Electricity production is up more than 50 percent, and international energy firms are bidding enthusiastically to help develop new oil fields in Iraq. The central government is sharing revenues, and responsibilities, with Iraq's eighteen provinces—even those dominated by Sunni and Kurdish communities. Politics are still rough and tumble, and the future is uncertain, so Iraq's progress has been surprising, but it is real. And however unpleasant they have been at times, debate and parliamentary maneuver and horse-trading, rather than violence and threats, became the main means of trying to resolve differences in Iraq. As Biden put it, "Politics has broken out."[20]

The politics of Iraq are still tough at times in America, too, and the administration has not always found the right words to describe developments. In early 2010 on *Larry King Live,* for example, Biden celebrated the Obama administration's success in Iraq, saying it could be one of the administration's "great achievements." That was too much for the likes of his predecessor, the former vice president Dick Cheney, who reminded Biden that he and President Obama had both opposed the surge that had led to the drop in violence and turnaround in Iraq more generally. Biden did not backtrack, but he did acknowledge the progress in Iraq achieved in the last two years of the Bush administration.[21] At other times, the administration was too bent on claiming it had fulfilled its campaign promises. Obama's Oval Office speech marking the end of the "combat mission" and the return of all combat troops from Iraq to the United States on August 31, 2010, was largely an exercise in semantics, since many well-armed American troops remained—and indeed continued to suffer casualties.[22] So the administration was not above playing politics, and some word games, on the issue. But by the end of 2011 it had truly if belatedly honored its campaign promise to get American forces entirely out of Iraq, so at this point it was no longer a matter of wording.

Despite these relatively minor Obama administration failings on Iraq policy, the policy itself has been reasonably successful. The president rode the war to political victory on a tsunami of partisan anger, but in office he forged a pragmatic and bipartisan policy with heavy reliance on holdover stars from George Bush's foreign policy team. And then he asked his experienced vice president to implement the details of the policy. The story of the new Iraq continues to unfold. But at least for most of Obama's first three years in office, it has been mostly a good news story, with the issue no longer driving a partisan wedge down the middle of the American polity.

The Obama administration's work is not done, however—and the issue may become partisan yet again, just in time for the 2012 elections. Countries recently experiencing civil war have a high likelihood of relapse—with one-third to one-half reverting to war. To the extent that Iraq's constitution and parliamentary democracy can be viewed as elements of a peace, it is a peace that has numerous frailties. Specifically, as Stanford professor Steve Stedman and other scholars show, countries with neighbors bent on wreaking havoc, with "spoilers" within their own country who prefer to defeat a peace accord, and with abundant natural resources that provide tempting targets for exploitation are particularly vulnerable to renewed violence. Iraq has all three factors.[23] In addition, while political science tells us that established democracies are prone to peace (with other democracies and also internally), young democracies are not—as the violence Iraq suffered after its election in 2005 suggests.[24]

As such, the complete departure of the remaining American forces in 2011 holds risks. Iraq has come a long way but is nowhere near to being out of the woods. Bombings and killings continue, with the potential to escalate to high-level assassinations or other tragedies. There is still a myriad of serious political problems, too. They include unresolved constitutional debates about how much power the central government should wield; uncertainty over the future of the Sons of Iraq (as well as the so-called Daughters of Iraq), most of them Sunni, who did so much to check al Qaeda in 2007 and 2008 but who worry that a Shia-based government will now find it convenient to forget them; residual pockets of al Qaeda; and insidious influences from Iran and other neighbors.[25] These collectively create a real risk of resumed hostilities.

It is not that U.S. forces were in a position to suppress any such violence if it occurred. The goal of the U.S. presence, rather, had been to exercise American influence with relevant Iraqi parties in a preventive and confidence-building fashion. This task was facilitated by U.S. troops, who helped man checkpoints, carried out joint patrols with Iraqi and Kurdish forces, and otherwise helped calm nerves and provide reassurance among still jittery Iraqis as the wounds of civil war began to heal. It is a different situation with them gone.

To what extent was their departure inevitable? Could Obama have done more to improve the odds of striking an acceptable deal with the Iraqi government that would have kept, say, 5,000 to 20,000 U.S. troops in Iraq for an additional period of time, perhaps up to several years? It is difficult to say. The Obama administration could not force the issue, as Secretary Gates realized in noting late in 2010 that the United States would be open to reconsidering the departure deadline but only if Iraqis made the first move.[26] It was at Prime Minister Maliki's insistence that the 2008 accord mandating this scheduled departure was reached, and it was the Bush administration, not the current U.S. government, that signed the bilateral deal. Iraqi domestic politics still contain a healthy dose of anti-Americanism, and Iraqis remain a proud people who want to run their own country without help.

There have been reports that the Obama administration signaled to Iraqis that it wanted any enduring American role to be quite modest—perhaps scaring away Iraqi leaders who would have been willing to lobby hard for a continuing U.S. military presence but only one large enough to make a major difference.[27] This fact may have contributed to the ultimate impasse in negotiations and thus the complete departure of American units from the country. If such reports are true, the Obama administration elected to take a gamble that perhaps was not necessary. To be sure, the administration tried to stay engaged in Iraq to an extent. There was Gates's attempt at subtle persuasion, as well as his successor Leon Panetta's blunter approach when on visiting Iraq shortly after becoming secretary of defense he counseled Iraqis to, "Dammit, make a decision."[28] But concerted diplomacy, including at the levels of secretary of state and president, was not as vigorous as it might have been.

As former prime minister Ayad Allawi put it, "The invasion of Iraq in 2003 may indeed have been a war of choice. But losing Iraq in 2011 is a choice that the United States and the rest of the world cannot afford to make."[29] We do not go so far in our criticism. The United States gave Iraq eight and a half years of military support, including nearly three on Obama's watch, when he had promised only sixteen months before being elected president. At some point, Iraqis must accept primary responsibility for their own future. And in the end, even if Washington's interest in staying engaged was known to be only lukewarm, it was the Iraqis and their new democratic government that insisted on terms—no legal immunity for American troops on Iraqi soil—that all knew in advance to be unacceptable to the United States. That said, Obama could have played it differently and perhaps improved the odds of keeping a residual American force, which could have been a form of insurance.

Still, Iraqis made the decision for the United States to go, as is their right, and it reflects in many ways a welcome confidence on their part. It is also useful for the United States to prove once again to the Middle East and the world that when asked to leave, we do in fact leave. That counters many myths about our supposedly imperial intent and discourages countries from taking our presence and our help for granted. On balance, this outcome appears a reasonable gamble on the part of Baghdad and Washington.

There are reasons to worry that the American withdrawal is leading to problems. Maliki is driven not just by understandable national pride and coalition politics but also by a personal tendency toward rash action, as indicated by two instances: in the spring of 2008, when he launched the campaign in Basra with virtually no planning or coordination with American forces, and in early 2010, when he tried to disqualify some legitimate opposition candidates for parliament. Maliki has also tried to consolidate many powers in his office, circumscribing the roles of parliament and other actors on matters such as who can propose legislation.[30] Sectarian tensions in Iraq remain only partially healed after the civil warfare of 2004–07 or so, and the possibility of future Arab-Kurd or Sunni-Shia conflict cannot be dismissed. The latter in particular could have severe regional implications, with its potential for spillover to other countries. And the events in the immediate aftermath of the U.S. troop departure have not been auspicious. Maliki immediately sought to arrest a vice president, to dismiss a deputy prime minister, and to turn up the political and legal pressure on his finance minister. These attempts against Sunnis arguably violated pledges to be politically inclusive and also constitutional restraints on his power as prime minister.

Further, Obama's celebratory words from the Oval Office, expressed just the week before all these events—during a visit to Washington by Maliki—now seem incongruous. Indeed, they were incongruous even at the time, as Obama was heralding the very milestone—the complete departure of U.S. forces from Iraq—that his negotiators had been working to try to avoid. In light of Americans' fatigue with Iraq, the temptation to celebrate the end proved irresistible for Obama on domestic political grounds. But it may have weakened his leverage with Iraqis and made him seem disconnected from the reality of the situation. Only future events will determine just how big a problem that will be.

In short, President Obama has handled Iraq imperfectly but still reasonably well to date. Yet the job is not done. The permanent withdrawal of all American troops opens up a new phase in the challenge of using Washington's influence to help Iraqis put back together the country that the last decade nearly ripped apart. A case in point is the planned sale of F-16 fighters to Iraq. It is difficult to see how Washington can or should countenance completing that transaction in the near future given Maliki's recent undemocratic and indeed perhaps illegal behavior. The administration needs to have the courage to make such tough calls: in the coming months it needs to condition cooperation with Baghdad, even if in doing so it complicates its own narrative about how it successfully concluded the Iraq war.

Beyond matters of troops, it appears that America made one major mistake in late 2010 that has contributed to the problems since. When former prime minister Ayad Allawi, whose Iraqiya Party won a plurality of seats in the March 2010 elections, could not find enough potential coalition partners to form a new government and Prime Minister Maliki was poised to then do so, Washington counseled Maliki to form a government of national unity that included Allawi's party, an alliance that would allow the latter to play a major role in the selection of defense and interior ministers. Unfortunately, that approach has led to paralysis and a breakdown in the functioning of much of the Iraqi government, as Allawi and Maliki have not been on speaking terms and the key security positions have not been filled. This backdrop contributed to the difficulty Iraqis had in deciding whether to request an extension of the American military presence beyond 2011, so the coalition strategy has been widely seen in retrospect as a mistake.[31]

With any opportunity to keep U.S. forces in Iraq beyond 2011 now lost, President Obama may have to step up his own personal involvement in the issue to compensate for the reduced leverage that the U.S. military departure will likely entail. Whatever his own druthers, he has no choice but to maintain his administration's focus on this important country.

AFGHANISTAN

From the beginning of his presidential campaign, Barack Obama made it clear that he viewed the Afghanistan conflict as the correct war to pursue in the aftermath of 9/11. He pledged to swing the focus from Iraq to Afghanistan and often spoke of adding at least two brigades of U.S. combat forces to the latter mission, as the Taliban regained strength during the second term of the Bush presidency.

Many onlookers suspected that this was partly politics. Being against Iraq was politically easy for a Democrat seeking support in primary elections, given the unpopularity of the incumbent president, and of that war itself, among Democratic voters. But looking ahead to a general election against the formidable war hero Senator John McCain—and especially in light of the fact that the three previous Democratic presidents were all frequently viewed as vulnerable on national security matters—some suspected that if Obama wanted to be against Iraq and also in favor of closing Guantanamo and of negotiating with dictators, he needed to support some other war. Afghanistan was the obvious choice. By this theory, his real commitment to that war might not have been expected to outlast the presidential campaign.

This theory appears to have been fully debunked by Obama's actual performance as president. Far more than deploying two more brigades to Afghanistan, on top of the four or so already there when he stepped into the White House, he in fact added eight. The United States had 30,000 troops in Afghanistan when Obama was inaugurated; it had 100,000 there by late 2010. Not only did Obama quickly turn to an Afghanistan policy review upon taking office, increasing that 30,000 figure to about 68,000 as a result, but he agreed to a second major review in the fall of 2009—and then doubled down his bets with a second troop increase. Some criticized Obama for taking too long to complete the second review, or for doubting his generals, or for asking tough questions in the course of his review before deciding on a course of action. But the fact remains that within a year of taking office he had authorized two major troop additions for the war—each as great in size as the entire U.S. force that was in Afghanistan when he took office.

Even with his decision in June 2011 to return U.S. force levels to 68,000 troops by the end of the summer of 2012, a decision that ISAF commander General David Petraeus publicly dissented from, Obama will have been rather resolute in his Afghanistan policy—and will ask voters to reelect him at a time the U.S. force there will be roughly twice what it was when he took office. Partly as a result of the intensified effort, more U.S. lives were lost under Obama's watch in Afghanistan in 2009 and 2010 than during the entire Bush presidency. That is hardly a virtue, but it is an indicator of commitment, especially by a commander in chief, who typically feels such losses personally and deeply in any war.

Moreover, the Obama team's initial wariness about the second proposed troop increase in the fall of 2009 was not hard to fathom. It is understandable why people like Vice President Joseph Biden, National Security Adviser James Jones, and Ambassador Karl Eikenberry would be skeptical about General Stanley McChrystal's proposal, backed up by General Petraeus, Admiral Mike Mullen, and Secretary Gates, for yet another addition of U.S. troops in the summer of 2009. Hadn't the military (even if not McChrystal himself, who assumed command in June 2009) just made that same kind of request half a year before, implying that its first request would provide ample resources, only to come back just a few months later with a plea for even more boots on the ground? Skeptics of another U.S. troop buildup argued that Afghanistan, with its tribal society and weak traditions of loyalty to the state, was not a promising place for a classic counterinsurgency operation. The twin goals of such an operation—protecting the population while building up Afghan security forces so they could do the job themselves—were seen as inconsistent with Afghanistan's history, culture, and society. NATO's role in the war's early years cast doubt on whether it could have played a constructive influence in the country, given its weak knowledge of the nation's anthropology.[32] It wound up inadvertently favoring some tribes and groups over others, leading to backlash by those left out and worsening corruption by pumping in too much money too fast.

In the end, however, Obama saw that McChrystal's skeptics did not really offer an alternative strategy so much as a damage-control effort. They may look prescient if the mission ultimately fails, since at least their approach would have limited America's investment in the war. They can also argue that al Qaeda in Afghanistan at present is minimal in size and scale, that other sanctuaries in places like Yemen have become comparably more useful to the organization, and that it may prove possible to split the Taliban from al Qaeda such that even if the former came back to power in Afghanistan, the latter might not benefit. This argument may be stronger in the aftermath of the death of Osama bin Laden, since his personal relationships with certain Afghan Taliban leaders have now been lost, perhaps weakening the bonds between the organizations—though to date the actions of the Haqqani network and other Taliban leaders since bin Laden's death suggest no greater moderation. That said, at least back in 2009 skeptical views evidently did not add up in Obama's mind to a plan for success in Afghanistan that would keep al Qaeda from reestablishing a sanctuary there.

Some observers, such as Bob Woodward in his intriguing book about the 2009 policy review process, allege that major figures in the Pentagon failed to provide Obama with a full range of options in requesting the second major installment of troops.[33] But that critique largely misses the point. It was Obama who emphatically favored a resolute and robust effort—and had said so all along.[34] One can disagree with the policy, but it is fairly clear that its parameters were established by the commander in chief.

There were indeed troubled communications between the military and the White House during the summer and early fall of 2009. That was partly because the military came back with a second request for a big troop increase so soon after the first. Again, while it was understandable why it did so, since before McChrystal no one had done a comprehensive assessment of mission requirements in Afghanistan, it was also natural for President Obama to place a higher burden of proof on military proponents of such an approach the second time around. Communications difficulties were also due to the fact that White House aides deliberately established a distance between General McChrystal in the field and President Obama. They felt that the weekly videoteleconferences that President Bush had held with General Petraeus (and Ambassador Ryan Crocker) in Iraq made for too close a relationship. They did not want to repeat the pattern. But here, their apparent antipathy for following a Bush precedent kept McChrystal and Obama out of touch during the crucial summer months, when the need for additional troops was being diagnosed in Afghanistan. That led to some unpleasant surprises and strained relations later on. On this point, the White House does deserve much of the blame for problematic communications. But the fall review process allowed the situation to be largely repaired.

On the substance of the decision, it might have been possible to craft a hybrid option that allowed more rigorous counterinsurgency efforts in some places before trying them throughout the key populated swaths of the south and east of the country. But in fact, McChrystal's request for 40,000 more troops (ultimately scaled back to 30,000) was itself a selective approach. It did not permit a fully resourced effort in the country's east, or in its north and west, which like Kabul itself were relatively secure but certainly not safe. Indeed, in his new plan and troop buildup, McChrystal placed primary emphasis on only about eighty districts and secondary emphasis on another forty—together, about one-third of the country. Given that the United States had attempted a "light footprint" strategy in the first term of the Bush administration, staying small and emphasizing counterterrorism operations did not offer much hope to Obama. It was in fact that very approach that allowed for the Taliban's comeback. Nor did Obama believe that there was much hope of successful negotiations with the Taliban. That group and the Haqqani network remained quite ideological and extreme—and were likely of the view that they were winning the war and had no need to compromise.[35]

The arguments that Afghanistan did not want a strong central government, that it could not afford a large army, and that its people and politicians did not wish to have a large foreign presence on their territory had a certain appeal and historical validity.[36] But a strategy based on such arguments was tried in the Bush administration (perhaps for other reasons as well, since Bush's focus on Iraq necessarily diverted resources from Afghanistan). And it failed, as evidenced by, first, a growth in Taliban strength from perhaps 5,000 fighters around 2005 to 25,000 by the time Obama took office, and, second, by trends in violence that saw U.S. fatalities grow from about 50 a year through 2004 to 99 in 2005, 98 in 2006, 117 in 2007, and 155 in 2008 (with even greater relative growth in insurgent attacks).[37]

Several key aspects of the Taliban's revival drove McChrystal's and Obama's thinking and show just how formidable the group had become over the years. Whatever their many flaws, the Afghan Taliban and other main insurgent groups are far smarter than, for example, al Qaeda in Iraq. The Taliban has rarely engaged in the brutal bombings that have plagued Iraq and to a lesser extent Pakistan. Instead, the Taliban's use of targeted assassinations, as well as threats in the form of anonymous "night letters" delivered to the homes of those loyal to the government, has discouraged many Afghans who want to help reform and rebuild their country.

The Taliban returned to influence through a combination of intimidation, cajolery, bribery, and selective violence. And its vision for the country, while still not preferred among Afghans who have seen Taliban rule before, nonetheless gained traction in certain areas, as the population became increasingly frustrated by the failures of the Karzai government as well as the NATO mission.

The rapid justice system the Taliban offers, or imposes upon, citizens in its areas of influence, while crude and sometimes brutal, is still often seen as fairer and more dependable than the government's. If this "kinder, gentler," more efficient Taliban might be willing to split from al Qaeda, it may be feasible to imagine a Taliban resurgence in Afghanistan. They may simply be clever tactics, however—reflecting an awareness on the Taliban's part of the importance of rehabilitating its image (even if its ideology or long-term goals might not have changed). Either way, they make enlisting the Afghan population against the Taliban, at least the Pashtun plurality of Afghanistan's population from which the Taliban draws virtually all of its support, quite hard.

Taliban and fighters in the Haqqani network also improved their battlefield tactics—by operating as a flexible, horizontal network rather than as a highly hierarchical organization.[38] Several years ago they might mass for battle but would lose the ensuing firefights—if not right away, then once NATO reinforcements arrived. For example, in 2006 the Taliban sought to establish control in a large swath of the south of the country but was defeated by a combination of Canadian and other NATO forces and Afghan forces.[39] Since then, the coordinated actions of large numbers of Taliban fighters have sometimes occurred—but generally in places where insurgent forces realized they could challenge a small NATO outpost, as with the summer 2008 battles in eastern Afghanistan (such as the Battle of Wanat) and a similar mass attack in the east on October 4, 2009. Most other operations have been conducted by small numbers of insurgents. Often their approach is a complex ambush, using the detonation of a huge roadside bomb to create initial injury and panic, quickly moving in with small arms fire against any incapacitated vehicles and their NATO or Afghan security force occupants, then breaking off contact before NATO reinforcements or airpower arrive.

The news from Afghanistan, however, is not all bad. Security trends in some areas—the north, northwest, south, and southwest—have been favorable in many ways in the latter part of 2011 (though the east has been an important exception). Living standards are better, even if much of the improvement is due to a temporary foreign presence, and the numbers of children in school, of accessible health clinics, and of cell phones in use have skyrocketed. Even today, moreover, Afghanistan is not a particularly dangerous place for normal citizens—compared at least with the typical standards of war-torn lands or even of high-crime countries such as South Africa, Nigeria, Mexico, and Colombia. Statistically, Afghanistan is no worse off than any of these places, and in per capita terms it is safer than most of them.[40] But the economic benefits have accrued unevenly to certain players and politicians and tribes. And as for violence, things are much worse than the broad numbers suggest for NATO and Afghan soldiers and police, as well as for Afghan political, religious, and tribal leaders outside of the insurgent ranks. Afghan security forces have been losing a thousand personnel a year to violence, for example, and this number was even higher in 2011. Assassinations of political, business, civic, and tribal leaders are up, too, with the 2010 weekly toll reaching a level of one or two in Kandahar alone and growing further in 2011.[41]

Against such a backdrop, as it appeared in 2009, Obama decided that he had little choice but to try a classic counterinsurgency approach. Even though his core goals were to prevent another al Qaeda attack on the United States, as well as the destabilization of a nuclear-armed Pakistan, he saw the stability of Afghanistan as crucial, given the potential for that country to otherwise offer safe haven to extremist groups like al Qaeda, the Pakistani Taliban, and Lashkar-e-Taiba. Counterinsurgency methods were seen as needed to achieve a counterterrorism objective.

Much of the purpose of the new troops Obama sent has been to establish substantial NATO troop concentrations in the key centers of the Afghan population and, most specifically, the Pashtun plurality in the south and east. Large numbers of added forces were sent to Helmand Province and Kandahar Province, the latter being the spiritual home and base of the Taliban, the former a major source of additional support as well as wealth from the opium trade. The addition of these troops has led to the high numbers of casualties under Obama, with U.S. fatalities in 2009 exceeding 300 and those in 2010 nearly reaching 500, before declining to 418 in 2011. But the areas are also now much improved, as reflected in a few key facts and figures—for example, in Helmand in 2011, 50 percent more children were in school than in 2009, nearly half the population considers the roads secure in contrast to a third who felt that way a year before, and government officials now travel locally by road rather than NATO helicopter.

Many of the additional U.S. and NATO forces are also being used to train the Afghan military and police forces. Going beyond what was done in Iraq, McChrystal emphasized not only good initial training for Afghan forces and the embedding of mentoring teams within army and police units thereafter but also a formal partnering of Afghan and NATO units. They now pair off as sister formations and train, plan, deploy, patrol, and fight together. About three-fourths of Afghan army units now have such a relationship with a NATO formation. This apprenticeship concept is the essence of the U.S. exit strategy and is a far more intense approach to training Afghan forces than had ever been used before. While there is a long way to go, this approach already resulted, for example, in Afghan forces providing about 60 percent of combined coalition manpower for the major operations in and around Kandahar in 2010, according to General Petraeus's congressional testimony of March 2011.

The administration did a solid job of getting American allies to help more in the mission. To be sure, Obama's more multilateral approach to American foreign policy hardly opened the floodgates to greater assistance from NATO and other allies. But the increment in help was impressive nonetheless and proved to be a tangible benefit of his approach to foreign policy, if not a transformational one. Agreeing to provide 30,000 of McChrystal's requested 40,000 troops from the U.S. armed forces, the president hoped that allies would make up the difference—and they did, more or less, even though the Netherlands later ended its role in the operation and Canada reduced its own dramatically. Those expecting the Obama magic to produce tens of thousands of additional foreign forces as a show of solidarity with a popular American president might have been disappointed. But most seasoned foreign policy analysts were impressed that Obama could get the allies to provide about 25 percent more troops than they had collectively done before.

Whatever one's views on the broad strategy, there have unfortunately been many tactical mistakes. Obama's team has had internal schisms that sometimes became public. That was true even before WikiLeaks, as a cable written by Ambassador Eikenberry that cast doubts on President Karzai's dependability was leaked by the administration. More broadly, the Obama administration has not maintained a consistent or constructive approach in dealing with Afghan president Hamid Karzai. Several administration officials, such as former national security adviser Jim Jones, Vice President Biden, and the late ambassador Richard Holbrooke, either excoriated the Afghan leader in public or had very heated exchanges with him in private, exchanges that negatively affected the broader relationship.[42] Looking back on the history, Secretary Gates declared that the United States had done a "lousy job" listening to the Afghan leader—even if the problem was clearly not all American made.[43]

Most important, Obama has failed to project resolve despite his strong decisionmaking on the war. His policies have been firmer than his words on the subject. In announcing his decision to increase troops a second time at West Point on December 1, 2009, Obama also pledged to begin removing U.S. forces from Afghanistan by July 2011. By itself, a plan to make any additional foreign military buildup in Afghanistan temporary should not have raised too many eyebrows; after all, President Bush did much the same thing with the surge in Iraq. But Obama seemed to be promising a fairly rapid end to the war overall—and that seemed to be the message he wanted the U.S. Congress and the American people, especially the antiwar base of his own party, to hear. Well aware of the nation's war fatigue, well aware of the analogies drawn between his war effort in Afghanistan and Lyndon Johnson's in Vietnam, Obama tried to have it all—being muscular enough to create a chance to succeed while hedging his bets and trying to keep the country's political left supportive at the same time. The frequent explanations from administration officials that any U.S. drawdown in July 2011 would be conditions based and responsible could not change the basic fact that people around the world thought they heard Obama promise a fairly rapid and *unconditional* American departure. President Obama's earlier message on March 27, 2009—when unveiling his first Afghanistan policy review—that his central goal in that country was to prevent another possible terrorist strike on the United States, also made many believe that his aspirations for Afghanistan were modest and his commitment temporary.

This effort to have a strong war policy but hedged rhetoric, however understandable in light of America's political challenges at home and Obama's advisers' deep doubts about the viability of the mission, proved to be counterproductive. In Afghanistan, many heard Obama's words as signaling the likelihood of a U.S. departure before the mission could be properly concluded, since the time scales for building Afghan security forces and achieving other key goals were more like three to five years than one or two. That may have motivated some Afghans to step up the pace of reform, as intended by Washington, but it also had many Afghan actors hedging their bets, unsure of what is coming next. And the central Afghan Taliban leadership as well as that of the Haqqani network hardly seem likely to make a peace deal under current circumstances, despite the initiation of talks through a Taliban office in Qatar, as the Taliban-directed assassination of former Afghan president Rabbani in Kabul in September 2011 would suggest. Rabbani was in charge of national reconciliation efforts at the time he was killed.

Setting a deadline had a similar effect in Pakistan, where the country's traditional support for the Afghan Taliban has continued. Some in Pakistan's military see the Afghan Taliban as their best guarantor against what could follow a premature U.S. and NATO/ISAF departure: either chaos or too much Indian influence in the country. That many of these fears are exaggerated or incorrect does not make them any less important.

At times, the Obama administration has tried to firm up perceptions of its resolve. But for each step forward, there has been a step back. After criticizing Karzai when the president flew to Afghanistan in the early spring of 2010, the administration then feted him on a trip to Washington that same May. Obama then relieved General McChrystal, the commander that Karzai had pleaded with President Obama to retain once the *Rolling Stone* article about General McChrystal's staff broke, even while keeping in place Ambassador Eikenberry, with whom Karzai had a very strained relationship. A few months later President Obama flew all the way to Bagram Air Force Base near Kabul to wish U.S. troops well during the holiday season, but when bad weather precluded a helicopter flight to visit with Karzai, Obama turned around and flew back to Washington without ever meeting with the man who was supposedly his close partner in a crucial counterinsurgency effort.

Beyond the matters of personal intrigue, confusing messages were sent about policy, too. The NATO Lisbon summit in November 2010, for example, conveyed alliance staying power. It emphasized the year 2014 rather than 2011 as the deadline for troop withdrawals—when the transition to Afghan leadership on security would be complete. But then in his 2011 State of the Union address, President Obama reverted back to the emphasis on starting to bring troops home by July 2011, with no mention of commitments in any subsequent years.[44] Vice President Biden told *Meet the Press* in December 2010 that the United States would surely be all the way out of Afghanistan by 2014, rather than remaining in a support role thereafter as previously stated; the fact that he corrected his statement on a trip to Kabul several weeks later repaired only part of the damage.[45] Secretary Gates, a stalwart of the war who had long promised that the United States would never again abandon Afghanistan as it had after the Soviets left in 1989, nonetheless gave a speech at West Point in February 2011 in which he said that anyone favoring another land war in Asia should "have his head examined." While he was speaking hypothetically about the future, such disdain for this type of mission made some wonder about his commitment to the present fight.[46] In short, Obama was deeply conflicted about the war, and his advisers were deeply divided. That frame of mind was inevitably manifested in the way policy was implemented and in the public explanations of it, to the inevitable detriment of the overall policy, as it caused doubts and reinforced hedging behavior among key groups in both Afghanistan and Pakistan.

It is too soon to know if Obama's policy gamble in Afghanistan will work. The weaknesses of the Karzai government jeopardize the mission, even though polls show that Karzai's personal popularity among his countrymen consistently exceeds 60 percent. NATO bears some responsibility for the weakness of the Karzai government, too, as outside forces have built up a logistics system for their militaries that fuels corruption. Further, the alliance has often been manipulated by tribal actors seeking to use outsiders to settle their internal scores.[47]

It is not clear if the remedial efforts to address these challenges will be too little, too late. Pakistan's continued ambivalence—tolerating sanctuaries for the Afghan Taliban and Haqqani network on its soil, perhaps as backup plans in case NATO leaves Afghanistan too soon or in case a future Afghan government would be too India friendly—is another major vulnerability. And it is difficult to defeat insurgencies that have such foreign bases as well as a border they can easily traverse.[48]

The death of Osama bin Laden in a bold, impressive raid on May 2, 2011, is quite likely to weaken al Qaeda. It seems less likely to facilitate a split between that group and the Afghan Taliban, but it has probably made America safer. It is possible that the Afghanistan war will take a decided turn for the better—perhaps not on the remarkable scale that followed in Iraq from the surge there but to an extent that creates a virtuous cycle. Success could then breed more success, as a sense of inevitability developed among both opponents and supporters of the Afghan government. Given that many of the insurgents in Afghanistan today are undoubtedly what David Kilcullen calls "accidental guerrillas"—motivated by money, or local rivalry, or a quest for personal vengeance more than by ideology—this effect would seem entirely possible.[49] Moreover, as NATO begins to stand down in the coming years, and Afghan security forces improve as a result of better training, better pay, and the partnering work noted above, the antiforeigner motivation of some insurgents may weaken.

Perhaps more likely, though, is a mediocre but still tolerable outcome whereby Afghanistan's government gradually gains enough military and police capability to handle more of the internal security challenge itself but fails to establish robust control of certain parts of its territory—after the United States and other foreign partners will have drawn down their forces too fast to accomplish that task themselves.[50] This need not be a wholesale change or a repudiation of the population protection strategy so much as an alteration in how the next steps are taken—and a bit of a pause in the clearing operations. Expectations would be lowered somewhat; the strategy would be modified but not discarded. Taking this approach will require Obama to develop a careful plan for downsizing the remaining U.S. forces in Afghanistan between September 2012, when they will reach their 68,000 interim level after a first round of downsizing, and the end of 2014, by which point NATO is to have taken most of its forces home. As this book was going to press on February 1, 2012, Secretary Panetta announced that the combat mission would formally end for U.S. troops by 2013 (underscoring that they would still conduct dangerous operations thereafter). The change in nomenclature does not yet answer the question of how many U.S. and other NATO troops will remain in Afghanistan; indeed, 50,000 U.S. soldiers remained in Iraq even after their combat mission was declared over in 2010. In making decisions on troop levels, Obama will have to exercise great care in consultation with his commanders and diplomats in the field.

Under such assumptions, the future of Afghanistan may then resemble what has been witnessed in places like Pakistan and Colombia, with an ongoing insurgency and certain areas largely beyond the control of the government. But at least Afghanistan will no longer be in Taliban hands or in an anarchic Somalia-like state; the areas where al Qaeda could seek to take sanctuary would be more limited and more vulnerable to government or NATO strikes. That would not be a risk-free result, but it would be far preferable to outright defeat. Whether or not such an outcome would be seen as worth the high costs of achieving it remains debatable, of course.

PAKISTAN AND BEYOND: THE BROADER "WAR ON TERROR"

As the nation's commander in chief, President Obama had a special responsibility for those operations that involved American combat troops. But of course both Iraq and Afghanistan were linked to a broader challenge. George W. Bush called it the war on terror, despite the fact that Saddam Hussein was not implicated in the 9/11 attacks. Barack Obama had never used that formulation, but he too recognized the transnational challenge that was posed by al Qaeda and related groups. The core rationale for the Afghanistan war was defined by both Bush and Obama in terms of the counter-terrorism agenda. And of course, that agenda extended far beyond Afghanistan as well—to Pakistan and certain other countries like Yemen and Somalia, to the homeland security agenda back in the United States, to the broader intelligence effort, and to the detention policy at Guantanamo Bay. It also extended to other areas of foreign policy beyond the hard-power instruments of military force, intelligence, and homeland security, and we address some of these other related subjects in the chapters on the Middle East.

Barack Obama accurately sized up the stakes in Pakistan. That country is in fact far more inherently important than is Afghanistan. In its northern and western tribal regions, near the Afghanistan border, al Qaeda's new top leader, Osama Ayman al-Zawahiri, is believed to reside. It is from there that recent attacks or attempted attacks against the United States and other countries—such as the 2006 London airplane bombing plot and attempted Times Square bombing in 2010—were launched. Pakistan is six times the size of Afghanistan in population and the second-largest Muslim majority nation in the world after Indonesia. It is nuclear armed and in fact has the fastest-growing nuclear arsenal in the world. It has fought India three times in their brief histories as independent states. It either provoked or contributed to at least three crises with India in the last dozen years (the Kargil crisis of 1999; the attack on the Indian parliament by terrorists with ties to Pakistan in 2001; and the Mumbai tragedy of 2008) that could have produced another war—this time among nuclear-armed states. Its economic fragility, high birth and unemployment rates, weak political traditions, unresolved ambitions toward Kashmir, and antipathy felt by most of its citizens and elites toward India make the prospects of instability forbidding.[51]

Against this backdrop, Barack Obama reached several correct conclusions about Pakistan's importance in the broader war on terror well before he became president. This started with the basic fact that, even after 9/11, Washington's focus on that country was inadequate to the scale of the problem. Yes, foreign assistance had increased substantially after 9/11, as Pakistan was rehabilitated in American eyes despite its past nuclear proliferation track record, nuclear weapons tests, and provocative behavior toward India. But the average funding level of about $1 billion a year was largely in the form of "coalition support funds" that compensated Islamabad for the wear and tear on the country's roads and ports imposed by the huge U.S./NATO logistics operation. In Pakistan's eyes, this payment was more of a toll than aid—miserly assistance for an ally that in fact helped the United States arrest 500 al Qaeda operatives in the aftermath of 9/11.[52] It was barely adequate for the direct costs incurred and was clearly inadequate when measured against the violence and disruption that occurred on its territory.

Pakistanis often blamed the United States for this violence, on the grounds that somehow the war in Afghanistan caused a spill-over effect. They saw the Afghanistan war as largely a problem of America's making, moreover, since the United States left the place in chaos after the Soviets were driven out in 1989. This interpretation of events begins with an accurate factual basis but then conveniently ignores that Pakistan's own cultivation of extremists, like the Taliban and Lashkar-e-Taiba, created terror networks that came back to bite the hand that had once fed them.[53] But in any event, Pakistanis believe the narrative. Former deputy secretary of state James Steinberg was surely right when he told Charlie Rose of PBS in June 2011 that "there is probably no more complex bilateral relationship in the world than the relationship between the United States and Pakistan."[54]

Barack Obama realized that to have any chance of eliciting greater support from Pakistan for shutting down the Afghan insurgent sanctuaries operating on its soil, more generous U.S. assistance was needed. The Kerry-Lugar-Berman bill (originally sponsored as well by then senator Biden and supported by then senator Obama) began to redress the situation, as did greater amounts of military aid.[55] Obama also appointed the formidable Richard Holbrooke as special representative for Afghanistan and Pakistan, a new position; encouraged his military leaders to expand their contacts in Pakistan; and asked Secretary Clinton and Secretary Gates to lead a strategic dialogue with their counterparts.[56]

But Obama had inherited such a tough problem in Pakistan that progress was bound to be slow and fitful.[57] The Mumbai attacks in late November 2008, after Obama was elected but before he was inaugurated, were linked to the Lashkar-e-Taiba group that Islamabad had supported in the past. These attacks brought Pakistan and India to the brink of war—and made it quite possible that India, despite its traditions of restraint, would retaliate if attacked again.[58] After the assassination of Benazir Bhutto and the decision by General Musharaf to step down from the presidency, Pakistan also gained a new leader in 2008, Asif Ali Zardari, the widower of Bhutto—but even more pointedly a man known for his corrupt ways. This context made it difficult for Obama to reach out enthusiastically to Pakistan even as some types of support and interaction were increased. Thus there was to be no "Obama effect" in Pakistan; America's popularity among the Pakistani people, already at abysmal levels, barely budged when a new American president with Muslim roots was inaugurated.[59]

Indeed, the passage of the Kerry-Lugar-Berman bill in 2009 was telling as much for the rancor it caused, with Pakistani critics believing it included too many conditions and demands on their country, as for any gratitude or improved relations that resulted. One of us, speaking with an ISI official in Rawalpindi, Pakistan, in March 2010 was struck to hear even this well-informed and senior government servant belittle U.S. aid as a "drop in the bucket." There was, however, a grain of truth behind the complaints. The legislation itself was solid. But the global economic downturn that began in 2008, largely due to U.S. financial transgressions, swamped the Kerry-Lugar-Berman aid in its magnitude. Pakistani GDP growth, which had been averaging almost 7 percent annually in mid-decade, fell to just 2 percent in 2008 and returned only to 3 percent in 2010. U.S. foreign investment in Pakistan also dropped by nearly a billion dollars a year.[60] Measured against a nearly $200 billion economy, this translated into roughly a $10 billion differential in annual growth from what Pakistan might have otherwise expected.[61]

Military cooperation improved at times—that is, within very specific and limited parameters. Pakistan has for the most part continued to allow major logistics operations into Afghanistan through its territory (even as NATO has diversified somewhat, using the Northern Distribution Network through Russia and neighboring states more than in the past). There was a disruption of cooperation at the end of 2011, when a mistaken American bombing raid killed twenty-four Pakistani soldiers near the border and produced a backlash from Islamabad that took several weeks to begin to ease. As of this writing, the immediate fallout from this crisis may be ending, though the broader relationship remains very troubled and fragile.

Aware in recent years of the threat the Pakistani Taliban poses to its own country and people and soldiers, Pakistan stepped up its operations against that group (the so-called TTP) in places like Bajaur, the Swat Valley, and South Waziristan, despite the terrible 2010 floods that complicated operations and diverted some of the military to relief efforts. Its performance in such efforts has had some successes and has shown improvement over time.[62] And Pakistan has tolerated large numbers of American drone strikes against Afghan insurgents who have moved into its tribal areas, particularly North and South Waziristan. Indeed, under Obama there have been more than 200 drone strikes (compared with 50 during the entire Bush presidency). The strikes have become increasingly precise and less likely to cause civilian casualties. But the Pakistani press continues to pillory the United States for these operations, meaning that the government's tolerance of them is a substantial act of assistance to the United States.[63]

Yet Pakistan has not moved its army into North Waziristan. Nor has it taken other major actions against the Afghan Taliban and Haqqani strongholds and headquarters in places such as Quetta and Miram Shah (in the province of Baluchistan and the tribal area of North Waziristan, respectively). More broadly, the tribal areas as well as Baluchistan remain severely underdeveloped and neglected by the government.[64]

Pakistan also provided insufficient help, at best, in recent years in the pursuit of al Qaeda. It did not turn over Osama bin Laden even as he lived for five years in the town of Abbottabad, near Islamabad, an urban area full of military personnel and hosting a military academy as well. The South Asia expert Steve Coll finds it incredible that no Pakistani government officials had knowledge of the site, and he suspects they may even have collaborated in its construction.[65] Thus Pakistan was not even seen as trustworthy enough to be told about the May 2011 raid in advance, out of fear that intelligence might be compromised and bin Laden allowed to escape.[66] This was hardly the first time Pakistanis told their American counterparts less than the full truth about a matter of major significance for U.S. interests.[67] But even so, the possibility that Pakistani officials actually knew where bin Laden was hidden yet chose not to inform the United States or take action themselves was deeply distressing.

Could Obama have done more on Pakistan? Could he still do more? The renewed focus on Pakistan is welcome and appropriate, but to date results have been meager, and perhaps there has been insufficient imagination. Are there any requests that Obama could have made, or might still make, of Islamabad that would be big enough to get Pakistan's attention and get its leaders to truly commit to partnership with the United States? In other words, rather than let the relationship deteriorate, can the United States do the counterintuitive thing and see if there is a way to build it up? It is possible that some progress will begin to occur without further big policy moves. The clarification at the November 2010 NATO Lisbon summit that the U.S.-led International Security Assistance Force mission will continue until 2014, and indeed beyond, may help Pakistan begin to see that the United States is not abandoning the region. Or at least that was the hope for a while. At this point in early 2012, such aspirations appear to be fading, and a more limited U.S.-Pakistan relationship may be all that is truly possible for the foreseeable future. Accordingly, our colleague Bruce Riedel advocates a refocused Pakistan policy, in which we expect less military cooperation from Pakistan, reduce aid to Pakistan's armed forces, and direct a higher percentage of our aid to strengthening the country's civilian government—however weak and flawed it may be. Obama could also offer Islamabad a much more expansive U.S.-Pakistan relationship, but only if it helps win this war. Three major incentives could have particular appeal to Pakistan. First is a major energy deal, perhaps nuclear related and perhaps not, depending on Pakistan's progress with export controls and on its willingness to curb production of nuclear weapons. Second is a free trade accord. Struggling economically, Pakistan needs such a shot in the arm, and with average tariffs on goods from Pakistan at 11.4 percent in the U.S. market, a trade deal could arguably do even more than aid at this point.[68] Third is debt forgiveness or other balance-of-payments help, partly in recognition of how much of Pakistan's current economic mess was exacerbated by the United States with the 2008 financial crisis and the ensuing global recession. Such American generosity would be sensible, and politically feasible in the U.S. Congress, only if Islamabad were to clamp down verifiably on terror groups operating on its soil, including al Qaeda and Lashkar-e-Taiba as well as the insurgent groups operating in Afghanistan. But Washington might consider making clear that it would be inclined toward such greater generosity if Pakistan can get off the fence in terms of its policies toward extremist groups. As suggested by Bruce Riedel, it is time for a message to Pakistani military and intelligence leaders that American support and collaboration cannot continue at previous levels absent a change in their actions.

Beyond Pakistan, the broader counterterrorism effort combines country-specific policies in places such as Yemen with matters of intelligence, homeland security, and detention policy. Under Obama, aid was significantly increased for the Saleh regime as it sought to pursue the twin goals of strengthening its security forces and bolstering development efforts in tribal regions, where the likes of Anwar al-Awlaki have operated. The latter figure, described by an American intelligence official in early 2011 as perhaps the greatest terrorist threat to the United States, was behind the Major Nidal Hasan murders of November 2009 at Fort Hood,

Texas, as well as the attempted Christmas Day 2009 "underwear bombing" of a jet by the Nigerian Umar Farouk Abdulmutallab. These early Obama administration efforts toward Yemen were pragmatic and reasonable.[69]

The Arab awakenings have turned this policy on its head, and a new approach to Yemen will be sorely needed in 2012 and beyond—though the September 2011 killing of Awlaki by a U.S. drone reduces at least some of the pressure. In particular, with President Saleh gone, it will be important to help a new government get on its feet. While "leading from behind" may overstate it, the administration is right to let Saudi Arabia and Yemen's other Gulf neighbors drive much of the process. That is especially so in states like Yemen, where American interests, though important, are not immediately vital.

Somalia is another important case. Not only do pirates continue to operate off its coasts, requiring a multilateral naval mission in the Gulf of Aden and leading to the deaths of some hostages, such as the four elderly Americans killed by pirates in early 2011. But even more consequentially, Somalia itself remains in chaos, with the resulting potential to provide harbor to transnational terrorists. A peacekeeping force made up largely of Ugandans and Burundians is attempting to shore up an extremely weak central government in the face of attacks by various militias as well as by the al-Shabab group, which has ties to al Qaeda. Perhaps scarred by how Somalia damaged another Democratic president early in his tenure—Bill Clinton in 1993, when the famous Black Hawk down episode led to the downfall of a defense secretary and the rapid departure of U.S. troops from the country—Obama has kept his distance from Somalia.

To some extent this is to his credit: prioritization is important in foreign policy, and for all its difficulties, Somalia has not yet produced the kinds of international terrorists threatening the West that Yemen, Pakistan, and Afghanistan have generated. Moreover, the Somali Transitional Federal Government (TFG) has been ineffective. But then again, Uganda and Burundi have been left largely on their own as they try to shore up the TFG and contend with powerful forces that have among other things attacked the capital city of Uganda in reprisal bombings.[70] Their valiant efforts have made some progress, but the mission could still fail, starvation could intensify, and the security situation in Somalia could again worsen.[71] Obama could have done more to strengthen African Union peacekeeping forces through training and arms transfers, through Africa Command as well as bilateral efforts—bolstering programs that date back to the Clinton administration. We discuss this issue again in chapter 7.

On the broad subjects of intelligence and homeland security, activities together costing the government some $120 billion a year, there is again little of a legacy to date. Obama has in fact maintained considerable continuity with his predecessor.

On intelligence, the 9/11 Commission and other investigations produced a proposal for major intelligence reform that was passed into law in 2004 and created a new position, the director of national intelligence. Obama still had his challenges. His first DNI, Admiral Dennis Blair, clashed with CIA director Leon Panetta, until the former was fired in the spring of 2010. There were also calls for reforms after U.S. intelligence failed to predict the winter of revolt in the Arab world in 2011. But Obama has been prudent, and conservative, perhaps recognizing that bureaucratic reforms are often disruptive.[72] Indeed, there is a good chance that the highly touted intelligence reform act of 2004 made things worse, not better, organizationally—and in any event it proved a major distraction for extremely busy analysts and leaders.[73] So Obama's approach seems generally reasonable, if not particularly innovative or transformative. The $75 billion annual price tag for intelligence seems exorbitant, and the growth in the intelligence community over the last decade excessive. Obama should probably chip away at this monstrous figure, but it is unrealistic to think that he could have gained much ground by this point.[74]

Similarly, and perhaps more surprisingly, homeland security has not changed radically. In 2003 a new department charged with this set of responsibilities was created, but that hardly ended the controversy. Critics argue that the department is under-resourced. Proposals abound for major increases in resources above the $40 billion annual budget, which became its typical funding level by mid-decade. The purpose of these funding increases would be, among other things, to protect chemical plants, to outfit first responders with gear to protect against weapons of mass destruction, and to inspect most cargo ships headed for U.S. destinations.[75]

But Obama as president has neither increased DHS's budget substantially nor proposed major new reforms. The 2010 *Quadrennial Homeland Security Review Report* under Secretary of Homeland Security Janet Napolitano emphasizes essentially the same core missions as had the Bush administration, and the 2010 national security strategy emphasizes the same core terrorist threats from "al Qaeda and its affiliates." That is all understandable in broad brush; somewhat more surprising though is that the *QHSR* calls for no major initiatives to redress any perceived major gaps in the country's defenses at all.[76] It is a solid but incrementalist piece of work.

Given the potential for homeland security efforts to gobble up enormous resources without producing much added security, that is mostly the right broad approach. And progress has occurred—not only at DHS but within the intelligence community and Department of State and other agencies—on crucial matters like integrating terrorism watch lists internally and, in conjunction with allies, training foreign law enforcement and counterterrorism officials and making sure all airline passengers are screened.[77] That said, it is not clear that the department is conducting enough bottom-up assessments of national vulnerabilities to identify and remedy any remaining gaps in protection.

Meanwhile, the threat remains. The late 2009 episodes reflect the potency of terrorism that is partly or entirely homegrown. Other near misses—like Najibullah Zazi, the Afghan-born American who sought to bomb the New York subway, and the Pakistan-born U.S. citizen David Headley, who played a role in preparing the devastating Mumbai attacks—show that the threat of terrorism by Americans may be growing. This threat picture still requires a broad agenda of policy response and shows that remaining gaps in homeland security should not be taken lightly.[78]

There are several relatively economical steps that merit consideration. Previous Brookings studies on the subject emphasize protecting against catastrophic attacks, in particular, as well as against the tactics most preferred by al Qaeda.[79] This framework does not answer all questions, and judgment must be used about the nature of the evolving threat as well. But it does lead to some useful ideas.

For example, more large metropolitan police departments should emulate New York City and develop local counterterrorism units; there has been some progress here, but not enough.[80] Large, iconic buildings should make commonsensical decisions about where they locate their HVAC intakes for their air circulation systems when being built or renovated; and some should install shatterproof glass in lower floors and employ more security for their underground parking garages that are contiguous to the building's foundations. Screening of shipping containers needs to become substantially more comprehensive as well, given the potential for nuclear materials to be smuggled into the country. Biometric indicators should probably be upgraded on driver's licenses. And gradual improvements should continue to be made in safety on subways and trains, despite the difficulty of making them truly secure—given al Qaeda's demonstrated interest in such targets.[81] This list does not feature dramatic changes or radically big ideas; alas, the nature of the homeland security effort necessitates slogging away.

Napolitano's tenure has, however, often been characterized by its focus on relatively second-order and third-order issues, like privacy associated with airport screening devices, color coding for terror alerts, and disputes over how well the homeland security system worked (or failed to work) regarding the attempted Christmas Day bombing.[82] The performance has been workmanlike but hardly distinguished or pathbreaking. There is room for low-cost improvement. The president will not pay a major political price for any lack of focus here unless there is another attack that is later deemed to have been preventable, but the risks of such an attack are real enough to warrant more national attention.

Compared to homeland security, Guantanamo Bay has been more challenging to the president and also to Attorney General Eric Holder. Perhaps here the electoral campaign really does haunt the president. His efforts to honor his pledge to close the detention facilities at Guantanamo within a year led to a sometimes frantic and feckless, and ultimately unsuccessful, effort to find other ways to handle terrorism suspects. This was partly Obama's fault; he attacked the symbol of Guantanamo and contributed to the partisan political environment that affected how the issue would play once he was in the White House. He might have argued about the policy instead—asserting that a process of largely arbitrary detention was inconsistent with American values and principles and needed more accountability and checks and balances. His ideas of trying suspects in criminal court in a place like New York City, or building a detention facility to replace Guantanamo within the United States, met with local and congressional disfavor and ultimately proved unworkable. There has nonetheless been quiet progress on the issue since Obama has been in the White House, with fewer than 175 prisoners left in detention at Guantanamo. But the facility itself remains in existence, and the legal framework by which terrorism suspects are held and tried remains underdeveloped.[83] This issue has probably dealt Obama his clearest defeat to date, at least at the symbolic and political level, on matters of counterterrorism.

CONCLUSION

President Obama has been a pragmatic and, so far, a successful president on the hard-power questions of waging war and protecting the country from terrorism. He has been characterized by patience but in the end decisiveness in leaving Iraq; by dogged determination in the pursuit for al Qaeda; and by persistence in beefing up the Afghanistan mission and support for Pakistan, albeit with mixed results and mixed public messaging about his commitment to these latter efforts to date. There have been spectacular successes, too, like the killing of Osama bin Laden, Anwar al-Awlaki, and other terrorist leaders. The homeland and core American interests have not suffered major attack—partly out of luck but also partly out of sheer effort and devotion of resources, time, and attention to the subject by the president himself as well as a focused and committed administration team.

The situation could still break, for better or worse, in any of the key overseas missions or on homeland security. So far, however, the Obama record is one of persevering in Afghanistan and Pakistan, ending the Iraq war, and decapitating much of al Qaeda. In the process, Obama has been tough. He has displayed no naïve expectations in the power of his personal charm or vision to resolve matters of war and peace and no notable softness in his approach. He has certainly not been apologetic about America or its interests during this fight, either.

There is not yet a distinctive Obama legacy in Iraq, Afghanistan, or Pakistan, where the situations remain in flux—no bending of history in the direction of justice. It is not yet clear if the president will succeed in balancing two competing goals, both of which he strongly supports—ending the wars soon, on the one hand, but doing so as carefully and successfully as possible on the other. On that front, big decisions lie ahead for whoever occupies the White House, including the crucial matters of how fast to bring U.S. troops home from Afghanistan and how to help Afghans politically as they prepare to choose a new leader in their crucial election year of 2014. In the interim, though, one conclusion is ineluctable. The United States has been generally kept safe on President Obama's watch, and that is itself a considerable feat

CHAPTER FOUR

MIDDLE EAST PEACEMAKING

NOWHERE IN OBAMA'S FOREIGN POLICY has the gap been wider between promise and delivery than in the Middle East. This is both surprising and ironic. During the presidential campaign, Obama had criticized George W. Bush for only taking up the effort to make Middle East peace in the last year of his second term in office; Obama vowed to make peacemaking a priority from day one of his presidency. Indeed, on his second day in office, Obama traveled to the State Department to witness his new secretary of state swear in George Mitchell, the former senator who had negotiated peace in Northern Ireland, as his special envoy for Middle East peace—a clear manifestation of this commitment to pursue, as Secretary Hillary Clinton put it, "a relentless diplomatic effort . . . to produce a lasting, sustainable peace."[1] Almost three years later, Obama has been unable even to sustain the Israeli-Palestinian peace negotiations that were routine during Bush's last year in office, let alone generate the final peace agreement that Obama had been so determined to achieve at the beginning of the first year of his presidency. Indeed, by May 2011, George Mitchell had resigned in quiet frustration, and Obama had issued instructions to his diplomats not to engage in any further efforts to resume the negotiations. American peacemaking diplomacy in the Middle East had reached a new nadir.

The failure of Obama's peacemaking effort is matched and inter-connected with his other Middle Eastern foreign policy failure: to improve America's standing in the Arab and Muslim world. As a candidate he had made much of the damage George W. Bush had done to America's reputation in the world, especially in the greater Middle East where U.S. troops were now involved in two wars. He announced early on that if elected, he would address the Muslim world and work to improve relations with its many disparate parts.

Obama believed that in the Middle East, there was a symbiotic relationship between peacemaking and public diplomacy: if he suc-ceeded in improving relations with the Muslim world, he would make it easier for Arab leaders to engage in the effort to resolve the Israeli-Palestinian conflict; if he succeeded in settling that conflict, it would make it easier to improve relations with the Muslim world for which the Palestinian issue had long been the "hot button." Yet, notwithstanding his good intentions and his appreciation of the interconnectedness of the Middle East's multiple maladies, by the end of his third year in office, Obama's approval ratings in the Arab world had ended up as low as Bush's.[2]

In a further irony, the one thing Obama seemed uninterested in—promoting democratic change in the Middle East—turned out to be the one thing that occurred on his watch anyway. The Arab awakenings that have swept the Arab world since the revolutions in Tunisia and Egypt at the beginning of 2011 were neither gener-ated nor anticipated by the Obama administration, although it was certainly cognizant of the problems that produced them.[3] While the president has embraced some of these secular, democratic rev-olutions and distanced himself from others, the Arab street has not shown any greater warmth to Obama or America as a result (although it is still early days).

Egypt, one of the long-standing pillars of American influence in the region, is shaking. The kings and sheikhs of Araby—on whom the United States relies for the production of over 20 percent of the world's oil—have escaped the contagion of instability for the moment, but how long that can last without serious efforts at political reform is highly questionable. The specter of an anti-American Muslim Brotherhood eventually taking power in Arab countries whose previous leaders had been staunch American allies has now become a real, though possibly misplaced, concern.

In the meantime, the United States became embroiled in a third war in the greater Middle East, this time in Libya, where Obama committed to Qaddafi's overthrow but left it to his NATO allies to provide the resources necessary to achieve it. While "leading from behind" was the correct approach, since no American national interest required the United States to get out in front, the gap between his declared objective and the means he was willing to commit to achieve it left Obama's foreign policy branded with this unfortunate and unfair label.[4]

There still remains the hope that the Syrian people will eventually overthrow the Assad regime and thereby deal a severe blow to Iran's efforts to use its alliance with Syria to promote its anti-American agenda in the Middle East heartland. But Obama is left with only limited means to influence the outcome there. And in the meantime, the failure to move the Israeli-Palestinian conflict toward resolution has left the United States poorly positioned to deal with the potential negative fallout from turmoil in a region vital to American interests.

The demise of the American-led Israeli-Palestinian peace process, the loss of Egypt as a reliable partner in promoting American interests in this volatile region, and the potential unintended impact on the stability of the two American-brokered peace agreements—between Israel, Egypt, and Jordan—may well generate the combination of circumstances that ends the era of *Pax Americana* in the Middle East. If that is the case, Obama will have succeeded in helping bend history in the wrong direction.

Where did it all go wrong? The blame cannot be apportioned to Obama alone. Certainly, he faced a steep uphill climb to achieve any of his objectives. By the time he entered the Oval Office, anger at the United States in the Muslim world was at its peak, fueled by the widespread belief that Bush's war on terror was in fact a war on Islam, and that America's true attitude to Muslims had manifested itself in the torture and humiliation of prisoners in Abu Ghraib and Guantanamo Bay. The fact that Obama was the first African American president, with a Muslim father and a Muslim name, generated enthusiasm in Africa and Indonesia, but it bought him only a little credit in the Arab world.

On the Israeli-Palestinian front, Obama also faced very long odds. Five years of the Second Intifada had left thousands killed and many more wounded on both sides, generating deep distrust in the intentions of the other. While majorities of Israelis and Palestinians still supported the two-state solution that Clinton had proposed at the end of his time in office and Bush had endorsed during his term, neither side believed the other wanted it or would be prepared to make the necessary compromises and sacrifices to achieve it.

Two months after Obama became president, Benjamin Netanyahu became prime minister of Israel, heading up a right-wing coalition that initially did not even accept the idea of an independent Palestinian state in the West Bank and Gaza. Meanwhile the Palestinians were deeply split both politically and geographically between a moderate Fatah leadership in the West Bank—headed by President Mahmoud Abbas (Abu Mazen) and Prime Minister Salam Fayyad—committed to peace with Israel, and a radical Hamas leadership in Gaza committed to Israel's destruction.

Hamas, along with Hezbollah in Lebanon, was backed by Iran, which had long been determined to use these two proxies to prevent any progress in resolving the conflict because that would reduce its ability to spread its influence into the Middle East heartland. By the time Obama came into office, Iran's efforts had been given a huge boost by Bush's failure to curb Iran's nuclear program, by his opening of the gates to Iranian influence in Iraq, as well as by his insistence on Palestinian elections that had led willy-nilly to Hamas's control of Gaza.

In these circumstances, it is by no means clear that any combination of benign intentions, skillful statecraft, and good fortune could have overcome the considerable obstacles Obama faced. No recent president had fared much better. Nevertheless, the way Obama went about it had the effect of compounding the difficulties rather than ameliorating them. An examination of his method reveals some of the underlying problems with his approach to foreign policy more generally that have served also to hold up his achievements elsewhere across the globe.

OBAMA'S "THEORY OF THE CASE"

As with so much else in Obama's presidency, the early days of his Middle East engagement seemed to hold out the hope of a bright new day in a region that had grown tired and cynical. Obama promised a new relationship with the Arab world, symbolized by his commitment to end the use of torture and close the Guantanamo Bay detention camp, and to withdraw American forces from Iraq. He also offered an outstretched and open hand to the Iranian regime, if it would unclench its fist. And he promised to resolve the Palestinian problem on his watch. But there was one constituency to whom Obama seemed to pay little heed as he painted his picture of a new Middle East at peace with America—Israelis and their fervent supporters in the American Jewish community.

During the presidential campaign, Obama had gone through the ritualistic paces of a Democratic candidate: meeting with American Jewish leaders, traveling to Israel, and speaking to the annual convention of the American Israel Public Affairs Committee (AIPAC—the vaunted "Israel lobby"). He overcame the fact that he was an unknown quantity to most American Jews by having leaders of the Chicago Jewish community vouch for him. He persuaded those who doubted his pro-Israel credentials by declaring to the citizens of the southern Israeli town of Sderot that he could identify with their existential dread by imagining putting his own daughters on the school bus there and wondering if he would ever see them again.[5] He swore to remain steadfast in his support for Israel's security. And he won a near record 78 percent of the Jewish vote and secured more than one-third of his campaign funds from American Jews.[6]

However, along the way there were signs, for those who cared to pay attention, that this was no ordinary Democratic candidate. At a meeting of Jewish leaders in Cleveland during the campaign, Obama inveighed against those in the pro-Israel community who insisted on the adoption of "an unwavering pro-Likud approach" and called for an "honest dialogue" about the best way to achieve peace.[7] And in a speech to AIPAC that touched all the usual pro-Israel themes, Obama also insisted that Israel "refrain from building new settlements." He scolded Bush—popular among many in the AIPAC audience for his staunchly pro-Israeli stance—for isolating the United States in the region, arguing that he had thereby jeopardized Israel's security. And he put them on notice that peacemaking was an American national interest that could not wait any longer.[8] While he also announced that he supported an "undivided" Jerusalem as Israel's capital, he would immediately afterward explain that he had misspoken and that Jerusalem's status needed to be negotiated.

Once in the White House, Obama would pay little attention to the American Jews who had done so much to put him there, meeting with their leadership only once a year and telling them in the first meeting that Bush's closeness to Israel (which they had greatly appreciated) had not helped the United States or Israel: "There was no daylight," Obama asserted, "and no progress."[9]

In Obama's mind, the way to handle Israel was not to embrace it warmly like Bill Clinton and George W. Bush had done, but rather to meet all of its security requirements. He would state repeatedly that the U.S. commitment to Israel's security was "steadfast," and he meant it. Under his instructions, the Pentagon, CIA, and State Department took security cooperation with their Israeli counterparts to new highs. Obama lived up to a commitment made by

George W. Bush in more profligate times to provide Israel with $30 billion of military assistance over the next ten years. He also requested from Congress an additional $300 million to pay for the Iron Dome short-range rocket defense system that would help protect civilians on Israel's southern and northern borders from Hamas and Hezbollah rocket attacks.[10] And he and his senior national security team would work hand-in-hand with their Israeli counterparts to deal with Iran's nuclear program. No matter the level of tension on the political level, there was never any hint from the Obama administration of withholding security assistance to Israel.

On the other hand, Obama was intent on pursuing the "other woman" in the U.S.-Israel relationship. He gave his first foreign interview as president to al-Arabiya, the Arab cable TV network; it would be another eighteen months before he granted an interview to an Israeli TV station, and he has yet to repeat the exercise. He made much of appointing a special envoy from the White House to be his ambassador to the Organization of the Islamic Conference in February 2010, but he did not replace Bush's ambassador to Israel until August 2011. He traveled the Muslim world from Ankara to Riyadh to Cairo and Djakarta. But he has yet to visit Jerusalem.

In his personally crafted Cairo speech to the Muslim world in June 2009, he channeled the Arab narrative that Israel's existence was a product of the Holocaust, making no reference to the centuries-old longing of Jews to return to their ancient, biblical homeland.[11] Moreover, he drew a parallel between Jewish suffering through the ages and Palestinian suffering at the hands of Israel, identifying with Palestinians who have had to endure "the pain of dislocation" and the "daily humiliations . . . that come with occupation."[12]

The "theory of the case" that Obama was prosecuting was all quite logical: the United States needed to repair its relations with the Arab and Muslim world because American troops were involved in two wars in the Middle East. And as he explained it to Israelis in that single Israeli TV interview, "My outreach to the Muslim community is designed precisely to reduce the antagonism and the dangers posed by a hostile Muslim world to Israel and to the West."[13] If he succeeded at that, he thought, he would make it easier for Arab leaders to engage with Israel and therefore easier for Israelis to take risks for peace.

Israelis and their American Jewish supporters, who had grown used to the unalloyed affection of two American presidents over the previous sixteen years, viewed Obama's intentions quite differently—as a deliberate effort by the new president to distance the United States from Israel in order to curry favor with the Arabs. And, security assistance and strategic cooperation notwithstanding, they really did not appreciate it.

This created a deeply problematic context for the showdown that Obama sought over Israeli settlement activity with the newly elected Likud prime minister, Benjamin (Bibi) Netanyahu. A majority of Israelis and American Jews do not support building more settlements in the West Bank, just as they had backed the evacuation of all of them from Gaza in the summer of 2005. But in his Cairo speech, Obama had declared that the United States did not accept "the *legitimacy* of continued Israeli settlements," and in his first meeting with Netanyahu in the White House in May 2009, he demanded a complete settlements freeze. As his secretary of state would elaborate in a Cairo press conference, "[The president] wants to see a stop to settlements—not some settlements, not outposts, not natural growth exceptions. We think it is in the best interests of the effort that we are engaged in that settlement expansion cease."[14]

Obama was seeking a settlements freeze that allowed no building at all, not even additional apartments or a school or synagogue, in existing settlements. That was something that might have been possible in 1977, when Menachem Begin agreed to Jimmy Carter's insistence on a three-month moratorium, because the West Bank settlement population numbered only some 50,000. Even in 1993, when Yitzhak Rabin froze all settlement activity in the West Bank, settlers numbered some 150,000. But today they number more than 300,000, rendering a total freeze unrealistic, especially for the

119

right-wing coalition that Netanyahu had assembled, which drew its support from the settler community and its supporters.

Moreover, all Israeli prime ministers since Israel annexed east Jerusalem in 1967 have encouraged vigorous building in the Jewish suburbs of east Jerusalem, and previous U.S. presidents had been loath to make an issue out of that because of the political sensitivities involved. In demanding a complete settlements freeze, Obama failed to make any distinction, thereby implying that building in east Jerusalem had to cease, too, and inadvertently encouraging the Palestinians to insist on that. In addition, labeling the settlements themselves "illegitimate" represented an important shift in U.S. language that implied the freeze was just the prelude to a demand for their complete dismantlement.[15] That, too, went beyond the Israeli-American Jewish consensus since it was generally assumed that the settlement blocs, where some 70 percent of the settlers were concentrated along the 1967 "green line," would be annexed to Israel in any final peace agreement.

Netanyahu bridled at the demand, believing in his more insecure moments that Obama's real intention was to cause a split in his right-wing, settler-allied coalition and either unseat him or force him into a new, more moderate coalition with his rival Tzipi Livni and her centrist Kadima Party. Nevertheless, he told Obama in their first meeting that if he could bring Saudi Arabia's King Abdullah to the table, Israelis would support a reciprocal gesture like the freeze that Obama had demanded.

PURSUING THE SAUDI MIRAGE

This concept of reciprocity—a favorite approach of Netanyahu in his dealings with the Arabs and the United States—was actually something that George Mitchell had been working on: in his first tour of Arab capitals as Obama's envoy, he heard from some leaders there that if Israel froze settlements, they would be prepared to take reciprocal steps of normalization (for example, reopening

Israeli interest sections or commercial offices, overflight rights for Israeli civilian aircraft, and tourist visas for Israelis).

Moreover, in 2002 Saudi Arabia's King Abdullah had launched the Arab Peace Initiative, which offered Israel peace and normalized relations with every country in the Arab world if it withdrew to the 1967 lines and made peace with the Palestinians and Syria. However, the Arab Peace Initiative had yet to be turned from a declaration of intent into a mechanism for Arab state involvement in resolving the Israeli-Palestinian conflict. Both Hillary Clinton and George Mitchell, in their early soundings in Gulf Arab capitals, had heard from the Arab leaders about their fear of Iran's hegemonic ambitions. Perhaps Obama could build on a common concern about Iran between Israel and the Saudi-led Gulf Arabs to activate the Arab state engagement that he believed would boost the prospects for peacemaking.

Moreover, recruiting the Saudi king had special appeal for Obama because it fit his "theory of the case." It could boost his credentials in the Muslim world and help him make peace at the same time. So when he heard from the Saudi ambassador in Washington that the king was keen for the president to visit Riyadh and would not let him go home empty handed, Obama imagined that the stage was set. In June 2009, a visit was hastily arranged en route to Cairo for his speech to the Muslim world.

However, for a Saudi king—the "Custodian of the Two Holy Mosques" in Mecca and Medina—to meet directly with an Israeli prime minister was not only unprecedented, it was highly unlikely. The Saudis had always kept their contacts with the Israelis under the table, and they had always preferred to be the caboose on the peace train. Were the gambit to succeed, it would require careful preparation. Yet Obama was so confident that he decided to perform this mission solo: his secretary of state and his Middle East envoy were instructed to rendezvous with him in Cairo. The only preparation he made was to send ahead John Brennan, his counterterrorism adviser, to confer with his Saudi counterpart about taking some of the Yemeni Guantanamo prisoners off U.S. hands. When Brennan reported agreement on that, the president was encouraged: surely his request for engagement with Israel would be treated in the same way.

When he made his presentation to King Abdullah at his horse farm outside Riyadh, however, Obama was reportedly stunned to discover that the monarch had not been briefed by his intelligence chief on the Yemeni prisoners. Surprise turned to dismay when the king told Obama that he trusted neither Netanyahu nor Abbas, and would certainly not meet with the prime minister of Israel. Worse, the king said he would not even contemplate positive steps toward Israel until after Obama had secured a final peace deal. And even then, he would only consider it; he would make no commitment in advance of the deal.[16]

This was a rude awakening for the president, one that led him to ask Dennis Ross, Bill Clinton's Middle East peace envoy, to move from the State Department to the National Security Council (NSC) to provide Obama with advice from an old hand to make up for his own inexperience. On the face of it, this was a sensible move: when Obama has seasoned policy experts by his side at the NSC to help implement his policy, he has been able to demonstrate considerable success. Michael McFaul on Russia, Jeff Bader on China, and indeed Dennis Ross on Iran were all able to help Obama develop his foreign policy in these areas with élan.

But when it came to peacemaking, Ross's recruitment only compounded the problem of delivery because he had a very different theory of the case. He believed that the only way to make progress was by working with Israel's prime minister and taking his coalition difficulties into account, and by building trust between the Israeli public and the president. In Ross's view, showing daylight between the United States and Israel would only encourage the Arabs to sit back and wait for the president to deliver Israeli concessions, rather than persuading them to step forward and engage with Israel.

That difference in approach was reinforced by the fact that during the Clinton years, when Netanyahu had been prime minister the first time around, Ross had developed a special relationship with Yitzhak Molcho, Netanyahu's closest adviser and his designated chief negotiator with the Palestinians. With Ross now in the White House, Netanyahu pursued a long-standing Israeli preference for direct communication with the president by activating this back channel, thereby circumventing and undermining the roles of Obama's secretary of state and his special envoy for Middle East peace.[17] The unintended consequence of Ross's reengagement in Obama's peacemaking effort was therefore to create a basic dysfunction at the heart of his operation.

THE SETTLEMENTS FREEZE FIASCO

Without a Saudi dividend, Netanyahu was less willing to risk jeopardizing his coalition to meet Obama's requirements. Instead, he began a long, drawn-out negotiation with George Mitchell over the terms of a settlement moratorium. This was a well-practiced Middle Eastern technique of dragging a would-be activist American president down into the weeds of a detailed negotiation over a subject in which his interlocutors had the advantage of local knowledge. It took seven months to reach a deal in which Netanyahu would freeze all new residential activity in the West Bank for a period of ten months. However, 3,000 housing units that were already in the planning stage would be grandfathered into the agreement. And there would be no formal restriction on building in Jewish suburbs of Arab East Jerusalem that had been annexed by Israel after the 1967 war.

On the face of it, this settlements moratorium was unprecedented—a Likud-led government had been persuaded to agree to freeze all residential building in the West Bank settlements for ten months. But when Secretary of State Clinton said as much in a press conference in Kuwait welcoming the agreement, she was met with derision across the Arab world, particularly among Palestinians in the West Bank.[18] They focused on the exceptions rather than the rule. Instead of triggering a series of reciprocal steps from the Arab states to create a more conducive environment for negotiations, not one of them was willing to step forward.[19]

Worse still, Abu Mazen now insisted that without a complete settlements freeze, including on building in East Jerusalem, he could not enter direct negotiations with Netanyahu. Seven months of U.S. diplomatic effort had been wasted and Obama's credibility damaged for no good purpose.[20]

Unfortunately, it did not end there. Now that Netanyahu had managed to convince his government to support a settlements moratorium, he needed the resumption of negotiations to show his people that he had gained something for it. Otherwise he feared he would look like a sucker. But in the meantime, Abu Mazen's own credibility and pride had been damaged by an episode in which he had tried to be responsive to Hillary Clinton's request that he delay consideration by the UN Human Rights Council of the Goldstone Report on war crimes allegedly committed by Israel during the 2006 Gaza war. This unleashed fury at Abu Mazen among Palestinians and across the Arab world; even the normally protective Egyptian and Jordanian governments condemned him. And in the midst of this furor, Israeli officials leaked tapes of Abu Mazen and other Palestinian officials during the 2009 Gaza war urging their Israeli counterparts to hit Hamas even harder. Deeply offended, Abu Mazen became even more unwilling to countenance Obama's request that he drop his full settlement freeze precondition and resume negotiations.

By the end of 2009, Obama was publicly admitting that he had underestimated the difficulty of resuming negotiations and had "overestimated our ability to persuade them to do so when their politics ran contrary to that. . . . If we had anticipated some of these political problems on both sides earlier, we might not have raised expectations as high."[21]

In an effort to circumvent the impasse over settlement activity, in March 2010 Mitchell proposed four months of "proximity talks," in which he would shuttle between the two leaders and discuss the critical issues of borders and security to facilitate a return to direct negotiations. Mitchell borrowed the concept from his successful experience in the Northern Ireland peace negotiations. But in the Arab-Israeli context it looked like a throwback to the proximity talks overseen by the United Nations in 1949. Israelis and Palestinians had been holding direct negotiations continuously for fifteen years (from 1993 to 2008). Abu Mazen's Mukata (the presidential compound) in Ramallah was a thirty-minute drive from the Israeli prime minister's residence in Rehavya, where Abu Mazen had negotiated for eight months with Ehud Olmert, Netanyahu's predecessor. To revert now to proximity talks amounted to more than just a lowering of expectations; it signaled a near breakdown of the negotiating process. And there was worse to come.

On March 9, 2010, the day after Mitchell's announcement, and the same day that Vice President Biden was making an official fence-mending visit to Jerusalem, an obscure planning committee in Israel's Ministry of Interior announced approval for 1,600 new housing units in Ramat Shlomo, a Jewish suburb in East Jerusalem. Although the move appears to have blindsided Netanyahu, it caused an immediate suspension of Palestinian engagement in the proximity talks and a major eruption in U.S.-Israel relations.

The committee's decision incensed Obama because he had been working on a private understanding with Netanyahu that his government would issue no new tenders for building in Jerusalem in 2010 in return for Abu Mazen agreeing to enter direct negotiations. His vice president had also been personally embarrassed. Obama instructed Biden publicly to condemn the decision while still in Jerusalem and Clinton to personally rebuke Netanyahu. The president also instructed Clinton to demand that Netanyahu take immediate steps to show his commitment to renewing negotiations and to warn him of specific consequences if he failed to do so, including the possibility of allowing condemnation of Israeli settlement activity in the UN Security Council. Their stormy conversation was then briefed to the *Washington Post*.[22] When Netanyahu visited the president in the White House two weeks later, he received a chilly reception—no official photograph in the Oval Office and no meal. While hanging tough did generate a commitment from Netanyahu to block construction in Ramat Shlomo for two years, enabling the proximity talks to get under way again, the incident deepened the divide between Obama and Israel and its supporters in the United States.[23]

Not surprisingly, in this atmosphere the proximity talks made little progress. Netanyahu insisted that he would only lay out his substantive positions on borders in direct negotiations, focusing the diplomatic exchanges instead on industrial zones, water, and economic issues. Abu Mazen, on the other hand, only wanted to focus on territorial issues in order to determine Netanyahu's intentions when it came to defining the borders of the Palestinian state.

Within weeks, on May 31, 2010, the indirect negotiations were disrupted again, this time by the Gaza flotilla incident in which Israeli commandos in international waters boarded a Turkish passenger ferry attempting to break the blockade of Gaza. In the melee that ensued, Israeli forces killed nine Turkish citizens. The simmering Obama-Netanyahu tensions were suddenly transformed into a full-blown crisis between Israel and Turkey, two long-time U.S. strategic allies in the Middle East.

This crisis required Obama to test the alternative theory of the case: working with Netanyahu rather than against him, in an attempt to ameliorate the crisis. (The alternative of condemning Israel would only have deepened the crisis and raised doubts about the credibility of Obama's "steadfast commitment" to Israel's security.) Within days he had managed to persuade Netanyahu to lift the ban on the flow of most goods into Gaza and had channeled the crisis in Israeli-Turkish relations into a special UN panel of inquiry into the raid. It was not quite peacemaking, but it did show a deft presidential diplomatic hand. This in turn produced a newfound comity in U.S.-Israel relations, crowned by an "excellent" White

House meeting in July between Obama and Netanyahu. The meeting included a working lunch as well as a photo opportunity and produced enough of an understanding between the two leaders actually to facilitate a return to direct negotiations.

On the Palestinian side, the flotilla crisis had created a new, more positive dynamic, too. Perhaps worried that the easing of the Gaza siege would advantage Hamas, Abu Mazen decided that he should see whether he could produce some gains from negotiations. He also seems to have come to appreciate, albeit belatedly, that the settlements moratorium had actually frozen most West Bank settlement activity. And he found his main Arab patrons, Egypt's Hosni Mubarak and Jordan's King Abdullah, keen for him to engage with Netanyahu because of promises that the Israeli prime minister had made to them that he would be forthcoming with Abu Mazen, including on Jerusalem.

At last, on September 2, 2010, after eighteen months of contentious preparatory work, with Egypt's President Mubarak and Jordan's King Abdullah looking on, Obama presided over a White House ceremony that launched direct negotiations between Bibi Netanyahu and Abu Mazen. The terms of reference for the negotiations were deliberately vague. As Obama outlined them, "These will be direct negotiations between Israelis and Palestinians. These negotiations are intended to resolve all final status issues. The goal is a settlement, negotiated between the parties, that ends the occupation which began in 1967 and results in the emergence of an independent, democratic and viable Palestinian state, living side by side in peace and security with a Jewish state of Israel and its other neighbors."[24]

There would be a one-year timeline for the negotiations, but Obama was silent on what would happen when Netanyahu's settlement moratorium expired in one month's time. Asked about that at a press conference after the opening ceremony, Obama explained that he had told the Israeli prime minister, "It makes sense to extend that moratorium so long as the talks are moving in a constructive way."[25] That might have made sense to Obama, but Netanyahu's right-wing coalition partners surely did not see things the same way: they had been promised by Bibi that the moratorium would be a one-time commitment, and they made clear they would hold him to it.

In any case, the talks did not move forward in a constructive way. Two weeks later, in their third meeting, at the prime minister's residence in Jerusalem on September 16, Abu Mazen presented Netanyahu with the formal Palestinian position on territory and other issues that he had previously given to Ehud Olmert. Bibi put this paper aside and instead gave Abu Mazen an elaborate lecture on Israel's security requirements in a final status agreement. Rejecting the idea of an international force in the Jordan Valley—something Olmert had accepted—Netanyahu explained in great detail why the Israeli army would have to remain there "for decades, *many* decades."[26] From this Abu Mazen understood that Netanyahu intended for Israel's military occupation of the West Bank to continue long after a final agreement had been struck. That was something he could not begin to countenance. He told Netanyahu to keep his occupation. The negotiations were over almost before they had begun.

The action shifted immediately to the UN General Assembly in New York, which convenes every year in the last week of September. The speech of the president of the United States always garners a great deal of attention from the heads of state and other high representatives of the international community assembled there. Obama knew he now had a problem with the negotiations faltering and the settlement moratorium about to expire. Nevertheless, when he addressed the UN General Assembly two days later, he highlighted the settlement issue by calling for an extension of the moratorium. And then he doubled-down: "When we come back here next year, we can have an agreement that will lead to a new member of the United Nations—an independent, sovereign state of Palestine, living in peace with Israel."[27]

It was not exactly a promise, but that's how the representatives of the international community in the General Assembly Hall immediately interpreted it. In particular, Palestinians and their

Arab supporters read it as the president of the United States opening the door to Palestine's entry into the United Nations as an independent state. The Palestinians had always enjoyed overwhelming
support at the UN, particularly in the General Assembly; it was
only the American veto that protected Israel in the Security Council, and Obama had already raised questions about that (which the
Palestinians would soon test by introducing a resolution condemning Israeli settlement activity). From this moment on, it seems, the
Palestinians began serious planning for a vote during the September 2011 UN General Assembly on Palestinian state membership,
not as the culmination of negotiations with Israel—as Obama had
intended it—but rather as a substitute for negotiations with Netanyahu, in whom they had lost all faith.

Behind the scenes in New York, Obama was focused on how to
persuade Netanyahu to extend the settlements freeze. The positive
experience of working with him on the flotilla crisis rendered the
president willing this time to listen to Dennis Ross, who resur-
rected an old technique that he had used in negotiations between
President Clinton and Netanyahu: a side letter of assurances. The
basic idea was to give Netanyahu something valuable on security
issues from the United States that he could use to persuade his
hard-line coalition partners to support extending the moratorium.
Since Obama had repeatedly vowed to do everything necessary to
support Israel's security, he had little objection to this approach.
However, the terms of the letter, as they emerged over another two
months of negotiations—including a seven-hour session between
Secretary of State Clinton and Netanyahu in New York on November 1—read like extortion when they were leaked to the media.

In return for Netanyahu extending the settlements moratorium
for ninety days, the United States would give Israel an additional
$3 billion in military assistance to pay for twenty more F35 Joint
Strike Fighter jets.[28] And the letter from the president would explicitly state that he would make no further request for extending
the moratorium when it expired again in three months, which of

course raised the question: what would happen in the likely event that there was no progress in the negotiations by then?

What looked like a bad deal was made even less attractive when Shas, the Sephardi orthodox party and a mainstay of Netanyahu's coalition, announced that notwithstanding the letter of assurance, it would not support the moratorium extension unless Netanyahu also committed to approving new building starts in Jewish suburbs of East Jerusalem. Without that commitment, Bibi did not have the votes in his cabinet; but if he made that commitment, he would not have a Palestinian partner in the negotiations. Obama quietly pulled the plug on the whole exercise.

In the meantime, the moratorium had expired at the end of September, and the Palestinians, as expected, had declared that unless it was extended, they would not continue the negotiations. Abu Mazen had now turned the extension of the settlements moratorium, which he had decried as inadequate until one month before its expiration, into the *sine qua non* of negotiations. Another year of intensive engagement had left Obama in exactly the same position as when he had expressed his disappointment to *TIME* magazine at the end of his first year in office.[29]

This time Obama left it to his secretary of state to announce the pivot. In a speech to the Saban Forum in early December 2010, Hillary Clinton explained that instead of direct negotiations between Israelis and Palestinians, she would engage in "substantive two-way conversations" on the core final status issues, "hopefully to find enough common ground on which to eventually re-launch direct negotiations." She promised that the United States would play an active role, pushing the parties to lay out their positions "without delay," asking the tough questions "and expecting substantive answers," offering "our own ideas and bridging proposals when appropriate," and measuring their seriousness "by their engagement on these core issues."[30] In other words, Obama was finally abandoning both the effort to achieve a settlements freeze and the effort to engage the parties in direct negotiations.

Notwithstanding Clinton's public commitment to substantive engagement, there was none. George Mitchell made one more visit to the region in December and was then not heard from again until he quietly resigned on April 6, 2011.[31]

OBAMA WALKS AWAY

In the meantime, the Palestinians sought to test whether the United States would be willing to separate from Israel in the UN Security Council. In February 2011, they introduced (through Lebanon, the Arab representative on the Security Council) a resolution that condemned as illegal all Israeli settlement activity, including in East Jerusalem, and demanded that Israel cease this activity forthwith.[32] Because the resolution was cosponsored by 120 states and supported by all the other members of the Security Council, Obama found himself in a difficult position.

If he let the resolution pass, he would go beyond his declared policy that settlements were "illegitimate" to brand them as illegal, facilitate the condemnation of a close U.S. ally in the Security Council, and insert the Security Council into the effort to resolve the Israeli-Palestinian conflict. But if he blocked the resolution, he would be casting the first Security Council veto of his presidency and thus isolate the United States in the most important world forum as a consequence of defending the very Israeli settlement activity that he fundamentally opposed. In the end, after a valiant effort by his UN ambassador to substitute a nonbinding presidential statement failed, Obama decided to veto. It was a bitter ending to a well-intentioned effort to improve the environment for a negotiated solution, which had instead reinforced the obstacles even to resuming the negotiations. And it was the harbinger of more UN-generated quandaries to come, since the Palestinians were now determined to seek recognition of their state at the next UN General Assembly opening meeting the following September, just as Obama had foreshadowed.

Given its fraught state, Middle East peacemaking could now no longer compete for the attention of a White House that quickly became preoccupied with dramatic developments elsewhere. At home, Republicans had taken control of the House in the 2010 midterm elections, not only creating immense complications for Obama's domestic agenda but also providing an opportunity for Netanyahu to circumvent him by mobilizing his strong ties to the Republican leadership. Meanwhile, in the Middle East, democratic revolutions were sweeping U.S. allies in Egypt and Tunisia from power, spreading instability across the region to the borders of Saudi Arabia, the world's largest oil producer. Obama no longer had the inclination or the time to be caught up in another futile effort to resume Israeli-Palestinian negotiations.

Instead, in January 2011, his aides began considering a different approach altogether. From the outset of his administration, Jim Jones, Obama's national security adviser, had pushed the idea of laying down "Obama parameters"—a detailed American plan for a settlement—and concerting international pressure on both sides to accept it. Several influential pundits—notably former national security advisers Brent Scowcroft and Zbigniew Brzezinski—promoted this idea in the public debate every time the peace process stalled.[33] Although Jones left the White House in October 2010, the idea gained new legs when Clinton raised it with Obama in January 2011, and he said that he would be willing to consider it, "at the right time." Planning began in earnest for a presidential speech in which he would lay out the parameters, but it soon became bogged down in an intense argument within the administration about whether to make the speech, when to do it, and what its contents would be.

The internal debate dragged on for months. It was not until mid-April 2011 that the president finally decided that he would give a speech on the Palestinian issue within the context of addressing the other dramatic developments in the Arab world.[34] By that time, cognizant of the deliberations within the Obama administration, Netanyahu had announced that he intended to make his own speech, and his friends in the Republican leadership in the House had invited him to deliver that address to a joint session of Congress. The timing was set for mid-May, to coincide with Netanyahu's appearance at AIPAC's annual convention. So the question then turned on whether Obama should deliver the speech before or after Netanyahu's visit to Washington. Eventually the White House decided that it should be delivered before, to prevent Netanyahu's address to Congress—which would inevitably be greeted with prolonged standing ovations—from boxing the president in. But given the president's other competing priorities and the lateness of his decision to give the speech, the timing was set for May 19, two days before Netanyahu arrived in Washington, creating the impression of dueling presidential and prime ministerial speeches.

The debate within the Obama administration about the substance of what he would say on the Palestinian issue raged until the last moment. Tom Donilon, the new national security adviser, and Dennis Ross argued that to put out detailed parameters in the context of the Arab uprisings that were occurring all over the Arab world risked another failure and further damage to Obama's credibility at a time when he could ill afford it. Secretary Clinton argued that to say nothing at this point about the Palestinian issue would make it look like Obama had abandoned a cause that was still fundamentally important to Arabs and would leave the United States unarmed in the effort to head off UN General Assembly action in September. In the end the president decided to go for a pared down version of the parameters, one that would put the United States on record as believing that "the borders of Israel and Palestine should be based on the 1967 lines with mutually agreed swaps" but would avoid saying anything substantive about other sensitive issues like Jerusalem and refugees.[35] However, Obama only cleared on this language at the last minute, leaving no time before delivery to prepare the ground with Netanyahu, Abu Mazen, or any of the many other world leaders with an interest in the Palestinian issue.

Netanyahu was incensed that Obama would stake out a position on borders that would favor the Palestinians just before he arrived in Washington.[36] Emboldened by his appearance at AIPAC the night before, and by the expectation that his Republican friends would ensure a warm welcome when he spoke before Congress the day after, Netanyahu decided to attempt to beard the president in the Oval Office. In the photo-op after their meeting, he upbraided the president for suggesting that Israel should return to the indefensible lines of 1967.[37] Obama sat next to him, staring at the ceiling in silence, even though he had said no such thing.

Now it was Obama's turn to be furious with Netanyahu. Always maintaining his cool demeanor, however, the president went to AIPAC's annual conference two days later and elaborated on the parameter that had ignited such controversy: "By definition it means that the parties themselves—Israelis and Palestinians— will negotiate a border that is different than the one that existed on June 4, 1967 . . . [that] allows the parties themselves to account for the changes that have taken place over the last forty-four years, including the new demographic realities on the ground."[38]

This was a way of indicating that Obama accepted the language of a letter President Bush had written to Prime Minister Ariel Sharon in 2004 to indicate that settlement blocs (that is, "demographic realities") should be incorporated into Israel when the borders were agreed on, something that the Palestinians had already accepted in principle.[39] However, this elaboration by Obama in front of AIPAC made it appear that the president was backing down in the face of pressure from the "Israel lobby."

Lost in the *sturm und drang* was the fact that the United States had for the first time put two parameters on the table: that the borders between the two states should be based on the 1967 lines, and that the "ultimate goal" of the negotiations should be "Israel as a Jewish state and homeland for the Jewish people, and the state of Palestine as the homeland for the Palestinian people." These two parameters were the very principles that each side had been demanding from Obama for much of the time that he had been engaged in the pre-negotiations: Abu Mazen had wanted the 1967 lines as the basis of negotiations; Netanyahu had wanted Palestinian recognition of the Jewish state as a goal of the negotiations. But absent from Obama's two speeches had been any mention of a mechanism that his administration would now employ to capitalize on his words. No envoys were dispatched to consult with the two sides; no invitations were issued to begin negotiations on the basis of these parameters. On the contrary, Obama issued instructions that no one from his administration should engage with either side.

Instead, Tony Blair, the Middle East Quartet's special envoy, and Catherine Ashton, the European Union's foreign minister, were given license to explore whether negotiations could be resumed on the basis of Obama's speech; but since they did not represent the United States, neither side would take them seriously. Both Netanyahu and Abu Mazen understood that Obama had checked out. From his point of view, Middle East peacemaking would have to await his reelection—that is, it was 2013 work.

Nothing could underscore that better than the speech Obama made before the UN General Assembly in September 2011, one year after he had raised the idea of UN membership for Palestine in front of the very same body. He had earlier indicated in his AIPAC speech that he would oppose any attempt to secure recognition of statehood for the Palestinians through the United Nations. Now he made clear that the only route the United States would support was direct negotiations and decried the idea of a UN "shortcut." Sounding very much like a candidate running for reelection, he emphasized his commitment to Israel's security. Instead of dwelling on Palestinian suffering, as he had in his Cairo speech two years earlier, he now dwelt on Jewish suffering, winning himself plaudits in Israel and among American Jewish leaders but lukewarm applause in a body with a well-established sympathy for the Palestinians.[40]

Behind the scenes in New York, Obama's diplomats had engaged in furious efforts to head off Abu Mazen's application to the UN secretary general for Palestinian admittance as a member state, but to no avail. Blair and Ashton had also worked hard to cobble together a Quartet statement that would at least form the basis for a resumption of negotiations. But in the end, Netanyahu would only accept the president's parameter on borders—the 1967 lines plus swaps—if Abu Mazen would accept the "Jewish state" as a goal of the negotiations. Abu Mazen would only countenance such language if there were a requirement for a full settlements freeze during the course of the negotiations. Seeing an opening to champion the Palestinian cause at U.S. expense, Russian foreign minister Sergei Lavrov also rejected any reference to the Jewish state in the Quartet statement.

There was little chance of untangling this mess without the president's active engagement, but his unwillingness to pay any further domestic political price, his refusal to revisit the settlements issue, and his opposition to Abu Mazen's UN gambit only added to the hurdles. In the end, the Quartet statement made no reference to the parameters the president himself had outlined in his May 19 speech; it referred only to a timetable for negotiations, which both sides knew from long experience would only be met in the breach.[41] That is how the peace process ended on Obama's watch: not with a bang but a Quartet whimper.

CONCLUSION

It was an ignominious conclusion to Obama's effort to resolve the Israeli-Palestinian conflict. Critics have been unanimous in declaring that the mistake was for the president to have focused on the unrealistic demand for a full settlement freeze. After all, the Palestinians had previously negotiated with Netanyahu and other Israeli prime ministers without a cessation of settlement activity. By insisting on it, the critics argued, Obama actually succeeded in driving Abu Mazen away from the negotiating table since he could not be seen to accept something less than the U.S. president had demanded of the Israelis. By focusing on it, Obama ended up wasting a good deal of time and energy, the one thing a four-year presidential term does not allow for. And by failing to achieve it, Obama damaged U.S. credibility as the mediator in the conflict—a problem that compounded the other challenges at home and abroad to "brand America."

There was, however, logic in Obama's demand—restricting settlement activity could have improved the environment for negotiations and reduced Palestinian mistrust of Israeli intentions. His call for a settlement freeze, including "natural growth," was neither unprecedented nor unreasonable in the context of a renewed effort to resolve the conflict through negotiations. It had been one of George Mitchell's principal recommendations when he had been tasked by President Bill Clinton to head an international inquiry into the causes of the intifada.[42] That recommendation had been turned into an Israeli obligation under phase one of Bush's October 2002 "Road Map for Peace," which then prime minister Sharon had accepted.[43] The Palestinian Authority had taken on reciprocal obligations to fight terror and dismantle its infrastructure, which it had been doing in the West Bank with increasing effectiveness on Bush's watch; it was logical for Obama to expect that Israel would now fulfill its obligations on settlement activity. American diplomats involved in earlier Israeli-Palestinian negotiations had all noted in retrospect that one of the greatest impediments to progress was settlement activity because it undermined the confidence of Palestinians in Israel's ultimate willingness to give up the territory that they were being built on. Menachem Begin had agreed to freeze settlement activity for three months; Yitzhak Rabin had frozen building in the West Bank for more than a year; Ehud Olmert had agreed with Bush not to build any new settlements.

On the other hand, when Bibi Netanyahu had been prime minister of a right-wing coalition in the 1990s and Bill Clinton had sought to persuade him to restrict settlement activity, Netanyahu had taken advantage of a "natural growth" exemption to expand significantly settlements in the West Bank. Two of Obama's closest advisers, Rahm Emanuel and Hillary Clinton, had both lived through that experience in Bill Clinton's White House and were determined to shut off that loophole the second time around. So there were multiple reasons for Obama to insist on a settlements freeze including "natural growth" in his first engagement with the newly elected Netanyahu. And to give Obama, Clinton, and Mitchell their due, they did succeed in getting Netanyahu to agree to a significant settlement moratorium.

What they failed to do, however, was to modify the declared objective once Obama, following his pragmatic instinct, had given Mitchell the green light to negotiate with Netanyahu for something less than a complete settlements freeze, including natural growth. As Abu Mazen has repeatedly explained, Obama's demand put him up in a high tree and Mitchell's moratorium ladder was too short to use it to climb down.

The signs of trouble had been there from the very beginning. In May 2009, on his first visit to Washington to meet with Obama, Abu Mazen told the *Washington Post* that he would not begin negotiations until Obama had forced Netanyahu to freeze all settlement activity.[44] And he repeated that position in a letter to the president in August. By that time, Mitchell knew that Netanyahu would only accept a moratorium if he were allowed to grandfather new building permits into the deal and exclude East Jerusalem.[45] Obama approved that deal even though he knew that, following his visit to Saudi Arabia, he could not sell it to the Arabs, let alone Abu Mazen.[46] At that point, in the summer of 2009, Obama needed to pivot—his favorite tactic, borrowed from his basketball experience—before all sides got locked into a self-defeating fixation on settlements. In hindsight, he would have been better off focusing on developing the terms of reference for the negotiations, which could have helped both Netanyahu and Abu Mazen go into the encounter with greater confidence about its outcome. His unwillingness to adjust his publicly articulated goal to the realities of what was achievable opened up a gap between his declared objective and his ability to deliver on it. The same was true of his speech envisaging a Palestinian state welcomed into the 2011 session of the UN General Assembly, an idea that he ultimately had to reject.

This has become a familiar hallmark of Obama's presidency. When it comes to speaking, his rhetoric is visionary; but when it comes to delivering, his approach is pragmatic. That generates an inevitable tension, which he seems unable to resolve. His willingness to compromise necessarily produces something less—often far less—than the expectations generated by his rhetoric. But he often fails to adjust his prophetic vision to the pragmatic outcome of his administration's diplomacy, and that produces inevitable disappointment.

This tension has expressed itself elsewhere, too. His theory of the case led him to focus his rhetorical skills on the Arab world while refusing to address the Israeli public. The content of his Cairo speech combined with his perceived unwillingness to visit Israel lost him Israeli public opinion very early on. His reception of Netanyahu on his second visit to Washington in July 2009 left Israelis with the impression that he regarded their elected leader as an unwanted guest, compounding the damage done by the Cairo speech. Consequently, he surrendered his leverage over Netanyahu, who follows the polls obsessively. The Israeli prime minister knew from bitter experience that the Israeli public would punish him for mishandling relations with a popular U.S. president, but he also knew that they would support him if he stood up to an unpopular U.S. president, which is what Obama fast became in Israeli eyes.[47] From all previous experiences, Netanyahu's upbraiding of the president of the United States in the Oval Office should have cost him dearly in Israeli public opinion; instead his ratings went up ten points.

The president had an array of advisers who were familiar with Netanyahu and the Israeli public—Vice President Biden had dealt with both for decades; Secretary of State Clinton had been the senator for New York, with its large American Jewish community, and is married to a president who was immensely popular in Israel;

Chief of Staff Rahm Emanuel had served in the Israeli army and was intimately familiar with Israeli politics; George Mitchell had dealt with Israel on Capitol Hill for many years; and Dennis Ross, Obama's Middle East adviser at the NSC, had worked closely with Netanyahu. All of them recommended that he take steps to address the Israeli public, either by visiting or through media interviews. Nothing happened for eighteen months until the president finally gave a convincing interview to Israeli TV; but inexplicably, he never followed up with another.

All of that might have been forgotten or forgiven if he had succeeded in bringing the Arab world around to embrace Israel. But the Arab street had become deeply cynical about leaders mouthing empty rhetoric. They cared less about Obama's distancing from Israel and more about whether he could use America's closeness to Israel—which they took for granted—to deliver concessions that would lead to the creation of the Palestinian state that he had promised them. But without the trust of the Israeli public, he could not hope to deliver those concessions. When Obama also failed to deliver on his commitment to close the Guantanamo Bay detention camp, the Arab street began to turn its back on him. And when he spoke of welcoming a Palestinian state into the United Nations community, and then vetoed a Security Council resolution that condemned Israeli settlement activity and threatened to do the same to a resolution that recommended UN membership for a Palestinian state, they gave up on him. Thus Obama has ended up with the worst of both worlds.

Whether he can redeem his promise of Israeli-Palestinian peace awaits both the outcome of the U.S. presidential election and conditions on the ground, should Obama have the opportunity to try again. Perhaps the Jordanian efforts at preliminary Israeli-Palestinian talks will succeed in laying the groundwork. But unless Obama develops a different theory of the case and works with Israeli and Palestinian partners who are willing to take risks for peace and defend the necessary, painful compromises, the result of a second attempt is unlikely to be much different from the first.

CHAPTER FIVE

THE ARAB AWAKENINGS

BY JANUARY 2011 THE PRESIDENT'S inability to make progress on the Palestinian issue and his loss of popularity on both sides of the Arab-Israeli divide had combined with a sluggish economy and a burgeoning debt problem to leave the United States poorly positioned for dealing with the unexpected problems or opportunities bound to arise in the unpredictable Middle East.

Nothing could have been more unpredictable than the uprisings that swept across the Arab world, beginning in January 2011 with the overthrow of the regime of Zine al Abedine Ben-Ali in Tunisia. North Africa—the Maghreb—had never featured prominently in American strategy for the Middle East. Except when King Hassan of Morocco had taken the lead in efforts to resolve the Israeli-Palestinian conflict and when Libya's Qaddafi had sponsored terror attacks on U.S. citizens or developed and then abandoned a nuclear weapons program, the Maghreb tended to be a sideshow for U.S. interests compared to the much larger stakes elsewhere in the Middle East.

Thus when Tunisian protesters succeeded in toppling one of the region's most repressive rulers in a matter of days, the ripple effects for the rest of the Middle East were not expected to be profound. Secretary of State Hillary Clinton remarked at the time of the Tunisian revolution, "Our assessment is that the Egyptian government is stable and is looking for ways to respond to the legitimate needs and interests of the Egyptian people."[1] But when tens of thousands of Egyptian demonstrators, inspired by their Tunisian counterparts, began to demand the ouster of Hosni Mubarak, President Obama started to pay keen attention.

In contrast to the Maghreb sideshow, Egypt is at the epicenter of U.S. strategic interests in the Middle East. It is the militarily most powerful and culturally most influential country in the Arab world, with an ancient civilization, a homogeneous population, and a history of 4,000 years of centralized rule. One in every four Arabs is an Egyptian. Its geostrategic location astride the Suez Canal and at the crossroads of three continents makes it an invaluable ally to the United States. And its peace treaty with Israel has served as the anchor of stability and the foundation of peacemaking in the Arab-Israeli arena; as long as the peace agreement holds, no other Arab state can rationally contemplate war with Israel. Egypt has therefore served for thirty-five years as a pillar on which the United States has built its position of influence in the region. And for thirty of those years, Hosni Mubarak ruled over Egypt with the firm grip of a pharaoh.

As a superpower, the United States has developed vital interests and alliances across the globe; as the world's leading democracy, the United States has also seen itself as the beacon of freedom to the world's oppressed. Each American president has had to strike a balance between protecting the national interest and promoting the nation's values. In the Middle East, however, every American president since Franklin Roosevelt has struck that balance in favor of the national interest, downplaying the promotion of America's democratic values because of the region's strategic importance. Successive presidents accepted a tacit deal with those Middle Eastern kings, sheiks, and military rulers willing to maintain stability in a volatile but vital region: the United States in return would leave them essentially alone to run their own internal affairs.

For a time, George W. Bush was the exception to this rule. After toppling Saddam Hussein in Iraq, he decided to promote a "freedom agenda" in the Middle East. As his secretary of state, Condoleezza Rice, famously argued in her own Cairo speech in 2005: "For 60 years, my country, the United States, pursued stability at the expense of democracy in this region, here in the Middle East, and we achieved neither. Throughout the Middle East the fear of free choices can no longer justify the denial of liberty."[2] Bush pressed Mubarak to open some political space for moderate, secular forces to emerge in Egypt and succeeded for a moment in convincing Mubarak to loosen his grip. But when Hamas won the Palestinian elections, Bush relented and returned U.S. policy in the Middle East to its default position.

Barack Obama, in his determination to distinguish himself from Bush, made clear during his campaign for president that he would not promote democracy in the Middle East—at least not the way Bush did. He portrayed himself as a realist in the Eisenhower-Kennedy-Reagan-Bush 41 tradition, rather than an idealist in the Bush 43 mold. His visionary rhetoric rarely included the word *democracy*. Many in the Arab world watched his Cairo speech carefully to see how he would handle Mubarak's increased suppression of opposition after Bush had backed off pressing him to reform.[3] In that speech he distanced himself from Bush by declaring that "no system of government can or should be imposed by one nation on any other." While he avowed his support for human rights, he noted that "there is no straight line to realize this promise."

His national security strategy white paper, issued in May 2010, buried the section on promoting democracy and human rights abroad on page 38 of a fifty-two-page document.[4] There Obama explains his approach of "principled engagement with nondemocratic regimes." His strategy would be to work with them on counterterrorism, nonproliferation, and economic ties but also "to create permissive conditions for civil society to operate and for more extensive people-to-people exchanges." If rebuffed, "we must lead the international community in using public and private diplomacy, and drawing on incentives and disincentives, in an effort to change repressive behavior." Not exactly a freedom agenda, his approach was typically progressive but pragmatic, working with the authoritarian regimes rather than supporting those who would overthrow them.

The White House published the white paper nine months after the Iranian regime had brutally suppressed widespread demonstrations provoked by its hijacking of the presidential elections. Obama hesitated to criticize Iran's bloody crackdown partly because of his desire to keep the hope of engagement alive and partly because he did not want to risk validating charges that the demonstrators were "American agents." He made no serious attempt to lead the international community in pressing for constraints on the regime's brutal crackdown.

THE EGYPTIAN REVOLUTION

Given this predisposition and the strategic insignificance of Tunisia, the rapid collapse of the Ben-Ali regime made a limited impression on Obama's White House. But on January 25 mass demonstrations occurred in Egypt's major cities, accompanied by violent clashes with the police that continued for days. On Friday, January 28, after the police failed to suppress the demonstrators with tear gas, water cannon, and occasional live fire, army troops were ordered into the streets of Cairo, and Egypt's Interior Ministry warned of "decisive measures."[5]

Obama publicly called that day on the Egyptian government to recognize its people's "universal rights" and to respond to their demands. But he ended his remarks by declaring that he intended to work *with* the Mubarak government "in the pursuit of a future, that is more just, more free, and more hopeful."[6]

However, in a press briefing on that same Friday afternoon, after the Egyptian troops had been deployed, Obama's spokesman, Robert Gibbs, did something quite extraordinary: he called on Egyptian security and military personnel "to refrain from violence" and warned repeatedly, "We will be reviewing our assistance posture based on events that take place in the coming days."[7] Asked whether that message had been communicated to the Egyptian military, he noted, "It has been communicated not just from this podium, not just in remarks from the secretary of state, but at levels within the Pentagon to the Egyptian military." Asked whether that message had been discussed with the president, he replied in the affirmative.

Since the 1978 signing of the Egypt-Israel peace treaty, the Egyptian military had received massive amounts of U.S. military assistance, enabling it to turn the army into an American-trained and American-equipped fighting force. That assistance was currently at $1.3 billion a year. But the message now being transmitted from American commanders to their Egyptian counterparts was, We are watching closely; if you fire on unarmed civilian demonstrators, American law will require an immediate suspension of military assistance.[8] Although they were little noticed in the American media at the time (the briefing occurred on a Friday afternoon), these verbal warning shots from the White House and the Pentagon clearly found their mark.

Three days later, on January 31, the Egyptian military declared in a televised broadcast ahead of "a million man" march called by the protest leaders for the next day, that it would not fire on the demonstrators. Describing the demands of the protesters as "legitimate," the military communiqué emphasized, "freedom of expression through peaceful means is guaranteed."[9] This statement represented a decisive move by the critical mainstay of Mubarak's regime. A mere six days of mass demonstrations had brought the Egyptian army to the side of the people. The declaration not only guaranteed freedom of expression, it also ensured that many more demonstrators would pour into the streets now, knowing that they had nothing to fear from the army. Obama immediately responded by praising the Egyptian military for their patriotism and for allowing peaceful demonstrations.[10] From that moment it was essentially all over for Mubarak.

As events unfolded in Tahrir Square, Obama's timely intervention had helped to ensure that rather than be drawn into a bloody civil war, the Egyptian military was preserved intact as an institution that—at least in theory—could serve as the midwife of a transition to democracy and yet still play a regional role in preserving stability and in maintaining the Israel-Egypt peace treaty, the foundation stone of *Pax Americana* in the Middle East. At the time of his intervention Obama had not yet reached the unsentimental judgment that regardless of America's debt to Mubarak for thirty years of dutiful friendship, he was finished. That would come soon enough in response to the rapid collapse of Mubarak's grip on power. Rather, Obama was acting to reinforce the Egyptian military's own instincts for self-preservation by pressing it to refrain from entering the fray.

At this stage, Obama's objective was an orderly transition to a democratically elected government. To help produce that, he approved an approach that would have Mubarak hand over power to a vice president (Mubarak had never appointed one before in his thirty-year reign), who would then oversee constitutional amendments and an eventual democratic election after secular parties had been given time to organize. This strategy, however, required Mubarak to stay in place as a figurehead president until the scheduled presidential elections took place in September. In the meantime, constitutional changes could be put into effect to ensure free and fair elections. If Mubarak resigned before then, the existing constitution required that presidential elections take place in two months. As borne out by subsequent events, the Obama administration had good reason to fear that a rapid election would advantage the Muslim Brotherhood, which was disciplined and well organized and had now joined the demonstrators.

On January 29, according to plan, Mubarak sacked his cabinet and appointed Omar Suleiman, his chief of military intelligence, to the post of vice president. Suleiman, on advice from the Obama administration, began a dialogue with leaders of the opposition. On January 30 the U.S. secretary of state appeared on the main

Sunday television news shows to articulate the objective of an "orderly transition" of power. But to achieve this would require Mubarak and Suleiman to get ahead of the crowd. Accordingly, Obama dispatched Frank Wisner, a veteran diplomat, to Cairo with instructions to persuade Mubarak to announce that neither he nor his sons would stand in the September presidential elections.

Wisner had served as U.S. ambassador to Egypt in the 1980s and had maintained a friendship with Mubarak since then. While Mubarak rejected Obama's message in his meeting with Wisner, he clearly gave it further thought. The next day, February 1, he announced to the Egyptian people that he would not stand for reelection.[11] Instead, he said he would stay in office until the elections were held in September to oversee changes in the constitution that would allow for independent candidates to run for president. But his tone was paternalistic, and the hundreds of thousands of demonstrators who were watching the speech on JumboTrons in Cairo's Tahrir Square were in no mood to trust his stewardship of the promised constitutional changes. It was clear that they would accept nothing short of Mubarak's immediate departure. That same evening, after a difficult conversation with Mubarak in which Obama tried unsuccessfully to persuade him to speed up the process, Obama chose to respond from the White House in his own televised address:

All of us who are privileged to serve in positions of political power do so at the will of our people. Through thousands of years, Egypt has known many moments of transformation. The voices of the Egyptian people tell us that this is one of those moments; this is one of those times. Now, it is not the role of any other country to determine Egypt's leaders. Only the Egyptian people can do that. What is clear—and what I indicated tonight to President Mubarak—is my belief that an orderly transition must be meaningful, it must be peaceful, *and it must begin now*.[12]

It seems Obama had decided that, constitutional requirements notwithstanding, the prospects for an orderly transition were less likely the longer Mubarak stayed in power. He wanted to make clear that he heard and identified with the demands of the demonstrators and supported their "universal rights" to freedom and democracy.[13] His speech said as much but in such a peremptory tone that it offended both Mubarak and his friends, the leaders of the Arab world. Israel's leaders too were deeply troubled by the way that the president seemed to be demanding that Mubarak step down and do it immediately.

The president had inserted himself directly in the contest for power that was unfolding in the streets of Cairo. And if anyone doubted his purpose, for good measure he sent his press spokesman out the next day to reinforce the message. Gibbs insisted that the president wanted the transition of power "to begin now."[14] He then added, "When we said now, we meant yesterday." To many of the region's leaders it sounded like the young president of the United States was ordering an old and proud Egyptian president to get out of the way and to hurry up about it.

Obama seemed insensitive to the public humiliation that he was seen to be inflicting on Mubarak, but he would soon get the message. King Abdullah of Saudi Arabia was furious; the much younger crown prince of the UAE was equally upset. If that is what Obama could do to a stalwart friend of the United States as soon as he faced demonstrations, what, they wondered, would he do to them in the event that they confronted similar circumstances? Didn't he understand that revolution in Egypt would produce a Muslim Brotherhood takeover, which could sweep them out of power too? They had entrusted their external security to the United States; now it looked like the president, in his newfound passion for universal rights, had turned America into a threat to their internal security. They both made their feelings clear to him in very difficult conversations.[15]

The dismay of America's Arab authoritarian allies made little immediate difference. Obama was determined to be on the right side of history. If the United States were to have any hope of shaping the post-Mubarak era in a country that would remain of critical strategic importance, he felt strongly that the United States needed to be on the side of the square not the palace. But the message was now ahead of the policy: a week later Secretary Clinton was still talking about an orderly transition that "takes time," while the White House press spokesman continued to insist that "an orderly transition must begin now, that it must produce without delay immediate and irreversible progress."[16]

In the following days, each time Mubarak or his vice president did something that did not comport with that message, the White House was quick to respond publicly.[17] On February 10, for example, Director of the CIA Leon Panetta testified to Congress ahead of a televised address that Mubarak was scheduled to make that evening. Asked what Mubarak might do, Panetta said that he expected the Egyptian president to announce his resignation. When Mubarak did not follow the script and instead spoke of continuing to shoulder his responsibilities until the transition took place in September, the Tahrir Square demonstrators erupted in anger.

Obama immediately issued a statement from the White House, making clear that he identified with the impatience of the Egyptian people: "We believe that this transition must immediately demonstrate irreversible political change and a negotiated path to democracy."[18] He reiterated his demands on the Egyptian government, and then he made a point of saluting the demonstrators: "In these difficult times, I know that the Egyptian people will persevere, and they must know that they will continue to have a friend in the United States of America."

Within twenty-four hours, sensing and fearing the anger of the crowd, the Egyptian military forced Mubarak to resign and depart for Sharm el-Sheikh. Obama wasted no time in heralding the moment from the grand foyer of the White House.[19] This was a historic moment for Obama, not just for the Egyptian people, signified by the linkage that he drew between their nonviolent revolution and the movements led by his heroes, Mahatma Gandhi and Martin Luther King. Obama noted, "For in Egypt it was the moral force of non-violence . . . that bent the arc of history toward justice once more." It was no coincidence that in marking the occasion he would choose to paraphrase his favorite quotation. As he noted, the Egyptian people had succeeded in changing their country, "and in doing so changed the world." That is what he had hoped his presidency would be about too, and for one bright moment it was.

Obama's public messaging had now raised expectations among disaffected Arab youth across the region that he would be just as outspoken in support of their aspirations for freedom. At the same time, by abandoning a long-time friend of the United States, he had managed to cause deep offense and raise serious doubts about his reliability among America's other authoritarian allies in the region. In recognizing the Egyptian revolution, Obama had embraced "that something in our souls that cries out for freedom." That would quickly put him back on the horns of a dilemma when it came to attempting to balance interests and values elsewhere in a Middle East now in turmoil.

THE BAHRAIN EXCEPTION

The first test came within days. Because of Egypt's role and influence in the Arab world, Mubarak's overthrow prompted further demonstrations across the Middle East, from Algeria and Morocco in the west to Yemen and Oman in the east. In Bahrain, demonstrators holding their own peaceful "day of rage" were immediately confronted by police using tear gas and rubber bullets. Obama was quick to urge King Hamad Bin Isa al-Khalifa "to get out ahead of change," and for a moment it looked like he was taking heed.[20] But two days later, in a predawn raid, police attacked demonstrators who had camped out in the country's main traffic roundabout, the Pearl Circle.

When the demonstrators attempted to retake the circle, security forces opened fire on them. This prompted the eighteen parliamentary members of the official opposition party, Al Wefaq, to resign and join the ranks of the dissenters. The crowd in Pearl Circle swelled to over 100,000—one fifth of the island's citizens. Some demanded that the king sack his government and remove his uncle from the office of prime minister, which he had held for four decades; others called for the overthrow of the monarchy.

At a similar moment in the Egyptian revolution Obama had publicly insisted that a leadership transition take place immediately. This time he kept out of the limelight: publicly, his spokesman expressed "deep concern"; privately, Obama phoned the king and urged him to exercise restraint.[21] What accounted for the difference in treatment between giant Egypt and tiny Bahrain?

The simple answer is Saudi Arabia, Bahrain's next-door neighbor and that other pillar of American influence in the Arab world. The largest state on the Arabian Peninsula, Saudi Arabia is also one of the largest oil producers in the world and the only one with the "swing" capacity capable of moderating the price of oil through increased production.[22] Since 1945, when King Saud al-Faisal and Franklin Roosevelt made their pact, the Saudis kept the oil spigot open, and U.S. armed forces provided for the security of the kingdom and the free flow of its oil through the troubled waters of the Gulf. That understanding reached its high point in 1991, under George H. W. Bush, who dispatched 500,000 U.S. forces to save the kingdom by evicting Saddam Hussein's army from neighboring Kuwait. It reached its low point twelve years later when George W. Bush overthrew Saddam Hussein and, in the service of democracy, encouraged a Shia government to take control in Baghdad. From the Saudi perspective, as the leaders of the Sunni world, Shias in the Arab world were merely extensions of their Persian masters.

Simplistic as it may seem to Americans, the Saudis had good reason to be suspicious of Iranian intentions, especially under the rule of the ayatollahs, who sought to extend their revolution to the Arab world and establish their dominance of the Gulf. Bush's emphasis on spreading democracy in the Middle East only deepened Saudi angst. Now they had to deal with a new American president who failed to fulfill his promise on the Palestinian issue and seemed to be transferring Bush's freedom agenda from Baghdad, where in Saudi eyes it had already done irretrievable damage, to Cairo, where it could destabilize the whole region.

King Abdullah had already expressed directly to Obama his deep unhappiness with the White House's treatment of Mubarak. From his perspective, the United States was responsible for the turmoil that followed. Although he understood the need for political reform in his highly conservative, orthodox religious kingdom, he was determined that it would happen slowly. If he responded too quickly to the secular demands of Western-educated, middle-class Saudis—especially for equal treatment of women—he could unleash a Wahhabi fundamentalist backlash that would be a gift to al Qaeda and its anti-American agenda.[23] He was therefore unwilling to countenance any possibility of popular dissent in Saudi Arabia. His way of "getting ahead of his people" was to offer them, at the outset of the troubles in Egypt, a package of benefits worth $37 billion in housing and new jobs; he would top that off with much more of the same, as the flames of instability started licking at almost all of Saudi Arabia's borders.[24]

Above all else, the one thing the Saudi king would not tolerate was the overthrow of the Al-Khalifa royal family in Bahrain. These Sunni sheikhs had ruled there for two centuries, dominating a Shia majority, which had now grown to more than 60 percent of the people. Deprived of equal rights and opportunities, the Shias had long sought representation in an empowered parliament. To satisfy these demands, King Hamad introduced constitutional changes in 2001 but, under Saudi pressure, failed to implement them. Since then, the Saudis kept a wary eye on this virtual satrapy out of two concerns about a Shia revolt there: that it could spill over into Saudi Arabia's oil-rich eastern province, where its Shia community—5 percent of its population—is concentrated; and that the Iranians would exploit the conflict to take control of Bahrain through Shia proxies and gain a foothold on the Arab side of the Gulf.

President Obama had good reason to take King Abdullah's concerns into account, even if the U.S. government saw no evidence of Iranian interference in Bahrain and could not have stopped the Egyptian revolution if it wanted to. The Arab awakenings had already caused the price of a barrel of oil to rise into the $90 range, and now strife in Libya would soon remove its supply of sweet crude from the market, which would drive the price even higher. Turmoil in Bahrain that spread to Saudi Arabia's eastern province and threatened Saudi oil exports could cause a panic in the market. Economists estimated that every $10 hike in oil prices shaved a quarter percent growth off the U.S. economy, with a similar impact on the global economy. With the U.S. economic recovery already sluggish, and Obama's reelection prospects hinging on growth that could generate jobs, he simply could not countenance instability in Saudi Arabia. Here was a case in which interests trumped values, regardless of whether Obama's soul cried out for freedom. That realist judgment governed Obama's approach to the revolt in Bahrain.

Thus on Friday evening, February 18, when it looked like a major confrontation between the armed forces and the demonstrators was about to take place, Obama called the king and urged him to show restraint. The next day, Crown Prince Salman bin Hamad al-Khalifa ordered the troops to leave the circle and offered a dialogue with the protesters. That cooled passions for several weeks, but the dialogue never got off the ground. Hard-line relatives, including the prime minister, pressured the crown prince to show no leniency. Meanwhile, the leaders of al-Wefaq became fearful of being outflanked by the harder line demonstrators, who insisted that the prime minister first resign before the dialogue took place.[25]

By Friday, March 4, the crowd in the circle had grown to some 200,000, and their demands had escalated, too—they now called for the overthrow of the king. Distracted by the rebellion in Libya, Obama had done little in the meantime to encourage the dialogue. However, on March 11, in the face of huge Friday demonstrations,

Secretary of Defense Robert Gates arrived in Bahrain to consult with the king.

The sheiks of Bahrain had developed a special friendship with the U.S. armed forces—seeing in them, like their Saudi big brothers, the ultimate source of their protection. They had provided a base for the U.S. navy since 1971, and it had been converted into the headquarters of the U.S. navy's Fifth Fleet in 1995. Gates was therefore well positioned to have a heart-to-heart conversation with King Hamad and Crown Prince Salman, since, as the U.S. secretary of defense, he could hardly have any interest in seeing the kingdom destabilized. According to Gates's account of the two-hour meeting, he told them that "baby steps" toward reform would be inadequate to meet the political and economic grievances of their people.[26] He also cautioned them that prolonging the reform process would provide an opportunity for Iran to become involved, creating more chaos and triggering sectarian warfare. He warned them, "Time is not our friend."

From the U.S. perspective, urging the king to make a serious and prompt effort to meet the reasonable demands of his citizens for constitutional reforms made eminent sense. Before the revolts broke out across the Arab world, Secretary Clinton had bluntly warned all the Gulf rulers that they risked "sinking into the sand" of unrest and extremism unless they liberalized their political systems.[27] Gates was following a Washington-designed script to help ensure that its Gulf Arab allies would survive the rising dissent in their neighborhood.

But that was not the way the king of Saudi Arabia saw it. If the Iranians were about to exploit the turmoil in Bahrain, the only remedy was to snuff out the revolt, not encourage the Shia demonstrators by offering them major reforms. He was already making contingency plans to that effect, mobilizing his troops and those of the UAE. Now claiming illness, he begged off seeing Gates or Clinton, who was heading to the region at that moment. But he conveyed to Obama through other channels a very clear warning:

if the United States tries to push the king of Bahrain from power it will cause a break in U.S.-Saudi relations.

On Sunday, March 13, the day after Gates departed Bahrain, thousands of protesters moved on Manama's financial district, shutting down the access roads and rebuffing efforts by the police to disperse them. That night the White House again publicly urged the king "to pursue a peaceful and meaningful dialogue with the opposition rather than resorting to the use of force."[28] But it was too late. Cutting off the financial district threatened Bahrain's economy—the banking sector accounted for 25 percent of the country's GDP. King Abdullah decided to move.

On Monday, March 14, a Gulf Cooperation Council (GCC) force of some 1,200 Saudi and 800 UAE troops advanced across the causeway linking Saudi Arabia to Bahrain and took up positions around government buildings, industries, and infrastructure. With this backing, the Bahrain armed forces, using tanks and helicopters, cleared the financial district and Pearl Circle of the demonstrators and for good measure demolished the 300-foot-high pearl monument that had given the park its name. Some thirty protesters were reportedly killed in the violent suppression. Widespread arrests followed, including all the opposition leaders and some of the doctors and hospital staff who had helped treat casualties. Emergency decrees were promulgated, and a nighttime curfew was enforced in downtown Manama.

Iran reacted with rhetorical fury but preferred to let Arab Shias take the lead in standing up for their coreligionists—Hezbollah and the Iraqi Shia parties were happy to oblige. In Saudi Arabia, Shia protests in the eastern province took place but remained peaceful. The Saudi king went on television to thank his citizens for not succumbing to the pressures to join the crowds around them and promised them another $93 billion in handouts!

From the distance of Washington, Obama's spokesman called for calm and restraint, placing the emphasis on a political solution that through dialogue could address "the needs of all Bahrain's

155

citizens." On her arrival in Cairo, Clinton criticized the use of force "from any source" and repeated the call for a dialogue, noting that she had called the Saudi foreign minister and told him that use of force "cannot be a substitute for a political resolution."[29] There was notably no call on the GCC to withdraw its forces or for the king of Bahrain to back off the violent suppression of peaceful, freedom-seeking demonstrators.

If the muted public criticism had little impact, the private exchanges were no more productive. Obama called the Saudi and Bahraini kings to deliver a message to them directly. In what his spokesman described as difficult conversations, the president stressed the need for a political process that would lead to a Bahrain "that is stable, just, more unified and responsive to its people." According to an Arab official briefed on the conversation, King Abdullah responded, "Saudi Arabia will never allow Shia rule in Bahrain—never."[30]

Obama left it to his secretary of state publicly to "deplore" the use of force and reiterate that political reform was the only way forward to resolve the legitimate differences of the Bahraini people.[31] Reform, not revolution; that remained the Obama administration's mantra on appropriate public occasions. For example, in his seminal May 19, 2011, Middle East speech, in which Obama declared that U.S. support for universal human rights in the Middle East would be a "top priority," the president criticized the Bahrain government for its mass arrests and use of brute force and again insisted that the only way forward was a dialogue with the opposition, pointedly adding, "and you can't have a real dialogue when parts of the peaceful opposition are in jail."[32] Three months later, the king released the leaders of the opposition, but notwithstanding Obama's call, the national dialogue is yet to resume.

Elections were staged to replace the eighteen Shia members of parliament, who had resigned in protest, but the opposition boycotted the election, and the newly elected members were denounced as fronts for the regime. And in the meantime, many Bahraini Shia demonstrators were sacked, and doctors and nurses were sentenced to severe prison terms for having tended to those wounded by the police. The King did establish an independent commission of inquiry and vowed to implement its recommendations, but, by the time of this writing, little had been done to redress people's grievances. As Obama noted in his May 19 speech, "there will be times when our short-term interests don't align perfectly with our long-term vision for the region."[33] The king of Bahrain's suppression of his people's "universal rights" was one of those times.

Notably missing from Obama's May 19 speech was any mention of Saudi Arabia, even though he knew that, with GCC troops still in Bahrain, the Saudi king was effectively in control of what the Bahraini king did with his opposition. There was more important business to transact there. Gates had finally met with King Abdullah on April 6 for an "extremely cordial, warm meeting," in which the secretary of defense admitted that he had not raised the Saudi-backed crushing of the Bahrain awakening.[34]

A week later, the president dispatched Tom Donilon, his national security adviser, to Riyadh for a two-hour meeting with the king, in which he delivered a personal letter from Obama. That, too, was an "excellent" meeting, producing joint cooperation to ease pressure on the price of oil, deal with the deteriorating situation in Yemen, and increase the pressure on the Assad regime in Syria and their common nemesis in Iran.[35] As Donilon's spokesman noted, "The discussion highlighted the importance of the U.S.-Saudi partnership rooted in strong historical ties and shared interests." The one place where they did not share interests—political reform in the kingdoms and sheikhdoms of the Middle East—appears to have been put aside in favor of the "short-term interests" Obama had allowed for in his speech.

Obama's pragmatism was on clear display. But in allowing for a Saudi exemption from his newly declared priority of promoting political reform across the Middle East, Obama was not just honoring a decades-old American presidential tradition of placing interests above values when it came to Saudi Arabia; he was now papering over a fundamental divide that had opened up between the United States and its most important remaining Arab ally.

"LEADING FROM BEHIND" IN LIBYA

Fortunately, King Abdullah and President Obama were in greater agreement about what should be done in the case of those Arab republics whose leaders have been difficult partners or even adversaries of both Saudi Arabia and the United States. Libya's Muammar Qaddafi and Syria's Bashar al-Assad have long been the Arab world's bad boys from the perspective of the palace in Riyadh, and that has essentially been true for Washington as well. So when revolts broke out in Libya and Syria following the revolution in Egypt, it was more possible to find common ground. And this proved particularly useful for Obama, as he struggled to find ways to support the Libyan rebels and the Syrian revolutionaries.

Given that Libya borders Tunisia to its west and Egypt to its east, the influence of the revolutions there on Libyans was bound to be profound, especially since they had suffered for four decades under the repressive and quirky rule of Muammar Qaddafi. Three days after Mubarak's overthrow, on February 17, 2011, Libyan demonstrators in Benghazi came out in large numbers to protest the regime's human rights abuses. The police responded with live fire, killing twenty-four demonstrators and provoking an armed rebellion.

Within days, major clashes erupted between Qaddafi's security forces, which were backed by African mercenaries, and protesters in Benghazi, Tripoli, and Misrata. As the death toll rose to 200, Benghazi fell to the rebels. By the end of February, Qaddafi had lost control of much of eastern Libya, including Ajdabiya, the refinery at Ras Lanuf, and the oil port of Brega. He responded with rage, declaring that he would track down and kill protesters "house to house." His son and heir apparent, Seif al-Islam, warned in a similar vein that the regime would "fight until the last man, the last woman, the last bullet." As the fighting intensified, the death toll rose dramatically, with the Italian foreign minister declaring that over a thousand civilians had been killed.[36]

Libya had not featured in Obama's foreign policy agenda at all up to that point. The Bush administration had normalized relations with Libya following Qaddafi's relinquishment of his nuclear program and his payment of full compensation to the families of the 190 American victims of Libya's terrorist attack on Pan Am flight 103 in December 1988. Qaddafi in the meantime had become a limited partner in the war on al Qaeda because Libyan jihadists were targeting his regime, too. The United States had reopened its embassy in Tripoli in 2006, and two years later Secretary of State Condoleezza Rice had even visited Tripoli. Qaddafi told her at the time that he "just wanted to be left alone," which suited U.S. interests well, as long as he continued to reciprocate.

By the time Obama came into office there was not much more to be done with this unsavory regime. American oil companies had found it difficult to do business in such an unpredictable and unfriendly environment; the Europeans seemed to fare better, perhaps because of their geographic proximity and greater willingness to engage. The simple reality was that as long as Qaddafi behaved himself, there was little American interest in this oil-rich North African desert state. Conversely, relations between Qaddafi and Saudi Arabia's King Abdullah had deteriorated dramatically at the same time as they had improved with George W. Bush.[37] An attempt to reconcile them at an Arab League meeting in 2009 ended in a shouting match, with Qaddafi walking out. Over the decades of his rule, similar antics had alienated most of the other Arab leaders, which left him quite isolated in the Arab world at the outset of the Arab awakenings.

So when Obama met with his national security team on February 23, it was the first time in his administration that Libya had been on the agenda. Before the meeting, Obama's spokesman condemned Qaddafi's violent response to the protests but—as with Bahrain— the president had stayed out of the limelight, in contrast to his bully pulpit approach to the revolution in Egypt. Now Obama denounced Qaddafi's onslaught as "outrageous and unacceptable," but at that point the president's focus was on evacuating over 600 American citizens and on "preparing the full range of options that we have to respond to this crisis."[38] Until all Americans were out of Libya, he was prudently buying time, intent on being circumspect to avoid any harm coming to them. However, he did send his diplomats to the UN and to Europe to influence the international reaction. As soon as the last Americans were on the plane, the White House announced unilateral sanctions against the Qaddafi regime, freezing $30 billion of its assets in the United States. And Obama's spokesman Jay Carney declared that Qaddafi's legitimacy "has been reduced to zero."[39]

Yet unlike the case of Egypt and Bahrain, from the beginning of the Libya crisis Obama sought a multilateral response to Qaddafi's brutality. On February 26, at U.S. urging, the UNSC imposed an arms embargo on Libya and referred Qaddafi to the International Criminal Court for investigation of war crimes; on February 27 the UN Human Rights Council opened its own inquiry into Qaddafi's actions and suspended Libya from participating in its deliberations. Similarly, the Arab League acted unanimously to suspend Libya's membership. As Qaddafi's brutal campaign of repression gained pace, so, too, did his regional and international isolation, and Obama took advantage of that.

On March 3, however, Obama went one rhetorical step further, getting out ahead of the rest of the international community. "Muammar Qaddafi has lost legitimacy to lead and he must leave office," the president declared in a photo opportunity in the Oval Office after a meeting with the Mexican president, Felipe Calderon.[40] This marked a continuation of the peremptory style he had just used with Mubarak but that King Abdullah had prevented him from using with the king of Bahrain. Though it was unlikely to cause the same offense to his Gulf allies, since they agreed with Obama in this case, it would put the president on record as seeking the overthrow of the Libyan dictator.

Qaddafi was undaunted; three days later his forces counterattacked the rebels, supported by tanks, artillery, war planes, and warships. In the next few days, they retook Ras Lanuf and Brega with relative ease, battled for control of Misrata, and advanced toward Benghazi. These events generated urgent calls for the international community to impose a no-fly zone over Libya to protect the civilians that Qaddafi had promised to eliminate.

As the killing continued, and the rebel leaders beseeched the international community for material help, an intense and surprisingly public debate broke out in Washington among the president's senior advisers. On the one side, Secretary Clinton announced that the option of imposing a no-fly zone was under "active consideration," and Senator John Kerry, chairman of the Senate Foreign Relations Committee, argued that it was appropriate, since the United States could not afford to stay on the sidelines. On the other side, Secretary Gates emphasized that now was not the time to get engaged in yet another war in Asia or the Middle East. Gates's public remarks became more strident as the pressure increased for Obama to do something to stop Qaddafi's advance on Benghazi: he argued in a speech at West Point that any U.S. president who decided to engage in another land war in the Middle East should "have his head examined"; and in testimony on the Hill, he pointed out that imposing a no-fly zone would have to begin with an attack on Libyan air defenses—an act of war.[41]

Obama was cautious, arguing to his aides that U.S. military intervention would skew the uprisings, making them look as if they were made in America rather than spontaneous outbursts of Arab popular dissent against brutal dictators. Nowhere in the administration's public statements was there any assessment of U.S. interests in Libya that would justify American military intervention. Yet Obama's public insistence that Qaddafi leave office led people to question what he was prepared to do to achieve it. This gap between declared objective and the means deployed to achieve it appeared in stark relief on March 10, when the White House announced a set of steps that amounted to providing aid and legitimacy to Qaddafi's opposition but nothing that would change the director of national intelligence's public assessment on the same day—that over time Qaddafi's regime was "likely to prevail."[42]

As the situation on the ground became more urgent, the Arab League—an institution with a well-deserved reputation for fecklessness—took an extraordinary step. On March 12, following the lead of Saudi Arabia, it called on the UN Security Council to impose a no-fly zone that would provide protection for Libya's civilians against the use of force by their government. Given the abhorrence of the Arab world for U.S. intervention in Iraq to overthrow Saddam Hussein, that twenty-two Arab countries would agree to call for outside military intervention in the affairs of another Arab country was quite extraordinary.

Even with that Arab invitation for military intervention, Obama was reluctant to act. At the G-8 meeting on March 15, no decision was taken to intervene despite French and British cajoling.[43] Russia and Germany were strongly opposed, and the United States remained noncommittal. But in days, Qaddafi's forces laid siege to the western city of Misrata and retook the town of Ajdabiyeh, leaving nothing standing between them and Benghazi except a ragtag group of poorly equipped rebels. In a radio broadcast, Qaddafi made it clear what he had in store for the people of Benghazi: "We will come house-by-house, room-by-room. It's over. The issue has been decided. . . . We will find you in your closets. We will have no mercy and no pity."[44]

The sense that a humanitarian atrocity was about to be committed in Benghazi tipped the argument in Washington in favor of the interventionists.[45] On March 17, Obama instructed Susan Rice, his UN representative, to seek a resolution that would provide cover for military intervention to protect Libyan civilians. But since this was a case of an intervention justified on moral grounds rather than national interest, and since French president Nicholas Sarkozy and British prime minister David Cameron were determined to take the lead, Obama decided to use it as a test case for the multilateralism that he had sought to promote elsewhere in adjusting to shifts in the global balance of power. He made clear that the U.S. military would take the lead only in the initial imposition of the no-fly zone and that there would be "no boots on the ground."[46] After U.S. military strikes on Qaddafi's air defense systems, which he limited to "days not weeks," others in NATO and the Arab League with greater interests at stake would have to take over responsibility.

Amazingly, given the time such multilateral action normally takes to negotiate, UN Security Council Resolution 1973 passed within hours, with Russia and China abstaining. It specifically provided for "all necessary measures" to be deployed "to protect civilians and civilian populated areas under threat of attack in the Libyan Arab Jamahiriya, including Benghazi." To be sure, the imminence of the expected massacre of possibly thousands of Libyan civilians, the fact that the Arab League had specifically requested the intervention, and the universal disdain for Qaddafi had all contributed to the willingness to act quickly. But now the UN Security Council decided to assume the "responsibility to protect" Libyan civilians against their government, and this represented a milestone for humanitarian intervention. And the willingness of Russia and China, as well as Brazil and India, to acquiesce indicated that there was now—for what turned out to be a fleeting moment—a degree of consensus about one of the pillars of the emerging global order that Obama was attempting to shape.

Indeed, in explaining to the American people his decision to commit U.S. military capabilities to the effort, Obama placed greater emphasis on the importance of not standing idly by "in the face of actions that undermine global peace and security" than he did on the need to support the universal rights of the Libyan people. Pointing to the Arab League and UNSC resolutions calling for the intervention, he observed, "This is precisely how the international community should work, as more nations bear both the responsibility and the cost of enforcing international law."[47]

However, there was nothing in UNSC Resolution 1973 that called for Qaddafi's removal, so Obama's insistence that he was implementing international law was at odds with his oft-stated insistence that Qaddafi had to go. Similarly, his emphasis on the strictly limited nature of the U.S. engagement highlighted the gap between the declared objective and the means applied to achieving it.

Not surprisingly, those in Washington who preferred a more robust, unilateral approach were quick to make the point.[48] And when one of Obama's senior advisers branded his strategy as "leading from behind," the gap widened further.[49] Obama's unwillingness to seek congressional authorization for his military action also reinforced the sense that the president was doing everything he could to avoid the perception that he had started another war in the Middle East, but he never explained how he hoped to get rid of Qaddafi without committing to support the rebels in their military campaign.

There were moments when it looked like the whole effort might fail because of a disorganized opposition movement with no experience in combating Qaddafi's well-equipped military forces, serious splits within the opposition leadership, and the constraints Obama placed on NATO's capabilities.[50] At those moments, the demand that Qaddafi should go looked unachievable; the chairman of the Joint Chiefs even publicly warned of a "stalemate."[51] That raised questions about U.S. and NATO credibility, questions that would not have arisen if Obama had stuck to the objective of protecting Libyan civilians while leaving the task of removing Qaddafi to the rebel forces.

Moreover, the repeated bombing of Qaddafi's command and control centers, including his compound in Tripoli, indicated that Obama was trying to use NATO airpower to achieve his declared objective. That strained the multilateral consensus achieved by the UNSC resolution by feeding Russian and Chinese suspicions that the West would always take permissive Security Council language and stretch its meaning well beyond its original intention—a problem that would come back to haunt Obama in his subsequent efforts to garner their support for dealing with two other Middle Eastern rogues—Iran and Syria.

And there were other unintended consequences. Saudi Arabia and the GCC sheikhs made a clever calculation that if they helped Obama with Qaddafi in the far-away Maghreb, they could expect him to lighten his pressure for political reforms in the closer-to-home Gulf. It was no coincidence that the commitment of UAE and Qatari aircraft and other resources to support the NATO operations and the opposition in Libya came at the same moment as Saudi-led GCC forces were entering Bahrain. As the *New York Times* reported on a meeting between Secretary of State Clinton and Foreign Minister Abdullah bin Zayed of the UAE, in Paris on March 14, "She criticized the foreign minister of the United Arab Emirates for sending troops to quash protests in Bahrain even as she pressed him to send planes to intervene in Libya."[52]

Nevertheless, this time Obama's theory of the case proved correct. Qaddafi's forces were turned back from Benghazi, and atrocities were prevented. As time wore on, opposition military capabilities grew, Qaddafi's financial resources were depleted, NATO air strikes significantly degraded Qaddafi's forces, and high-level defections signaled the approach of a tipping point. The rebellion spread from Benghazi in the east to the mountains in the west, eventually encircling Tripoli and cutting off Qaddafi's oil supply. At that point, the long-planned uprising in the capital was triggered, and Qaddafi's regime collapsed.

In the end, it only took six months to vindicate Obama's judgment that since no vital American interest was at stake, the promotion of universal rights in the Libyan case needed to be a multilateral effort.[53] As he noted on October 20, the day Qaddafi's death was announced, "the dark shadow of tyranny has been lifted," and in the process, "working with Libya's friends and allies, we've demonstrated what collective action can achieve in the twenty-first century."[54] No American lives were lost in the process, and the Pentagon estimates that the cost of the U.S. contribution was only

$1.1 billion, a small price to pay for the removal of one of the Arab world's worst dictators.[55]

Yet, during that time, Obama's repeated insistence that Qaddafi had to go but that it was up to others to accomplish that objective highlights again the vexing gap between his high-principled rhetoric and the means he was willing to deploy. That, too, would have its consequences when it came to dealing with the next Arab awakening, in Syria.

THE ROAD TO DAMASCUS

Libya and Bahrain are on the periphery of the Arab world; Syria is at its center. President Bashar al-Assad's father, Hafez al-Assad, who ruled Syria with an iron grip for three decades until his death in June 2000, liked to boast that Syria was the beating heart of pan-Arabism. A resource-poor, middle-sized country with a population of 21 million people, Syria's geostrategic location (bordering the three regional powers of Turkey, Israel, and Iraq) and ideological influence enabled it to punch above its weight in regional affairs. Its ancient capital of Damascus had for millennia dominated the region known as the Levant, which encompasses Lebanon, Syria, Jordan, and Palestine. Israel's creation on its southern border consolidated its regional role as a front-line state in the Arab-Israeli conflict.

Syria's modern history, dating from its independence in 1946, was until 1971 marked by political turmoil and coups. But since 1971 Syria has been ruled by the Assad family, an Alawite regime in a predominantly Sunni country.[56] Representing a minority sect, they were able to retain control through emergency rule, a repressive state apparatus, and the ideological purity of the Ba'ath Party, a secular, socialist party. In 1981 the Muslim Brotherhood led a Sunni Islamic uprising against the regime from its base in the city of Hama, which the Assads crushed a few months later, killing perhaps as many as 25,000 of their citizens and quieting the rest of Syria's Sunnis for decades.

There were no indications of dissent when Hafez al-Assad died and his son Bashar al-Assad took over, even though he had no credentials other than the family name to justify his assumption of power. He consolidated his rule by introducing some limited economic reforms, which benefited the Sunni business elites in Damascus and Aleppo (and enriched his own family). The young, British-educated ophthalmologist also gained credibility by promising political reform, but he ended the Damascus Spring, a brief interlude of liberalization, a year after he introduced it. Since then Assad has talked a good game—especially with Western visitors—but in substance has done nothing to change his repressive rule.

Instead, he solidified Syria's alliances with Iran and Hezbollah, the Shia powers in his neighborhood, turning Damascus into the conduit for Iranian influence into the Arab heartland and a source of support for the anti-American insurgency in Iraq, which Iran also promoted. They shared a common interest in Lebanon, too, especially after the March 2005 Cedar Revolution, a popular uprising that forced Assad to withdraw Syrian troops, which had been deployed in Lebanon for more than thirty years, thus reducing Syria's dominance of Lebanese politics. Working with Iran and Hezbollah, Assad was eventually able to regain control of Lebanon via a Hezbollah-dominated government, which took power in January 2011, just as the demonstrations were breaking out in Tunis and Cairo. Damascus has also long housed the headquarters of Hamas, the Palestine Islamic Jihad, and other Palestinian rejectionist and terrorist groups, manifesting its ideological credentials on the Palestinian issue. As Hamas took control of Gaza and split the Palestinian national movement, Bashar deepened his involvement with the Damascus-based Hamas external leadership, the better to interfere with reconciliation efforts that helped prevent the Palestinians from achieving their independence.

Because of Syria's centrality to the regional balance of power, the idea of luring the Assad regime out of the radical, Iranian-led camp into the American-led peace camp has long been attractive to

strategic thinkers in Washington.[57] Hafez al-Assad was always willing to play this game, understanding that holding out the prospect
of shifting camps improved his leverage with both sides. The key
to maintaining Syria's role was never fully to commit to either side:
his alliances with Iran and Hezbollah were tactical; his willingness
to commit to peace with Israel a carefully maintained mirage.

Bashar al-Assad was less politically agile than his father and
more attracted to the radical camp, especially as his circumstances
became more difficult because of pressure from the Bush administration, which was more interested in changing the regime in Damascus than in making peace with it. But in a shrewd move, Bashar
took the proffered hand of neighboring Turkish prime minister
Erdogan, thus forming a new partnership with an old adversary.
Erdogan and his foreign minister, Ahmet Davutoglu, were intent
on engineering Turkey's reentry into the Arab world using their
Muslim Brotherhood credentials. At a time when Bashar al-Assad
had isolated Syria from the Sunni Arab world, his relationship with
Turkey provided him with "Sunni depth" to counterbalance his
alliance with Shia Iran, which was important for the stability of his
rule over a predominantly Sunni population.[58]

Although at the outset of his administration Obama made improving relations with Iran a priority, he sought to engage with Assad,
too. As usual in the U.S.-Syrian relationship, the president's desire to
resolve the Palestinian problem led him to view Damascus through
the prism of the peace process. While former senator George Mitchell focused on the Palestinian track, his deputy, Fred Hof, worked
quietly but assiduously with the advisers to Assad and Netanyahu
to develop a formula that would enable the resumption of Israeli-
Syrian negotiations. But Assad's insistence on a prior Israeli commitment to full withdrawal from the Golan Heights and Netanyahu's
unwillingness to accept such a precondition made progress impossible. The Turks weren't able to help out, as they had previously with
then Israeli prime minister Ehud Olmert and Assad, because of the
deterioration in Turkish-Israeli relations that began with Erdogan's

harsh criticism of Israel's military operations in Gaza in December 2008 and escalated over the Turkish flotilla incident in May 2010.

Obama and Clinton were nevertheless willing to explore the possibility of improving the bilateral U.S.-Syrian relationship, encouraged by Senator Kerry, who had cultivated a relationship with Bashar and his British-educated wife. While maintaining the sanctions on Syria because of its support for terrorism, in July 2009 Obama decided to expedite waivers for sales of aircraft spare parts, information technology, and telecommunications equipment. In June 2010 the State Department sponsored a high-level business delegation visit to Damascus—with representatives from Dell, Microsoft, and Cisco Systems—to discuss high-tech private sector cooperation. In January 2011, after a six-year hiatus, Obama sent a U.S. ambassador back to Damascus; Robert Ford assumed his duties just as the revolutions broke out in North Africa.

True to form, Assad pocketed these gestures and continued with business as usual, providing more advanced rocket systems to Hezbollah, failing to deliver on promised political reforms, and completing his reassertion of control in Beirut at about the same time as Ford turned up to present his credentials in Damascus.[59]

At the outset of the Arab awakenings, Assad was so confident that the protests would not spread to Syria that, at the end of January 2011, he gave a rare interview to the *Wall Street Journal* in which he boasted about his open-mindedness and his reform credentials and scoffed at the idea of contagion: "We have more difficult circumstances than most of the Arab countries, but in spite of that Syria is stable." Justifying the nonexistent pace of Syrian reform, Assad noted that it would take a generation to build the institutions of democracy. "People are patient in our region," he claimed, seemingly impervious to the revolutions that were taking place in Egypt and North Africa. What they cared about, he averred, was whether things were moving, not how fast they moved. And in any case, he claimed, political reform wasn't the people's first priority.[60]

Evidently the people of the southern Syrian city of Dara'a viewed things differently. On March 18 they came out in the thousands to protest the regime's arrest and brutal treatment of teenagers who had spray painted anti-Assad graffiti on some walls. In a response that would set a pattern, Assad's security forces in Dara'a opened fire on the demonstrators, killing sixty-one over the course of the next week and provoking deep anger. Meanwhile, in Damascus Assad promised a series of reforms, including greater press freedom, political parties, and a reconsideration of emergency rule.

Unlike the Egyptian revolution, in which the protesters—eventually in the millions—congregated in Cairo's Tahrir Square, the Syrian revolt worked its way from the periphery to the center. What started in Dara'a soon spread to other cities on Syria's borders, from Latakia on the Lebanese border, to the Kurdish villages on the Iraqi border, and to many nearby towns. By mid-April thousands of demonstrators were regularly protesting after Friday prayers in at least twenty cities and towns across Syria and in the outer suburbs of Damascus. Security forces responded with live fire in most cases. On Friday, April 22, the day after Assad announced the lifting of emergency rule, at least eighty-one people were killed.

In May the demonstrations spread to Syria's larger cities, Homs and Hama. The Assad regime responded by deploying its tanks and instituting a harsh military crackdown, claiming that it was confronting an armed insurrection of fundamentalists, terrorists, criminals, and smugglers. Amnesty International documented 580 deaths in the seven weeks since the uprising began. More than ten thousand Syrians had been arrested.[61]

Meanwhile, in Damascus Assad announced the beginning of a "national dialogue" with the opposition, now holding out the prospect of a new electoral law that would end the Ba'ath Party's monopoly. On May 31 he announced a general amnesty. In June the revolt spread to the Turkish and Israeli borders. In the north the Syrian army deployed helicopter gunships and tanks to stamp out protests in two border towns. For the first time there were reports of army defections in the fighting. As the death toll mounted, thousands of Syrian refugees crossed the border into Turkey, where they were provided with safe haven in hastily erected tent camps.

At the same time, in the south Assad made good on his warning that trouble in Syria could have implications for regional stability by encouraging hundreds of Palestinians from refugee camps in Syria to rush the Golan Heights border fence with Israel on the anniversary of the 1967 Six Day War. The Israeli army opened fire on those who tried to climb over the fence; the Syrian government claimed that twenty-two were killed and many more wounded. Again, on June 20, in the face of mounting international pressure, especially from Turkey, Assad offered a national dialogue with a hundred leaders of the opposition in order to agree on changes in the way the country was governed. Given the disparity between the repeated promises of reform and the growing brutality of his repression, which had by this time caused over a thousand deaths, the protests only intensified as the uprising entered its fourth month. At that moment, the Assad regime took a puzzling step, withdrawing its military and security forces from Hama, one of Syria's largest cities and the site of the notorious massacre by Hafez al-Assad of some 20,000 Sunnis in 1982. For several weeks, the city reveled in its freedom. But it was a short-lived respite; Assad was just regrouping his forces.

At the end of July, and the onset of the holy month of Ramadan, Assad ordered his military and security forces to undertake what he must have hoped would be a decisive campaign to suppress the revolt. He deployed hundreds of tanks and thousands of soldiers. They moved simultaneously into the major cities of Homs, Latakia, Hama, and Deir al-Zour, firing at random from tanks and with snipers and arresting thousands in house-to-house raids. Over 300 protesters were killed, provoking a widespread international outcry. Images of destruction in Hama, where over 76 people were killed in one day, provoked fears of another atrocity. In Latakia, tanks shelled a Palestinian refugee camp, and activists reported gunfire from Syrian navy ships off the coast.

Assad responded to the international outcry by telling the UN secretary general Ban Ki-moon that all military operations against the opposition had ended and inviting him to send a UN team to Syria to investigate. The team traveled to Hama and was welcomed by thousands of demonstrators. As soon as they left, security forces opened fire. By mid-August the now familiar pattern of widespread demonstrations after Friday prayers met by indiscriminate shootings continued, as the death toll crossed the 2,000 mark. The UN high commissioner for human rights issued a damning report, accusing the Syrian regime of committing crimes against humanity, including the summary executions of over 350 named victims.

It had become too much even for Assad's allies. Iran's foreign minister Ali Akbar Salehi and Hezbollah chief Hassan Nasrallah both urged Assad to respond to the legitimate demands of the Syrian people "as soon as possible."[62] And Assad went on TV to express confidence that the crisis in Syria would end and promising yet again vague political reform measures.

This pattern of promised reform followed by brutal crackdown continued through the summer and fall, as the death toll of Syrian protesters inexorably approached the 3,000 mark, many more than Qaddafi had killed in Libya. Yet for the first six months of the Syrian revolution, in stark contrast to his approach to the Egyptian and Libyan rebellions, Obama deliberately adopted a low profile. The president avoided making public statements about the unfolding events, and his spokesman refused to call for Assad to step down. It took the White House almost five months to declare that Assad had "lost legitimacy" and another month till Obama finally decided to call for Assad's departure. What accounted for the delay? Administration spokesmen were quick to explain that Libya was a special case—urgent military intervention was required to stave off a humanitarian disaster. But as time wore on and the Syrian death toll mounted, that explanation became increasingly implausible.

The contrast becomes even starker when strategic interests are taken into account. Qaddafi's Libya was of little strategic import to the United States. In contrast, Assad's Syria was Iran's ally and the co-patron of its Hezbollah and Hamas proxies: Damascus provided the conduit for increasingly sophisticated arms to Hezbollah and a home for Hamas's external headquarters. Syria under Assad was nothing less than Iran's forward operating base for its efforts to challenge U.S. interests in the Arab-Israeli heartland. Syria therefore presented a rare case in which American interests and values coalesced. Helping the Syrian people achieve freedom from a brutal autocratic regime would also deal a severe setback to Iran's grandiose Middle East ambitions. Why then would Obama be so hesitant to seek Assad's overthrow?

The explanation lies in other differences between Libya and Syria. First, the United States had limited tools available to effect change in Syria. Comprehensive unilateral sanctions had already been imposed because of Assad's support for terrorism and his efforts to suppress democracy in Lebanon. Military intervention was not a serious option, given the capabilities of the Syrian army, its alliances with Hezbollah and Iran, and the fact that U.S. forces were now engaged in three wars in the Middle East already. Moreover, unlike in Libya, the U.S. ambassador to Syria was reporting that opposition leaders made clear they did not want U.S. military intervention.[63] With Libyan-style intervention effectively off the table, Obama was determined not to repeat his Libyan experience and declare an objective—Assad's ouster—that he felt he had no means to achieve. That would only unleash criticism from congressional hawks like John McCain and Joe Lieberman for looking weak and unwilling to back his objective with force. Instead, he decided to leave policy to his diplomats.

Secretary Clinton took up the challenge, but she had her own serious reservations about allowing a gap to open up between administration rhetoric and the results it could hope to deliver. She had heard from representatives of Syria's Christian minority community, who had expressed grave concern about their future if the Assad regime were to collapse. That concern was reinforced by meetings she held with representatives of the Syrian opposition, who left her impressed by their courage but depressed by their woeful lack of organization. "There is a lot of sort of beginning sprouts of such an opposition," she said. "But there's no address for the opposition. There is no place that any of us who wish to assist can go. So part of what we've been encouraging and trying to facilitate is for the opposition to become unified."[64]

Clinton also discovered early on that, unlike with Libya, it would be very difficult to generate an international consensus in favor of strong measures against the Assad regime. Although the leading Arab states hardly appreciated Assad's long-standing alliance with their Iranian archrival, they were unwilling to countenance the consequences of another revolution in the heart of the Arab world. They knew all too well that Assad's Alawite regime would not go quietly into the night. With its back against the wall it was more likely to perpetrate a slaughter that could provoke a civil war along sectarian lines.

Similarly, Turkey had invested a great deal in its newfound relationship with Syria, and Erdogan preferred to try his hand at convincing Assad to end the violence and pursue genuine political reforms. More than the Arab leaders, he was reluctant to countenance a descent into civil war that would provoke a refugee crisis across Turkey's southern border with Syria. Obama understood that Turkey, with its large and capable army and a long border with Syria, held the key to exerting real pressure on Assad. Accordingly, Obama took Erdogan's frequent phone calls and agreed to hold off on ratcheting up pressure until the Turks had an opportunity to try to convince Assad to undertake serious reforms. That served as an additional brake on Obama's road to abandoning the Syrian regime.

Russia and China presented the biggest problem. Deeply resenting the way the United States and its NATO allies had exploited their acquiescence in the Libyan military intervention, they were determined not to allow a repeat of the exercise in Syria. Moscow's relationship with Damascus—a socialist relic of the cold war bolstered by arms sales and access to the Syrian port of Tartus for the Russian navy—was one of the few it retained in the Arab world after the collapse of the Soviet Union, and it was not about to abandon it in favor of Western intervention. Instead, the Russians blocked any serious action in the Security Council and even responded positively to urgent requests from the Assad regime for replenishment of arms for use against the demonstrators.

With the Russians providing cover, the Chinese could revert to their default position of opposition to interventionist tendencies by the international community. And with the split so evident among the permanent members of the Security Council, the emerging regional powers—South Africa, Brazil, and India—which all happened to have seats on the Security Council, were unwilling to support a robust condemnation either. It took the all-out assault on Hama in early August, which conjured up memories of the massive slaughter in the same city thirty years earlier, for the Security Council finally to agree on action. But even then, all it could produce was a watered-down presidential statement—which had none of the implications of a UNSC resolution—condemning Assad's use of force against his people and calling on him to address the "legitimate aspirations and concerns of the population."[65]

Two months later, in the face of continued violent suppression and with a real concern that civil war was looming on the horizon, the United States, France, and Britain tried to pass a UN Security Council resolution that would give a little more moral force to the words of the international community. The Europeans watered down the resolution to avoid any implication of sanctions in an effort at least to secure Russian and Chinese abstentions. It made little difference. Russia and China vetoed the resolution while India, Brazil, and South Africa abstained. Rather than speaking with one voice, the international community sent a signal to the Assad regime that no matter its resort to violence used against its own people, it could still avoid international intervention. If Libya represented the high-water mark for concerted international action in support of an emerging global order, Syria represented its low point, and there was little that Obama seemed willing to do about it.

Instead, the president maintained a low profile, while the White House carefully calibrated the rhetoric of the statements it issued in his name to prevent Obama from getting out ahead of the little they thought could be delivered. Criticism and condemnation of Assad's brutality was coupled with calls on him to end violence and undertake reform, even though it was blindingly obvious that he had no intention of doing so. In Obama's May 19 speech, with its inspirational rhetoric about U.S. support for the Arab peoples' demand for freedom and a particular commitment to bear witness on behalf of the Syrian people, he stuck with that formula, even though it was expressed in more forceful terms: "President Assad now has a choice: He can lead that transition, or get out of the way."[66]

Predictably, that made little impression on a Syrian regime that was fighting for its survival. So Obama and Clinton began to deploy targeted sanctions. But out of a mistaken belief that Assad might actually embark on meaningful political reforms, the first round of these sanctions focused on Assad's henchmen but left his name off the list. More killing of protesters made that approach untenable, so on May 18, in advance of his Arab Spring speech, Obama finally designated Assad for targeted sanctions, too.

It was only a matter of time before Assad's brutal repression led Obama to declare that enough was enough and that Assad should go. But because of the concern about the rhetoric/results gap, the administration needed to come up with something credible to back up that determination. Oil sanctions provided the answer. The United States imported no oil from Syria, but Europe consumed 90 percent of Syrian oil exports; European oil sanctions could have a real impact on an economy already strained by countrywide rebellions. Clinton worked with her British, French, and German counterparts to ensure that they called for Assad to step down when Obama did and then that they imposed oil sanctions. The rollout began in late July 2011, after Assad sent tanks into Hama to open fire on the demonstrators there. By that time, Obama had declared that Assad had lost all legitimacy, saying that "President Assad is not indispensable, and we have absolutely nothing invested in him remaining in power."

The final break came in early August, after a dramatic escalation of violence in Homs, Hama, and Deir al-Zour resulted in King Abdullah recalling the Saudi ambassador from Damascus and calling on Assad "to stop the killing machine and end the bloodshed." Bahrain and Kuwait also withdrew their ambassadors, and Egypt's foreign minister warned that Assad was heading toward "the point of no return."

Obama accepted Turkish prime minister Erdogan's appeal to hold off while he sent his foreign minister to Damascus for one last attempt at persuading Assad to end the fearsome crackdown. But Davutoglu was roundly rebuffed and subsequently issued a "final word" to Assad that if he didn't end the violent assaults "immediately and unconditionally" there would be "nothing more to discuss about steps that would be taken."

Finally, on August 18, 2011, the same day that the UN high commissioner issued a damning report accusing Assad of crimes against humanity, the White House issued a statement in which Obama declared that Syria's future must be determined by its people, that Assad has failed to lead them, and that for their sake, "the time has come for President Assad to step aside."[67] The statement also announced the freezing of all Syrian assets within American jurisdiction, banned Syrian oil imports, and barred American citizens from having any dealings with the Syrian government.

Consistent with his low-profile approach to Syria, however, Obama did not come out and say it himself. Instead, it was left to his secretary of state to put a human face on the newly declared policy. In front of the cameras, she declared that "the transition to democracy has begun, and it's time for Assad to get out of the way."[68] To protect against any pressure for Libyan-like military intervention to back up this assertion, she noted "the strong desire of the Syrian people that no foreign country should intervene in their struggle, and we respect their wishes." Pointing out that the United States had "all along . . . backed up our words with action," she detailed the ratcheting up of sanctions and the multilateral efforts to isolate the Syrian regime.

The leaders of Britain, France, Germany, the EU, and Canada followed suit in calling on Assad to step aside; a week later they imposed similar sanctions, including on imports of Syrian oil. A few weeks after that Turkey also broke with the Assad regime, imposed its own sanctions, and provided a platform in Istanbul for the disparate Syrian opposition forces to join together in a semblance of unity, and a safe haven near the Syrian border for military defectors to organize "the Free Syrian Army."[69]

It was clearly going to take time for sanctions to have sufficient impact that Syria's Sunni business elites would break with the regime and for the opposition to organize a coherent political front. It would also take time for the military to crack under the strain of constant suppression of its own people: by October there were already some signs of significant military defections, and by the end of the year attacks on Syrian military installations had begun.[70] And it will take time for Russia and China to recognize that they can no longer justify the Assad regime's brutality.[71]

In the meantime, the Arab League, with Saudi backing, is taking the lead in threatening Assad with sanctions and expulsion from its ranks unless his regime stops the killing of its people. Similarly, Turkey's leadership is threatening sanctions and military intervention to create humanitarian corridors if the killing does not cease. But Assad continues his game of promising moderation while prosecuting a bloody campaign of brutal suppression; by year's end the death toll surpassed 5,000, while Assad played a cat-and-mouse game with Arab League observers dispatched in an attempt to persuade the regime to pull back its armed forces from the main cities of the revolt.

At some point, as his kill-or-be-killed approach causes ever more civilian casualties, Assad's isolation will be complete, and UNSC sanctions will likely result. But absent Turkish military intervention and a more systematic morphing of the opposition from peaceful to armed resistance (with a consequent much higher casualty toll), it is difficult to see how the Assad regime will be removed. Nevertheless, the confluence of U.S. interests and values in the promotion of Syrian regime change is sure to abide. And while the circumstances make U.S. military intervention unlikely, there are all manner of ways to increase pressure on Assad, from overt and covert support for the Syrian opposition to the concerting of efforts with Turkey, Saudi Arabia, and Europe. While the arc of the Syrian revolution is likely to be a long and bloody one, the outcome—Assad's overthrow—seems very likely if not necessarily imminent.

CONCLUSION

Because the course of revolutions is so unpredictable and, in the case of the Arab awakenings, so varied, it is difficult to forecast how it will all work out in the end. Therefore only historians will be able to render judgment on Obama's handling of the events that are now shaking the Middle East. In the short term, he has managed the turmoil and tensions relatively well, recognizing that these revolutionary stirrings were not about the United States and that he would therefore have limited ability to affect their outcomes. He certainly helped promote popular demands for freedom and democracy across the Arab world, protected civilians in Libya, and assisted in toppling unpopular dictators in Egypt, Libya, and Yemen, while doing his best to protect American interests in stability in the Gulf. There were tactical missteps—the humiliation of Mubarak, the failure to push effectively for meaningful reforms in Bahrain, the gap between means and objective in Libya, and the consequent slowness to push for Assad's ouster in Syria. But overall Obama's innate pragmatism has served him well in tempering his instinctive idealism.

It is, however, too soon to assess the strategic consequences for the United States in the Middle East. In Egypt   the most important strategic test—Obama's preservation of the military's role was important to achieving a quick start to the transition process, but betting on the Egyptian military as the midwife of Egyptian democracy has also proved problematic. While the Supreme Council of the Armed Forces (SCAF) has reiterated its intention to honor all of Egypt's international obligations, including the peace treaty with Israel, it has proved feckless in handling the competing political demands of the street and protecting the rights of Egypt's Coptic Christian minority. Worse than that, instead of ensuring the orderly transition that Obama sought from the early days of the revolution, the military has sought to protect its special interests and place itself above the constitution.

At year's end SCAF's use of force against demonstrators in Tahrir Square—the very thing Obama helped deter the military from doing at the outset of the revolution—earned it a rebuke from the White House similar to that deployed against Mubarak. In a hastily released statement, Obama called on the Egyptian military to swiftly begin a "full transfer of power" to a democratically elected civilian government in a "just and inclusive manner."[72] The use of the word *inclusive* signaled the SCAF that its American patron expected it to accept Islamists in an empowered, civilian government. But when the Muslim Brotherhood took 47 percent of the votes in the first post-Mubarak parliamentary elections and the more extreme Salafis took another 25 percent, inclusion took on new meaning.

Obama is betting that rather than attempting to impose Sharia law and customs on a quarter of the Arab world's population, the Muslim Brotherhood's need to generate tangible results for those who voted for it will lead it to prefer the stability that comes from cooperating with the United States and preserving the peace treaty with Israel. Obama has made a judgment that it will be less damaging to U.S. interests to try to shape this dramatic development than to support its suppression by military means. His administration is certainly engaged in a determined effort, from coaching the SCAF to engaging the Muslim Brotherhood and providing economic assistance that can help generate jobs. But it is a gamble. Suddenly, standing on the right side of history means accepting that the cornerstone of America's strategic position in the Arab world will likely be in the hands of democratically elected Islamist religious parties that are at their core opposed to liberalism, secularism, and Zionism.

The shakiness of the U.S. strategic relationship with Egypt is offset, however, by the strategic windfall that comes from the increasingly embattled state of Iran's ally in Damascus. Cutting off the Syrian conduit for Iran's meddling in the affairs of the Arab-Israeli heartland would represent a major strategic setback for Iran. Already Assad's international isolation and his preoccupation with severe internal challenges significantly reduce his ability to support Iran's proxy Hezbollah in maintaining its grip on Lebanon. Meanwhile Hamas is busy moving out of the Iranian orbit and into the Egyptian camp as the influence of its Muslim Brotherhood patron rises there, manifested in the shifting of Hamas's external headquarters out of Damascus and the cutting off of Iranian aid.

Libya was always a strategic sideshow. Obama helped achieve the relatively low-cost overthrow of a brutal dictator while avoiding responsibility for the aftermath. But the indirect costs were significant. By repeatedly calling for Qaddafi's overthrow when the UNSC resolution that justified NATO's military intervention provided for no such thing, Obama confirmed Russian and Chinese fears that the West would always distort the intentions of UNSC resolutions for its own purposes. The unintended consequence was that Russia and China, as well as the emerging powers on the Security Council (India, Brazil, and South Africa), are no longer willing to countenance UNSC resolutions that could lead toward their again acquiescing in military intervention to overthrow regimes elsewhere in the Arab world. This has made it more difficult for Obama to isolate the Assad regime within the strategically far more important Arab heartland. Obama's efforts to set a precedent in Libya for international intervention to protect civilian populations against their governments proved to be short-lived. As he would be the first to admit, shaping the emerging international order had proved yet again to be hard work.

Meanwhile, in the Gulf, Obama's balancing of American interests and values is likely to be put to the test sooner rather than later. Saudi Arabia seems determined to slow roll political reform at home, prevent it altogether in neighboring Bahrain, and carve out and pay for an exemption for all the kings and sheikhs in its wider neighborhood.[73] This effort to erect a wall against the political tsunami sweeping across the Arab world cannot work as a long-term solution, even though the kings and sheikhs enjoy greater tribal and religious legitimacy among their people than the pharaohs and generals who ruled in other parts of the Arab world.

In Bahrain the situation is tenuous. The only chance for meaningful reconciliation between the king and his deeply alienated Shia citizens lies in the implementation of the recommendations of the Bahrain Independent Commission of Inquiry, which has documented the government's systematic human rights abuses. King Hamad has promised to implement the recommendations but faces strong resistance from his uncle, the prime minister, and others in the royal family who enjoy the strong backing of Saudi Arabia. If Bahrain blows, it will be hard for Saudi Arabia to prevent its own Shia citizens from demanding equal rights.

Indeed, it seems likely that no Arab authoritarian regime will remain immune for long from the demands of its people for political freedom and accountable government. The idea of democracy, transmitted across Arab borders via cable television and the Internet, when it is combined with large-scale unemployment or underemployment, has proved to be a lure to the young generation in Arab monarchies as much as in Arab republics. In the end, their longing will not be suppressed by economic bribes or police-state tactics.

Notwithstanding Saudi objections, the kings of Jordan and Morocco recognize this reality and have attempted meaningful political reforms intended to set their countries on the road toward constitutional monarchies with empowered, democratically elected legislatures. But closer to home, the Gulf monarchies are adhering to the Saudi model, even though their younger leaders understand its limitations. They are all too aware that the Saudi system is fragile, with power concentrated in the hands of a king and his brothers who are old and ailing. And the Saud family's legitimacy depends in significant part on its pact with a fundamentalist Wahhabi clergy deeply opposed to basic political reforms, such as equal rights for women.[74]

Obama's inclination to leave well enough alone is understandable, but his decision to defer to "short-term interests" might well end up as shortsightedness unless he can find a way to negotiate a new compact with Saudi King Abdullah. Obama needs to convince the king that defining a road map that leads to constitutional monarchies in his neighborhood, first in Bahrain but eventually in Jordan and other GCC states, is the better way to secure his kingdom and the interests of his subjects. Abdullah has been willing to undertake important reforms in the past. But if the king is to be persuaded to embrace this strategy, he will need to know that the president will provide a safety net. Such a compact would be difficult to negotiate in the best of times. It could not even be broached in current circumstances unless the basic trust between the president and the king can be reestablished.

In many respects the Arab awakenings have changed the nature of the "great game" in the Middle East. For the time being at least, the Palestinian issue has been sidelined, and the strategic rivalry between the United States and Iran, which has dominated Middle Eastern dynamics for the last two decades, is morphing into a new rivalry between Shias and Sunnis, backed by Iran on one side and Saudi Arabia and Turkey on the other. This divide is opening up in Syria, Iraq, and Bahrain. It could spread to Kuwait and ultimately to Saudi Arabia itself. Obama's withdrawal of U.S. forces from Iraq, combined with his circumspection in Syria and his discretion in Bahrain, has reduced American influence in this particular competition. He will need to depend on Turkey and Saudi Arabia to carry much of America's water. Appreciating the importance of Turkey's role as a secular democracy headed by a moderate Islamist party, Obama has gone to considerable pains to build a relationship of trust with Turkey's Erdogan. He will need to make the same effort with Saudi Arabia's leadership.

Bending history's arc has proven particularly difficult and complicated in the Middle East, whether through Obama's attempts to make peace or his attempts to promote political freedom. It will be made even more difficult if Obama fails to curb Iran's nuclear program, for that could lead to a regional nuclear arms race or an Iranian-Israeli war. Either one would engulf the region and divert attention again from the urgent task of political reform. It is to the subject of dealing with Iran's nuclear ambitions that we now turn.

CHAPTER SIX

THE ROGUE STATES

SHAPING AN EMERGING GLOBAL ORDER required Obama to develop a strategy for dealing with those states that were determined to remain outside it or were fixated on doing battle with its norms and institutions. In earlier eras the great battle between empires or ideologies made the whole notion of international society a contentious one. But with the collapse of the Soviet Union, the end of the cold war, and the onset of globalization, the potential for building an international consensus around such norms while reforming existing institutions or building new ones to reflect them became a lot more possible, even though hardly less daunting. If through collective efforts by the leading members of the emerging order the so-called rogue states could be persuaded to accept the prevailing rules of the game, international society would be strengthened both from the experience of working together on a common project and from the conversion of those who had opposed it. Conversely, if the effort to reform, or "graduate," the rogues failed, the order itself would be challenged in ways that could shake its foundations.

Obama's efforts to engage with the outliers of the international system have their origin in his efforts during the presidential campaign to distinguish himself both from George W. Bush and from the other candidates by arguing the need for engaging with nations with which we disagree. His "theory of the case," however, had deeper foundations in his grander ambition to bend history in the direction of a more secure and peaceful world.

Obama articulated this vision early on in his administration, in his April 2009 Prague speech, with its ambitious call for a world without nuclear weapons and its four-part agenda for disarmament: reducing the role of nuclear weapons in U.S. national security strategy; negotiating a new strategic arms reduction treaty with Russia; achieving a global ban on nuclear testing and the production of fissile materials for nuclear weapons; and strengthening the Non-Proliferation Treaty (NPT).[1]

As it happened, the two most prominent rogues—Iran and North Korea—posed the greatest challenge to the nonproliferation regime because of their ambitious nuclear programs. By the time Obama took his presidential oath, North Korea had already withdrawn from the NPT and had embarked on a new uranium enrichment project that would provide a more reliable source of fuel for its nuclear weapons program. Iran was still a member of the NPT but had already raised grave doubts about its real intentions, sufficient for it to be reported by the International Atomic Energy Agency (IAEA) to the UN Security Council, which had already imposed mandatory sanctions.[2] If the international community did not succeed in curbing the Iranian and North Korean nuclear programs, they could do irreparable damage to the nonproliferation regime and to the cause of nuclear disarmament. Indeed, they could trigger nuclear arms races in the Middle East and Northeast Asia, perhaps the two most sensitive security arenas on the globe.

In his Prague speech Obama made clear how he intended to deal with both of these states. In the case of North Korea, which tested a long-range missile on the very morning of his speech, he insisted, "Rules must be binding. Violations must be punished. Words must mean something. The world must stand together to prevent the spread of these weapons." He foreshadowed an effort in the UN Security Council to impose harsher sanctions on Pyongyang. In

Iran's case, he noted that it had not yet built a nuclear weapon. Consistent with his campaign pledge, and his inauguration speech in which he offered to "extend a hand if you are willing to unclench your fist," Obama emphasized that he sought a dialogue with Iran that would present it with a clear choice: either membership in the community of nations with the right to peaceful nuclear energy under safeguards or increased isolation and international pressure. Obama saw this as a balanced deal: Iranian "rights" as a full-fledged member of international society would be respected as long as Iran took its "responsibilities" to that society seriously.

From an American perspective, it looked like a genuine offer to turn a new page in relations with both Iran and North Korea if they would only accept the norms of the emerging global order. But it would prove insufficient to the tasks of overcoming their ambitions and suspicions and persuading them to adhere to American-sponsored norms.

IRAN

By the time Obama entered the Oval Office, Iran had an established record of flouting the will of the international community. As an Islamist revolutionary republic, run by a clergy-dominated regime that was deeply anti-American and highly suspicious of Washington's motives, it had a preference for hostile relations with the United States. That hostility had been sustained for more than three decades in the face of American sanctions. There had been occasional efforts by one side or the other to attempt a rapprochement, but mutual suspicion and domestic politics had thwarted them every time: the United States and Iran were like ships passing in the night.[3]

In January 2009 the prevailing views of the leadership in Tehran vis-à-vis the United States were certainly permeated with hostility and distrust. The Supreme Leader, Ayatollah Ali Khamenei, was deeply suspicious of the United States and saw little value in a rapprochement. He had effectively thwarted the efforts by presidents

Mohammad Khatami and Bill Clinton in the 1990s to normalize relations. When George W. Bush labeled Iran part of the "axis of evil" in 2002, Khamenei was content to maintain the default position of hostile relations.

Mahmoud Ahmadinejad, Khatami's successor as president, had a more ambitious agenda: he sought to challenge American dominance of the Middle East. Before he was elected, in June 2005, the United States had already done him the favor of overthrowing both the Taliban in Afghanistan and Saddam Hussein in Iraq. To have "the Great Satan" remove hostile regimes from two of Iran's borders free of charge had the potential to transform Iran's strategic circumstances. But those regimes had been replaced by some 200,000 American troops in Iraq and Afghanistan, on Iran's eastern and western borders. Given Iran's suspicions of U.S. intentions, this presented a new threat and one that had to be neutralized. Coordinating strategy with its Syrian ally on the other side of Iraq, Tehran was able to promote both Sunni and Shia insurgencies there, which pinned down and debilitated U.S. forces. With Washington preoccupied, Ahmadinejad then used Iran's relations with the Shia parties, which dominated the newly elected Iraqi government, to build Iran's influence in Baghdad.

At the same time, American intervention in Iraq tarnished its reputation in the Arab world, creating a conducive environment for the spread of Iranian influence. Bush's insistence on his "freedom agenda" created an opportunity for Iran to pursue its agenda through the American-dictated ballot box, when Iran's proxy, Hamas, won the Palestinian elections and subsequently took control of Gaza. At the same time, Ahmadinejad's alliance with Bashar al-Assad in Syria enabled him to use Damascus as a conduit to support Hezbollah's control of southern Lebanon, including the provision of 40,000 rockets capable of reaching Israel's major cities. Tehran's proxies were now on the northern and southern borders of Israel, and the regime had secured an ability to interfere in Palestine and Lebanon, the two most sensitive areas in the Middle East.

Sure enough, Hezbollah provoked a war with Israel in the summer of 2006, and Hamas followed suit in December 2008, enhancing Iran's standing in the Arab world as their backers.

And at the same time as this great game between Iran and the United States for dominance in the Middle East was unfolding, Tehran was advancing its nuclear program, stockpiling enriched uranium, developing ballistic missiles, designing warheads, and building clandestine underground facilities. From Ahmadinejad's perspective, with George W. Bush's help Iran was successfully challenging American dominance in the Middle East, building an alternative narrative that violence and terrorism—not negotiation and compromise—was the way to redeem Arab dignity and Palestinian rights. And it was working. In a poll of public opinion in six Arab states, Ahmadinejad was more popular than any Arab leader, including Iran's proxy, the Hezbollah leader Hassan Nasrallah, and he was certainly more popular than the American president.[4]

By the time Obama offered to engage with Iran's revolutionary leaders, Ahmadinejad felt they could do so as equals. From his perspective, negotiations would not be about submitting to the rules of an American-dictated international order; rather, they would be about dividing the Middle East between the United States and Iran, with the United States acknowledging Iranian dominance of the Persian Gulf and accepting Iran's right to a nuclear weapons threshold capability. The grandiosity of Ahmadinejad's ambitions was on display each time he turned up in New York for UN General Assembly meetings, to stand up to the "Great Satan" on his home turf—or in Caracas, Baghdad, Damascus, or Beirut, the capitals of his partners—in the effort to construct an Iranian-led international order. Whereas for three decades American presidents had faced a blanket refusal by the Iranians to engage in any official bilateral dialogue, Ahmadinejad succeeded in convincing a suspicious Khamenei that now Iran's position of strength allowed it to agree to such a dialogue. Thus in January 2009 the Iranian president wrote a congratulatory letter to the new American president, opening the door to increased contact and cooperation and declaring that "Iran would welcome major, fair and real changes in policies and actions, especially in this region."[5]

In February, when Vice President Biden publicly previewed Obama's approach and expressed a willingness to talk to Iran, Ahmadinejad responded three days later that "the Iranian nation is prepared to talk." Despite appearances, however, the Obama administration did not view this as an auspicious beginning. Talking with Iran was one thing, talking to Ahmadinejad, another; the latter had become the world's leading Holocaust denier and repeatedly threatened to wipe Israel off the map. Instead, in public Obama addressed the Iranian people; in private he wrote a personal letter to Khamenei; and his secretary of state invited the Iranian government to participate in a security summit on Afghanistan. Ahmadinejad's overtures were ignored.

Obama's public appeal came in a special speech to the Iranian people in March 2009, on the occasion of Nowruz, the Iranian celebration of the new year. Obama made a point of addressing the people and leaders of "the Islamic Republic of Iran," thereby putting the United States on record as recognizing the revolution. He praised Persian civilization and spoke of a new day in U.S.-Iranian relations, in which "lesser differences" would be left behind in favor of a future based on shared values. To achieve that he called for "engagement that is honest and grounded in mutual respect." Iran, he said, would be welcomed back into the community of nations as long as it was also ready to assume the "responsibilities" of membership.[6]

Around the same time as the public appeal, the Swiss ambassador in Tehran delivered a letter from President Obama to the Supreme Leader, the Ayatollah Khamenei, in which he expressed America's respect for the Islamic republic and his desire for the reestablishment of relations. Obama apparently laid out the prospect of "cooperation in regional and bilateral relations," offered a resolution of the dispute over Iran's nuclear program, and suggested that discrete bilateral negotiations begin.[7]

It took some time, but in May the Supreme Leader did respond. Despite a tortuous repetition of Iran's grievances, the letter nevertheless indicated openness to dealing directly with the United States. Obama took some encouragement from this and quickly responded with suggestions for the modalities of the bilateral negotiations that he now expected would soon get under way. While Obama waited for a response, he made sure to reinforce his message in his Cairo speech to the Muslim world on June 4. Reiterating his interest in putting the past behind them and moving forward into a dialogue "without preconditions on the basis of mutual respect," he emphasized that the issue he cared about was Iran's nuclear program. He underscored Iran's "right" to peaceful nuclear power, as long as it fulfilled its "responsibilities" under the NPT.

Iran's answer came in an unexpected form. On June 12 the Iranian people went to the polls in massive numbers to vote for a new president. Within a day, while the votes were still being tallied, the regime announced that Ahmadinejad had won in a landslide, garnering 63.8 percent of the vote. The appearance of a stolen election generated a massive peaceful protest that went on for weeks, with hundreds of thousands of demonstrators filling the streets of downtown Tehran, as the Green Movement challenged the regime. Khamenei and Ahmadinejad responded to the demonstrations with brutal beatings, widespread arrests, and sniper fire. Troops of young thugs on motorcycles—the *basij*—broke up the crowds and beat the protesters. With the prospect of negotiations still up in the air, Obama hesitated to condemn the crackdown. He explained publicly that "despite numerous differences, there is still room for cooperation." So the most he was willing to do initially was to express "deep concern." There was another consideration: he did not want the United States to be accused of meddling in Iran's affairs; privately the administration had heard from some people in the Green

Movement that the regime would be able to discredit them as American agents if Obama's embrace of them was too warm.

Nevertheless, as the crackdown continued it seemed to trigger the "inner Obama." On June 20 he called on the Iranian government to stop all violence and respect the universal rights of its people. And for the first time in a Middle Eastern context—eighteen months before the Egyptian revolution—he quoted Martin Luther King Jr.: "The arc of the moral universe is long, but it bends toward justice."[8] However, he confined the U.S. role to "bearing witness." A few days later, as the regime stepped up its crackdown, he sided with the Iranian demonstrators, noting that "those who stand up for justice are always on the right side of history." He finally expressed outrage and strongly condemned the regime's "unjust actions."[9] The Supreme Leader responded with a public denunciation of the president of the United States. From that point on, Obama quietly dropped any talk of a bilateral dialogue.

Obama still faced the challenge of heading off Iran's nuclear program. Since he had always viewed dialogue with the Supreme Leader as a long shot, Obama had at the same time been lining up international support for his broader strategy of placing before the Iranians a choice on their nuclear program. Because he understood that an Iran with nuclear weapons would be a game changer for the nonproliferation regime, triggering either an Israeli preventive strike or a nuclear arms race in the Middle East, and because that would represent a major setback to his global order agenda as well as to U.S. vital interests, he had developed a two-track strategy. On the first track he would pursue negotiations with Tehran over its nuclear program via the EU 3+3 format (France, the United Kingdom, and Germany plus Russia, China, and the United States), which had been used in the past; on the second track he would seek to generate a common response from the international community if Iran did not comply with its obligations.

The advantage of this parallel-track approach was that the offer of negotiations in a format that included all five permanent members of the UNSC would show Russia and China that he was genuinely open to a deal with Tehran. But the disadvantage was that such an offer scared the daylights out of America's Arab allies in the Gulf and made the Israelis even more nervous. The Israelis were convinced that the Iranians would play out the clock in the negotiations until they crossed the point of no return in their nuclear program. In the process, Israel would have lost its opportunity to take military action. The Gulf Arabs, on the other hand, were convinced that a naïve American president was about to sacrifice their interests on the altar of a U.S.-Iranian deal that would acknowledge Tehran's dominance in their region. This fear was exacerbated by the rebuffing of repeated requests by the Gulf Cooperation Council to be represented in the negotiations.

Calming the Israelis down was an important priority for Obama, because any military action on their part against Iran's nuclear facilities would inevitably drag the United States in, and that was the last thing Obama needed, given the exposure and difficulties facing American troops across Iran's borders in Iraq and Afghanistan. In his first meeting with Benjamin Netanyahu in May 2009, Obama reassured him that he would set a deadline of the end of the year for assessing the progress of negotiations. In public he rejected the idea of setting an "artificial deadline" but noted, "We're not going to create a situation in which talks become an excuse for inaction while Iran proceeds with developing . . . and deploying a nuclear weapon."[10]

Then the president ordered his national security team to engage intensively in consultations with the Israelis at all levels. The twice-yearly strategic dialogue talks conducted by Deputy Secretary Jim Steinberg and his counterpart, Deputy Foreign Minister Danny Ayalon, were complemented by three other more intensive exchanges: National Security Adviser Jim Jones met every month with Uzi Arad, his Israeli counterpart; Admiral Mike Mullen, chairman of the Joint Chiefs, also met every month with General Ashkenazi, the IDF chief of staff; and every other month Secretary of Defense Robert Gates conferred with Defense Minister Ehud Barak. Thus even though Obama's relationship with Netanyahu would rapidly deteriorate because of differences over the peace process, their closest advisers remained in intensive contact over Iran's nuclear program.

Out of those exchanges, and intensified intelligence cooperation, the Israelis came to understand the Obama administration's approach and also to influence it. This proved important to the overall effort. On the intelligence level, cooperation is reported to have produced a computer virus—Stuxnet—that severely impaired the functioning of Iran's centrifuges and bought an additional two to four years before the Iranians would have the ability to produce enough weapons-grade uranium for several bombs; time enough to give tougher, targeted sanctions a chance to affect the Iranian calculus.[11] The Israelis also helped identify Iranian economic vulnerabilities that could be targeted with those sanctions. Together the two countries also developed an approach designed to test Iranian nuclear intentions, a test that would come in handy sooner than expected.

Meanwhile, Obama essentially left to the U.S. military the task of reassuring the Gulf allies. After his ill-fated encounter with King Abdullah in June 2009, he seemed to want to stay away from these potentates. Instead, Gates and General David Petraeus, at the time the commander of the U.S. Central Command (CENTCOM), took several measures designed to reassure them, including deploying advanced Patriot air defense systems to protect the Gulf states from a potential Iranian missile strike and bolstering the U.S. fleet presence in the Gulf with its antimissile capabilities. The fact that the bilateral dialogue effort with Khamenei ended almost before it started also served to calm them down.

Perhaps Obama's greatest diplomatic achievement on this front, however, was with the Russians. As part of his efforts to repair damage done by his predecessor, Obama declared after his first meeting with Russian president Dmitry Medvedev, on April 1, 2009, on the margins of the London G-20 summit, that he sought a "fresh start" in bilateral relations. What subsequently became known as the "reset" in U.S.-Russian relations had a higher strategic purpose. Together with Secretary of State Hillary Clinton, Obama set about assiduously recruiting Russian president Medvedev to his nuclear disarmament agenda.

First, Obama removed the thorn from the side of the U.S.-Russian strategic relationship by agreeing not to deploy antimissile systems in Poland and a radar system in the Czech Republic. By doing this, Obama was not only able to show sensitivity to Russian strategic concerns that Bush had dismissed, he was also able to persuade the Russians to take seriously Iran's nuclear program because he insisted that it was America's central strategic concern.

Second, he committed to engage in a serious and prompt negotiation of a new strategic arms reduction treaty (New START). By April 2010 the deal had been signed, and by December 2010 the Senate had ratified it, after a drawn-out fight with Republican opponents, which nevertheless proved to the Russians that Obama could deliver at least on this issue. The agreement provided for a 30 percent cut in strategic nuclear warheads, to 1,550 deployed by each side, also lending credibility to Obama's nuclear disarmament agenda.[12] But the true advantage of this deal for Obama's relations with the Russians was that it demonstrated to a once great superpower that this U.S. president regarded them as equals on strategic matters.

Third, in an exception to his normally cool and distant relationships with other world leaders (particularly transatlantic allies like Gordon Brown, Angela Merkel, and Nicholas Sarkozy), Obama built a close and personal rapport with his Russian counterpart. Perhaps it was because they were both lawyers who came from the same younger generation of leaders and defined themselves as pragmatic reformers. Whatever the explanation, Obama invested in his relationship with Medvedev and in each of their eight meetings emphasized the vital importance to the United States of Iran's nuclear program.

Finally, Obama treated Medvedev as a partner in the development of strategy toward Iran, which paid big dividends in recruiting Russia to the cause of curbing Iran's nuclear program.

Obama did not have the same warm relationship with Chinese president Hu Jintao, but he used a modified version of the tactics he had deployed with the Russians. Certainly, he emphasized the centrality of relations with China to his agenda of shaping the emerging global order, but, as observed in earlier chapters, the Chinese were suspicious of his real intentions. Nevertheless, he was able to persuade Hu Jintao that Iran's nuclear program was a "core interest" of the United States and that if China expected the United States to take its core interests into account Beijing needed to reciprocate on this issue.

Obama's argument was reinforced by a message delivered by his aides—Tom Donilon, Jeffrey Bader, James Steinberg, and Dennis Ross—on a series of visits to Beijing in which they briefed their Chinese counterparts on the nature of the Iranian nuclear program. The argument that seemed to make a significant difference to China's calculations was that a failure to curb the program could result in an Israeli military strike or a nuclear arms race in the Middle East. Either way, the stability so essential to the extraction and shipment of oil supplies from the Gulf to China would be placed in severe jeopardy. With 60 percent of China's oil imports coming from the Gulf, this argument concentrated the minds of Beijing's leadership. Obama's aides also succeeded in recruiting Saudi Arabia and the UAE to the cause: they offered China a guarantee of alternative supplies of oil so that Beijing would not need to fear Iranian retribution if it joined the sanctions effort.[13]

Obama had a much easier time of it with the Europeans. They shared his concerns about Iran's nuclear ambitions; Sarkozy struck a tougher posture than Obama, threatening at various points to take military action if the Iranians didn't comply with the demands of the international community. The key three—Britain, France, and Germany—had also gone through the experience of attempting to negotiate curbs on Iran's enrichment program during the Bush era, to no avail. When he assumed the presidency, Ahmadinejad had accused the earlier Iranian negotiators of treason. So the Europeans were entirely skeptical about the prospects for a new negotiation with the harder-line leadership in Tehran. With Russia and the Europeans in harness, and China on the bandwagon, the Obama administration succeeded in recruiting all the permanent members of the UN Security Council to its strategy—a formidable achievement. And with the Gulf Arabs and Israel all cooperating in the cause, Obama had reason to be satisfied.

The coalition would quickly be put to its first test. Once he succeeded in suppressing the demonstrators after his June election swindle, Ahmadinejad clearly felt the need to try again to engage Obama and the West, perhaps seeking to refurbish his tarnished image. The initiative this time came in the form of an Iranian request to the IAEA, in June 2009, to purchase fabricated fuel assemblies abroad—including from the United States—for the Tehran research reactor (TRR). The reactor was apparently running low on fuel and needed new fuel rods to produce nuclear isotopes for medical purposes.

Working with the Israelis and Russians, the Obama administration came up with a counterproposal: Iran should ship out its stockpile of 1,200 kilograms of low-enriched uranium or LEU (5 percent), which would be enriched further in Russia (to 20 percent), fabricated in France, and shipped back as fuel rods to Iran for use in the TRR. The cleverness of this proposal was that it would serve as a test of Iran's real intentions. If, as its leaders averred, it was seeking nuclear capabilities only for peaceful purposes, then it should have no objection to shipping out its stockpiled nuclear fuel to Russia—with which Iran had relatively good relations—for processing into fuel rods that would be returned to Iran for use in a civilian reactor (Iran had no known ability to extract or reprocess the fuel in the rods). And in the meantime, with most of Iran's stockpile shipped out of the country, the rest of the world could be more relaxed about the risk that Iran would be able to produce a nuclear bomb. Time would also have been bought to negotiate further curbs on Iran's enrichment program and perhaps to build mutual confidence in the process, as Iran saw the value of accepting multilateral control of the nuclear fuel needed for its reactors. And if the Iranians rejected the offer, then Obama would have a stronger case to make to Russia and China about Iran's true purposes. It was a win-win arrangement.

The Iranians agreed to send their nuclear negotiators to meet on October 1, in Geneva, with representatives of the EU 3+3 to discuss the TRR deal. However, one week beforehand, the Iranians suddenly informed the IAEA of the existence of a hitherto secret enrichment facility that they were constructing deep inside a mountain on an Iranian Revolutionary Guards Council (IRGC) military base called Fordow, near the holy city of Qom.

This announcement was a godsend for Obama, coming at a moment when the world's leaders were all assembled in New York for the UN General Assembly and just ahead of a G-8 summit in Pittsburgh. Together with UK prime minister Gordon Brown and French president Nicholas Sarkozy, Obama hastily convened a press conference to denounce Iran's deceptiveness for building a clandestine enrichment facility too small for generating enriched uranium for civilian purposes but ideal for generating smaller amounts of highly enriched uranium (HEU) for bomb-making purposes.[14] Obama demanded immediate inspection of the facility and declared an end-of-year deadline for Iran to show cooperation with the international community or face tougher sanctions.

It soon became clear that the United States and its allies had been watching the Iranians build this facility for two years and had been holding back the information to use as a possible trump card when it came time to expose Iran's real intentions. But the Russians knew nothing about it, and Putin in particular felt blindsided because he had been vouching for Iran's peaceful nuclear intentions.

Placed on the defensive for the first time in years, in Geneva on October 1 the Iranians quickly agreed to the immediate inspection of the Qom clandestine enrichment facility. They also accepted the TRR proposal without argument, agreeing to ship out of the country Iran's stockpile of LEU. Technical experts were to meet in Vienna two weeks later to agree on the details of implementing the TRR arrangement, and the American and Iranian negotiators also agreed to meet within weeks to discuss broader nuclear issues as well as how to improve the bilateral relationship.

It certainly looked like a breakthrough. A week earlier, Ahmadinejad made clear in an interview with the *Washington Post*'s Lally Weymouth that Iran intended to accept the TRR offer and made a point of emphasizing that, as a gesture to Obama, he wanted the enriched fuel to come from the United States.[15] However, as soon as news of the deal reached Tehran, all hell broke loose. Ahmadinejad was assailed by his conservative opponents in the regime, such as Majlis speaker Ali Larijani, for making the unacceptable concession of shipping out of the country most of Iran's stockpile of enriched uranium. Others objected to putting their uranium stockpile in the hands of countries like France and Russia, which had been unreliable in their trade relations with Iran.[16]

Supreme Leader Khamenei had originally gone along with Ahmadinejad's agreement to accept the deal, but now his suspicions got the better of him. He ordered his technical experts to stay away from the meeting in Vienna, and on October 29 Iran informed the IAEA that it could not accept the deal. Khamenei's rejection of the TRR proposal, together with his failure to respond to Obama's second letter suggesting that the two sides meet, created the pivot point for Obama to cross over to the second track of sanctions and isolation—the "growing consequences" of recalcitrant behavior that Obama had warned Iran about. Obama also ratcheted up his rhetorical posture. Whereas previously he described Iran's acquisition of nuclear weapons as "unacceptable," he now declared that he was determined to prevent Iran from acquiring nuclear weapons.[17]

The threat of military consequences was then given a doctrinal foundation in April 2010 when the White House released its Nuclear Posture Review, which drew a distinction between non-proliferators and rogues: the former would be given a guarantee that regardless of their behavior on other issues, as long as they adhered to their NPT commitments they would not be subjected to a first strike or retaliation with American nuclear weapons. Pointedly, no such assurance was given to Iran and North Korea.[18]

With Obama's focus now on enhanced sanctions in the UN Security Council, Russia's role became critical. Since Britain and France were already on board, if Russia voted in favor, or simply abstained, it was highly unlikely that China would veto, since it always avoided standing alone in this supreme international forum. Previously, the Russians had staunchly opposed additional sanctions. However, Putin's anger with the Iranians for embarrassing him over the clandestine Fordow enrichment facility was now complemented by wounded pride caused by the implication that Iran could not trust Russia to handle its fuel.

The event that seems to have served as the last straw for Putin and Medvedev, though, was Ahmadinejad's declaration in February 2010 that Iran would produce its own fuel for the TRR by enriching its LEU to 20 percent. That move, if implemented, would bring the Iranian stockpile a lot closer to weapons-grade material, because it takes much less effort and time to jump from 20 percent to the 90 percent needed for HEU than to enrich LEU to 20 percent. The Russian government declared Iran's move "wholly unjustified" and, for the first time, joined the United States and France in encouraging the IAEA to report Iran to the UN Security Council.

It therefore proved relatively easy for Obama to convince the Russians to support a resolution, even though the new language required among other things an enhanced arms embargo. That could force the cancellation of a series of Russian arms contracts with Iran, including one for their most sophisticated S-300 anti-aircraft missile system, worth some $800 million.[19] Obama and Medvedev reached an understanding in which, in return for Russia supporting the new resolution, the United States would lift sanctions against Russian companies that had previously transferred sensitive technology to Iran and would make no mention in the resolution of the S-300 sale. Russia wanted to avoid the impression that the new sanctions would harm the Iranian people, many of whom had just made clear their opposition to their government. Obama agreed with that approach. Consequently, the resolution targeted the IRGC and its front companies that were responsible for the nuclear program. It was short on other specifics, resorting instead to generic language that gave blanket permission to member states to impose additional unilateral sanctions.

This approach made it easier to bring China on board. The Chinese were loath to cancel any of the contracts they had negotiated for investing in Iran's oil sector or for purchasing Iran's oil. Instead of insisting on something they would not agree to do, Obama focused on securing an understanding from Beijing that it would not seek to fill the gap left by other countries and companies pulling out of Iran.

Realizing that Obama had succeeded in garnering support for tougher sanctions from all five permanent Security Council members, Ahmadinejad tried a last-minute sleight of hand. Playing on the desire of Turkey's prime minister Erdogan and Brazil's president Lula to assert their influence as emerging powers at a time when they were both members of the UN Security Council, in May 2010 Ahmadinejad offered them acceptance of the TRR deal that Khamenei had rejected in October 2009. The deal that Lula and Erdogan negotiated included an Iranian willingness to escrow 1,200 kilograms of LEU in Turkey—an idea that the Obama administration had itself proposed after the Iranians rejected the original offer.[20]

This last-minute effort to forestall a new sanctions resolution placed Obama in a dilemma. Brazil and Turkey were important players in the new global order that he was attempting to shape. He had conferred with them before they launched their mediation, including writing Lula a letter outlining his requirements and "suggesting a way ahead," which they had specifically pursued in the deal that they signed with Ahmadinejad. Lula and Erdogan were both leaders with outsized egos who would not take kindly to American rejection at a moment when they believed their intervention was saving the world.

On the other hand, if Obama allowed them to divert his carefully and painstakingly orchestrated strategy for new sanctions at the very moment that he had managed to line up Russia and China for "sanctions with teeth," the consensus would undoubtedly quickly unravel. Essentially, Obama had to choose between working with the emerging powers or sticking with the deals he had negotiated with the established powers.

To be sure, the deal that Lula and Erdogan had negotiated was problematic. Ahmadinejad had slyly inserted into the agreement recognition of Iran's right to enrich uranium, something Obama might have been ready to concede once a more comprehensive agreement was struck, dealing with all of Iran's other violations of the NPT, but something he was not willing to concede at the outset, as part of the TRR deal. In addition, the Brazil-Turkey-Iran deal required shipment to Turkey of only the same 1,200 kilograms of LEU that had been envisaged in the original negotiations, the previous October. But Iran had continued to enrich uranium since then and had doubled the quantity in its stockpile.[21]

Obama could have sent Lula and Erdogan back to Tehran to try to fix these problems, but that would have guaranteed a long, drawn-out negotiating process with uncertain prospects of success just at the moment Obama had managed to achieve a rare consensus among the permanent five members of the Security Council. Instead, on May 19 Secretary Clinton announced agreement among the major powers on a new sanctions resolution.[22] Not surprisingly, Lula and Erdogan were upset at Obama's rejection and duly voted against UNSC Resolution 1929, which nevertheless passed with twelve votes in favor—including all five permanent members—on June 9, 2010.

Obama had yet again made a pragmatic, realist's calculation, choosing the bird in his hand over the bird in the bush, favoring bigger powers over smaller ones, and preferring punishing sanctions on Iran to further engagement with Ahmadinejad. In the circumstances, it was probably the right choice to have made, but it underscored just how far Obama had come from that heady moment of his inauguration, when he offered an outstretched hand to the Iranian regime.

The damage done by the negative votes of Turkey and Brazil was soon forgotten in the cascade of actions that followed. First, the U.S. Treasury announced sanctions on more than a dozen Iranian companies and individuals with links to the country's nuclear and missile programs, including a major bank and front companies for Iran's state shipping line. Then the EU announced its own, additional sanctions, which would inhibit trade with Iran and impose harsh restrictions on Iranian banks and shipping. A week later Congress passed and Obama signed into law the Comprehensive Iran Sanctions, Accountability, and Divestment Act, which requires the imposition of U.S. sanctions on companies investing in Iran's energy sector or exporting refined oil products to Iran and on banks engaged in financial transactions with the Iranian regime or the IRGC and its front companies. This resulted in a host of European and even Russian companies announcing that they would stop doing business in Iran, causing the suspension of some $60 billion of foreign investment in the Iranian energy sector and restricting the import of refined gasoline, cars, trucks, and tractors.[23] Then, in perhaps the harshest blow of all, Medvedev announced in September that he had issued a decree banning the sale to Iran of the S-300 antiaircraft missiles systems.

Predictably, the Iranians responded with defiance: the Supreme Leader denounced Obama, the regime continued its refusal to answer the IAEA's questions about its nuclear program and banned two of its most experienced inspectors from entering the country, enrichment continued apace, and further evidence emerged of Iran's ongoing efforts to build a nuclear weapons capability.[24]

Obama still hoped that the pressure of these new sanctions would drive Tehran back to the negotiating table where a chastened regime might be willing to negotiate curbs on its nuclear program. His administration therefore continued to signal to Iran that the door to negotiations was open and continued to consult with the EU, Russia, and China about terms that might be presented to the Iranians if they ever showed up.[25] When their nuclear negotiator, Saeed Jalili, did show up, however, for a meeting in Istanbul with the EU 3+3 in January 2011, he insisted that there had to be recognition of Iran's right to enrich uranium and the lifting of sanctions before he would negotiate over the nuclear program. As for the fuel-swap deal, Jalili told his counterparts that Iran was "no longer interested."[26]

Nevertheless, Obama could still afford to wait for the sanctions to have their intended effect. The various efforts to slow Iran's nuclear progress had been sufficiently successful that Secretary Clinton could declare, "the sanctions are working."[27] Even the head of Israel's Mossad spy agency stated with confidence that Iran would not be able to construct a bomb until 2015 at the earliest.[28] But that was in January 2011, just before the revolutions broke out in Tunisia and Egypt.

Initially, the Arab awakenings advantaged Iran, even though the demonstrators looked to the West, not Tehran, for inspiration and support. Their demands were decidedly secular and democratic: an end to tyranny, free and fair elections, accountable and transparent government. The regime in Tehran, with its recent suppression of its own people, could hardly lay claim to leadership of the Arab awakenings, even though it tried.[29] Nevertheless, with instability in Libya and Bahrain causing the price of oil to spike at $120 a barrel, the effect of the sanctions on Iran's economy was vitiated. Moreover, as noted earlier, the toppling of Mubarak and the spread of the uprisings to all of Saudi Arabia's borders advantaged Iran in the geopolitical competition with the United States. Unrest among Shias in Bahrain, in particular, gave Iran the potential for gaining a foothold at the most sensitive point on the Arabian side of the Gulf.

Iran was suddenly feeling more confident, and its defiance of the United States increased. In June 2011, Fereydoon Abbasi, the new head of its atomic energy agency, announced that Iran would step up its production of 20 percent enriched uranium, doing so with a new generation of centrifuges in the Fordow underground facility it had earlier been caught building near Qom. In September, Abbasi announced that the new IR-2 centrifuges had started production there. This proved to be an exaggeration, but by November the IAEA was reporting that two cascades of IR-1 centrifuges were in place and ready to be switched on at the Fordow plant, with a third cascade almost completed. In the meantime, according to the IAEA, Iran had stockpiled 4,900 kilograms of LEU and 70 kilograms of 20 percent enriched uranium at its large-scale enrichment facility at Natanz.

More alarming still was the IAEA's conclusion that Iran was continuing its work on "the indigenous design of a nuclear weapon, including the testing of components." The report documents Iran's work on computer models of nuclear explosions, its experiments on nuclear triggers, and its completion of advanced research on a warhead that could be delivered by a medium-range missile.[30] And with the Fordow plant about to become operational, Iran's ability to protect its efforts to acquire weapons-grade uranium would increase considerably. Sanctions and subversion efforts notwithstanding, Iran was clearly making slow but steady progress toward a breakout nuclear weapons threshold.[31] As Ehud Barak warned in November 2011, it might only be nine months before Iran's attempt to acquire nuclear weapons moved into a "zone of immunity."

This reality, together with growing pressure from the U.S. Congress and Republican presidential candidates, led Obama to conclude that he needed to ratchet up the pressure from sanctions even further. In early 2012 he signed into law sanctions that could be imposed on any foreign banks transacting with Iran's central bank to pay for imports of Iranian oil. These sanctions have the potential of cutting Iran's oil revenues by some 50 percent. The sanctions would not go into effect until mid-2012, providing time for the oil markets to adjust, for countries dependent on Iranian oil imports to find alternative suppliers, and for Saudi Arabia to increase its production to make up for any shortfall. Nevertheless, Iran's economy is already reeling: in December 2011 its currency plunged to its lowest level ever, its deputy oil minister confirmed that oil production had declined to 3.5 millions of barrels a day (from 4.2 millions of barrels a day a year earlier) because of the withdrawal of the European and Russian companies that had been investing in oil recovery in Iran, its central bank governor warned that the country was "under siege," and its foreign minister admitted for the first time that sanctions were having an effect.[32]

These adverse economic circumstances coincided with regional setbacks, which increased Iran's international isolation. At the time of this writing, Iran's ally, Syria, is imploding, and its proxy, Hamas, is breaking ranks. Turkey's turn against Syria is generating friction between Ankara and Tehran, underscored by Prime Minister Erdogan's agreement in September 2011 to host a radar system for NATO's antimissile system specifically designed to defend against an Iranian attack. And Saudi Arabia is becoming more active in its efforts to counter Iran's ambitions in the Arab world.

Whether this combination of adverse circumstances will prove sufficient to bend the will of the Iranian regime to the demands of the international community for stringent curbs on its nuclear program remains uncertain. Observing NATO's military intervention in Libya to help topple Qaddafi, Iran's Supreme Leader might well have concluded that Qaddafi should never have given up his nuclear weapons program and that Iran needs them now more than ever. Certainly, Iran's response so far to its growing isolation and the pressure of sanctions has been to strike back rather than offer to compromise on its nuclear program. Its attempt to assassinate the Saudi ambassador to the United States in a Washington restaurant in June 2011, its attack on the British embassy in Tehran in November 2011, and its threat to close the Hormuz Straits (through which flow 20 percent of the world's oil supplies) in December 2011 underscore this tendency to react aggressively when the regime feels cornered.

On the other hand, with Iran's position in the Arab heartland under threat, sanctions severely constraining Iran's ability to do business with the world, and the international community so apparently united against his regime, Khamenei might yet conclude that tactical concessions were now worth making if only to buy some time.

Three years into Obama's term, the effort to curb Iran's nuclear enthusiasm continues. Iran's nuclear program has been sabotaged and slowed, its intentions laid bare, its oil production reduced, its military embargoed, and its banking and shipping constrained. Obama deserves credit for all this, especially for his successful effort to rally the international community against Iran and force it to face the growing consequences of its rogue behavior. His strategy has depended in particular on working closely with the Russians and the Israelis. It is not clear, however, whether that approach can be sustained, given the leadership transition in Russia and an Israeli defense establishment growing increasingly anxious as Iran seems to draw ever closer to developing nuclear weapons. Obama has certainly succeeded in strengthening the commitment of other powers to his broader effort to make nonproliferation a pillar of the emerging global order, but he has so far failed to prevent Iran from advancing to the nuclear weapons threshold.

Some will argue that Obama should have been less hasty in abandoning his policy of engagement and switching to tougher sanctions, that he should have taken up Ahmadinejad's various offers of dialogue, or that he should have worked with Lula and Erdogan rather than rejecting their initiative. Others will counter that Ahmadinejad demonstrated in the TRR episode his inability to deliver and that the brutal suppression of Iranian protesters made continuation of the policy of engagement with Khamenei simply untenable. We shall simply never know whether an alternative approach would have been more successful.

What is clear, however, is that in choosing sanctions over engagement as his method for preventing Iran from acquiring nuclear weapons and thereby undermining the nonproliferation regime, Obama was striving for a better world through a realist's application of power and diplomacy. Before his first term as president concludes, this approach could well bring him to the point where he has to make a fateful choice between bombing Iran's nuclear facilities and allowing Iran to acquire a nuclear weapons capability, with grave implications either way. It would be ironic indeed if Obama were to end the war in Iraq only to start a new one with Iran. But if it comes to that, he will be acting in defense of the non-proliferation regime and in support of a more stable international order as much as he will be seeking to protect America's Arab and Israeli allies. And in the process he will have used power in support of principle as well as in protection of interests.

NORTH KOREA

With North Korea, Obama faced a similar challenge, except by the time he came into office, Pyongyang had already acquired and tested nuclear weapons. Nevertheless, containing North Korea's nuclear program required a strategy similar to that with Iran. In this case, substitute China for Russia as the key power and substitute the Republic of Korea (ROK) and Japan for Israel and the Gulf Arabs as America's nervous allies.

Like Iran's, North Korea's national leadership has enormous pride and regards development of nuclear weapons as core to its survival.[33] But unlike Iran's, it is presiding over a highly dysfunctional political and economic system. The country's GDP is so inconsequential that it has no positive economic leverage or impact in the region or farther afield.[34] As a state it has to barter, bargain, bribe, beg, backtrack, and brutalize to access the resources and opportunities necessary to ensure its survival. Indeed, its importance stems from its development of nuclear and missile capabilities, its willingness to defy all international norms and conventions, and its weaknesses.[35] Each of these creates significant challenges for Obama's foreign policy.

The late Kim Jong-il, North Korea's doughty former leader, saw himself as surrounded by hostile powers and unreliable friends. He, moreover, confronted a world of relative giants—South Korea, Japan, China, Russia, and the United States. He seemed early on to have decided that he must ascertain and exploit to the full the underlying tensions among these major players. He, moreover, appears to have concluded that making concessions under pressure signals weakness, which will only lead to greater pressure to make more concessions. When confronted by external pressure, his modus operandi therefore was to escalate the situation to the point at which the issue was no longer in the comfort zone of the other country, which then was willing to compromise. Kim always exacted a price (often a monetary one) for his own compromises, and he then had a tendency to adhere to his share of the agreement only in part, using his violations as bargaining chips to exact the next compromise or to illicitly build North Korea's capabilities.[36]

Kim proved himself an astute observer of tensions among the major powers with which he dealt but a far less capable analyst of the domestic politics of other countries. He therefore repeatedly and skillfully played off one major power against another, but he also miscalculated when he sought to manipulate the domestic politics of other countries to North Korea's advantage. After the great famine of the mid-1990s, he pursued all of this with a strategically weak hand, the consequences of a puny domestic economy and disastrous food scarcities. His conventional armed forces, over time, became weaker compared to those of the major powers.[37]

Strategically, Kim Jong-il appears to have played his hand badly, missing major opportunities to reduce the threat to his country and to elicit aid commitments and diplomatic progress. Tactically, though, he was tough and astute (given his own analytical framework) and gamed all of his neighbors at various times to keep them at odds with each other and prevent any one of them from gaining substantial leverage over North Korean actions.[38]

For the Obama administration, North Korea presents problems in five major contexts: proliferation, alliance relations with South Korea and Japan, U.S.-China relations, multilateral cooperation in Northeast Asia, and the potential for chaos in North Korea with direct major U.S. and Chinese military involvement. There are other North Korea issues that get attention from U.S. policymakers, such as counterfeiting, narcotics, money laundering, and cyberwarfare. North Korea is active in each of these issues, and the United States has devoted focused attention to each. But this chapter is concerned only with the more strategic issues that North Korea, as a rogue state, places on the Obama administration's agenda.

Nuclear Proliferation

North Korea is the only country ever to withdraw formally from the NPT.[39] It has for many years, moreover, engaged in nuclear proliferation activities, sometimes in combination with missile technology proliferation. Pyongyang, for example, appears to have acquired nuclear capabilities from Pakistan's A. Q. Khan network, at least in part in exchange for providing Pakistan with enhanced missile capabilities.[40] In Syria, North Korea provided the technology to build a clandestine nuclear reactor, which Israel took preemptive military action to destroy before it became operational.[41]

North Korea developed a nuclear weapons capability via a plutonium program that is decades old and appears as of 2012 to be largely defunct. Pyongyang has tested two bombs produced through this program and likely has an uncertain number remaining in storage.[42] More ominously, North Korea has surreptitiously carried out an HEU program in direct violation of the major international commitments it made in the Six-Party Talks.[43] By mid 2011 that program may well have produced enough weapons-grade material for a uranium bomb, which generally is a simpler and more reliable device than a plutonium weapon. Despite winding down the plutonium program, therefore, North Korea may now have moved onto a path of sustained production of nuclear weapons.

Given its foreign policy record, moreover, there is good reason for concern that North Korea would sell weapons-grade material (or the bombs themselves) to another rogue state or even a terrorist network. This would be an extremely high-stakes gamble, as any use of that weapon (or of fissionable materials for a dirty bomb) would likely be traceable to its North Korean origins. But the possibility cannot be ruled out. North Korea has proven willing in the past to proliferate the technology for building bombs, and it evidently has no inhibitions about dealing with the highest bidder.

The HEU program, moreover, complicates the nonproliferation effort tremendously because the locations of what are likely to be several production sites (other than the site at Yongbyon) are unknown.[44] It is hard to imagine the circumstances under which Pyongyang would be willing to identify the location of all such sites in order to allow for full international inspections as part of the nonproliferation regime.

In sum, North Korea has technology, weapons-grade material, and possibly nuclear weapons themselves that it might sell. It has no apparent problems in principle with dealing with terrorist organizations and rogue states. Additionally, North Korea has deep experience in running drug smuggling, international counterfeiting, and other types of illicit operations that have given it extensive contacts with criminal organizations on a global scale.[45] Preventing North Korea from proliferating nuclear weapons must, therefore, be a major priority of any American administration.

North Korea also holds the world's third-largest chemical weapons stockpile and possibly also possesses biological weapons. Given its needs for cash, extensive ties with criminal organizations, and own history of state-sponsored terrorism, the proliferation concerns North Korea poses must extend beyond nuclear and missile technology to include assets in the chemical and biological weapons spheres, too.

Alliance Relations with South Korea and Japan

North Korea has from the start played a pivotal role in the U.S.-ROK alliance, and it has also factored heavily into the content and dynamics of the U.S.-Japan alliance, especially in recent decades. Pyongyang has worked hard over time to identify and exacerbate underlying disagreements between the United States and the ROK and between the United States and Japan over policy toward North Korea. In addition, generally friction-ridden relations between the ROK and Japan have further complicated matters for American policymakers.

Both the ROK and Japan are now under the North Korean missile threat, with a rapidly increasing potential for North Korea to be able to mount a nuclear weapon on those missiles.[46] As this North Korean threat has grown, Japan has become increasingly inclined toward robust missile defenses.[47] It has also squeezed down North Korea's ability to receive cash transfers from its friends in Japan to the point at which these evidently are negligible, and there is no Japan–North Korea trade to speak of.[48]

In addition to Japan's concerns with North Korean missiles and nuclear weapons, Tokyo also pays close attention to resolving the issue of kidnapped Japanese citizens who were brought to North Korea as part of its program to develop the capacity to train and plant agents in Japan.[49] Kim Jong-il ran this program and in 2002 provided Japan with some information on it.[50] He eventually yielded to Japanese pressure to permit the return of those kidnapped Japanese who North Korea admitted were still alive. But North Korean accounting for these individuals is still deemed unsatisfactory in Tokyo, and no full normalization of relations is politically feasible in Japan without satisfactory resolution of this issue. Japan, therefore, always presses the United States to support its concerns about this emotional issue, even as North Korea wants normalization of relations with Japan in substantial part because it expects Japan as part of any normalization deal to make billions of dollars in reparations payments to North Korea for the damage done during the Japanese colonization of Korea, which spanned more than thirty years and concluded only at the end of World War II.[51]

For the ROK, the North Korea issue is deeply intertwined with matters of national identity, domestic politics, economic opportunity, and fear of either the precipitous collapse of North Korea or a rapid Korean unification (both of which would entail huge and unpredictable costs). South Korea's fundamental approach to dealing with North Korea has shifted significantly over time. During 1998–2008 two presidents successively implemented what Kim Dae-jong termed a "sunshine" policy.[52] This policy was based on the premise that North Korea is fundamentally driven by fear, distrust, and insecurity and that an effective way to overcome these emotions would be to preemptively provide various concessions to North Korea to build mutual trust and confidence.[53] The current Lee Myung-bak administration, however, came into office on the basis of rejecting the sunshine policy as having enabled Kim Jong-il to manipulate South Korea to obtain resources and concessions while not following through on his own commitments. Lee, therefore, determined to take a far tougher line, according to which North Korea would receive no concessions without taking tangible reciprocal measures of its own.[54]

Both the ROK and Japan, under threat from North Korea's nuclear weapons, agreed on the need to address that issue effectively. But for both the ROK and Japan, the nonproliferation issue has never been as central as have been the other concerns just noted. These and other differences have provided fertile ground for exploitation by Kim Jong-il over the years, and the Obama administration had to find ways to cope with this reality. For various reasons, both Seoul and Tokyo felt that the Bush administration had not consulted closely enough with them on America's shifting negotiating tactics in dealing with North Korea.

U.S.-China Relations

Because China has closer and more extensive relations with North Korea than does any other country, the United States has seen Beijing as key to shaping North Korean policy so that Pyongyang moves away from further acquisition of nuclear weapons capabilities.[55] China does indeed have a strong interest in the elimination of the North Korean nuclear weapons program for a variety of reasons: it does not want another nuclear power in Northeast Asia, especially one that might some day unite with South Korea; it is concerned that ongoing development of North Korean nuclear capabilities might provoke Japan or South Korea to develop similar capabilities, which would have deeply adverse implications for China's own security; and it does not like being boxed into defending North Korea when Pyongyang is so widely seen as a bad actor in the international arena primarily because of its nuclear program.[56]

But China also has other considerations. It highly values North Korea as a strategic buffer state and is unwilling to apply pressure that risks bringing the demise of the North Korean regime. It also fears the consequences of regime collapse: additional evidence that autocratic regimes are not viable in the twenty-first century; possible chaos and huge refugee flows across the border into Yanbian Prefecture, an ethnically Korean area of Northeast China; potential unrest in North Korea that could lead to People's Liberation Army (PLA) or U.S. and ROK military intervention in the North; or actual unification of the peninsula under ROK auspices and in close alliance with the United States.[57] All of these outcomes are, for Beijing, far worse than the continuation of North Korea as a rogue state.

Beijing's hope is to encourage Chinese-style reforms in North Korea that would preserve an authoritarian system there while improving the viability of the regime.[58] There is apparently some calculation that as North Korea improves its economy and establishes significant ties with other countries, it will act more responsibly and perhaps even cut back or eliminate its nuclear program so as to avoid economic and other sanctions. In pursuit of this objective, Beijing repeatedly hosted Kim Jong-il for tours of areas in China that highlight the results of its own economic reforms, and China has proven eager to train North Korean specialists in the various skills they would need to move in a Chinese-style reform direction.[59]

In short, China shares the key nuclear goals of the United States vis-à-vis North Korea but is far more concerned with preserving North Korea as a viable authoritarian state than is the United States. Beijing is deeply chagrined that North Korea's activities put China in a difficult position, as it seeks to limit the external pressures on the North without at the same time undermining its own relations with the ROK, Japan, the United States, and others. Of course, North Korea has seen complicating China's relations with these other countries as very much in Pyongyang's interests, and it has "played" Beijing as much as it has Washington, Tokyo, and Seoul.[60]

Multilateral Cooperation in Northeast Asia

Northeast Asia is unique in the extent to which it is a focal point of involvement by the major powers (primarily the United States, China, Japan, and the ROK, but also, to some extent, Russia). This group contains one of the world's largest energy exporters and four of the world's largest energy importers. It includes the states with the top four militaries in the world by capability, three of which are nuclear powers. And it is a region of enormous historic tensions and animosities.

It makes great sense to begin to develop some sort of diplomatic community in Northeast Asia that could in turn address such shared concerns as energy security. Given historic animosities and current levels of distrust, any such initiative would require a great deal of time to build something meaningful, and it would be difficult to move far down this road. But a multilateral forum for the United States, China, Japan, and the ROK (and possibly Russia) could help reduce misunderstanding and encourage cooperation.

The major problem in moving in this direction to date has been North Korea, which would view any such effort as being directed against its interests. China, having sponsored the Six-Party Talks, would prefer that this forum evolve to a broader agenda once it has resolved the North Korean nuclear issue. But the prospects for a near-term resolution via the Six-Party Talks are remote. The North Korea issue is, therefore, serving as a significant obstacle to the development of multilateral approaches to deal with other issues in the region.[61]

Chaos Leading to Intervention in North Korea

The George W. Bush administration, during its first term, at times regarded the potential for regime change in North Korea with relish, evidently reflecting a presidential judgment that no good could come of an agreement with Kim Jong-il and that the only hope for resolving the nuclear and related threats from North Korea was to enhance the potential for a collapse of the North Korean regime.[62] This approach always contained three flaws: Kim Jong-il's regime had more survival capability than Washington assumed, and thus the Bush administration's approach guaranteed acute hostility from Pyongyang without achieving its political objectives; Beijing, for the reasons noted above, would seek to prevent pressure on North Korea from reaching destabilizing levels; and the Bush administration assumed without evidence that regime change in North Korea would be relatively peaceful and would lead to a more constructive leadership there.[63]

As of early 2012 the danger of a North Korean regime collapse appears greater than was the case in the early 2000s. Kim Jong-il's death in December 2011 has resulted in his youngest son,

Kim Jong-un, assuming the mantle. But his son is only in his late twenties, has not built up his own power base, and is unlikely to be regarded as a real leader among the old military warhorses who wield the power under North Korea's military-first policy.

Kim Jong-il promised the people of North Korea that 2012, the hundredth anniversary of his father Kim Il-sung's birth, is the year when North Korea achieves genuine prosperity. The reality is that the North Korean economy is in shambles, and food scarcity remains a pressing problem. Further, the revelation of its HEU program has isolated North Korea more than ever from the international community.

North Korea faces some serious risks: failure to improve living standards by late spring, as promised by Kim Jong-il (or to improve them by extraordinary measures in 2012, only to have them decline precipitously in 2013), may sap regime credibility; the succession process in the wake of Kim Jong-il's death may go off track in any number of ways; and internal tensions among top military and security officials over how to manage a critical situation without Kim Jong-il at the helm to enforce discipline could produce severe fissures in the power structure. Some combination of these developments—further enhanced by the spreading information revolution in North Korea—could produce massive instability and regime collapse. While this outcome is not probable, it is sufficiently feasible that the United States and others in the region must consider the scenarios that might unfold rapidly and how best to plan for them.

Those scenarios are very worrisome. North Korea has nuclear weapons and nuclear materials, but presumably nobody outside of the country knows exactly where they are located and who controls them. In the event of regime collapse there will be justifiable concerns that some of these assets can find their way to other rogue states or criminal or terrorist organizations.[64] There will be a great premium on securing all of these assets as quickly as possible, but there is little reason to think that China, the ROK, and the United

States will agree on how best to do so and on who should take charge of the assets once they are located.

Civil war in North Korea between military factions who disagree on the best course for the future is also a possibility. In that case, it is possible that one or more factions would claim control over North Korea's WMD assets and invite outside assistance by the PLA, ROK forces, or the U.S. military. Other factions could seek outside support for their own cause. The potential permutations are varied and dangerous. In any of a number of ways, in short, PLA, U.S., and ROK forces might be drawn directly into North Korea to establish order, secure WMD assets, and even affect the course of internal hostilities there. The potential for clashes of interests, misunderstandings, and even hostilities among those forces may be high, depending on the circumstances. A North Korean collapse could prove, in short, enormously consequential for peace and stability in Northeast Asia.

Obama Administration Strategy

The Obama administration entered office determined not to repeat a cycle in which North Korea ratchets up tension, then negotiates payment for reducing tensions and for promising progress on dismantling its nuclear program, then reneges on at least part of its agreement, and then again ratchets up tensions in order to start the sequence all over again. President Obama wanted real progress in curtailing and eventually dismantling North Korea's nuclear capabilities, but he was prepared to exercise patience and to avoid rewarding bad behavior on Pyongyang's part.[65]

President Obama also well understood the importance of reducing to a minimum the daylight between the United States, South Korea, Japan, and China in dealing with North Korea. While he consistently encouraged close cooperation with Beijing, he made clear that negotiations could resume only when North Korea came into compliance with the obligations it had already taken on and indicated its intention to move forward from that point.[66] In short, the United States would not participate in the Six-Party Talks only to have them negotiate again commitments that North Korea already made during the Bush administration.

Knowing full well the likely limits to which China would go to constrain North Korean behavior, President Obama focused especially on building a rapport with Lee Myung-bak of South Korea and on moving forward in close coordination with America's South Korean ally. Lee, as noted above, took the position that North Korea had to earn any new concessions from the ROK, as in his view the sunshine policy had produced only North Korean deviousness in eliciting support from South Korea without making any substantial changes in its own behavior.

Kim Jong-il seems to have miscalculated in his reading of the new president's thinking. Still weak from his stroke of the previous summer, Kim decided to establish his credentials with Barack Obama as someone who could not be bullied or pushed around. North Korea began visibly to prepare for a new test of its Taepodong-2 missile, with a potential range that could reach American territory. It used the transparent ruse of putting an object in the nose cone so that it could call this a "satellite" test (which was permitted) and not a ballistic missile test (which was banned under UN sanctions).[67] On a technical level, this is a distinction without a difference, and the Obama administration reacted accordingly, by suspending the step-by-step process the Bush administration had negotiated to work toward dismantlement of North Korea's plutonium facility at Yongbyon.[68]

North Korea conducted its test on April 5, 2009. The first two stages of the missile reportedly worked well, but the third stage failed.[69] The United States in response took the issue to the United Nations, where it cajoled China and Russia into supporting a president's statement condemning the test.[70] While a President's Statement is not at all equivalent to a sanctions resolution, the fact that the net result put China and Russia on record as indicating that a "satellite launch" violated the restrictions on a North Korean ballistic missile test was significant. In what would become a fairly regular pattern, North Korea's bad behavior enabled the United States to achieve important diplomatic progress (albeit not always with China on board).

Pyongyang responded, as it frequently had in the past, with escalation. It denied IAEA inspectors continued access to its Yongbyon facility, made clear that it would enrich uranium, warned it would carry out a nuclear test, and indicated it would continue development of its ICBM capabilities (potentially bringing the United States into reach of North Korea's nuclear capabilities).[71] The Obama administration quickly muted its enthusiasm for returning to the Six-Party Talks (which Beijing wanted) and also warmly embraced Lee Myung-bak.[72]

North Korea's next move, on May 25, was to conduct its second nuclear test. As indicated in chapter 2, this gave the Obama administration an opportunity to make the case clearly to China and to the ROK and Japan that North Korea's deployment of a nuclear weapons and ICBM capability, by directly threatening American territory, would be a game changer for U.S. security interests. Given this prospect, the United States would have to take appropriate measures to defend American citizens, including moving necessary assets, such as additional missile defense capabilities, to Asia. Such U.S. defensive moves would inevitably complicate China's own nuclear deterrence strategy. Deputy Secretary of State James Steinberg conveyed this assessment in a June trip to Japan, South Korea, and Beijing.[73]

Washington followed this up with negotiations to have the UN Security Council adopt a strong sanctions resolution in response to the North Korean nuclear test.[74] After strenuous efforts, the Obama administration persuaded China and Russia to support a resolution that was significantly more stringent than any previously adopted against North Korea. The purpose of this resolution was to make it far more difficult for North Korea to earn the hard currency—and to carry out the activities—necessary to strengthen its

nuclear and missile programs and also to tighten the antiprolifera-
tion regime directed against it.[75]

The fundamental pattern of North Korean provocations continued throughout 2010, as summarized in chapter 2. As also
explained there, China on balance opted to protect North Korea
at considerable cost to Beijing's relations with the ROK and the
United States. It was only at the end of 2010 that Beijing appeared
to have taken a tougher line in its internal communications to
Pyongyang, making clear that its patience was nearly exhausted.

As of early 2012, the Obama administration has not succeeded
in bringing North Korea back to the negotiating table. Two bilateral discussions and a third scheduled for late December 2011
sought to get Pyongyang's agreement on the preliminary steps that
the Obama administration had outlined. These were a moratorium
on missile and nuclear tests, adherence to the 2005 Joint Statement and the Armistice, and a freeze on North Korea's enriched
uranium program with international inspection of sites. The South
Koreans were apparently also talking to the North about buying up
the used Yongbyon fuel rods. None of this was agreed upon when
Kim Jong-il's death on December 17, 2011, put all such talks on
hold, as North Korea announced a period of mourning and focused
wholly on managing its domestic power transition.

Thus there have been various ups and downs, as there always are
when dealing with North Korea, but the situation on the ground
regarding nuclear and missile development has not improved.
Indeed, with a robust HEU program now apparently fully in place,
arguably the dangers from North Korea's nuclear program have
grown since the Obama administration took office.

President Obama now has to confront significant uncertainties
about North Korea's stability and intentions under a new leadership. Kim Jong-il's sudden death rattled Beijing, which wants
stability above all else in the North. China's early reaction not
surprisingly included elaborate condolences to North Korea, along
with strong support expressed in various ways for Kim Jong-un

as the legitimate successor. China is therefore, as of early 2012, less likely than ever to prove willing to impose tougher sanctions on Pyongyang; indeed, Beijing may welcome new opportunities during 2012 to demonstrate the value of its support to the new North Korean leadership. Over the long run, China continues to prefer to stop any North Korean proliferation activities, provocations against the South, and continuation of its nuclear and missile programs. But Beijing, at least until Hu Jintao's successor is in power, is likely to focus first and foremost on cementing its ties with Kim Jong-il's successor and preventing any major instability on the peninsula.

China may, in addition, be deeply uncertain about America's ultimate objectives in North Korea, especially given Secretary Clinton's December 2011 trip to Burma to encourage democratic reforms there and the greater prominence of America's global democracy agenda in the Obama administration's foreign policy following the Arab awakenings. Washington's overall promotion of the integrated Asian strategy described in chapter 2 may, moreover, intensify China's wariness regarding U.S. motives toward North Korea during 2012.[76]

The key question is, What opportunities and risks will Kim Jong-il's death create? Although Kim had a far shorter time than his father enjoyed to secure the succession for his son, early indications suggest that he used this time well and that, at least initially, Kim Jong-un will acquire the top political offices and the sworn allegiance of the military. Kim Jong-il worked during 2009–11 to revivify the Korean Workers Party as an important political organization and to bring younger talent into key positions in the Central Military Commission and the civilian party leadership.[77] Kim's younger sister and her husband also played vital roles while he recovered from his 2008 stroke, and they appear to be part of the new power structure that will incorporate Kim Jong-un as the public face. The younger Kim's real power is unclear and will almost certainly evolve over time.

While the early indications suggest a smooth succession, a lot can happen as the new leadership has to make hard decisions on military expenditures, economic and social policies, and domestic and international politico-military issues regarding its nuclear and missile programs. There is clearly the potential for positive change over time in North Korean priorities as well as for the infighting that leads to renewed external hostility or a breakdown in the system itself. In short, the Obama administration must prepare for a range of contingencies in the absence of reliable information as to the relative likelihood of any particular one of them coming to pass.

Quite rightly, Obama, immediately upon hearing of Kim Jong-il's death, talked with Lee Myung-bak to assure him that the United States stands ready to assist if North Korea initiates any provocations or worse. Presumably, the Obama administration is also working to make sure that the ROK response to any such action would not itself easily lead to uncontrolled escalation. The administration also immediately contacted Japan and consulted with China's foreign minister.

As long as the succession appears to be moving ahead reasonably smoothly, the Obama administration should maintain the set of conditions it had previously put on the table and seek to renew bilateral discussions as soon as North Korea is ready to do so. Hopefully, those discussions will lead quickly to resumption of the Six-Party Talks on the basis of the conditions the administration previously set out. This is also likely an appropriate time to lay out a more ambitious set of long-term goals, including full removal of sanctions, normalization of diplomatic relations, a formal end to the Korean War (with a peace treaty to replace the armistice), and energy assistance and economic aid as part and parcel of North Korea's enjoying normal relations with the international community. This package should be available only if North Korea gives up its nuclear program and weapons-grade material, allows full international inspections to verify its adherence to that commitment, and begins to improve its treatment of its own population.

The recommendation here is thus not to begin to provide North Korea with these opportunities but rather to articulate these ultimate goals now so as to make as clear as possible the benefits that the new leadership of North Korea can enjoy if it adopts the appropriate policies. Given North Korean sensitivities, moreover, the Obama administration should take particular care to avoid statements that North Korea considers insulting at this politically sensitive time.[78] A strategy to nurture constructive change in North Korea should give prominent place to working with Beijing toward that goal. China is more trusted in North Korea than any other country, and Beijing likely has better information than does any other government on developments unfolding there. China also has an interest in promoting economic reform in North Korea and diminishing the threat Pyongyang's nuclear program poses.

More important, effective U.S.-China communication and mutual trust will be vital if the North Korean succession unravels and there is a systemic breakdown in the country. It is therefore critically important that President Obama press Hu Jintao to permit secret talks between U.S. and Chinese representatives to explore the thinking on each side on North Korean contingencies, including the possibility of massive instability. A complete breakdown of authority in North Korea, producing armed conflict among military units and uncertainty as to who controls nuclear materials, runs a substantial risk of provoking intervention by China, the United States, and the ROK.

While presumably the United States and the ROK have consulted on potential responses to various contingencies, it appears that to date Beijing has been unwilling to have discussions with the United States on this topic. Given Beijing's strong desire not to alienate the new North Korean leadership (and given the recent U.S. experience with Wikileaks), it will likely require a personal effort by Obama to convince Beijing that any such discussions can be held in total secrecy. That effort should begin immediately.

If there are initial signs of increasing political discord in North Korea, moreover, the administration must have a clear internal point of view as to whether it should seek to stoke those tensions and attempt to create widespread unrest (as some in the United States and perhaps in the ROK will encourage) or to tamp them down and avoid the tremendous risks attendant on massive destabilization of the North (as Beijing will try to do). Given the huge uncertainties that instability would entail and the likelihood that North Korea ultimately will be able, despite tensions and disagreements, to keep its internal differences at a manageable level, President Obama is wise to opt for encouraging stability.

Our point is that it is important to forge clear agreement across the White House, State Department, Defense Department, and other relevant agencies on this objective—and to work accordingly with Congress to prevent this issue from becoming a political football in the 2012 election year. The Obama administration must also in all circumstances continue to take every measure to prevent North Korea's proliferation activities and to increase the chances that Pyongyang will negotiate restraint on—and eventual dismantlement of—its nuclear program.

CONCLUSION

North Korea again highlights the difficulty in achieving core goals against rogue states. The nuclear and related missile programs are central to North Korea's political and security strategies, and there is a question as to whether any feasible approach will produce a decision to dismantle those efforts.[79] The best hope is to nurture greater flexibility among the post–Kim Jong-il leadership, but the chances of success and even the best approach to take to improve the odds are uncertain.

In short, the collective efforts of the international community led by the United States have not to date led North Korea to accept the prevailing rules of the game. It remains to be seen how important the impact of this failure will be in terms of challenging the global nonproliferation order that President Obama has sought to develop as a major pillar of his effort to bend history. It appears, moreover, that the lessons of North Korea's nuclear development and the inability of the United States to stop it—potentially reinforced by developments in Libya in 2011—may not have been lost on Tehran.

But the Obama administration has handled the North Korea issue in a way that has at least generated other important diplomatic benefits for the United States in the region. Through its clear articulation of the consequences of ongoing nuclear and missile development for the U.S. deployment of military assets in Northeast Asia, the administration has increased Chinese incentives to try to constrain North Korea. The White House has also very adeptly worked with South Korea to unify thinking on how to handle the North Korea issue, and as a consequence the U.S.-ROK alliance is probably as strong as it has ever been. Extensive consultations with Japan have also been a factor in improving American relations with the DPJ government and strengthening the U.S.-Japan alliance overall.

North Korea under Kim Jong-il thus inadvertently helped the Obama administration strengthen its alliance relations in Northeast Asia, which the administration had in any case sought to do as part of its overall strategy toward providing regional reassurance in the face of China's rise. At the same time, the North Korea problem has also exacerbated China's relations with both the ROK and Japan (as explained in chapter 2).

The Obama administration has not succeeded in shifting Beijing's calculus away from protecting North Korea from the full diplomatic wrath that its actions have provoked. But the administration on balance worked reasonably effectively with Beijing to craft some limited UNSC actions on North Korea. In 2011 there was obvious debate among foreign policy elites in China over the best strategy to pursue toward North Korea, and the Kim Jong-il succession will probably sharpen these. But Kim Jong-il's death just before the 2012 year of political succession in China has very likely, as noted above, reduced the already slim chances of a significant shift toward a tougher stance in China's North Korea policies before the new Chinese leadership is in place.

At one level, the Obama administration's experience with North Korea has thus failed to deal with the central aim of policy—to constrain and eventually eliminate North Korea's nuclear and missile programs. But the administration has pursued this objective in ways that have enabled it to reap substantial diplomatic and security benefits in the region via skillful responses to North Korea's various provocative actions. North Korea remains a very dangerous place because of its growing nuclear and missile capabilities, the ongoing potential for it to proliferate technologies and assets to rogue states and terrorist groups, and the possibility that it will generate a massive crisis as a consequence of its own domestic tensions. Nevertheless, the North Korea issue has on balance significantly strengthened United States relationships and America's overall position in Northeast Asia.

Three years into Obama's term, both Iran and North Korea are proceeding with their nuclear and ballistic missile programs, both are enriching and stockpiling uranium, and both are thumbing their noses at the international community and generating tensions with their neighbors. But they are also facing the "growing consequences" that Obama warned them about in his Prague speech. And through painstaking diplomatic efforts, Obama has succeeded in convincing China and Russia to cooperate with his broader arms control agenda as well as with UN Security Council efforts to inflict increased costs for Iran's and North Korea's recalcitrance. That, together with other measures, has forced Iran's leaders to contemplate the dire consequences of its nuclear advance and possibly persuaded North Korea to contemplate again the steps necessary to reactivate the Six-Party talks.[80]

In addition, Obama's actions have alerted others that the route of rogues is costly. Although there have been no breakthroughs to disarming the world as yet, Obama has strengthened the international community's commitment to nonproliferation and nuclear disarmament and has forged a new consensus with emerging and established powers about the unacceptability of Iran's and North Korea's behavior. Consequently, these rogue states face growing isolation from the emerging global order that Obama has helped shape.

CHAPTER SEVEN

THE "SOFT SECURITY" AGENDA: ENERGY, CLIMATE, AND WEAK STATES

BEYOND COPING WITH THE REALITIES of a China in ascendance, an Afghanistan and Pakistan in turmoil, and a Middle East in revolution, Obama has had to deal with other tectonic shifts at work in the world. Promisingly, powers like India, Indonesia, Turkey, and Brazil are getting their own houses in order, tapping into global investment and trade opportunities to innovate and grow, and reshaping regional power balances in the process. As a result, hundreds of millions of people are being lifted out of poverty in an ongoing trend that represents an often underappreciated and hugely encouraging development in the current era of human history. Yet at the same time, huge numbers of people around the world continue to subsist on meager incomes. Trends in globalization are threatening the stability and exacerbating the problems of certain countries, such as Mexico, with considerable impact on the United States due to criminality, drugs, illegal immigration, and other illicit activities. Also at the top of the twenty-first-century agenda is the interrelated set of problems concerning energy use and climate change. The very trends in economic development and growth that are lifting so many out of poverty are also leading to much greater energy consumption.

In a serious and systematic way, from early on in his national political career, Barack Obama sought to address this mélange of issues, which he clearly saw as crucial to the planet's long-term health and thus to American national security. Indeed, the first half of his main chapter about foreign policy in his 2006 book *The Audacity of Hope* uses lessons from his years growing up in Indonesia as a template for understanding the world and its challenges, before he even mentions Iraq or nuclear nonproliferation or defense spending. He concludes the chapter with a final section on the portion of foreign policy "that has less to do with avoiding war than promoting peace," underscoring again how central such matters are to his worldview. As then senator Obama put it, if the United States is to "serve our long-term security interests—then we will have to go beyond a more prudent use of military force. We will have to align our policies to help reduce the spheres of insecurity, poverty, and violence around the world, and give more people a stake in the global order that has served us so well."[1] Collectively, these sorts of issues might be termed the soft security agenda because they do not generally constitute clear and present dangers to the United States, yet they do affect its broader national security, especially over the longer term.

For Obama, while all of these new threats and opportunities did not supplant the traditional national security agenda, they were central to the planet's future. The president's "theory of the case" was that these issues were too important to ignore or even be deferred for very long in his first term. His "theory of the politics" seemed to be that by making sure that he addressed the wars and core economic issues successfully, he could also address nontraditional threats without appearing weak on national security. To recall another one of his favorite Martin Luther King phrases, he sensed "the fierce urgency of now" in regard to these matters and spoke of them frequently in major speeches on the campaign trail. Iraq, Afghanistan, Pakistan, the Middle East peace process, the rise of China, Iran's and North Korea's nuclear programs—none of these would be relegated to lesser importance, but none of them would be allowed to displace attention to the soft security agenda either.

Beyond the campaign speeches, some of his administration's key doctrinal and planning documents underscored the significance of this nontraditional security agenda in Obama's eyes. For example, the 2010 *Quadrennial Diplomacy and Development Review,* a new planning document developed by Secretary of State Clinton's State Department, summarized the president's views rather well:

> We must remain vigilant against the traditional interstate threats of war and aggression. In the 21st century, however, we also face new types of emerging threats that transcend regional boundaries and imperil the global community.
>
> First, the threat of terrorism and violent extremism has become more acute and more immediate. . . . Second, as President Obama has made clear, one of today's most immediate and extreme dangers is the proliferation of nuclear materials, particularly to terrorist organizations. . . . Third, while the global economy has helped lift millions around the world from poverty and has fueled American prosperity, the interconnected global economic system also creates new transnational challenges. . . . A fourth threat is the specter of irreversible climate change. . . . A fifth threat is the cybersecurity risk that comes from our dependence on technology and online networks. . . . A sixth growing threat is transnational crime, which directly threatens the United States as well as governance and stability in foreign countries. . . . Finally, while pandemics and infectious diseases have existed for millennia, today they are more potent and potentially devastating.[2]

Clinton's language echoed what the president had himself written in the preamble to his *National Security Strategy,* released in May 2010: "The international order we seek is one that can resolve the challenges of our times—countering violent extremism and insurgency; stopping the spread of nuclear weapons and securing nuclear materials; combating a changing climate and sustaining global growth; helping countries feed themselves and care for their sick; resolving and preventing conflict, while also healing its wounds."[3]

The items on these lists can be subdivided into two broad categories: those concerning the hard power issues of counterterrorism, nuclear security, and homeland security, discussed elsewhere in this book, and those relating to energy, economics, epidemics, state weakness, civil conflicts, and crime. The soft security issues of greatest concern to the United States and its core interests are, first, energy (including nuclear energy, especially the issues of nonproliferation and safety) and climate change and, second, global poverty and criminality (with a particular focus on pivotal states such as Mexico). Both sets of issues have been very important to Barack Obama. The first concerns the basic economic security of the United States as well as the inherent livability of the planet over time. Obama sees the second set as crucial for creating a more just and inherently more stable international order. In dealing with these challenges, some of which could pose threats to the international system and perhaps even the very survivability of the planet, how well is President Obama doing?

The short answer is: President Obama has had some limited successes but has not yet bent history in any major way on this set of issues. He tried and failed to adopt a new energy policy, which had a direct and negative impact on the pursuit of his goals at the global summit on climate change in Copenhagen in 2009. His nonproliferation efforts have moved the ball forward in significant ways; however, in terms of nuclear capability, the world is likely as dangerous in early 2012 as it was at the beginning of 2009.

Mexico is more troubled than when Obama took office, and the related challenge of illegal immigration in American politics has not proven amenable to his hopes of forging a post-partisan style of policymaking. Global antipoverty efforts are in fact making some headway, but less because of what Obama had hoped to do by doubling foreign aid or breaking down trade barriers than because developing countries themselves are making sounder choices about their policies, a trend that began before he was elected. Challenges from failed or failing states such as the Democratic Republic of Congo have not been alleviated on Obama's watch. With the active support of the administration, the G-8 economic forum has been largely replaced by the G-20, which is movement in the right direction, but a reformed UN Security Council is as distant as ever.

That Obama has been largely frustrated in these matters does not make him unique among American presidents. But on balance the soft security agenda has not been an area of major accomplishment for a president who had harbored a big vision—one who had inspired grand hopes from Jakarta to Berlin to many other places around the world.

ENERGY AND CLIMATE

President Obama came into office riveted on two huge concerns about the nature of America's and the world's consumption of energy resources. First, like many presidents before him, he recognized the vulnerability of U.S. access to oil. Second, even more than Presidents Jimmy Carter and Bill Clinton, he was of the view that global warming poses a major peril to the country's and planet's very viability, amounting to a major national security threat.

Energy Demand and Traditional National Security

Worrying about energy security *and* climate change makes the policy challenge extremely complex. For example, to address energy security, an "energy nationalist" might encourage all-out development of American offshore oil as well as coal, natural gas, Canadian oil sands, and related sources of hydrocarbons.[4] But for climate change activists, fuels like coal and oil sands in particular are problematic. Because coal emits a large amount of carbon dioxide per unit of energy (the latter typically expressed in terms of British Thermal Units or BTUs), it verges on taboo for those focused mostly on the climate issue—at least until technologies can be developed that would increase combustion efficiency or sequester the carbon dioxide in permanent underground repositories. There are also large health costs associated with coal and its pollutants.[5] Even natural gas is problematic for those focused on mitigating climate change since it produces about 45 percent as much carbon dioxide on average as coal or oil per BTU. An energy economy based largely on natural gas would not likely achieve the dramatic reductions in emissions required to meet the goals considered necessary by climate scientists (discussed below).[6]

The world's basic energy facts might be summarized as follows. Oil, which powers the overwhelming majority of the world's vehicles, is presently pumped at the rate of about 85 million barrels a day worldwide.[7] The United States consumes about a quarter of that total, the majority of which is from imports. Most American oil imports do not come from the Middle East any more; North America and some countries in Africa provide the bulk of it. But oil is fungible, and the world economy does depend disproportionately on Middle Eastern (as well as Russian) oil, with about a third of all current production and nearly two-thirds of estimated global reserves located in the broader Persian Gulf region.[8] Notably, China today gets just under half its oil from the Middle East, India nearly 65 percent, South Korea almost 75 percent, and Japan about 80 percent.[9]

And the Middle East region, as recent history demonstrates, is as volatile as it is vital. By some estimates, the United States spends at least $50 billion a year maintaining the military forces required to help protect the free flow of oil out of the Persian Gulf region.[10] In addition, the United States is winding down what has been a trillion-dollar war to overthrow Saddam Hussein's regime and then help develop a new, stable government in Iraq; nearly 5,000 Americans have died in the effort as well. That war was not over oil per se, but many of its antecedents lay in the world's economic dependence on the Gulf region.

Beyond these actual costs, there is also the risk that an event such as a revolution in Bahrain or a succession crisis in Saudi Arabia or all-out war between neighboring states in the region could badly disrupt global oil markets for an extended period of time, making the $145 per barrel prices of 2008 seem a bargain by comparison. In 2011 instability in the region caused prices to jump to $120 a barrel before settling down, at least temporarily, at roughly two-thirds that level (though closer to $100 as of this writing in early 2012). These increases are already estimated to have shaved about 1 percent off the growth rate as the U.S. economy was struggling to emerge from recession. Such developments highlight the dangers of America's and the world's overseas oil dependencies.[11]

Oil constitutes about 40 percent of all American energy sources but accounts for more than 95 percent of all transportation fuels in America. By contrast, energy sources for heating and electricity generation are led by coal, natural gas, nuclear power, and hydroelectric power, with oil as well as wind and solar energy providing modest contributions.[12] Overall, the world uses about 500 quadrillion BTUs of energy a year, with about 35 percent from oil, roughly 25 percent from coal, just over 20 percent from natural gas, about 10 percent from renewables, and about 6 percent from nuclear power plants.[13] In comparison to oil, these other sources of energy are also more widely distributed around the world.[14]

Traditional national security considerations place a premium on mitigating foreign oil dependence through whatever means, including development of North American energy resources with high carbon content. President Obama, like most American politicians, adopted the autarkic language of national energy self-sufficiency and other traditional national security considerations in making his case on energy. For example, in his second debate with John McCain in Nashville in the fall of 2008, he described energy policy as a higher priority than health care reform or education:

> Energy we have to deal with today, because you're paying $3.80 here in Nashville for gasoline, and it could go up. And it's a strain on your family budget, but it's also bad for our national security, because countries like Russia and Venezuela

and, you know, in some cases, countries like Iran, are benefiting from higher oil prices. So we've got to deal with that right away. That's why I've called for an investment of $15 billion a year over 10 years. Our goal should be, in 10 years' time, we are free of dependence on Middle Eastern oil.[15]

In reality, given the country's huge foreign oil dependence, autarky has been less realistic a goal than a diversification of supplies to minimize the nation's dependence on any one region and particularly the Middle East. And the world as a whole cannot realistically aspire to eliminate its dependence on Middle Eastern oil anytime soon, even if the United States now has that option. Regardless, U.S. energy policy has been based on an approach that advocates diversity of supply and domestic (North American) production of as many resources as possible.

The Climate Change Factor

What distinguished Obama from other presidents was his additional focus on climate change. He was persuaded by the scientific consensus on the subject. The Intergovernmental Panel on Climate Change had estimated that an average worldwide temperature rise of about 2 degrees Celsius would pose a great cause for concern. That means an increase of 3.6 degrees Fahrenheit, of which 1.3 degrees has already occurred, due largely to the rapid increase in industrial activity over the last century.[16]

Increases in carbon dioxide emissions are the chief human contribution to climate change. The carbon dioxide concentration is now at 385 parts per million in the atmosphere, up by 100 parts per million relative to the nineteenth-century baseline, and is rising at 2 parts per million per year. If carbon dioxide levels reach roughly 400 parts per million, a 2 degrees Celsius temperature increase will likely occur. There is uncertainty in these numbers, to be sure, but the general scientific realities they depict are widely accepted.

To keep Earth's atmosphere at or below that threshold requires reducing current annual global carbon dioxide emissions from 30 billion to 15 billion tons. That would have to happen even as estimated global energy use grows by more than 50 percent over the coming decades.[17] Since carbon dioxide is gradually absorbed or otherwise removed from the atmosphere, such a reduced rate of emissions would stabilize the concentration of atmospheric carbon dioxide and thus potentially stabilize the global climate.[18]

Were carbon dioxide concentrations to exceed 400 parts per million, and average temperatures to increase by more than 2 degrees Celsius relative to a century ago, the results could be perilous. They would likely include the very significant further melting of the ice covering Greenland (temperature changes due to greenhouse gas emissions are even greater at the poles) and expansion of ocean water volume due simply to the higher water temperatures, resulting in rising ocean levels and flooding in low regions around the world; changes in weather patterns, including increased drought in already dry areas around the globe; and greater frequency of extreme weather conditions.[19] There is some debate about how much temperature increase will result from given levels of carbon dioxide and other greenhouse gases in the atmosphere, as well as about the specific consequences of any such increases. But the linkage between the release of greenhouse gases due to human activity and global warming no longer is questioned in mainstream science, even if it is rejected out of hand by a significant portion of America's political leadership.

There may be mitigating steps that could be taken to address global warming, such as artificially placing more soot-like particles in the upper atmosphere to simulate the cooling effects of volcanic eruptions. But scientists are concerned about the many unknown indirect consequences of such actions, such as a possible increase in the acidity of the oceans as the particles return to Earth. So such measures are at best risky last resorts.

International versus Domestic Politics

Motivated by these scientific findings, Obama sought to accomplish two big things in 2009 and 2010: an international accord at the Copenhagen climate change conference, and "cap and trade" legislation at home designed to introduce a system of carbon-emissions permits that would lead to a 17 percent reduction in carbon emissions by 2020 and an 83 percent (or five-sixths) reduction in U.S. carbon emissions by 2050.[20] Of course, these two efforts were linked; any international accord would require American action as an integral part of the plan. And in the run-up to Copenhagen, as explained in chapter 2, foreign actors watched with great interest whether the president appeared to have the political skills and clout at home to implement whatever he promised in multilateral treaty talks. No one had forgotten the Kyoto experience of the Clinton years, when domestic politics prevented ratification of a treaty that Washington had done so much to promote in the first place.

Also, countries such as China did not relish the notion of giving up their Annex II status under Kyoto since that exempted them from international obligations to limit greenhouse gas emissions. Beijing instead declared that its domestic priority was shifting from reducing the "energy intensity" of GDP (that is, the amount of energy required to produce a given amount of national economic output) to reducing its "carbon intensity." Thus Beijing has proven unwilling to commit to an absolute reduction in greenhouse gas emissions.[21]

Indeed, some Chinese leaders suspected a White House conspiracy: Obama would pressure them to promise reductions in carbon dioxide emissions at Copenhagen, then go home and fail to get congressional approval for legislation to have the United States hold up its end of the bargain. The net effect would be that China would be forced to reduce emissions, America would not, and as a result China would be disadvantaged in its economic competition with the United States.

At Copenhagen no binding international agreement to reduce carbon emissions could be reached. But Obama helped salvage a fallback accord that asked every country to develop its own plan for limiting emissions and declare it to the international community.[22] He did so in large part by joining a freewheeling meeting of Premier Wen Jiabao from China with leaders from India, South Africa, and Brazil on the final Friday evening of the Copenhagen conference and cajoling them into an agreement. The nature of this improvised meeting meant, among other things, that Europe did not have a direct voice in this last-minute accord, even though European nations had done more than the United States to control their emissions and focus international attention on the issue.

This Copenhagen Accord was not a hugely significant outcome, perhaps, but it was better than the absence of any agreement. It was also more realistic than an agreement locking the United States into a concrete commitment that Congress might then refuse to back up with implementing legislation back home. And its framework for encouraging efforts by all countries, including the United States and developing nations, made it preferable to the 1997 Kyoto accord from an American perspective. China and India both subsequently satisfied the requirement of registering their targets in the annex to the Copenhagen Accord by January 31, 2010. Neither agreed to reduce overall emissions, but both did commit to reduce the "carbon intensity" of their GDP, meaning that in effect they would move to cleaner energy overall.[23] China had already demonstrated its ability to reduce the energy intensity of GDP in its 2006–10 Five-Year Plan, even if its progress was somewhat tougher sledding than initially anticipated.[24] The December 2011 South Africa climate conference sustained a similar spirit, aspiring to a future accord that would involve binding commitments from all parties, including developing countries.

Obama was thus partially effective in an element of his foreign policy that had been important to him and important for the times. Beyond addressing the energy issue specifically, his policy also accorded greater responsibilities to—and expected greater contributions from—developing countries and in particular the emerging new powers. Obama viewed the Copenhagen Accord as important to bringing not only China but also India, Brazil, Turkey, Indonesia, and South Africa into the elite group of influential states on matters of global decisionmaking. His emphasis on the G-20 rather than the G-8 to address the global fiscal crisis was another manifestation of this shift. However, some aspects of this approach, such as the promise to push for permanent membership for India on the UN Security Council, have been more rhetorical than real. Regardless, on the climate issue, Obama helped convince developing countries that they must develop their own plans and submit them to at least a sharply delimited degree of international oversight and monitoring—even if they could not be expected to achieve actual reductions on carbon emissions, as were the established industrial powers.[25]

However, after the Copenhagen agreement, the United States itself failed to do its part, as energy legislation stalled in the United States in 2010. This made the international accord much less meaningful since the world's leading economy and number two carbon dioxide emitter became less credible on its own obligations.

What happened? The U.S. Senate proved unwilling to pass a binding policy on carbon emissions. But the executive branch was partly to blame for this outcome, as Obama decided to make health care reform a higher legislative priority. The administration also began to suffer from the perception that it was doing too much and spending too much. This further undermined its ability to push energy legislation.

The Obama administration also made numerous tactical mistakes while working with Congress on the cap-and-trade legislation. Rather than negotiate carefully to form a Senate coalition that could pass the legislation, Obama gave away concessions that his congressional allies on the issue needed to retain as bargaining chips to gather enough votes for energy legislation. These included entertaining some drilling off the U.S. Atlantic coast and expanding federal guarantees for loans related to nuclear reactor construction. The administration also failed to maintain support from Senate majority leader Harry Reid. Reid ultimately decided to prioritize immigration reform, given his challenges in gaining reelection in Nevada, meaning that he was unwilling to push energy legislation at a crucial moment. The administration also undercut key allies such as Senator Lindsey Graham through clumsy public relations that portrayed Graham as supporting new energy taxes when that was not a stance Graham could survive politically.[26]

Critically, Obama's decision to try to pass energy legislation indirectly through a cap-and-trade system that few understood was riskier than many appreciated. In an effort to avoid the traditional and highly controversial approach of proposing a carbon tax, the administration arguably committed the even greater mistake of trying to reshape the core of the American economy in a way that critics could deride as a stealthy plan for imposing huge *hidden* taxes. Indeed, it risked imposing indirect costs on the economy that critics argued would be in the trillion-dollar range.[27]

The goal of an 83 percent reduction in carbon emissions by 2050 was so ambitious, moreover, that it clearly reflected little more than an inherent hope that the economic incentives created by cap and trade would produce fundamentally new types of energy technologies. The long time horizon of the deadline defused the revolutionary quality of the proposal for some, but the idea itself was still remarkably audacious. The goal reflected more of a faith in the influence of science combined with the power of the free market rather than any hard evidence that such reductions would be attainable.[28]

Alternative Energy Options and Policies: Limits and Risks

In principle, renewable energy sources could replace all existing sources of American electricity, and most vehicles could be made to run on batteries. But in fact, all renewables would be very challenging to scale up dramatically today, and at the level of national need, they would typically be several times more expensive than the direct costs of existing energy production from coal or gas plants.[29] Since the United States already spends several hundreds of billions of dollars a year on energy, one can see how critics of cap and trade estimate the costs of such approaches in the range of $1 trillion a year or more.

Breakthroughs may well occur by 2050 that make some of the above options affordable and otherwise desirable. But assuming a more than 80 percent reduction in carbon emissions is more a hope than a solid and tangible policy. For example, the Obama administration's regulations on car mileage could reduce average vehicle emissions by half eventually, but not by anything approaching five-sixths.[30] And the Obama administration has taken only modest steps to increase the odds that technological breakthroughs in energy sources will occur. It has increased funding for energy research somewhat, but on balance the effect is limited: the roughly $5 billion a year now being spent on energy research in the United States is only about half as much in real dollar terms as that spent in the late 1970s.[31] The Solyndra scandal gave federal loan guarantees to green energy firms a bad name. Nor has Obama come up with any particular initiative to promote use of ethanol—a fuel hyped a bit in the latter part of the Bush administration but frequently under fire for diverting corn supplies away from food needs at home and abroad. Obama might have, for example, spurred research to encourage biomass fuel *not* from corn and *not* produced on viable farmland.

The administration has not made any real headway on nuclear power, either. The challenges on this front are at least as large as with "greener" renewables. In the aftermath of the 2011 Fukushima Daiichi disaster, it may be necessary to ensure that all future nuclear plants have passive cooling and other safety features, rather than depending on continuous sources of electricity and consistent direct human oversight.[32] The huge costs of building plants must become more widely acceptable to investors than they generally are today.[33] On balance, nuclear energy is hardly more poised to make a more substantial contribution to the nation's energy portfolio than it was when Obama took office.

Perhaps most important, the proliferation risks must be addressed in any plan to expand use of nuclear power at home and abroad. During the Bush administration, a number of proposals were developed to address concerns that the spread of nuclear energy technologies could give more foreign states easy access to materials needed to build nuclear bombs. These included the general consensus that the "Additional Protocol"—allowing international inspectors to monitor more of a country than just its declared nuclear facilities—should be made standard on International Atomic Energy Agency (IAEA) monitoring agreements. Other suggestions included the Bush administration proposal of not allowing any additional countries to develop enrichment capacity (instead being sure they could buy any needed fuel through guaranteed sources); then IAEA director Mohammed El Baradei's idea that any future enrichment plants be multilaterally owned and operated; and suggestions to ban any further production of highly enriched uranium or construction of any new plutonium reprocessing facilities (in effect, a toughened-up version of a fissile material cutoff treaty, though not necessarily an idea that would need to await formal negotiation of such an accord).[34]

The Obama administration has taken only modest steps on its watch, however. It has helped establish a nuclear fuel bank to reduce other countries' needs to have—or excuses for creating—their own enrichment capabilities, and this program may help modestly in the future.[35] The administration fared less well in convincing the Nuclear Suppliers Group to adopt tighter restrictions on the transfer of enrichment and reprocessing technologies. It also was unable to prevent China from aiding Pakistan's nuclear ambitions outside of such guidelines.[36] It has sustained the Bush administration's sensible Proliferation Security Initiative and also increased funds for securing nuclear materials at research reactors and similar sites while adding about 10 percent to aggregate nonproliferation funding in the process.[37] In addition, the administration proposed a plan whereby Russia and France would provide enriched uranium fuel for Iran's research reactor, but Tehran rejected the idea. Obama's other efforts, including support for the (moribund) talks on a fissile material cutoff treaty, add up to a workmanlike policy and not a bold or historic one.[38]

There are many other things a president viewing energy as among his three highest priorities might have done. Some would have been small fare; others, potentially more significant.[39] For example, Obama could have organized a clearinghouse where consumers could gain quick and vetted advice on which contractors in their areas could install solar panels and related technologies for home and office. He could have pushed for substantial subsidies for hybrid or plug-in cars and encouraged greater production of flexible fuel vehicles. And he could have asked for a direct tax on carbon, promising to reduce income taxes commensurately in the process so as not to stall the economic recovery.

But he generally has not led with such approaches either. Rather, he has tried to use the Environmental Protection Agency, and its powers under the Clean Air Act, to control greenhouse gas emissions through regulation and to impose steeper demands on car manufacturers to improve fuel efficiency over the coming decades. The latter policy has been implemented, though its benefits will only be realized over time. The former approach, though still in a relatively formative state of play, has already met opposition in Congress, where Republicans have sought to deny appropriations needed to carry it out.[40]

Obama has not failed completely on energy, but certainly his overall record to date has been disappointing—not least of all when measured against the standards he himself set out and the theory of the case he developed going back to his Senate days.

POVERTY, CIVIL CONFLICT, AND CRIME

Since the cold war ended, some analysts of American national security theory and strategy have argued that the combination of overseas poverty, civil conflict, failed and failing states, and transnational crime has become a top-tier national security concern for the United States. This agenda was inspired by concerns that everything from the global drug trade to the spread of epidemic disease to human trafficking to massive refugee movements could all become much worse in an era of globalization and burgeoning populations. It was further driven by the view that frustration and anarchy in key developing countries could provide motivation, recruits, and sanctuaries for international terrorism.

To be sure, humanitarianism has a key role in motivating attention to these issues, along with security concerns.[41] Dramatic increases in the number of people displaced by war, scares over new diseases, like AIDS and severe acute respiratory syndrome (SARS), and pathogens, such as West Nile virus, and the extreme violence of narcotraffickers operating just south of America's borders have all significantly heightened worries over the past two decades.[42] In the first instance, the international community has responded in recent years with record numbers of international peacekeepers to address civil conflicts.[43] But the problems remain enormous.

This "new" security agenda has not been compelling to everyone. For example, during the 1990s, the Republican-led Congress was particularly wary about foreign aid spending as well as overseas peacekeeping. Texas governor George W. Bush famously campaigned against the notion of U.S. troops participating in peacekeeping missions as an ill-advised form of international charity, and Condoleeza Rice wrote an article in *Foreign Affairs* in 2000 arguing that American GIs should not be walking little kids to their school buses around the world.[44] Bush's views changed in regard to Iraq and Afghanistan, of course, but only because he saw these two places as specific and acute security threats.

Yet this new security paradigm *was* compelling to Obama. As a senator he focused on several parts of Africa, particularly places where conflict was severe. As a presidential candidate he devoted several major speeches to the problems of weak states and their links to American security, and he wanted to double foreign aid to help developing countries. And as president he remained focused intently on these issues in his *National Security Strategy* and *Quadrennial Diplomacy and Development Review*.[45] His perspective was that this agenda could not wait.

Thus, in a major foreign policy speech in Chicago in April 2007, Obama argued that

> I believe that the single most important job of any President is to protect the American people. And I am equally convinced that doing that job effectively in the 21st century will require a new vision of American leadership and a new conception of our national security. . . . In today's globalized world, the security of the American people is inextricably linked to the security of all people. . . . Whether it's global terrorism or pandemic disease, dramatic climate change or the proliferation of weapons of mass annihilation, the threats we face at the dawn of the 21st century can no longer be contained by borders and boundaries.[46]

Some of Obama's views about how to pursue this vision are unrealistic and somewhat misguided. For example, his pledge to double foreign aid as a key, perhaps the key, to addressing global poverty was never very plausible and, under current budget conditions, is entirely impractical. His focus on aid itself, moreover, is questionable. He inherited a world, for example, in which the major emerging market economies, including Brazil, India, and China, went from producing 6.3 percent of global output in the 1960s to more than 22 percent by 2008–09, as measured in purchasing power parity terms. These same emerging economies also provided almost all global growth in the recession years of 2008–09.[47] Their dramatic takeoff over the last three decades was largely attributable to trade, investment, and related opportunities from globalization.[48] Although global aid flows did increase by half during the Bush years (even excluding funds for Iraq and Afghanistan), trends in globalization as well as the policy reforms of emerging states were even more consequential. For example, total foreign investment in developing countries roughly quadrupled over the decade before Obama took office.[49]

Meanwhile, the Obama administration during its first two years focused far less attention and effort on the important realm of trade policy. Faced with U.S. unemployment rates hovering around 10 percent due to the great recession he inherited, Obama did not feel strongly positioned to push for passage of the Colombia, Panama, or South Korea free trade accords, which finally cleared Congress and were signed into law only in October 2011. Other useful initiatives such as a revised and renewed North American Free Trade Agreement (NAFTA) or a free trade pact with beleaguered Pakistan have not received serious attention. These moves could likely have done much more for global growth as well as U.S. security interests than would a doubling of American foreign aid.[50]

To be sure, foreign assistance still has its place. Priorities, ranging from debt relief for reformist states in Africa, to greater security cooperation with states like Mexico, to expansion of health initiatives across the developing world, remain in need of resources.[51] The weakest and poorest states are less well positioned to tap into global trade and investment flows than are emerging markets, so assistance is still especially important for them. In addition, the growth of private aid—estimated at more than $30 billion a year from the United States and another $15 billion from other donors in aggregate—also has been important in addressing various specific needs in health, agriculture, and other sectors around the world.[52]

Beyond economic policy, most other priorities, including Obama's "soft security" agenda, have been given short shrift. Like every modern president, Obama has faced the challenges of state weakness and collapse in a number of places around the world. The issues were most acute in Sudan, the Democratic Republic of Congo, and Somalia. He also has had to wrestle with troubles closer to home, in countries like Colombia and Mexico, whose problems of crime, drug-related violence, and illegal migration could affect American well-being in a direct and concrete way. Fortunately, the level of civil conflict around the world has declined by about half since the end of the cold war.[53] But the remaining challenges are still serious. How has the president fared in dealing with these matters?

Conflict and Weak States in Africa

Some point to the 2011 Libya operation as proof of a break-through in the approach to addressing the problems of civil conflict and state weakness. Certainly, in his response to the Libya crisis, President Obama—assisted by the tireless efforts of Secretary Clinton and UN Ambassador Susan Rice—succeeded in passing a UN Security Council resolution that enshrined the principle of the "responsibility to protect" as part of Security Council action. He enlisted not only NATO but at least two Arab states in the effort to implement the resolution. Gaining the participation of key regional players was smarter than other approaches that might have been considered, such as seeking the approval of a Western-dominated community of democracies for key decisions on the use of force—which could have unnecessarily and unproductively exacerbated tensions with China and Russia.[54]

But compared with other human tragedies of the day, the Libya crisis was relatively minor. The breakthrough associated with the Libya intervention has been modest and certainly no greater than the international community's growing acceptance of a "responsibility to protect" that occurred during the tenures of the two previous American presidents.[55] The operation was pragmatically handled, but it has provided no paradigm for future action, no indicator of a future Obama doctrine of humanitarian intervention that will now be widely applied throughout the world. It could actually set back that broader cause because the original mission to protect Libyan citizens, as authorized under UN Security Council

Resolution 1973, morphed into an effort to remove Qaddafi from power. Russia, China, India, and Brazil stridently objected, ensuring that the same principle of "responsibility to protect" was not extended by the international community to the people of Syria in their revolt against a brutal regime (though by late 2011 the Arab League had begun to take action on that issue).

In Sudan, where the northern and southern parts of the country have gone their separate ways, the Obama administration got off to a slow start but then played a significant role in late 2010 and 2011 by providing diplomatic support to the process. Historically, the U.S. role in the Sudan peace process has been a limited one. Yet the 2005 Comprehensive Peace Agreement—the key accomplishment that mandated the recent 2011 referendum on separation that led to the creation of Southern Sudan on July 9, 2011—was negotiated with active participation by the Bush administration.

Despite the fact that Senator Barack Obama expressed a major interest in Sudan, the Obama administration did not make much headway in facilitating the implementation of this agreement. This is unfortunate because lingering disputes over territory and oil could produce bloody conflict between the two states. The basic situation, in which northern Sudan controls the only pipeline to the sea but the less populous southern Sudan possesses most of the oil, can work only if the two sides see each other as necessary partners. President Omar Hassan al-Bashir's actions could lead South Sudan to build a pipeline bypassing the north while claiming all rights of ownership to the oil.[56] Furthermore, escalating conflicts could arise from residual territorial disputes, such as the still unresolved status of the Abyei region, or over a specific region inside Khartoum's territory but adjoining South Sudan, such as Nuba or the Blue Nile State.[57]

Dealing with a government run by an accused war criminal is hardly an easy diplomatic task. Nevertheless, given Obama's focus on humanitarian intervention, applied so effectively in the case of Libya in 2011, it would seem that an equal amount of attention should be devoted to a place that has been far bloodier in recent times. For too long the administration's role was less energetic, dynamic, and preventive in character than it might have been.[58] In addition, the Obama administration appeared too reliant on positive incentives, such as debt relief and an end to sanctions, and not willing enough to toughen sanctions on Khartoum or support further International Criminal Court indictments in the event of violence by Bashir and his cronies.[59]

From late 2010 into 2011, the Obama administration worked on its Sudan diplomacy more energetically through envoy Princeton Lyman and also promoted a UN peacekeeping force for the disputed area around Abyei (the status of which is still not resolved). As of this writing, the future of both Sudans looks more promising, and the prospects for avoiding all-out civil war—if not preventing some ongoing atrocities—have possibly improved, but not dramatically.[60]

By some measures, the Democratic Republic of Congo has suffered more war-related deaths than any other place on Earth over the last fifteen years—due not so much to direct killing as to the resultant breakdown of the state and of health care and nutrition. Reliable estimates put the mortality figures at nearly three million over this time period.[61] While the violence has subsided some in recent years, the lack of effective governance in the country ensures that the lethality of this war remains considerable.[62] Yet the Obama administration's policies have done little to repair the situation.

The administration, for example, did not act on recommendations to beef up the UN peace mission or seriously engage to help reform and professionalize the Congolese security forces.[63] UN troop numbers have increased slightly over the Obama administration's time in office, with mission strength increasing from about 17,000 to 18,000—in a country several times the size of Iraq or Afghanistan with twice the population of either.[64] U.S. direct assistance has remained around Bush-era levels.[65] No substantial initiatives have been undertaken to help other Congolese institutions, such as the judiciary and legislative branches of government, function more effectively.[66] And the November 2011 parliamentary and presidential elections occurred with many irregularities, in part due to weak, ineffectual international engagement in election preparations. The contrast between how the Obama administration spoke out about Egyptian and Russian elections in that same time period versus its minimal response to the Congo elections suggests drift in current American policy in this arena, though Secretary Clinton's December statement on the subject mitigated the problem somewhat.

One more important case—an especially delicate one for a Democratic president—is Somalia, where Bill Clinton encountered huge problems after the Black Hawk down tragedy of October 1993. Since that time, Somalia has teetered between being a failed state and a non-state. In recent years, it has also become a haven for two groups that can threaten Western interests: the extremist al-Shabab militia and bands of pirates who traverse the ocean waters off Somalia's coast looking for booty and occasionally killing innocent seafarers in the process. The Obama administration inherited this set of problems and has taken no major steps to address them. A 2011 famine has killed tens of thousands of Somalis and put hundreds of thousands in dire peril.[67] In humanitarian terms, the magnitude of the Somalia tragedy is almost surely greater than the humanitarian challenges in any Arab state, including Libya, during 2011 or 2012.

An African Union peacekeeping mission exists in Somalia, made up primarily of Ugandan and Burundian soldiers, to try to strengthen the Transitional Federal Government as it seeks to extend control within and beyond the capital city of Mogadishu. But the international effort remains underresourced, and the U.S. role minimal. Total troop strength gradually grew from about 5,000 in early 2009 to almost 10,000 by 2011. But part of this was natural growth for a mission that began only in 2007, and current force levels remain below the UN-approved expansion to 12,000 and the goal of 20,000 promoted by some African governments. Funds for salaries for the mission are sometimes in short supply as well.[68] U.S. direct monetary assistance to Somalia has remained less than in the later Bush years.[69]

Total troop rosters for the transitional government list around 10,000 Somali fighters, perhaps, but as salaries are rarely paid, actual fighting strength is typically far less.[70]

All is not lost in Somalia. UN forces have indeed made some headway, and the roles of neighboring Ethiopia and Kenya have increased, possibly for the better. The regions of Somaliland and Puntland in the north are reasonably effective and stable autonomous areas. Some have suggested that as an alternative to trying to recreate a strong central state, working with more local autonomous actors—particularly the less corrupt ones—could be a preferable alternative.[71] It also may be possible to prod the Transitional Federal Government, seen by many Somalis as an Ethiopian proxy, to increase its domestic legitimacy by working cooperatively with some insurgents other than the core of the al-Shabab movement.[72] In any event, even though it would be unfair to attribute Somalia's difficulties to a specific failure of Obama's policy, it is a fact that the current underresourced effort has not been a success for the Obama administration.

Security Concerns South of the Border

Closer to home, and even more directly consequential for American national security policy, the Obama administration has made relatively few overtures toward Latin America. It began with considerable goodwill in the region and has not entirely lost that, but it has yet to be associated with a major policy initiative or accomplishment.[73] There have been steps forward, as with the U.S.-Brazil Defense Cooperation Agreement of 2010, for example, but these have generally been modest in scope and scale. Fortunately, the region itself is doing better. Almost all of South America has been growing faster than the global average over at least the last decade.[74] Democracy is thriving, especially in most of the larger and more important states, but such progress is much more the result of long-standing trends and actions by the leaders and peoples of the region than because of any recent U.S. initiative. Also, conflict remains severe, income inequality problematic, and crime serious in much of the region.[75] And problems with violence and crime remain direct threats to American interests, especially in Mexico and Central America.

Haiti is the exception. It suffered a historic tragedy with its 2010 earthquake. The Obama administration, and America more generally, responded generously with emergency relief (even if all continue to struggle with the age-old dilemma of how to help the Haitian state function more effectively). The administration stepped up in a major way here.

The same cannot be said of the U.S. response to the problems in Mexico. Secretary Clinton described the drug violence in Mexico as verging on an insurgency like that of Colombia's in previous times, a comparison that Mexico did not appreciate and that President Obama felt obliged to recant.[76] There also were serious difficulties in the relationship between President Felipe Calderón and Carlos Pascual, the American ambassador, culminating with the latter's departure in early 2011. Mexican domestic violence has continued at extraordinarily high levels, with roughly 10,000 individuals a year losing their lives due to the drug trade in most of the last few years and even more in 2010 and 2011. That trade is fueled by American demand, and the killing occurs quite often with American guns. These are issues that the Obama administration has been unable to address through any significant domestic legislation.[77] Even though Mexico has captured or killed at least twenty-one out of a list of thirty-seven top drug kingpins since 2009, the rate of violence has not yet declined.[78]

U.S.-Mexico trade has increased in recent decades, from less than $100 billion a year before NAFTA entered into force in 1994 to $350 billion in 2008, including a large volume of Mexican oil exports to the United States. However, Mexico has experienced a decade of mediocre growth, and the recent recession only punctuated what had become a disturbing stagnation in its economic trajectory.[79] Under Obama there has been no major initiative on trade relations of the type (a revised NAFTA) that he had promoted on the campaign trail, or on immigration reform within the United States, which might regularize the process whereby more Mexican immigrants send remittances back home.[80] The only noteworthy mitigating accomplishment was the overdue accord to allow Mexican trucks to cross into the United States (rather than transfer their cargo to American vehicles at the border) and vice versa.[81]

The State Department's Merida Initiative is the current U.S. response to the drug violence and criminality afflicting Mexico. It calls for support for Mexico's security forces and other instruments of law and order. The Obama administration has sustained it, and in fact boosted funding in 2010, temporarily raising annual aid by more than $300 million.[82] But overall, the current U.S. effort with Mexico appears relatively weak, with few major initiatives or breakthroughs on matters such as gun control, immigration policy, trade, and border security. And Mexico's existing strategy for countering violence and criminality appears quite troubled. Something akin to a robust counterinsurgency strategy may be needed—even if it is not called that—with primary effort and resources coming from Mexicans themselves, but with a more substantial amount of American assistance for several years, as well. It would be somewhat analogous to what has been done in Iraq and Afghanistan, though perhaps more similar to recent efforts in Colombia. That means reform and better support for the army, police, judiciary, and intelligence services, as well as something akin to an "inkspot" strategy for gradually expanding security in the country.[83] Efforts to date have been limited in scale and scope.[84]

There has been, by contrast, little need for a new, bold initiative on Colombia given how much progress that country has made in recent years. Most of the credit goes to Colombia, notably its previous leader, President Alvaro Uribe.[85] But the United States has played a strong supporting role over the last two administrations.[86]

Colombia still has a long way to go, however, and the United States has an important, ongoing role to play. Washington has finally come through on ratification of the U.S.-Colombia free trade accord. An aid package that increased economic assistance at least modestly might also help President Juan Manuel Santos improve governance, take on land reform, and otherwise increase Colombia's emphasis on economic development and human rights to complement the successful but primarily security-oriented Uribe legacy.[87] Instead, overall aid totals have slipped somewhat under Obama, and no major new initiative has been developed.[88]

Other Approaches

In sum, the Obama administration does not have many signature accomplishments to date regarding key states posing threats to their own peoples, their neighbors, and in some cases the United States. But have there been any broader policy changes that might prepare the United States and international community to respond more effectively to these kinds of challenges in the future?

As for the machinery of government, there are a number of ideas Obama could have pursued, based on years of previous scholarly and government work that had identified future avenues for cost-effective initiatives. For example, the administration could have promoted beefing up UN capacities for mediation in advance of conflicts; created planning cells at NATO, the African Union, and the United Nations for possible peacekeeping missions; and helped establish a standing, deployable headquarters of international civil-military experts to run missions. It could have substantially expanded the fledgling capabilities within the State Department for related purposes, within the Office of Reconstruction and Stabilization or the Office of Transitional Initiatives or through related mechanisms.[89] The administration could have promoted a major expansion of the Global Peace Operations Initiative (GPOI), by which the United States helps train potential peacekeepers in other countries. Perhaps GPOI could have gone beyond previous approaches to include transfers of major military equipment, including weaponry.[90]

In these areas, Obama has achieved no breakthroughs. That does not mean his administration's efforts have been nonexistent, only that they have been more incrementalist than visionary. The administration did provide increased funds to repay arrears at the United Nations in peace operations accounts, adding several hundred million dollars in 2009 to an annual contribution that now typically exceeds $2 billion. This was consistent with campaign rhetoric as well as subsequent language in the 2010 *National Security Strategy* that promised to strengthen the United Nations.[91] It also sustained ongoing efforts by the Bush administration in areas such as the GPOI and continued the gradual, modest growth in size and funding of civilian response capabilities within the Department of State.[92] It has also made a number of practical improvements in how the interagency process is coordinated for dealing with complex operations abroad.[93] And it responded vigorously to the 2010 Haiti earthquake, the subsequent 2010 floods in Pakistan, as well as the 2011 Japan tsunami and nuclear disaster.[94] But it did not break major new ground.

CONCLUSION

On what might be loosely called the "soft security agenda," Barack Obama campaigned as a candidate of transformation. For various reasons, however, including not least the nation's dire economic and budgetary dilemmas, he has had significant difficulty delivering on this promise.

Although previous presidents had devoted considerable attention to the energy security agenda, Obama intensified the political focus on global warming in a manner not seen before. His plan for mandating gradual reductions in U.S. carbon dioxide output by

83 percent by 2050 through a cap-and-trade system was extremely ambitious, and he failed in his attempt to work with congressional allies to make it happen. He has pursued initiatives of lesser magnitude, largely through regulation, but been constrained by Congress even in these efforts. Therefore, he has fallen far short of being a transformational leader on international action to deal with climate change.

Barack Obama's vision for foreign policy also included a fervent desire to address the problems of international poverty, state weakness, civil conflict, and crime. For Obama these were both humanitarian and major security concerns—especially when the foreign countries in question include nearby states such as Colombia and Mexico. On the campaign trail, candidate Obama promised a doubling of foreign aid, major presidential attention and action regarding states like Sudan and Congo, and a more cooperative and sympathetic approach in which new powers would be treated with greater respect and accorded greater roles in the key decisions of the international community.

President Obama has made only modest headway on this agenda. For example, he has helped expand the role of the G-20 group of nations in addressing various international problems. Particularly in his first year in office, he helped mobilize substantial international cooperation to address the global financial crisis and recession and thereby helped prevent catastrophe. Beyond these accomplishments, however, the Obama administration has been fundamentally cautious on matters ranging from the civil wars in Africa to the stability of Mexico to improving the multilateral military and police capacity to handle future security challenges.

In sum, Obama has not accomplished more than other recent American presidents when dealing with this set of admittedly almost intractable problems. And when measured against his own standards, he has made disappointing headway in dealing with energy, climate change, global poverty, international crime, and substate conflict.

CHAPTER EIGHT

THE ARC OF HISTORY IS LONG

BARACK OBAMA'S FOREIGN POLICY TO date has been more pragmatic than visionary. It has displayed eminently competent stewardship of the nation's interests on most issues, though lacking—with the notable exception of the elimination of Osama bin Laden—in signature accomplishments that might create a distinctive historical legacy. Keeping the country safe and helping prevent an even worse economic meltdown are considerable feats. But they are measured mostly against negative counterfacts—bad things that could have happened but were prevented, such as another big terror strike or another great depression. They are also less momentous achievements than Obama set for himself, and are not the kind of historic breakthroughs that he might have envisioned for his foreign policy at the outset of his administration.

The record also leaves no clear Obama road map for the future, no particularly compelling overall strategy for how he would advance American interests, or bend history. As he prepares to run for reelection, the difference between the agenda that he presented the nation and the world in his first campaign and what he will likely do in his second is significant. Obama evoked very big dreams in 2007 and 2008 in a way that he will not be able to do in 2012.

The visionary speeches have already been given and cannot make news the second or third time around the way they did initially. That is especially true because they would not be clearly connected to how he has governed on most issues. Indeed, however well crafted, those speeches have become somewhat of a liability for this president. The gaps between his grand visions and how he actually conducts foreign policy have become clear, breeding some degree of cynicism and disappointment among his audiences at home and abroad. This is the result of his practical need to confront the world's problems as he found them once in office, and he is not unusual among presidents in governing differently than he campaigned. Nonetheless, he conjured up hopes and expectations in more sweeping ways than the typical presidential candidate. As such, the distance between his original goals and his actual accomplishments has become quite considerable.

The situation can be remedied, at least partially. The president's own views of what matters most to him—a gradual readjustment of America's leadership role in an emerging global order that fits the straightened economic circumstances in which the United States finds itself—suggest the direction that he should propose taking the country if reelected. Much of the advice we offer would apply equally well to a Republican president.

OBAMA'S FOREIGN POLICY RECORD

Barack Obama's foreign policy has numerous elements of continuity with his predecessors. The continuity is perhaps greatest with the first Bush and Clinton administrations. But even relative to the latter days of the administration of George W. Bush, many policies have been sustained or modified only modestly, notwithstanding Obama's determination to set a different course. Ironically, the continuity from George W. Bush to Obama has been most evident in regard to war fighting on the one hand and democracy promotion in the Middle East on the other. To be sure, there has been no new case of preemption. Arguably, Obama's greatest concrete foreign policy accomplishments have been on the battlefield in the war against terrorism—the arena that was the central focus of the Bush presidency. The killing of Osama bin Laden in May 2011 and, more generally, the decimation of much of al Qaeda's leadership abroad, including Anwar al-Awlaki in Yemen, were primarily a credit to the American intelligence operatives and the Special Operations Forces who painstakingly pursued these individuals and then carried out operations to kill them. But President Obama deserves personal credit for devoting substantial resources to the effort, for his cool-headed and tough-minded determination in ratcheting up the resources that he inherited from his predecessor, and for his decision to dispatch commandos against bin Laden rather than bomb him from afar.

A significant accomplishment—and a supreme irony—of this presidency is that Obama has managed to isolate certain extremist actors more effectively than George W. Bush did. In dealing with North Korea and Iran—Bill Clinton's rogue states, George W. Bush's "axis of evil"—Obama has found his way to a reasonably effective approach. His initial efforts to extend a hand to leaders in Tehran and Pyongyang were rebuffed. But that predictable outcome did not amount to a complete failure by any means. When, in response to the new American president's entreaties, Kim Jong-il and Ayatollah Khamenei refused to unclench their own fists as Obama in his inaugural address had called on them to do, the United States was better placed to persuade others to tighten sanctions on these countries. Here Obama was more effective than Bush at pursuing Bush's own agenda. Of course, both countries have continued to develop their nuclear weapons programs despite the sanctions. Obama's accomplishments are thus better understood as effective damage control than historic breakthroughs. That said, in foreign affairs, limiting the fallout from problems—practicing the art of the possible—is more productive than attempting the impossible and failing.

President Obama has made other good decisions, too. They began with placing experienced and effective individuals in key jobs. Retaining Bush's secretary of defense, Robert Gates, was a wise and unprecedented move. The appointment of his political rival Hillary Clinton as secretary of state unified the Democratic Party while giving the nation a highly effective and diligent lead diplomat whose political skills proved critical in sustaining the president's determination to improve America's standing in the world. Obama has made good use of General David Petraeus as well, first in Afghanistan and now as director of the Central Intelligence Agency.

The Obama administration also has displayed a degree of flexibility and adaptiveness—on-the-job learning, so to speak—on numerous matters. On Iraq policy, for example, the president slowed down the U.S. troop withdrawal substantially—in contrast with his campaign promises—honoring most of the spirit of his earlier pledge without being bound by every letter. And when he finally brought the troops home in late 2011, according to a schedule first designed and agreed upon by President Bush and Prime Minister Nouri al-Maliki back in 2008, he again was being pragmatic, even though the move elicited howls of protest from the right of the U.S. political spectrum. It is hard to see how an American president could have—or should have—retained U.S. forces abroad in a country that was not willing to take proper steps to invite them to remain under a normal legal framework. As Obama's critics sometimes fail to acknowledge, the Iraqi democracy that we helped create has a right to make its own decisions, and—as Obama would be the first to recognize—Washington has limits on its influence, even with Baghdad.

Obama's rhetoric has sometimes been misplaced, as when he declared the return of all U.S. troops from Iraq a signature accomplishment of his administration, even though his administration was on record as trying to reach an accord with Iraqis to keep them deployed there longer. But, on balance, we believe it is better for the future of U.S. military intervention abroad that the United States reestablishes its reputation for leaving when asked than for remaining where it is not wanted. The United States has spent a fortune in treasure and the blood of American soldiers to give Iraqis a chance to stand on their own feet. Now Obama must figure out how to deal with an increasingly autocratic Maliki; at a minimum, business as usual on matters like the pending U.S. sale of F-16s to Iraq should be suspended until Maliki honors his previous political pledges and constitutional obligations.

In the case of China, when initial efforts to encourage Beijing to assume greater responsibility on global issues proved disappointing, and when Beijing became more muscular in a variety of ways in Asia, the Obama team responded with effective initiatives throughout the region. Obama's experience of tensions with China was hardly unique among modern American presidents, but his task was complicated by an increasingly confident Chinese leadership that perceived an America moving toward economic and strategic decline. He did much to strengthen America's commitment to a leadership role in Asia—though his rebalancing toward Asia is not a complete answer to the need for a forward-looking relationship with China that must be partly competitive yet also cooperative and collaborative. Obama handled the immediate challenges well in 2010 and 2011, but the natural trajectory of his recent policies leaves him with serious unresolved dilemmas as to how to handle relations with the world's predominant rising power in 2012 and beyond.

When global climate change talks in Copenhagen were foundering in December 2009, most visibly over differences between the United States and China, Obama responded flexibly and creatively. Caught in the difficult position of being unable to push for a comprehensive agreement at Copenhagen because of his inability to overcome his own domestic constraints, Obama successfully engaged China, Brazil, India, and South Africa to produce an "accord" that delivered what he needed domestically, put the

United States in a relatively positive light at the conference, and brought the Chinese farther along than they had planned. Presidents less in control of their emotions might have personalized the U.S.-China disagreement in a way that would have taken months or years to mend. Although unable to make big changes at home on energy policy, Obama did substantially toughen longer-term gas mileage requirements for future automobiles and used the Environmental Protection Agency's authority in other areas, steps that will yield important benefits down the road.

The "Russia reset" policy, even if always subject to reversal given Moscow's mercurial nature, has clearly yielded dividends. Obama's willingness to reach out to Russia—lightening (though not abandoning) the criticism on human rights and political freedoms, reengaging in formal strategic arms control talks, and acknowledging Russia's concerns about a planned missile defense system in Europe, without going so far as to give Moscow a veto over future missile defense decisions—has worked to a degree. It produced the New Strategic Arms Reduction Treaty to reduce the U.S. and Russian nuclear arsenals. Even when Russia and the United States disagree these days, as they do over Libya and Syria and other matters—including missile defense—the tone of disagreement is more subdued and contained. Meanwhile, the reset policy has made a significant difference in tightening international sanctions on Iran and in opening up northern supply routes through Russia and former Soviet republics into Afghanistan to lessen NATO's logistical dependence on Pakistan.

Generally speaking, President Obama has remained disciplined and prioritized his own use of time. He has given top attention to the key issues of the day—not only the rise of China but Iraq, Afghanistan, and Pakistan; counterterrorism and nuclear nonproliferation; the Arab awakenings; and the woes of the global economy. He has for the most part avoided getting bogged down in secondary matters or policy ruts. For example, he was not lured into counterproductive spats with President Hugo Chávez of

Venezuela, President Robert Mugabe of Zimbabwe, or the junta that ran Burma. He harbored no illusions that the simple fact of his election would quickly turn around America's relationships with such tyrants, any more than with the leaders of Iran and North Korea. Yet he has kept the door to improved relations open enough that, as of this writing in early 2012, progress appears possible, at least with Burma and perhaps with North Korea under its new leadership.

Obama's response to the Arab revolutions of 2011 was also prudent. The president did not claim greater responsibility for events than was warranted and maintained a more or less appropriate balance between protecting U.S. interests and promoting American democratic values in volatile and immensely complicated situations. At critical moments, inspired by the courage of common people demanding their freedom, his rhetoric got the better of him. But he correctly recognized that these revolutions are not about the United States and therefore avoided trying to push the process from Washington in ways that could have been counterproductive. He rightly recognized that America would be most influential by working in unison with key allies in the region and beyond and supporting their initiatives when U.S. interests did not require taking the lead.

While the Obama approach has been nonideological and pragmatic, it has nonetheless been informed by a realistic overarching sense of America's role in the world in the early twenty-first century. The tone has been neither one of American triumphalism and exceptionalism nor one of decline and despair, avoiding tendencies that afflict certain parts of the American political spectrum today. For example, on Libya the president was prepared to let others lead the military effort, even at some risk of mission stalemate or mission failure, because he wanted to encourage more burden sharing and because Libya was a second-tier issue for American interests. But on Afghanistan and the broader war on al Qaeda, Obama has recognized the enduring and irreplaceable significance of American leadership and kept the United States in the driver's seat. He has beefed up the role of the G-20 group of nations in global decision-making and lent at least rhetorical support to reform of the UN Security Council that might eventually make India, Japan, and perhaps others permanent members. At times he has also found a way to welcome greater roles in international affairs for emerging powers like Turkey and Brazil, though the process has often been challenging and halting. Taken together, this is not quite enough to make for a "made in America" new world order, but it does suggest the direction that Obama would like to take the international system and provides some guide to what he would likely seek to do in a second term.

Obama has hardly been an apologist for America or a wobbly national security leader, as some of his critics have alleged. It is not serious to make such a claim about a president who ordered U.S. Special Operations Forces to violate unilaterally Pakistani airspace to kill Osama bin Laden and who had American drones attack other extremists at five to ten times the rate of the Bush administration. Critics making this case fail to understand how effectively Obama has pivoted from briefly reaching out to extremist leaders to then pursuing punitive measures against them—or simply ignoring them, as the case may be. And for every June 2009 Cairo speech asking foreign audiences for a new beginning, there is a December 2009 Oslo speech (accepting the Nobel Peace Prize) underscoring his clear appreciation of his responsibilities to protect the United States and its allies, with lethal force if necessary. Indeed, Obama's style on balance has been effective, conveying a degree of openness to the views of other leaders and the interests of other nations while still projecting confidence and leadership.

Outcomes have been disappointing regarding the global economy. But Obama's basic understanding of America's role in the world and thus his approach to the economic crisis have been firmly grounded in reality. For example, he recognized the interdependence of the U.S. and Chinese economic systems and avoided acting as if he was alone in the driver's seat in that aspect of the relationship. He has pushed hard and steadily on the currency issue, pressuring China to appreciate its currency, without overplaying his hand. He also did not shirk from recognizing that the global economic crisis required American leadership and that only Washington could really galvanize a coordinated international response. Furthermore, Obama's openness and multilateral approach to global issues, both on the campaign trail and once in the Oval Office, may have helped defuse what otherwise might have been a fairly substantial amount of anti-Americanism. The global recession clearly had its roots in earlier mismanagement of the American financial system and could have caused a greater backlash against the United States with a different leader in the White House.

The above enumeration of competent management of most major foreign policy issues, while significant, may strike some as damning with faint praise. We sense that Obama himself might react that way. Certainly, his ambitions have been grand, and simply managing well an overwhelming inbox would probably not strike him as enough. Yet that has been the major thrust of his record to date.

Obama's vulnerability to criticism very much reflects his rhetoric, on the campaign trail but also well into 2009 as president, which was more evocative of Kennedy or Reagan than of anyone since. He mapped out a vision of where he would like to see the world move—of how he would like to bend history in the direction of justice—in ways designed to convey seriousness and to demand consideration from audiences at home and abroad. His ambitions have extended to matters of global economic inequality, war and peace, cross-cultural and interreligious harmony, energy, and the environment. Certainly, his rhetorical skills are among the most impressive in modern American presidential history, and his ideas on big issues of the day are as seriously reasoned as those of any recent president. He has laid out those visions in his public addresses as explicitly as any president has ever done. As one White House aide put it to us, if you want to know what President Obama thinks, read his speeches.

But his visionary goals have not been realized and in most instances are not measurably closer to success than was the case in early 2009. They are, moreover, quite often not a particularly meaningful guide to the policies Obama has pursued. This is clearly the case with regard to his loftiest aspirations, such as those for a nuclear-weapons-free world and for a planet with far less poverty. Pursuing the former agenda aggressively is impractical in a world of huge superpower arsenals and multiple nuclear powers, most of whom want their weapons even more than Obama believes the United States needs its own. Pursuing the latter agenda with big ideas or expensive policies is impractical in light of domestic budgetary and economic realities. Obama's speeches have also failed to have much impact on such critical matters as bridging the divide with the Muslim world and engaging extremist states.

Indeed, the speeches are often academic both in the good sense of being serious, thoughtful, and provocative, and in the more pejorative sense of having little clear connection to actual policy. Worse, they have raised hopes that the president's policies were then unable to deliver upon, disappointing many around the world and leading them to wonder if the speeches had been seriously intentioned in the first place. While inspirational words have their place in politics, there is a threshold beyond which aspirations become false hopes—and the conveyor of those visions sets himself up for resentment and a sense of betrayal on the part of those who once believed in him.

The expectations held for Obama as he entered the White House in January 2009 thus became a major challenge for the president. He had raised hopes so high on matters such as repairing the breach between the United States and the broader Islamic world, or ending the nation's wars, or resolving the Israeli-Palestinian conflict that disappointment was bound to occur as inherited problems and difficult leaders proved more intractable than expected. One might blame Obama's audiences for their naïveté in thinking that he could quickly provide the antidote to many of the world's ills—after all, hadn't he warned that change would not come easily? Indeed, the decision of the Nobel Committee to award Obama the Nobel Peace Prize after less than a year of his presidency symbolized the degree to which a breathless hopefulness accompanied his inauguration, even in normally tight-buttoned countries abroad. But notwithstanding his occasional caveat, Obama himself had cultivated that sense of hope, change, and historic transformation, not only on the campaign trail but in places like Prague in April and Cairo in June of 2009. So he bears some of the responsibility for the unrealistically inflated expectations, even if he might have always known better than to expect that an Obama presidency could change the world as rapidly as he led many others to believe.

At home, Obama has failed to fulfill his aspiration to be a post-partisan politician and to realize his prediction on the campaign trail that he could bridge the American political divide. Part of the reason, to be sure, has been Republican recalcitrance, but Obama has not been blameless. Most of this dynamic arose in regard to domestic policy. But his handling of several foreign policy issues also was afflicted by more partisanship than was necessary.

Iraq is a case in point. Obama was certainly on reasonable ground in having opposed the war in the first place, but his refusal to acknowledge the progress of the surge for so long created bitterness and some suspicions across the political aisle. This may come back to haunt him as critics (perhaps excessively) suggest that he was not really interested in finding a way to keep any U.S. forces in Iraq after 2011, thereby risking all the hard-fought gains of previous years. Again, Obama did give Iraqis twenty more months of military support than originally intended, did follow George Bush's schedule for withdrawing American forces, and in fact did offer to keep troops deployed longer if acceptable terms could be offered by Iraq's parliament. On top of that, it is possible that Iraqi politicians would have escalated their rivalries even with U.S. forces present; after all, they had taken almost a year to form a governing parliamentary coalition in 2010 due to standoffs between different parties and factions. Nonetheless, critics sensed that Obama was going back to his roots on the subject, revealing a certain disinterest in Iraq that he had simply masked for the first three years of his presidency, and his confused rhetoric on the subject fed into this interpretation. In addition, Obama talked about Guantanamo for so long that he hardened political divisions on the subject. Unable to persuade Congress or state and local officials to locate a new facility on American soil, he failed to honor his campaign pledge and his promise to the Muslim world that he would close down the detention facilities within a year of his inauguration. In effect, he has had to retain this aspect of Bush counterterrorism policy.

Energy and climate policy provide another example. Obama's initial aspiration in 2009 to negotiate binding commitments on greenhouse gas emissions on all countries was serious and even noble at one level, reflecting a sobriety about the problem of climate change that convinced the president to go for a major success rather than window dressing. However, the cap-and-trade approach he advocated for limiting U.S. emissions failed in part because it was, in the eyes of many Republicans, a tax in disguise. As such, it engendered an increasingly vitriolic opposition from Republicans who had vowed to defeat him from the very beginning of his presidency. When combined with a combative approach from Speaker of the House Nancy Pelosi, and a focus on passing health care reform as well as the economic stimulus and bank bailout efforts, it sealed Obama's identity in conservative eyes as a traditional big-government liberal and severely complicated his efforts to stimulate economic growth.

Failure to promote consensus at home in support of his ambitious domestic agenda negatively affected Obama's image abroad as the U.S. economy took far longer than expected to recover, feeding the perception of a weak president leading a stumbling giant. And that in turn made it more difficult for Obama to get his way with foreign leaders.

There have been problems with the internal bureaucratic process, too. President Obama centralized foreign policy decision-making within the White House and encouraged a deliberative process that often resembled a debating society when issues did not need an immediate decision, resulting in last-minute presidential judgments that left little time for consultation with the affected parties. The most unfortunate manifestation has been in his handling of Middle East peace, where the president had a theory of the case that was fundamentally flawed. His determination to ignore Israeli public opinion even as he cultivated the Arab street meant that he relinquished his one source of effective leverage on a recalcitrant Israeli prime minister. In so doing, he thereby set up the peace process for almost certain failure—and in turn, he ultimately produced disillusionment in the Arab world, so that now his poll numbers there are as low as George W. Bush's had been before him.

The Arab awakenings presented Obama with multiple challenges to the very foundations of American influence in the Middle East. And they required him to reconcile his inner idealistic urge to promote freedom and justice with his outer realism about the dangers to U.S. interests in doing so. His idealistic instincts led him to want to get on the right side of Egyptian history, and unsentimentally abandoning Mubarak and helping to protect the role of the Egyptian military demonstrated a realist's understanding of the critical role Egypt plays in the larger Middle Eastern balance.

Where U.S. interests were less significant—in Libya—he was able to stand up for American values in a more simple and straightforward fashion, helping the people there overthrow a brutal dictator. But where U.S. interests were more at stake—in Bahrain—Obama's unwillingness to stand by the protesters opened him to the charge of hypocrisy. And where U.S. interests and values coincided—in Syria—he proved somewhat irresolute and slow to act, perhaps missing an opportunity early on both to support peaceful protest and deal a strategic setback to Iran. A similar inability to manage effectively the tension between his idealistic desire to support Palestinian statehood and his need to present himself as the defender of Israel led to the administration's efforts to prevent the Palestinian leadership from pushing for Palestinian statehood at the United Nations in the fall of 2011, an idea he had first raised at the UN General Assembly a year earlier.

On balance, it is not clear that a more consistent American policy would have produced measurably different results in the Middle East since the awakenings began. America's influence has been inherently limited in most cases. But the net effect of the tumultuous developments in the Arab world, when combined with Obama's failure to achieve an Israeli-Palestinian peace deal and Turkey's determination to play a leadership role in the Arab world at the expense of its relationship with Israel, has left the United States without an effective strategy beyond reacting to the crosscutting currents of unpredictable events. All the traditional pillars of America's strategic position in the Middle East—the alliance with Egypt, the Egypt-Israel peace treaty, the pact with Saudi Arabia, the Turkish-Israeli strategic relationship—are now shaky. The only silver lining in this is that Iran faces a worse problem with its Syrian ally, the main pillar of its failing strategy for challenging American dominance in the Arab world.

If he has a second term, Obama will need to devise a replacement for the *Pax Americana* strategy that has guided most American engagement in the Middle East since the eviction of Saddam Hussein's army from Kuwait and the collapse of the Soviet Union in 1991. He or his possible Republican successor will need to steward carefully the relationship with an emerging democracy in Egypt while reaching a better understanding with Saudi Arabia's leaders about the path of political reform for Arab monarchies and concerting policy with an increasingly influential Turkey (especially in regard to pressuring and perhaps even toppling the Assad regime in Syria). And he will need a better understanding with Israel—especially with Israel's public—about how to move the Palestinian issue toward resolution.

There also have been cases when running foreign policy out of the White House worked reasonably well. When the president had an appropriate theory of the case for what he was doing and a good person on the National Security Council staff that he trusted to help him implement the policy, he often did very well. Delegating responsibility to Vice President Joe Biden on Iraq policy in the first eighteen to twenty-four months of the administration also proved to be a wise and effective move.

But in many other situations, the president either did not have a clear and compelling sense of his own goals or worked in some ways at cross-purposes with others in his administration. Cases here include not just the Middle East but also Afghanistan and Pakistan. In relations with both countries, Obama made initial policy decisions to devote far more resources than his predecessor to the challenges but allowed deep divisions within his team to undermine the effort. Different advisers—Special Representative Richard Holbrooke, Ambassador Karl Eikenberry, military leaders, Clinton, Gates, National Security Adviser Jim Jones—adopted different substantive priorities and political approaches to dealing with key leaders such as Afghan president Hamid Karzai. As a result, regional leaders could never quite figure out if the United States was staying or going, if Washington saw them as friends or foes, and if the administration wanted them to be successful or to be forced from power. This naturally engendered hedging behavior from key Afghans and Pakistanis, and the threats to American security from that part of the world were not mitigated as much as hoped.

Having invested so much in a robust Afghanistan strategy that sought to weaken the insurgency while building up state institutions, Obama now needs to engineer a carefully designed troop drawdown schedule for the period through 2013 and 2014—when Afghan forces assume primary responsibility for security throughout their country. There is room for debate about what this strategy means for the pace of future drawdowns, once American troops reach 68,000 in number at the end of September 2012. But there is little room for debate that Obama must convey clarity and conviction in setting out the strategy, avoid giving any sense of a rush for the exits, and keep his team unified in making and then implementing the plan.

The Afghanistan issue was one of several that revealed a problem for this president: his perceived aloofness. This is the unfortunate flip side of his calm and cool demeanor that has served him well in other ways. At a human level, there is something refreshing about a president who does not revel in the trappings of office, but at a leadership level, this detachment can come across as coldness.[1] When so much of diplomacy depends on personal relationships with world leaders, a reluctance to engage on a human level inevitably limits the effectiveness of the presidency. Obama has demonstrated this feature of his personality when dealing with President Karzai of Afghanistan, whom he has kept at arm's length. His disdain for Israeli prime minister Benjamin Netanyahu has cost him support among both Israelis and their avid supporters in the United States. This gained him no credit with Arab leaders, who themselves place a high premium on their personal relationships with the U.S. president. And when they saw how he publicly humiliated Hosni Mubarak, they wondered whether they, too, would receive the same treatment.

AN OBAMA DOCTRINE?

Beyond this point-by-point assessment of the president's record, there is a broader question: is there an Obama doctrine, and if so, does it meet the requirements of an American approach to the challenges of the twenty-first century in international affairs? It is incumbent on the president as strategist-in-chief to establish priorities as well as plans for pursuing those objectives. And only with a strategy can the president explain where he is actively trying to take the country and world on his watch—rather than where he is hoping the world will someday wind up in the longer term.

So far Obama's foreign policy includes a resolute approach to wars, including ending them in the greater Middle East, a balanced yet forward-looking relationship with China, modest headway with several of the world's other rising powers, about as good a "reset" as could realistically be expected with Russia, and serious but incomplete efforts on the nuclear arms control and nonproliferation front. It features no breakthroughs but at least stronger sanctions in regard to Iran and North Korea, generally prudent if sometimes inconsistent responses to the 2011 Arab awakenings, a very disappointing experience to date on Middle East peacemaking, a spotty record on energy and climate, and a fairly undistinguished record on dealing with weak or troubled states, including Mexico. Finally, Obama has avoided national and global economic collapse but without yet moving either the country or the world onto the path to sustained economic recovery. Given the degree of difficulty associated with this era's monumental challenges and tasks, Obama's foreign policy record is thus sensible and serious but not pathbreaking. The nation's interests have been well protected, but the promise of a new world order shaped by American leadership is far from being achieved.

How does the record cohere when viewed as a whole? Several proposals have been offered about an Obama grand strategy, all of them interesting but none that we think hits its mark. One scholar depicts an administration focused on counterpunching, but counterpunching at best is a tactic and not a strategy.[2] Another prominent writer suggests we abandon the search for an Obama doctrine because the world has become too complicated for any president to have the luxury of such a simple, clear, and consistent guide to most decisionmaking.[3] A third notion, suggested recently by an anonymous senior White House adviser, is that this administration has been trying to "lead from behind"—at least on matters such as the Libya intervention and the Tunisian and Egyptian revolutions. But while this approach may work for second-order issues or in cases where American influence is inherently limited, it is hardly a viable way for a country that remains far and away the world's most powerful actor to play its global leadership role. It is also poor domestic politics and disastrous branding.

Certainly, coherence is confounded by the nature of the world Obama confronts: more complex problems, more actors intent on asserting their own prerogatives and their own leadership rather than following Washington, and, of course, a far more onerous set of economic challenges than Obama expected when he chose to run for the highest office in the land. As a result, in our view there can be no concise definition of an Obama doctrine to rival George Kennan's "containment," John Kennedy's "bear any burden," Richard Nixon's detente, Ronald Reagan's "morning in America," or George W. Bush's preemption paradigm and freedom agenda.

Nevertheless, handling one's inbox issue-by-issue will not suffice for the leader of what is still the strongest country in the world. A strategic set of priorities is needed to guide how the nation's scarce resources and policymakers' limited time and energies should be best allocated. Publics at home and abroad also expect more guidance on how to understand U.S. goals and priorities.

Our judgment is that in fact Obama has done better than most of the bumper stickers that distill his foreign policy into simple terms would imply.[4] He has prioritized some issues, including those that we address in this book, because they are inherently more important than many others. Thus he has made America's security and its economic recovery paramount on his own short list of key matters on which he spends his time, and has avoided preoccupation with his more idealistic visions of a nuclear-free, poverty-free world featuring better relations between Islam and the West as well as better ties between "rogue states" and the United States. Obama has hired good people, and his team has worked competently and diligently on most things. His policies suggest a president who is more than a global carpenter, repairing the world here and there, and more than simply a reluctant realist pursuing George Bush's hard-nosed security agenda—more effectively than Bush himself in many ways—though he is that, too.

THE PROGRESSIVE PRAGMATIST

As this analysis reveals, Obama is a progressive pragmatist, competently managing today's problems and threats while seeking to advance a larger vision and create a better world where possible. At times the progressivism has been constrained by the weight of immediate challenges or the compromises that pragmatism requires—and at times by Obama's mistakes as well. He is trying to bend history in the direction of justice while prioritizing the promotion of the nation's prosperity and protecting its citizens in the process.

The potential larger strategy to be developed from all this is only now emerging as time and events have created a broad direction to Obama's foreign policy. Should he have the opportunity to pursue it in a second term, the rebalancing or "pivot" toward Asia, rolled out at the end of his third year in office, could undergird a broader Obama strategy. With regard to key regions and countries, it consists of a reaffirmation of America's purpose and leadership role internationally for many years to come, in the form of promoting trade and investment rules; making our military more flexible, lean, and interoperable with others; and creatively reshaping international organizations to more effectively match his vision of a progressive international system.

The elaboration of this strategy is made possible by Obama's ending of the war in Iraq and drawing down of troops in Afghanistan, which together free up resources and time to focus on the new and increasingly important challenges, especially in Asia. In strategic terms, it could be reinforced by the elimination of America's dependence on Gulf oil, making the United States—though not the global economy—somewhat less vulnerable to the chronic instability of that troubled region. This rebalancing toward Asia should allow the United States to give greater priority to integrating China and India into the emerging global order, just as the political and economic weakening of the EU will lend greater urgency to the effort.

But whether Obama can, in fact, develop this approach as a broad strategy in a possible second term will also depend on at least two other factors. The first will not be up to him alone: if Iran decides to acquire nuclear weapons in the face of Obama's concerted efforts to dissuade it from that course, and Israel launches a preventive strike, then he may well end up dealing with another significant conflict in the greater Middle East just as he is ending the other two wars there, confounding his rebalancing efforts.

The second factor, however, is likely to be much more amenable to his will and critical to history's judgment of his foreign policy. It will lie in his ability to strengthen America's domestic economic circumstances and overcome the enormous structural problems created by low growth, high unemployment, and a massive debt burden.

The debt crisis of the summer of 2011 added an exclamation mark to what much of the world and particularly rising Asia has seen as an ongoing narrative about Obama's first three years: he articulated seemingly sensible domestic priorities but then failed to engage in the day-to-day political maneuvering necessary to give his prescriptions for tackling them a chance of success; he exhibited questionable timing in the domestic interventions he made, and, when he lost the initiative, he in the end largely acceded to the points his opponents demanded; throughout it all he personally stuck to the narrative that there is a middle way that can garner sufficient support from reasonable people on all sides. As a result of all of the above and more, America has done what it should not be doing to have a chance at sustained global primacy in the future: it has been disinvesting in infrastructure, disinvesting in education, walking away from serious programs for clean energy, failing to address its social divisions, and making only partial fixes to the financial system that produced the crisis of 2008.

Although there are kernels of truth in the above narrative, it contains substantial simplification and caricature. It also overstates its impact on the president's standing overseas: for example, in Europe, Obama remains popular with more than a 70 percent favorable rating in a recent poll, and certainly voters on that continent see as many weaknesses in their own economies as in America's. But the problem, largely if not entirely one of perceptions, is still real. Obama himself has contributed to the perceptions. For example, he diluted the focus on rapid economic recovery in 2009 by introducing many longer-term issues, and his efforts on energy policy and health care reform sapped momentum from his approach to economic recovery. And when his own bipartisan deficit commission issued its report in the fall of 2010, he ignored it when there may have been a window of opportunity to build a bipartisan approach to the problem—or at least to put the onus for squandering that bipartisan opportunity on those from the other side of the aisle.

Nevertheless, the broad challenge remains. Bending history during a second term requires repairing the nation's economy—and with it the nation's self-confidence at home and its reputation and clout abroad. That is the sine qua non of an effective foreign policy strategy for Obama or whoever else inhabits the White House in 2013. America urgently needs to rebound, and it can only do so by effectively dealing with the current fiscal mess, promoting a positive trade policy agenda, carefully streamlining military defenses as well as other foreign policy instruments, and sustaining domestic investments that are needed to thrive in tomorrow's global economy.

Some scholars and policymakers would support a vigorous assertion of American primacy to make the U.S.-centric international order thrive again, as there is no clear alternative power center or leader. Others would advise that rather than try to reinvigorate American primacy, the United States should simply accept the reality of supposed American decline and try to manage it as best as we can. This point of view might counsel a major U.S. retrenchment from leading the international system, especially in security affairs.

We do not share these polar views. Rather, we believe that even though the world is undergoing rapid, sometimes tumultuous change, it is doing so in ways that are broadly compatible with the American-designed post–World War II order, and that America is well placed to manage the ongoing changes in the international system as long as it remains strong, respected, and confident.[5] Over a period of decades, the postwar global system the United States engineered the conditions that allowed for the development and rise of other powers, from Europe to Japan to the rest of East Asia and India. Gradual, managed change that accords greater constructive roles to others as they become successful economies and polities is very much in America's national interests. President Obama understands this well but needs to develop and convey his emerging strategy to Americans. And he will need to find practical, step-by-step ways to share burdens—such as protecting the global commons militarily—with allies and neutral states alike. Such a strategic road map, with its strong emphasis on American economic renewal as a key component of a successful, evolving international system, is much more relevant to the next decade or two of U.S. foreign policy than many of Obama's big themes of his first campaign.

From a foreign policy and national security perspective, there are no compelling arguments against either modestly higher taxes or modestly lower entitlements. As politicians consider the foreign policy aspects of their political platforms, they should bear in mind that, in foreign policy and national security terms, effective compromise that brings down the deficit and enhances growth is far more important than preventing any modest tax increase or entitlement reforms. We make this argument based not only on our own admittedly centrist politics, but even more so on our collective sense of how foreign powers view the United States at this moment in history. Their uncertainty about future American power derives not from an assessment of whether its marginal tax rates or cost-of-living adjustments for entitlements are properly calibrated, but from a perception that the nation is losing its ability to make tough decisions and get its finances and economic fundamentals in order.

We believe that proportionate budget reductions, commensurate with those in other parts of the federal budget, can be responsibly envisioned in federal spending on defense, intelligence, diplomacy, development, and democracy promotion. We do not believe, however, that defense and foreign policy accounts can make disproportionately large contributions to fiscal discipline without seriously jeopardizing U.S. interests abroad. Reductions of some 10 percent in the annual budgets are manageable, constituting up to half a trillion dollars in ten-year savings. But reductions approaching a trillion dollars over that period (as sequestration from the August 2011 debt deal and ensuing November failure of the so-called Supercommittee would require) would likely prove ill-advised.

Despite the claims of some pundits, even 10 percent reductions cannot be accomplished just by cutting easily identifiable and extractable waste, fraud, and abuse in places like the Pentagon budget. Such wasteful spending is often hard to locate and very difficult to eliminate. Cuts in muscle will be needed, too. And some calculated risks to the country's foreign policy interests will have to be accepted. But with good planning, those risks can be managed, and the nation's longer-term foreign policy interests can be advanced through a broad deficit reduction effort that strengthens the nation's economic fundamentals. The strategic defense review released in January 2012 moved in this direction, among other things singling out the ground forces for somewhat larger cuts than other parts of the military on the premise that large-scale counter-insurgency operations will be less likely in the future. This basic approach seems sound.

Put simply, the current weakening of America's economic foundations is incompatible with maintaining sufficient long-term national power and poses a national security threat itself, as Admiral Mike Mullen, former chairman of the Joint Chiefs of Staff, and others have rightly pointed out. The question is thus one of balancing risk, not of pretending we can eliminate it. At the end of the day, as foreign policy practitioners and scholars, we would argue strongly that foreign policy budgets can and must contribute their fair share to fiscal discipline.

Still, it is important to underscore at a strategic level what *cannot* be cut. We do not believe, for example, that it is sound to reduce military and diplomatic vigilance toward either the Persian Gulf region *or* the Western Pacific. The Obama-Panetta defense framework of January 2012 makes a similar argument. Forces will be substantially reduced in the broader Middle East region as the Afghanistan operation is downsized, and that is not only acceptable but desirable; however, ongoing vigilance and military presence, focused on naval and air capabilities primarily, remain important. Both of these theaters are crucially important to U.S. interests, and both are significantly challenged at present—one by a demonstrably hostile Iran, the other by an increasingly powerful People's Republic of China. Nor can the North Korean threat be dismissed. Various challenges in the broader Middle East and South Asia can be anticipated as well.

Any defense cuts will have to be made, therefore, by becoming more creative and efficient rather than fundamentally scaling back the nation's role in the world. But there is lots of room for rethinking current approaches at the Pentagon, as Secretary Panetta has correctly deduced.

Consider as a key example the nation's ground forces. As the wars wind down, it becomes feasible to consider cutting the standing size of the U.S. Army and Marine Corps. Returning to Clinton-era 1990s ground force numbers would mean a cut of roughly 15 percent relative to current combat force structure. There was in fact a reasonable amount of bipartisan consensus on those earlier levels, with defense secretaries Aspin, Perry, Cohen, and Rumsfeld all supporting them over a ten-year period.[6] Former secretary Gates proposed going almost halfway in this direction by 2015, with reductions of around 6 percent relative to current levels. But larger reductions make sense as part of an integrated national deficit reduction plan—perhaps somewhat larger, in fact, than Obama now envisages.

Reduced ground forces would not be large enough to handle another decade like the one we have just experienced without reverting to unpalatable policies such as 50 percent deployment rates for individual soldiers (for example, only a year at home after one twelve-month deployment and before another).[7] Nonetheless, a serious case can be made for such smaller forces. They would be adequate for a single, sustained, large operation on the scale of either Iraq or Afghanistan at their respective maximum sizes. They would also be a sizeable and probably adequate deterrent against the threat of a North Korean attack on South Korea.

Even for missions like helping to stabilize a large collapsing state, such as Pakistan, smaller U.S. ground forces could well prove sufficient as part of a coalition. That is, they might suffice if part of the security forces of the state at issue remained intact (and invited outside help), or if a broader international coalition of states contributed to the operation. If the United States does wind up at war or in a major operation again in the future, there will need to be a plan in place to start increasing the size of the ground forces immediately.

That is one more way in which the risk associated with a smaller standing U.S. Army and Marine Corps could be mitigated.

Closing bases abroad in theaters where U.S. forces have been stationed for years is not a very good way to save money because the added costs of these overseas units are generally modest. The additional costs of stationing forces in places like Germany and Japan, above and beyond their likely costs if they were located in the United States, are in the range of a couple of billion dollars a year worldwide, in total—and in fact, in the case of Japan in particular, it may actually be *less* expensive to keep forces there given Tokyo's generosity in paying the local costs of base real estate, operations, and construction.[8] Yet we can find more efficient ways to maintain our foreign military presence. For example, the U.S. Navy might try to maintain forward deployments by leaving certain ships overseas for longer stretches while rotating crews by airplane when sailors reach the end of their six-month at-sea cycles. This kind of approach can allow the United States to maintain its current capabilities in the Persian Gulf and Western Pacific with a somewhat smaller fleet.

Some savings are likely feasible in diplomacy and development accounts, too. The Bush and Obama administrations have worked hard to restore appropriate resources to the State Department, Agency for International Development, and related parts of the government after a decade of fairly severe neglect, and the recent progress should not be jeopardized. Protecting diplomacy and foreign assistance is not just a matter of humanitarianism. Missions like helping stabilize nuclear-armed Pakistan, enabling Afghan government forces to provide more of their nation's own security so that NATO troops can do less, promoting democratic transitions in the Arab world, and helping Mexico reduce the strength of its drug cartels and their extreme (and proximate) violence all require budgetary resources. There are no easy fixes here. Defeating insurgencies, extremists, and drug syndicates in weak states requires more capable police forces, stronger systems of law and order, more effective delivery of services by the state, and better economic opportunity.[9] Other aspects of diplomacy and international economic management require resources as well.

It is not clear that aid resources need to increase. Candidate Obama promised a doubling of foreign aid, and that seems even less plausible now than when he first said it. The last Bush administration budget, for fiscal year 2009, allocated some $37 billion in foreign aid, and the Obama administration figure had grown by $2 billion by 2010.[10] But in places like Africa, good governance and new technological opportunities, combined with rescheduled debt burdens and better investment and trade possibilities, are the keys to growth, even more than aid is. And because there has been substantial headway in these realms as well as in aid centralization and coordination, many countries are doing much better than before.[11] So a big increase in foreign aid does not seem useful, given current budget realities. That said, the United States and other donors still do have a crucial role in these countries, especially in terms of basic human needs, like health care and agricultural development, and in support of governments that have reformed their economic policies to be able to make good use of assistance. The Millennium Challenge Corporation, a Bush administration innovation, demonstrates the effectiveness of greater selectivity in allocating aid resources, mitigating previous concerns that foreign aid is often wasted. Given this progress, aid budgets, modest to begin with, should not be allowed to decline precipitously.

As noted above, American leaders must understand that how we handle our domestic economy will prove crucial to America's security and global position. There are many dimensions to this issue, but gaining control over our fiscal challenges while making investments that nurture our capacity to adapt and compete in the future are critical components of any serious program. For instance, only with a strong domestic consensus in favor of open trade and investment can America's economy thrive. Furthermore, with such policies we can help countries like Pakistan and Mexico—so crucial to our safety here at home—to succeed, or contemplate big ideas like a free trade accord with India or Brazil, or completion of the Trans-Pacific Partnership agreement.[12]

Developing a politically sustainable, pro-trade agenda in a time of high unemployment at home will be hard. It will require compensating and retraining workers displaced by trade more effectively than at present—for example, through a program of "wage insurance" that would partially compensate workers who take a job at a lower salary than what they earned before.[13]

Even more essential are steps to nurture the foundations of a stronger domestic economy so that American firms and workers can compete globally—and regain their confidence that they can do so as well. But the ability to implement this kind of pro-growth agenda at the same time that the domestic discretionary budget is dramatically reduced, as some deficit-reduction plans would require, will be limited.[14] Therefore excessive cuts in domestic discretionary accounts need to be avoided if we wish to nurture American competitiveness.

As this book is being written, a myriad of proposals for improving the economy and fiscal health of the country are being debated, and resolution will not come quickly or easily. Furthermore, this volume is not the place to reprise major arguments in this domestic debate. But the authors cannot stress strongly enough that far more than America's domestic well-being is at stake. The global system is based on American strength politically and economically, as well as militarily. That strength is now being called into question, and the very public domestic political dysfunction in the United States is affecting expectations about the future around the world. It is far too early for anyone either at home or abroad to reach final conclusions about the American future, but the decisions made about "domestic" policies will influence profoundly the evolution of the international system and America's role in it.

The broad challenge facing Barack Obama—how to right America's course and sustain its vital role in the world is not just his alone, but the country's. The United States has been in precarious situations before, but it has found its way out in the end. Can it do so again, at a time when no obvious threat scares the population into response, when America's politics are dysfunctional, when the American dream of leaving a better life to one's children seems in jeopardy for perhaps the first time in the country's history, and when a culture of entitlement, a federal budget dominated by those entitlements, and a tax system shaped by special interests hamstring leaders?

For all its economic travails at present, the United States has many strengths. It has the strongest armed forces in the world and will continue to do so for the foreseeable future. It continues to lead the world in research and development, higher education, innovation, and high-tech manufacturing. Its melting-pot demographics and slow but relatively balanced population growth work to its advantage. A transparent political system and reliable rule of law attract investment and earn the United States the highest overall "competitiveness" ranking of any large country in the world today.[15] America's rich resources, vibrant civil society, and vast experience in global leadership add to its prospects.

Yet many trends are heading in the wrong direction, and the country's economic future remains at risk. If President Obama cannot repair this, he cannot hope to repair the world, for he will have failed to address not only the chief domestic political test but also the major foreign policy challenge of his day. And the consequences for the United States and the world will reach far beyond his reelection prospects or his particular place in history.

NOTES

NOTES TO CHAPTER 1

1. This concept of an arc bending toward justice is Obama's favorite metaphor, appearing often in his most important speeches and even embroidered on the rim of his Oval Office rug. It comes from a speech by Martin Luther King in Montgomery, Alabama, on March 21, 1965, in which he answered the rhetorical question, "How long will it take?" His answer was taken from an earlier speech by Robert Parker, a nineteenth-century champion of social progress: "Not long, because the arc of the moral universe is long but it bends toward justice." See David Remnick, *The Bridge: The Life and Rise of Barack Obama* (New York: Alfred A. Knopf, 2010); "Oval Office Rug Gets History Wrong," *Washington Post*, September 4, 2010.

2. Barack Obama, "Renewing American Leadership," *Foreign Affairs* 86, no.4 (2007).

3. "Barack Obama's New Hampshire Primary Speech," *New York Times*, January 8, 2008.

4. He presented his biography to the American public in the following way: "I am the son of a black man from Kenya and a white woman from Kansas. I was raised with the help of a white grandfather who survived a Depression to serve in Patton's Army during World War II and a white grandmother who worked on a bomber assembly line at Fort Leavenworth while he was overseas. I've gone to some of the best schools in America and lived in one of the world's poorest nations. I am married to a black American who carries within her the blood of slaves and slave-owners—an inheritance we pass on to our two precious daughters. I have brothers, sisters, nieces, nephews, uncles and cousins, of every race and every hue, scattered across three continents, and for as long as I live, I will never forget that in no other country on Earth is my story even possible. It's a story that hasn't made me the most conventional candidate. But it is a story that has seared into my genetic makeup the idea that this nation is more than the sum of its parts—that out of many, we are truly one." "Barack Obama's Speech on Race," *New York Times*, March 18, 2008 (www.nytimes.com/2008/03/18/us/politics/18text-obama.html).

5. Cited in Remnick, *The Bridge: The Life and Rise of Barack Obama*, p. 552.

6. At the November 10, 2007, Jefferson-Jackson dinner in Iowa, in a speech widely viewed as contributing importantly to his subsequent victory in the Iowa caucuses, he said: "I am running for President because I am sick and tired of Democrats thinking that the only way to look tough on national security is by talking, and acting, and voting like George Bush Republicans. . . . When I am this party's nominee, my opponent will not be able to say that I voted for the war in Iraq."

7. Barack Obama, "My Plan for Iraq," *New York Times,* July 14, 2008.

8. See "McCain and Obama Mix It Up," Associated Press, September 26, 2008.

9. "Remarks of Senator Obama: The War We Need to Win," Washington, August 1, 2007 (www.barackobama.com/2007/08/01/the_war_we_need_to_win. php [February 10, 2011]).

10. "Remarks of Senator Barack Obama to the Chicago Council on Global Affairs," Chicago, April 23, 2007 (http://my.barackobama.com/page/content/ fpccga/ [February 8, 2011]).

11. Barack Obama, "A World That Stands as One," speech, Berlin, July 24, 2008 (www.huffingtonpost.com/2008/07/24/obama-in-berlin-video-of_n_114771. html [February 9, 2011]).

12. "Remarks of Senator Barack Obama to the Chicago Council on Global Affairs."

13. Andy Merten, "Presidential Candidates Debate Pakistan," *NBC News,* February 28, 2008 (www.msnbc.msn.com/id/23392577/ns/politics-decision_08/t/ presidential-candidates-debate-pakistan/).

14. Congressional Budget Office, *The Budget and Economic Outlook: An Update,* (September 2008), in particular "Selected Tables" (www.cbo.gov/ftpdocs/97xx/ doc9706/Selected_Tables.pdf [February 14, 2011]).

15. Warren Buffett, interview by Susie Gharib, *Nightly Business Report,* January 22, 2009 (www.calculatedriskblog.com/2009/01/pbs-interview-with-warren-buffett.html [February 14, 2011]).

16. Congressional Budget Office, *The Budget and Economic Outlook: Fiscal Years 2011 to 2021* (January 2011), pp. 30–34 (www.cbo.gov/ftpdocs/120xx/ doc12039/01-26_FY2011Outlook.pdf [February 14, 2011]).

17. Michael Mussa, "World Recession and Recovery: A V or an L?" paper presented at the Fifteenth Semiannual Meeting on Global Economic Prospects, Peterson Institute for International Economics, Washington, April 7, 2009 (www.iie. com/publications/papers/mussa0409.pdf [February 14, 2011]); M. Ayhan Kose and Eswar S. Prasad, *Emerging Markets: Resilience and Growth Amid Global Turmoil* (Brookings, 2010), pp. 34–36, 124–26.

18. C. Fred Bergsten, "Needed: A Global Response to the Global Economic and Financial Crisis," testimony before the Subcommittee on Terrorism, Nonproliferation and Trade, House Committee on Foreign Affairs, 111 Cong. 1 sess., March 12, 2009 (piie.com/publications/testimony/testimony.cfm?ResearchID=1146 [February 14, 2011]). Some countries, such as Germany, demurred regarding the scale preferred by the United States.

19. CNN World, "G20 Pumps $1 Trillion into Beating Recession," April 2, 2009 (http://articles.cnn.com/2009-04-02/world/g20_1_new-world-order-global-international-banking-system?_s=PM:WORLD [February 14, 2011]); Colin I.

Bradford and Johannes F. Linn, "The April 2009 London G-20 Summit in Retrospect," April 5, 2010 (www.brookings.edu/opinions/2010/0405_g20_summit_linn. aspx?p=1 [February 15, 2011]).

20. Brian Montopoli, "Obama Calls Three Foreign Leaders," *CBS News,* January 23, 2009; Reuters, "Obama Starts First Major Foreign Trip," March 31, 2009; Glenn Kessler, "Japan Premier Cautious on N. Korea—Economy Restricts Options, Aso Says," *Washington Post,* February 25, 2009; "Obama Tackles Thorny Economic, Military Issues in Canada Trip," CNN, February 19, 2009.

21. CNN Politics, "Full Text of Obama's Speech to UK Parliament," May 25, 2011 (http://articles.cnn.com/2011-05-25/politics/obama.europe.speech_1_magna-carta-english-bill-uk-parliament/3?_s=PM:POLITICS).

22. White House, Office of the Press Secretary, "Remarks by President Barack Obama in Prague as Delivered," April 5, 2009 (www.whitehouse.gov/the_press_office/Remarks-By-President-Barack-Obama-In-Prague-As-Delivered).

23. "Text: Obama's Speech in Cairo," *New York Times,* June 4, 2009.

24. Robert McNamara remained secretary of defense after John F. Kennedy was assassinated, ultimately serving both Kennedy and Johnson for comparable lengths of time until resigning over the Vietnam War, but both these presidents were Democrats.

25. These included Richard Danzig, former secretary of the navy; John Hamre, former deputy secretary of defense; former senator Sam Nunn; Senator Carl Levin; and former soldier and current senator Jack Reed, among others.

26. Jonathan Alter, *The Promise: President Obama, Year One* (New York: Simon and Schuster, 2010), p. 48.

27. His 2010 Quadrennial Defense Review did not depart notably from those of the previous two decades, preserving a basic U.S. defense posture not unlike those dating back to secretaries of defense Cheney, Aspin, Perry, and Cohen. See Robert Gates, *Quadrennial Defense Review Report* (Department of Defense, February 2010), pp. v, 46–47.

28. Those weapons included, in 2009, the F-22 air superiority fighter, the DDG-1000 destroyer, the presidential helicopter program, the so-called transformational satellite, much of the Army's Future Combat System program, the Airborne Laser and a high-speed interceptor missile defense system, and then, in the following years, the C-17 transport aircraft, the Marine Corps Expeditionary Fighting Vehicle, as well as a second engine program for the F-35 multipurpose combat aircraft. See Office of the Under Secretary of Defense (Comptroller), "Overview: United States Department of Defense Fiscal Year 2012 Budget Request" (February 2011), pp. 4-1 through 4-4; Gordon Adams, "Secretary Gates Outlines Changes to Major Defense Weapon Systems," April 6, 2009 (www.stimson.org/budgeting [April 9, 2009]).

29. William Branigin and Walter Pincus, "Lawmakers Grill Pentagon Officials on Defense Spending Cuts," *Washington Post,* January 27, 2011; Donna Cassata, "Pentagon Chiefs: Don't Cut Defense Too Deeply," Associated Press, February 16, 2011; Office of Management and Budget, *Fiscal Year 2012 Budget of the U.S. Government: Historical Tables* (Government Printing Office, February 2011), pp. 100–03.

30. Alter, *The Promise,* pp. 67–76.

NOTES TO CHAPTER 2

1. David Barboza, "China Passes Japan as Second-Largest Economy," *New York Times*, August 15, 2010. For military capabilities in terms of defense spending, see "The World's Biggest Defence Budgets," *Economist Online*, March 9, 2011 (www.economist.com/blogs/dailychart/2011/03/defence_budgets).

2. See Spencer Swartz and Shai Oster, "China Tops U.S. in Energy Use," *Wall Street Journal*, July 18, 2010; "China Overtakes U.S. in Greenhouse Gas Emissions," *New York Times*, June 20, 2007.

3. For text of Zoellick's speech, see "Whither China: From Membership to Responsibility?" (www.ncuscr.org/files/2005Gala_RobertZoellick_Whither_China1.pdf).

4. Kenneth Lieberthal, "The U.S.-China Relationship Goes Global," *Current History* (September 2009): 1–20.

5. For the most systematic statement of this vision more than two years into the Obama presidency, see Hillary Rodham Clinton, "America's Pacific Century," *Foreign Policy*, November 2011 (www.foreignpolicy.com/articles/2011/10/11/americas_pacific_century?page=full).

6. Liu Jianfei, "Zhanlue jiyuqi' yu zhong Mei guangxi" [The period of strategic opportunity and Sino-American ties], *Liaowang* [Outlook magazine], January 23, 2003 (www.xslx.com/Html/gjzl/200301/2960.html).

7. Generally, Beijing has been more comfortable with conservative Republicans than liberal Democrats in the United States. The former have supported free trade, been pro-business, and concentrated on hard power. The latter have constituencies that put more emphasis on human rights, soft power, and "fair" trade—all of which lead to nettlesome issues in relations with China.

8. Kenneth Lieberthal, *Managing the China Challenge* (Brookings, 2011).

9. Seung-Wook Baek, "Does China Follow 'The East Asian Development Model'?" *Journal of Contemporary Asia* 35, no. 4 (2005): 485–98 (http://search.proquest.com/docview/194233624/130479457631AB39530/20?accountid=26493).

10. Ed Steinfeld, *Playing Our Game* (MIT Press, 2010).

11. Yang Yao, "Beijing's Motives Are Often Just Pragmatic," *Financial Times*, February 6, 2011; Zheng Yongnian, "China's Model of the U.S., Which Is More Effective in Coping with the Financial Crisis?" *People's Daily Online*, May 12, 2009 (http://english.peopledaily.com.cn/90001/90780/91344/6655878.html).

12. Keith Bradsher, "China's Unemployment Swells as Exports Falter," *New York Times*, February 5, 2009.

13. Dexter Roberts, "China's Stimulus Package Boosts Economy," *Businessweek*, April 22, 2009.

14. Victor Shih, "China Takes the Brakes Off," *Wall Street Journal*, July 22, 2009; David Barboza, "China's Boom Is Beginning to Show Cracks, Analysts Say," *New York Times*, June 21, 2011; Kelvin Soh, "Chinese Banks Falter as Slowdown, Tightening Bite," Reuters, June 21, 2011.

15. Central People's Government, People's Republic of China, "China's Peaceful Development," white paper, September 6, 2011 (www.gov.cn/english/official/2011-09/06/content_1941354_2.htm).

16. Dong Wang and Li Kan, "Eying the Crippled Hegemon: China's Grand Strategy in the Wake of the Global Financial Crisis," paper prepared for the annual meeting of the American Political Science Association, Washington, September 1–4, 2010; Wang Jisi, "Zhongguo de guoji dingwei wenti yu 'taoguang yanghui, you suo zuowei' de zhanlue sixiang" [The issue of China's international status and the strategic thought of "lay low and bide one's time while getting something done"], *Guoji wenti yanjiu* [International studies], Issue 2, 2011.

17. Kenneth Lieberthal, "Is China Catching Up with the U.S.?" *Ethos,* no. 8 (August 2010): 12–16.

18. Kenneth Lieberthal and Jisi Wang, "Understanding and Dealing with U.S.-China Strategic Distrust" (Brookings and Peking University, 2012). To see the specific application of this in China's views on U.S. actions in the climate change arena, see Kenneth Lieberthal and David Sandalow, *Overcoming Obstacles to U.S.-China Cooperation on Climate Change* (Brookings, 2009).

19. For a brief overview of the history, structure, and functioning of the G-20, see www.g20.org/about_what_is_g20.aspx.

20. Sarah Marsh, "Europe to Urge Exit from Stimulus Schemes at G20: Merkel," Reuters, June 19, 2010.

21. Ariana Eunjung Cha and Maureen Fan, "China Unveils $586 Billion Stimulus Plan," *Washington Post,* November 10, 2008.

22. Ding Qingfen and Wang Bo, "U.S.-China Conflict May Be Central at G20 Summit," *China Daily,* October 23, 2010 (www.chinadaily.com.cn/world/2010-10/23/content_11448522.htm).

23. White House, Office of the Press Secretary,"U.S.-China Joint Statement," November 17, 2009 (www.whitehouse.gov/the-press-office/us-china-joint-statement).

24. Helene Cooper, "China Holds Firm on Major Issues in Obama's Visit," *New York Times,* November 17, 2009; Barbara Demick, "China Not in a Gift-Giving Mood," *Los Angeles Times,* November 18, 2009.

25. Tony Karon, "When it Comes to Kyoto, the U.S. Is the 'Rogue Nation,'" *Time,* July 24, 2001; Lloyd de Vries, "Bush Disses Global Warming Report," *CBS News,* June 4, 2002; Sheryl Gay Stolberg, "Bush Proposes Goals on Greenhouse Gas Emissions," *New York Times,* June 1, 2007.

26. "China Strives for Renewal of Kyoto Protocol," *China Daily,* June 9, 2011 (www.chinadaily.com.cn/world/2011-06/09/content_12669445.htm). The first crack in China's position on this issue occurred at the Conference of Parties in Durban, South Africa, in 2011.

27. Kenneth Lieberthal, "U.S.-China Clean Energy Cooperation: The Road Ahead," Policy Brief 09-07 (Brookings, September 2009).

28. Personal communication.

29. Edward Wong and Jonathan Ansfield, "China Insists That Its Steps on Climate Be Voluntary," *New York Times,* January 29, 2010.

30. This was one of the clear lessons the Obama administration learned from the fate of the Kyoto Protocol, which Vice President Gore actively helped to negotiate but then never came close to receiving the approval of the U.S. Senate.

31. The text of the Copenhagen Accord is available at http://unfccc.int/resource/docs/2009/cop15/eng/l07.pdf. The Accord was endorsed but not formally adopted

by the conference as a whole. Even these changes produced unprecedented open dissension within the Chinese delegation during this negotiating session, with a key member of the delegation shouting his dissent from his premier's compromises. Reflecting how controversial Premier Wen's approach was, his voluble critic in the delegation did not suffer any subsequent career consequences for his open display of pique with his own leader. Based on Kenneth Lieberthal's interviews with participants at this Friday night meeting.

32. Jonathan Pollack, "An Assessment of U.S. Strategy on Korea and a Policy Agenda for the Next Administration," *Strategic Asia 2008–09* (Seattle: National Bureau of Asian Research, 2008), pp. 135–64.

33. See Jonathan Pollack, *No Exit: North Korea, Nuclear Weapons, and International Security* (New York: Routledge, 2011). Pollack demonstrates in detail how central the nuclear program was to North Korea's security strategy. The history he reconstructs suggests very strongly that North Korea cannot be enticed to fully relinquish its military nuclear capabilities.

34. Blaine Harden, "Defiant N. Korea Launches Missile," *Washington Post*, April 5, 2009; "North Korea Conducts Nuclear Test," BBC, May 25, 2009.

35. Choe Sang-hun, "North Korea Claims to Conduct 2nd Nuclear Test," *New York Times*, May 24, 2009.

36. UN Security Council Resolution 1874, adopted June 12, 2009. For full text, see "Security Council, Acting Unanimously, Condemns in Strongest Terms Democratic People's Republic Of Korea Nuclear Test, Toughens Sanctions" (www.un.org/News/Press/docs/2009/sc9679.doc.htm). See also Bonnie S. Glaser, "China's Policy in the Wake of the Second DPRK Nuclear Test," *China Security*, no. 14 (2009) (www.chinasecurity.us/index.php?option=com_content&view=article&id=287&Itemid=8).

37. Chris Buckley, "China Vows to Stand by Isolated North Korea," Reuters, October 5, 2009.

38. "China and North Korea Defence Ministers Pledge Ties," BBC, November 23, 2009.

39. See chapter 6 for details.

40. Based on interviews by Kenneth Lieberthal.

41. Central People's Government, "China's Peaceful Development."

42. Such announcements can be—and often are—delayed for a period of time at the discretion of the secretary of the treasury.

43. President George W. Bush shifted this process from an annual review to an episodic decision on no particular timetable in order to reduce the annual spike in tensions that this issue created. But arms sales to Taiwan continue to rankle U.S.-China relations in a major way, and various advocates ensure that every year or two it comes up with sufficient attention to become an active irritant in U.S.-China relations.

44. The Dalai Lama had visited Washington in October 2009, and President Obama had refused to see him then; it was a month before the November summit, and the White House wanted to avoid "poisoning the waters." This decision was harshly criticized by many in the United States.

45. Actually, the January announcement was about *approval* for Taiwan to purchase a certain array of military items from the United States. For details, see Helene

Cooper, "U.S. Approval of Taiwan Arms Sales Angers China," *New York Times,* January 29, 2010. For the fallout from the Dalai Lama's visit, see John Pomfret, "Obama Meeting with Dalai Lama Complicates U.S. Ties with China," *Washington Post,* February 19, 2010.

46. See "China Denounces U.S. Arms Sales to Taiwan," *China Daily,* January 9, 2010 (www.chinadaily.com.cn/china/2010-01/09/content_9291821.htm); Huang Xiangyang, "Deplorable for Obama to Meet Dalai Lama," *China Daily,* February 3, 2010 (www.chinadaily.com.cn/china/2010-01/09/content_9291821.htm); "Jiu Mei shou Taiwan wuqi tichu yanzheng jiaobu he kangyi"aqi tichu 2010uld expend sufficient political capital to have cap and trade legislation adopted by the Senate [Stern statements on and protests of U.S. arms sales to Taiwan], *Renmin wang* [People's daily online], January 31, 2010 (http://politics.people.com.cn/GB/1026/10888178.html); Xing Shiwei, "Waijiaobu: Aobama huijian Dalai yanzhong sunhai Zhong Mei guanxi" [Ministry of foreign affairs: Obama's meeting with Dalai Lama seriously harms Sino-U.S. relations], *Beijing bao* [Beijing news], February 20, 2010 (http://news.sina.com.cn/c/2010-02-20/012619700995.shtml).

47. David Drummond, "A New Approach to China," Official Google Blog, January 12, 2010 (http://googleblog.blogspot.com/2010/01/new-approach-to-china.html).

48. "U.S. Treasury to Delay Currency Report to Congress," Reuters, April 8, 2010.

49. U.S. Department of State, "The Deputy Secretary's Trip to the Balkans and Asia," FPC Briefing, March 29, 2010 (http://fpc.state.gov/139203.htm).

50. Keith B. Richburg, "President Hu Jintao of China to Attend Nuclear Summit in Washington," *Washington Post,* April 2, 2010.

51. The report was released in July: "U.S. Treasury Releases Delayed China Currency Report," BBC, July 8, 2010.

52. Edward Wong, "China Sees Separatist Threats," *New York Times,* January 20, 2009; "U.S. Show of Force in Asian Waters a Threat to China: Magazine," Xinhua, August 15, 2010 (http://eng.mod.gov.cn/Opinion/2010-08/15/content_4184307.htm).

53. Martin Fackler, "Cables Show U.S. Concern on Japan's Disaster Readiness," *New York Times,* May 3, 2011.

54. Brendan Nicholson, "U.S. Forces Get Nod to Share Our Bases," *The Australian,* November 6, 2010 (www.theaustralian.com.au/national-affairs/us-forces-get-nod-to-share-our-bases/story-fn59niix-1225948576258); Jayshree Bagoria and Esther Pan, "The U.S.-India Nuclear Deal," Council on Foreign Relations Backgrounder, November 5, 2010 (www.cfr.org/india/us-india-nuclear-deal/p9663#p8).

55. U.S. Marine Corps, "Air-Sea Battle Concept Summary," November 10, 2011 (www.marines.mil/unit/hqmc/Pages/TheAir-SeaBattleconceptsummary.aspx); "U.S. Pledges Wider Military Presence across Pacific Rim," BBC, June 4, 2011; "Viewpoint: A New Sino-U.S. High-Tech Arms Race?" BBC, January 11, 2011. The term "area denial" has been used in U.S. Defense Department publications to describe PLA strategy, but Chinese sources have not adopted this terminology and question the applicability of the concept.

56. "Aobama huo dui Tai jun shou huijian Dalai 2010 nian Zhong Mei kong fanlian" [Obama likely to sell arms to Taiwan and meet Dalai Lama; Sino-American

relations in danger of 2010 fallout], *Huanqiu shibao* [Global times], January 4, 2010 (http://mil.huanqiu.com/Taiwan/2010-01/677702.html); "Yi wangle ziyou mingyi Meiguo gonggu wangluo baquan" [In the name of Internet freedom America strengthens its cyber hegemony], *Guangzhou ribao* [Guangzhou daily], January 31, 2010 (http://news.xinhuanet.com/mil/2010-01/31/content_12905749.htm).

57. Office of the Secretary of Defense, "Military and Security Developments Involving the People's Republic of China 2010" (www.defense.gov/pubs/pdfs/2010_CMPR_Final.pdf).

58. "'North Korean Torpedo' Sank South's Navy Ship—Report," BBC, May 20, 2010; Jack Kim and Lee Jae-won, "North Korea Shells South in Fiercest Attack in Decades," Reuters, November 23, 2010; Seo Yoonjung and Keith B. Richburg, "2 Civilians Killed in North Korea Artillery Attack," *Washington Post,* November 24, 2010.

Dr. Siegfried Hecker informed the White House of North Korea's new nuclear facility shortly after his November 12 visit to the plant. See David E. Sanger, "North Koreans Unveil New Plant for Nuclear Use," *New York Times,* November 20, 2010.

59. "'North Korean Torpedo' Sank South's Navy Ship," BBC.

60. Chico Harlan and Colum Lynch, "U.N. Security Council Condemns Sinking of South Korea Warship," *Washington Post,* July 10, 2010; UN Security Council, "Statement by the President of the Security Council," July 9, 2010 (www.security-councilreport.org/atf/cf/%7B65BFCF9B-6D27-4E9C-8CD3-CF6E4FF96FF9%7D/NKorea%20S%20PRST%202010%2013.pdf).

61. North Korea's calculations are unclear. The attack may have been partly an effort by Kim Jong-un to establish his bona fides as being sufficiently tough and skillful to warrant succeeding his father, and partly a strategy to initiate an action so startling that it would almost certainly drive a sharp wedge between Beijing on the one side and the United States and South Korea on the other. North Korea has always proven ruthless and skillful in dividing those who might otherwise unite to pressure it.

62. Martin Fackler, "U.S. and South Korea Begin Joint Naval Exercises," *New York Times,* November 27, 2010.

63. "China Calls for Restraint from DPRK and ROK," *China Daily,* November 24, 2010 (www.chinadaily.com.cn/china/2010-11/24/content_11604656.htm).

64. Kim Jong-il arrived in China on May 3, 2010; see Blaine Harden, "Kim Jong Il Visits China, Shows Persisting Frailty," *Washington Post,* May 7, 2010. His second trip to China occurred less than four months later, on August 26, 2010; see "North Korean Leader Kim Jong-il 'Pays Visit to China,'" BBC, August 26, 2010. Kim visited China again on May 20, 2011; see "Top DPRK Leader Kim Jong-il Visits China," Xinhua, May 26, 2011 (http://news.xinhuanet.com/english2010/world/2011-05/26/c_13895772.htm).

65. See chapter 6 for details.

66. John Pomfret, "U.S. Concerned about New Japanese Premier Hatoyama," *Washington Post,* December 29, 2009.

67. Ibid.

68. "China, Japan and the Sea," *New York Times,* September 24, 2010; Yuka Hayashi, "Japan's Defense Minister Seeks Stronger Military Ties to U.S.," *Wall Street Journal,* April 23, 2011.

69. Kyodo World Service in English (Tokyo), March 7, 2010.

70. See, for example, Kyodo World Service in English (Tokyo), January 17, 2010.

71. *Mainichi Daily News,* June 23, 2010.

72. Kyodo World Service in English (Tokyo), April 13, 2010; International Institute for Strategic Studies, "Chinese Navy's New Strategy in Action," *IISS Strategic Comments* 16 (May 2010) (www.iiss.org/EasysiteWeb/getresource.axd?AssetID=40229).

73. Keith Bradsher, "Amid Tension, China Blocks Rare Earth Exports to Japan," *New York Times,* September 22, 2010. China denied that it had cut off rare earth metal exports to Japan, and it also stressed that it had sought to handle the case of the captain through normal diplomatic channels until the Japanese referred the case to a local judicial authority in Okinawa, thereby making it a test of claims of sovereignty.

74. Tomohisa Tsuruta, Shuhei Kuromi, and Toshimitsu Miyai, "Public Opinion of China Slumps," *Yomiuri Shimbun,* October 5, 2010 (www.yomiuri.co.jp/dy/national/T101004003738.htm).

75. Alister Doyle, "World Seabed Disputes Face U.N. Deadline," Reuters, May 12, 2009.

76. The pertinent claims and issues are concisely summed up in Michael D. Swaine and M. Taylor Fravel, "China's Assertive Behavior: Part Two: The Maritime Periphery," *China Leadership Monitor,* no. 35 (Summer 2011) (www.hoover.org/publications/china-leadership-monitor).

77. "China Accuses Vietnam in South China Sea Row," BBC, June 10, 2011; Andrew Quinn, "U.S. Backs Philippines as S. China Sea Tensions Flare," Reuters, June 23, 2011; "Q&A: South China Sea Dispute," BBC, June 13, 2011.

78. See "Chairman's Statement, 17th ASEAN Regional Forum, Hanoi, July 23, 2010" (www.aseansec.org/24929.htm).

79. Hillary Rodham Clinton, "Remarks at Press Availability," Hanoi, Vietnam, July 23, 2010 (www.state.gov/secretary/rm/2010/07/145095.htm).

80. Secretary Clinton had planned to brief Foreign Minister Yang a day in advance on her prepared remarks but then canceled this meeting due to another obligation.

81. One American diplomat who participated in this meeting commented to Kenneth Lieberthal that Yang had in twenty minutes undone ten years of Chinese diplomacy that had sought to allay any fear of Chinese bullying in Southeast Asia.

82. As seen by many in the region, China's position amounts to saying that China can exploit what is China's and that China can jointly develop what belongs to other countries.

83. Ben Bland, "Vietnam Seeks U.S. Support in China Dispute," *Financial Times,* June 12, 2011; Andrew Quinn, "U.S. Backs Philippines as S. China Sea Tensions Flare," Reuters, June 23, 2011.

84. "China, Vietnam Agree to Resolve Maritime Dispute through Negotiations," Xinhua, June 26, 2011 (http://news.xinhuanet.com/english2010/china/2011-06/26/c_13950640.htm); Office of the President of the Philippines, "Philippines-China Joint Press Statement," July 8, 2011 (www.gov.ph/2011/07/08/philippines-china-joint-press-statement-july-8-2011/).

85. Swaine and Fravel, "China's Assertive Behavior."

86. Ibid.

87. Thom Shanker and Mark Mazzetti, "China and U.S. Clash on Naval Fracas," *New York Times,* March 10, 2009.

88. "China Asks U.S. to Prevent Illegal Entry to Its EEZ," *China Daily,* May 6, 2009 (www.chinadaily.com.cn/china/2009-05/06/content_7750820.htm); Peter Dutton, ed., *Military Activities in the EEZ: A U.S.-China Dialogue on Security and International Law in the Maritime Commons* (Newport, R.I.: U.S. Naval War College, China Maritime Studies Institute, December 2010).

89. Kenneth Lieberthal and Peter Singer, "Cybersecurity and US-China Relations" (Brookings, forthcoming).

90. Tom Gjelten, "Cyberattack: U.S. Unready for Future Face of War," NPR, April 7, 2010.

91. Siobhan Gorman, August Cole, and Yochi Dreazen,"Computer Spies Breach Fighter-Jet Project," *Wall Street Journal,* April 21, 2009.

92. Ron Deibert and Rafal Rohozinski, "Shadows in the Cloud: Investigating Cyber Espionage 2.0," April 6, 2010 (www.scribd.com/doc/29435784/SHADOWS-IN-THE-CLOUD-Investigating-Cyber-Espionage-2-0).

93. David E. Sanger and John Markoff, "I.M.F. Reports Cyberattack Led to 'Very Major Breach,'" *New York Times,* June 11, 2011.

94. Ben Worthen, "Wide Cyber Attack Is Linked to China," *Wall Street Journal,* March 30, 2009; Ariana Eunjung Cha and Ellen Nakashima, "Google China Cyberattack Part of Vast Espionage Campaign, Experts Say," *Washington Post,* January 14, 2010.

95. Michael Martina, "China Says Makes Progress on Use of Copyrighted Software," Reuters, April 21, 2011.

96. Kenneth Lieberthal, "The U.S. and China—Mending Fences," *Los Angeles Times,* January 17, 2011.

97. According to Wang Tao, an economist at UBS, "As a share of G.D.P. it [China's trade balance] should be below 4 percent this year. At its peak in 2007, the trade surplus was equal to 9 percent of G.D.P." Quoted from David Barboza and Bettina Wassener, "China Posts Trade Deficit of $7.3 Billion in February," *New York Times,* March 10, 2011.

98. U.S. Department of the Treasury and Federal Reserve Board, "Major Foreign Holders of Treasury Securities," August 15, 2011 (www.treasury.gov/resource-center/data-chart-center/tic/Documents/mfh.txt); Office of the U.S. Trade Representative, "China" (www.ustr.gov/countries-regions/china).

99. In reality, the undervaluation of the renminbi has had, for complex reasons, considerably less impact on the bilateral trade deficit than members of Congress believe. But this undervaluation has contributed substantially to harmful global imbalances. See Wayne M. Morrison and Marc Labonte, "China's Currency: An Analysis of the Economic Issues," Congressional Research Service Report for Congress, January 12, 2011 (www.fas.org/sgp/crs/row/RS21625.pdf); Ian Talley, "IMF: Chinese Yuan Substantially Weaker Than Fundamentals Warrant," *Wall Street Journal,* April 11, 2011.

100. U.S.-China Business Council, "Issues Brief: China's Domestic Innovation and Government Procurement Practices," March 2011 (www.uschina.org/public/documents/2011/innovation_procurement_brief.pdf).

101. Ryan Ong, "Tackling Intellectual Property Infringement in China," *China Business Review Online* 36, no. 2 (2009) (www.chinabusinessreview.com/store/product/view/384).

102. Nick Carey and James B. Kelleher, "Special Report: Does Corporate America Kowtow to China?" Reuters, April 27, 2011.

103. American Chamber of Commerce in the People's Republic of China, *American Business in China: 2011 White Paper* (Beijing: 2011).

104. Tan Yingzi and Chen Weihua, "U.S. Firms Vent Frustration over China Trade," *China Daily,* November 18, 2010 (www.chinadaily.com.cn/world/2010-11/18/content_11572573.htm).

105. Andrew Batson and Andrew Browne, "Wen Voices Concern Over China's U.S. Treasurys," *Wall Street Journal,* March 13, 2009 (http://online.wsj.com/article/SB123692233477317069.html); Daniel H. Rosen and Thilo Hanemann, "China's Changing Outbound Foreign Investment Profile: Drivers and Policy Implications," Policy Brief PB09-14 (Washington: Peterson Institute on International Economics, June 2009); Ding Qingfen, "China Urges U.S. to Reduce Investment Barriers," *China Daily,* November 2, 2010 (www.chinadaily.com.cn/china/2010-11/02/content_11487348.htm); "Ministry: U.S. Export Control Disappoints China," *China Daily,* June 29, 2011 (www.chinadaily.com.cn/china/2011-06/29/content_12797349.htm); Joe McDonald, "China Warns U.S. Currency Bill Might Harm Ties," *Washington Post,* September 30, 2010.

106. U.S. Department of Commerce, "21st U.S.-China Joint Commission on Commerce and Trade Fact Sheet" (www.commerce.gov/node/12467).

107. White House, Office of the Press Secretary, "Fact Sheet: U.S.-China Economic Issues," January 19, 2011 (www.whitehouse.gov/the-press-office/2011/01/19/fact-sheet-us-china-economic-issues).

108. Phil Stewart and Chris Buckley, "China Media Says Gates Visit Alone Cannot Heal Ties," Reuters, January 11, 2011.

109. "U.S., China Discussed North Korea, Maritime Security in Talks," Reuters, December 10, 2010.

110. Dai Bingguo, "Stick to the Path of Peaceful Development," Xinhua, December 6, 2010 (http://news.xinhuanet.com/english2010/indepth/2010-12/13/c_13646586.htm).

111. White House, Office of the Press Secretary, "Press Conference with President Obama and President Hu of the People's Republic of China," January 19, 2011 (www.whitehouse.gov/the-press-office/2011/01/19/press-conference-president-obama-and-president-hu-peoples-republic-china); "Building a China-U.S. Cooperative Partnership Based on Mutual Respect and Mutual Benefit," speech by Hu Jintao, Xinhua, January 20, 2011 (http://news.xinhuanet.com/english2010/china/2011-01/21/c_13700418.htm).

112. The 2006 reception of President Hu was marred by serious protocol and other gaffes. See Joseph Kahn and Christine Hauser, "China's Leader Makes First White House Visit," *New York Times,* April 20, 2006.

113. U.S. Department of the Treasury, "Third Meeting of the U.S.-China Strategic and Economic Dialogue Joint U.S.-China Economic Track Fact Sheet," May 10, 2011 (www.treasury.gov/press-center/press-releases/Pages/tg1170.aspx); U.S. Department of State, "U.S.-China Strategic and Economic Dialogue

2011 Outcomes of the Strategic Track," May 10, 2011 (www.state.gov/r/pa/prs/ps/2011/05/162967.htm).

114. On the Strategic Security Dialogue, see Department of State, "U.S.-China Strategic and Economic Dialogue 2011."

115. On the Biden trip, see Edward Wong, "Cooperation Emphasized as Biden Visits China," *New York Times,* August 18, 2011.

116. Based on interviews by Kenneth Lieberthal.

117. U.S. Department of State, "State Department Daily Press Briefing, May 31," May 31, 2011 (http://translations.state.gov/st/english/texttrans/2011/05/2011 0531171907su0.9079663.html); U.S. Department of State, "Presents Jeffrey Bader with the Secretary's Distinguished Service Award," May 8, 2011 (www.state.gov/secretary/rm/2011/05/162896.htm).

118. Mark Landler, "Republicans and Obama Can Agree on Criticizing China's Trade Practices," *New York Times,* November 21, 2011.

119. See Office of the Press Secretary, The White House, "Press Briefing by Press Secretary Jay Carney, Deputy National Security Adviser for Strategic Communications Ben Rhodes, and NSC Senior Director for Asia Danny Russel," November 16, 2011 (www.whitehouse.gov/the-press-office/2011/11/16/press-briefing-press-secretary-jay-carney-deptuy-national-security-advis). For remarks by the secretary of state, see U.S. Department of State, "America's Pacific Century," November 10, 2011 (www.state.gov/secretary/rm/2011/11/176999.htm); "Remarks with Nina Easton of Fortune Magazine at the CEO Summit on Women and the Economy," November 11, 2011 (www.state.gov/secretary/rm/2011/11/177032.htm); "Press Availability Following the APEC Ministerial Meetings," November 11, 2011 (www.state.gov/secretary/rm/2011/11/177030.htm); "Presentation of the Order of Lakandula, Signing of the Partnership for Growth and Joint Press Availability with Philippines Foreign Secretary Albert Del Rosario," November 16, 2011 (www.state.gov/secretary/rm/2011/11/177234.htm); "Remarks at ASEAN Business and Investment Summit," November 18, 2011 (www.state.gov/secretary/rm/2011/11/177349.htm).

120. Raul L. Cordenillo, "The Economic Benefits to ASEAN of the ASEAN-China Free Trade Area (ACFTA)," January 18, 2005 (www.asean.org/17310.htm); ASEAN Secretariat, "ASEAN-China Free Trade Area: Not a Zero-Sum Game," January 7, 2010 (www.asean.org/24161.htm).

121. White House, Office of the Press Secretary, "Remarks by President Obama at APEC CEO Business Summit Q&A," November 12, 2011 (www.whitehouse.gov/the-press-office/2011/11/12/remarks-president-obama-apec-ceo-business-summit-qa).

122. Office of the U.S. Trade Representative, "Outlines of the Trans-Pacific Partnership Agreement" (www.ustr.gov/about-us/press-office/fact-sheets/2011/november/outlines-trans-pacific-partnership-agreement [December 6, 2011]).

123. Jackie Calmes, "Obama and Asian Leaders Confront China's Premier," *New York Times,* November 19, 2011.

124. "South Korea Ratifies Long-Delayed US Trade Deal," BBC News, November 22, 2011.

125. White House, "APEC CEO Business Summit Q&A."

126. Chris Buckley, "China, U.S. Grapple with Tensions at Trade Talks," Reuters, November 20, 2011.

127. White House, Office of the Press Secretary, "Remarks by President Obama and Prime Minister Gillard of Australia in Joint Press Conference," November 16, 2011 (www.whitehouse.gov/the-press-office/2011/11/16/remarks-president-obama-and-prime-minister-gillard-australia-joint-press); U.S. Department of State, "White House Briefing on President Obama's Trip to Asia-Pacific," November 23, 2011 (http://iipdigital.usembassy.gov/st/english/texttrans/2011/11/20 111123120030su0.9150769.html#ixzz1fxYmEopv).

128. Karen Parrish, "Panetta Outlines Goals for Asia Trip," American Forces Press Service, October 21, 2011 (www.defense.gov/News/NewsArticle.aspx?ID= 65762); White House, Office of the Press Secretary, "Remarks by President Obama to the Australian Parliament," November 17, 2011 (www.whitehouse.gov/the-press-office/2011/11/17/remarks-president-obama-australian-parliament).

129. Ibid.

130. White House, Office of the Press Secretary, "Statement by President Obama on Burma," November 18, 2011 (www.whitehouse.gov/the-press-office/2011/11/18/statement-president-obama-burma).

131. Edward Wong, "U.S. Motives in Myanmar Are on China's Radar," *New York Times,* November 29, 2011.

132. On December 14, 2009, U.S. Trade Representative Ron Kirk notified Congress of President Obama's intent to enter the TPP negotiations. The president decided in the summer of 2010 to have the United States join the East Asian Summit.

133. Chris Buckley, "Analysis: China Gameplan in Question as Obama Pivots to Asia," Reuters, November 24, 2011.

134. "China: United States Begins 'Pacific Century,' Online Nationalism Follows," *Global Voice Online,* November 20, 2011 (http://globalvoicesonline.org/2011/11/20/china-us-begins-pacific-century-online-nationalism-follows/).

135. Jackie Calmes, "Obama's Trip Emphasizes Role of Pacific Rim," *New York Times,* November 18, 2011.

136. David E. Sanger, "In World's Eyes, Much Damage Is Already Done," *New York Times,* July 31, 2011.

137. Joint Select Committee on Deficit Reduction, "Statement from Co-Chairs of the Joint Select Committee on Deficit Reduction," November 21, 2011 (www.deficitreduction.gov/public/index.cfm/pressreleases?ID=fa0e02f6-2cc2-4aa6-b32a-3c7f6155806d).

138. Ian Johnson and Jackie Calmes, "As U.S. Looks to Asia, It Sees China Everywhere," *New York Times,* November 15, 2011.

139. According to a Defense Department report, China's military budget "continues more than two decades of sustained annual increases. . . . Analysis of 2000–2010 data indicates China's officially disclosed military budget grew at an average of 12.1 percent in inflation-adjusted terms over the period." See U.S. Department of Defense, "Annual Report to Congress: Military and Security Developments Involving the People's Republic of China 2011" (www.defense.gov/pubs/pdfs/2011_CMPR_Final.pdf). See also "Li Zhaoxing: China's Defense Budget Set to Increase by 12.7% in 2011," Xinhua, March 4, 2011 (http://news.xinhuanet.com/mil/2011-03/04/c_121148771.htm).

140. "China at Key Stage of Reform, Development," Xinhua, October 18, 2010 (http://news.xinhuanet.com/english2010/china/2010-10/18/c_13561781.htm).

Some of these undesirable outcomes include extreme disparities in wealth, pervasive problems with product and food safety, increasing corruption, catastrophic environmental degradation, decreasing returns to investment, and a widespread feeling that the system itself has become unfair.

141. As of 2011, China's per capital GDP ranks number 126 among the countries of the world. U.S. Central Intelligence Agency, "CIA World Factbook: China" (www.cia.gov/library/publications/the-world-factbook/geos/ch.html). See also Central People's Government, "China's Peaceful Development."

142. Kenneth Lieberthal and Jisi Wang, "Understanding and Dealing with U.S.-China Strategic Distrust."

143. Andrew Jacobs, "Chinese Government Responds to Call for Protests," *New York Times,* February 20, 2011; Peter Ford, "Report on China's 'Jasmine Revolution'? Not If You Want Your Visa," *Christian Science Monitor,* March 3, 2011; Geoff Dyer and Kathrin Hille, "Beijing Stamps on Calls for Revolution," *Financial Times,* February 23, 2011.

144. Administration policy toward the Arab world is discussed in chapter 5.

145. Jeremy Page, "Call for Protests Unnerves Beijing," *Wall Street Journal,* February 21, 2011.

NOTES TO CHAPTER 3

1. "President Obama on the Way Forward in Afghanistan," June 22, 2011 (www.whitehouse.gov/blog/2011/06/22/president-obama-way-forward-afghanistan).

2. Elisabeth Bumiller, "Panetta Says Defeat of al Qaeda Is 'Within Reach,'" *New York Times,* July 10, 2011, p. 11.

3. Peter Bergen, testimony before the Subcommittee on Emerging Threats, House Armed Services Committee, June 22, 2011 (newamerica.net/sites/newamerica.net/files/profiles/attachments/Bergen_HASC_June_22_Testimony.pdf).

4. John O. Brennan, "Ensuring al Qaeda's Demise," remarks, Paul H. Nitze School of Advanced International Studies, Washington, June 29, 2011; Bruce Riedel, *Deadly Embrace: Pakistan, America, and the Future of the Global Jihad* (Brookings, 2011), pp. 99–114.

5. Marvin Kalb and Deborah Kalb, *Haunting Legacy: Vietnam and the American Presidency from Ford to Obama* (Brookings, 2011), pp. 246–47.

6. Barack Obama, "My Plan for Iraq," *New York Times,* July 14, 2008.

7. Kimberly Kagan, *The Surge: A Military History* (New York: Encounter Books, 2009); Stephen Biddle, Michael E. O'Hanlon, and Kenneth M. Pollack, "The Evolution of Iraq Strategy," in *Restoring the Balance: A Middle East Strategy for the Next President,* edited by Richard N. Haass and Martin Indyk (Brookings, 2008), pp. 33–40.

8. Jason Campbell and Michael O'Hanlon, "The Iraq Index, July 31, 2008" (Brookings), p. 4 (www.brookings.edu/~/media/Files/Centers/Saban/Iraq%20Index/index20080731.pdf).

9. Ed Hornick, "Democrats Voice Concerns on Obama's Iraq Drawdown Plan," CNN, February 27, 2009.

10. Conversations between MNF-I personnel and O'Hanlon, Baghdad, February 2009.

11. Ian Livingston and Michael O'Hanlon, "The Iraq Index, January 31, 2011" (Brookings) (www.brookings.edu/~/media/Files/Centers/Saban/Iraq%20Index/index.pdf).

12. Anthony Shadid, "Ambassador Leaves Iraq with Much Still Unsettled," *New York Times,* August 12, 2010.

13. Senator Joseph R. Biden Jr. and Leslie H. Gelb, "Federalism, Not Partition," *Washington Post,* October 3, 2007.

14. Carol E. Lee, "Biden Makes Surprise Visit to Iraq," *Politico,* January 12, 2011.

15. "U.S. Vice-President Biden in Iraq Amid Election Deadlock," BBC, July 3, 2010.

16. Emma Sky, "Iraq: From Surge to Sovereignty," *Foreign Affairs* 90, no. 2 (2011): 127.

17. Steven Lee Myers, "Vote Seen as Pivotal Test for Both Iraq and Maliki," *New York Times,* February 28, 2010.

18. "Biden's Iraq Visit Conveniently Timed for Crisis," *Weekend Edition Sunday,* NPR, January 24, 2010.

19. Scott Wilson, "U.S. Withdrawal from Iraq Will Be on Time, Vice President Biden Says," *Washington Post,* May 27, 2010.

20. Vice President Joe Biden, "Remarks by Vice President Joe Biden at the Veterans of Foreign Wars 111th National Convention," Indianapolis, August 23, 2010 (www.whitehouse.gov/the-press-office/2010/08/23/remarks-vice-president-joe-biden).

21. Jake Tapper, "Political Punch," *ABC News,* February 11, 2010; Carol E. Lee, "Biden 'Happy' to Thank Bush," *Politico,* February 14, 2010 (www.politico.com/blogs/politicolive/0210/Biden_happy_to_thank_Bush_on_Iraq.html); Peter Wehner, "A Stroll Down Memory Lane," *Commentary,* July 30, 2010 (www.commentarymagazine.com/blogs/index.php/wehner/335756).

22. President Barack Obama, "Remarks by the President in Address to the Nation on the End of Combat Operations in Iraq," White House, August 31, 2010 (www.whitehouse.gov/the-press-office/2010/08/31/remarks-president-address-nation-end-combat-operations-iraq).

23. Stephen John Stedman, "Policy Implications," and George Downs and Stephen John Stedman, "Evaluation Issues in Peace Implementation," in *Ending Civil Wars: The Implementation of Peace Agreements,* edited by Stephen John Stedman, Donald Rothchild, and Elizabeth M. Cousens (Boulder, Colo.: Lynne Rienner, 2002), pp. 54–61, 666; for related ideas, see William J. Durch with Tobias C. Berkman, "Restoring and Maintaining Peace: What We Know So Far," in *Twenty-First Century Peace Operations,* edited by William J. Durch (Washington: U.S. Institute of Peace, 2006), pp. 1–48.

24. Edward D. Mansfield and Jack Snyder, "Turbulent Transitions: Why Emerging Democracies Go to War," in *Leashing the Dogs of War: Conflict Management in a Divided World,* edited by Chester A. Crocker, Fen Osler Hampson, and Pamela Aall (Washington: U.S. Institute of Peace, 2007), pp. 161–76.

25. Kenneth M. Pollack and others, *Unfinished Business: An American Strategy for Iraq Moving Forward* (Brookings, 2011), pp. 35–60; Timothy Williams and Durad Adnan, "Sunnis in Iraq Allied with U.S. Rejoin Rebels," *New York Times,* October 16, 2010.

26. Donna Miles, "Robert Gates: U.S. Open to Talks on Post-2011 Presence in Iraq," American Forces Press Service, November 9, 2010 (http://thesop.org/story/20101109/robert-gates-us-open-to-talks-on-post2011-presence-in-iraq.html).

27. Kenneth M. Pollack, "With a Whimper, Not a Bang," October 21, 2011 (www.brookings.edu/opinions/2011/1021_iraq_pollack.aspx_).

28. Elisabeth Bumiller, "Panetta Presses Iraq for Decision on Troops," New York Times, July 12, 2011, p. 8.

29. Ayad Allawi, "The Forgotten Battlefield," Washington Post, September 1, 2011, p. A15.

30. Sometimes Maliki has the help of Iraq's courts in this process. Michael S. Schmidt and Jack Healy, "Maliki's Broadened Powers Seen as a Threat in Iraq," New York Times, March 6, 2011.

31. Michael S. Schmidt and Tim Arango, "Bitter Feud between Top Iraqi Leaders Stalls Government," New York Times, June 26, 2011.

32. On intelligence, see Adam Cobb, "Intelligence in Low-Intensity Conflicts: Lessons from Afghanistan," in Victory Among People: Lessons from Countering Insurgency and Stabilising Fragile States, edited by David Richards and Greg Mills (London: Royal United Services Institute, 2011), pp. 107–26; Michael Flynn, Matt Pottiner, and Paul Batchelor, "Fixing Intel: A Blueprint for Making Intelligence Relevant in Afghanistan" (Washington: Center for a New American Security, 2010).

33. Bob Woodward, Obama's Wars (New York: Simon and Schuster, 2010), pp. 234–40.

34. Michael O'Hanlon and Bruce Riedel, "Plan A-Minus for Afghanistan," Washington Quarterly 34, no. 1 (2011): 123–32. Riedel was the coordinator of the first Afghanistan policy review of the Obama administration.

35. On the thinking of Haqqani leaders, see, for example, David Rohde and Kristen Mulvihill, A Rope and a Prayer: A Kidnapping from Two Sides (New York: Viking, 2010), pp. 71–96, 238–49.

36. For a good history, see Thomas Barfield, Afghanistan: A Cultural and Political History (Princeton University Press, 2010); for a description of what happened in the early period after 9/11, see James F. Dobbins, After the Taliban: Nation-Building in Afghanistan (Washington: Potomac Books, 2008).

37. General Stanley McChrystal, "COMISAF Initial Assessment," unclassified version, Washington Post, September 21, 2009; Ronald E. Neumann, The Other War: Winning and Losing in Afghanistan (Washington: Potomac Books, 2009); Seth G. Jones, In the Graveyard of Empires: America's War in Afghanistan (New York: W. W. Norton, 2009); on troop fatalities, see Ian S. Livingston, Heather L. Messera, and Michael O'Hanlon, "The Afghanistan Index, February 28, 2011" (Brookings) (www.brookings.edu/~/media/Files/Programs/FP/afghanistan%20index.pdf).

38. Stanley McChrystal, "How to Fight in Afghanistan," Foreign Policy, March/April 2011, pp. 66–70.

39. Carl Forsberg, "The Taliban's Campaign for Kandahar" (Washington: Institute for the Study of War, 2009), pp. 24–27; Ashraf Ghani, "A Ten-Year Framework for Afghanistan: Executing the Obama Plan . . . and Beyond" (Washington: Atlantic Council, 2009), pp. 1–3 (www.acus.org).

40. Livingston, Messera, and O'Hanlon, "Afghanistan Index, February 28, 2011."
41. Ibid.
42. Ahmed Rashid, "How Obama Lost Karzai," *Foreign Policy,* March/April 2011, pp. 71–76.
43. Donna Cassata, "Gates Says US Did 'Lousy Job' Listening to Karzai," Associated Press, March 2, 2011.
44. President Barack Obama, "State of the Union Address," Washington, January 25, 2011.
45. *Meet the Press,* NBC, December 19, 2010.
46. Remarks of the Secretary of Defense, West Point, February 25, 2011 (www.defense.gov/speeches/speech.aspx?speechid=1539).
47. Sarah Chayes, *The Punishment of Virtue: Inside Afghanistan after the Taliban* (New York: Penguin, 2006).
48. Seth G. Jones, *Counterinsurgency in Afghanistan* (Santa Monica, Calif.: RAND, 2008), p. 21; Christopher Paul, Colin P. Clarke, and Beth Grill, *Victory Has a Thousand Fathers: Sources of Success in Counterinsurgency* (Santa Monica, Calif.: RAND, 2010), pp. 50–51.
49. David Kilcullen, *The Accidental Guerrilla: Fighting Small Wars in the Midst of a Big One* (Oxford University Press, 2009).
50. For a more radical version of this kind of new possible approach, see Bing West, *The Wrong War: Grit, Strategy, and the Way out of Afghanistan* (New York: Random House, 2011); for a more moderate, evolutionary version, see Michael O'Hanlon and Bruce Riedel, "Plan A-Minus for Afghanistan," *Washington Quarterly* 34, no. 1 (2011): 123–32.
51. Stephen P. Cohen, *The Idea of Pakistan* (Brookings, 2004).
52. George Tenet with Bill Harlow, *At the Center of the Storm: My Years at the CIA* (New York: HarperCollins, 2007), p. 229.
53. Daniel Byman, *Deadly Connections: States that Sponsor Terrorism* (Cambridge University Press, 2005), pp. 164–65, 323–24.
54. Deputy Secretary of State James Steinberg, interview, *Charlie Rose Show,* June 24, 2011 (www.charlierose.com/guest/view/3378).
55. Riedel, *Deadly Embrace,* pp. 119–25.
56. Huma Yusuf, "U.S.-Pakistan Strategic Dialogue," Atlantic Council, October 25, 2010 (www.acus.org/new_atlanticist/us-pakistan-strategic-dialogue).
57. David E. Sanger, *The Inheritance: The World Obama Confronts and the Challenges to American Power* (New York: Broadway, 2010).
58. Stephen P. Cohen and Sunil Dasgupta, *Arming without Aiming: India's Military Modernization* (Brookings, 2010), pp. 53–70.
59. Riedel, *Deadly Embrace,* p. 122.
60. Nancy Birdsall, Wren Elhai, and Molly Kinder, "Beyond Bullets and Bombs: Fixing the U.S. Approach to Development in Pakistan" (Washington: Center for Global Development, 2011), p. 29 (www.cgdev.org/content/publications/detail/1425136).
61. For the GDP figures, see International Monetary Fund, *World Economic Outlook* (Washington: April 2010), p. 160 (www.imf.org/external/pubs/ft/weo/2010/01/pdf/text.pdf).

62. Shuja Nawaz, "Learning by Doing: The Pakistani Army's Experience with Counterinsurgency" (Washington: Atlantic Council, 2011) (www.acus.org/publication/learning-doing-pakistan-armys-eperience-counterinsurgency).

63. Peter Bergen and Katherine Tiedemann, "The Year of the Drones" (Washington: New America Foundation, 2010) (counterterrorism.newamerica.net/drones); Bill Roggio and Alexander Mayer, "Charting the Data for U.S. Airstrikes in Pakistan," *Long War Journal,* January 14, 2010 (www.longwarjournal.org/pakistan-strikes.php); Ian Livingston and Michael O'Hanlon, "The Pakistan Index, February 24, 2011" (Brookings) (www.brookings.edu/~/media/Files/Programs/FP/pakistan%20index/indes.pdf).

64. Joshua T. White, "Pakistan's Islamist Frontier: Islamic Politics and U.S. Policy in Pakistan's North-West Frontier" (Arlington, Va.: Center on Faith and International Affairs, 2008), pp. 3–9.

65. Steve Coll, president of the New America Foundation, testimony before the Subcommittee on Oversight, Investigations, and Management, House Committee on Homeland Security, June 3, 2011, p. 5 (newamerica.net/sites/newamerica.net/files/profiles/attachments/Coll_Homeland_Security_Testimony_June_3.pdf).

66. "CIA Director Leon Panetta Feared Pakistan 'Might Alert' bin Laden of Raid," *New York Post,* May 3, 2011.

67. Stephen J. Solarz, *Journeys to War and Peace* (Brandeis Press, 2011), p. 160.

68. Riedel, *Deadly Embrace,* pp. 119–44; Birdsall, Elhai, and Kinder, "Beyond Bullets and Bombs," p. 27.

69. Charlie Szrom and Chris Harnisch, "Al Qaeda's Operating Environments: A New Approach to the War on Terror" (Washington: American Enterprise Institute, 2011), pp. 18–22.

70. International Crisis Group, "Somalia: The Transitional Government on Life Support," Africa Report 170 (Brussels: International Crisis Group, 2011) (www.crisisgroup.org/en/regions/africa/horn-of-africa/somalia/170-somalia-the-transitional-government-on-life-support.aspx).

71. Jeffrey Gettleman, "African Union Force Makes Strides Inside Somalia," *New York Times,* November 24, 2011.

72. Richard K. Betts, *Enemies of Intelligence: Knowledge and Power in American National Security* (Columbia University Press, 2007); Paul Pillar, *Terrorism and U.S. Foreign Policy* (Brookings, 2001).

73. Michael V. Hayden, "The State of the Craft: Is Intelligence Reform Working?" *World Affairs,* September/October 2010, pp. 35–47.

74. Dana Priest and William M. Arkin, "A Hidden World, Growing beyond Control," *Washington Post,* July 19, 2010.

75. Clark Kent Ervin, *Open Target: Where America Is Vulnerable to Attack* (New York: Palgrave Macmillan, 2006); Stephen Flynn, *America the Vulnerable: How Our Government Is Failing to Protect Us from Terrorism* (New York: Harper Collins, 2004).

76. Secretary Janet Napolitano, *Quadrennial Homeland Security Review Report: A Strategic Framework for a Secure Homeland* (Department of Homeland Security, February 2010) (www.dhs.gov/xlibary/assets/qhsr_report.pdf); White House, *National Security Strategy,* May 2010 (www.whitehouse.gov/sites/default/files/rss_viewer/national_security_strategy.pdf).

77. John O. Brennan, assistant to the president for homeland security and counterterrorism, "Ensuring al-Qaeda's Demise," speech, School of Advanced International Studies, Johns Hopkins University, Washington, June 29, 2011 (www.sais.jhu.ed/bin/a/h/2011-06-29-john-brennan-remarks-sais.pdf); Hillary Rodham Clinton, "Smart Power Approach to Counterterrorism," speech, John Jay School of Criminal Justice, New York, September 9, 2011 (www.state.gov/secretary/rm/2011/09/172034.htm).

78. Bruce Hoffman, "American Jihad," *National Interest,* no. 107 (May/June 2010): 17—27.

79. Michael E. O'Hanlon and others, *Protecting the American Homeland: One Year On* (Brookings, 2003), pp. 1–11.

80. Secretary Napolitano, "Strength, Security, and Shared Responsibility: Preventing Terrorist Attacks a Decade after 9/11," speech, NYU School of Law and the Brennan Center for Justice, New York, June 7, 2011 (wwwdhs.gov/ynews/speeches/sp_1307479636063.shtm).

81. Michael d'Arcy, "Conclusion," in *Protecting the Homeland 2006/2007,* edited by James B. Steinberg and others (Brookings, 2006), pp. 184–92.

82. ABC News, *This Week,* December 27, 2009; Julie Mianecki, "8 Years on, DHS Weighs Successes, Shortcomings," *Baltimore Sun,* March 2, 2011, p. 10.

83. Benjamin Wittes, *Detention and Denial: The Case for Candor after Guantanamo* (Brookings, 2011).

NOTES TO CHAPTER 4

1. U.S. Department of State, "Secretary Clinton with Vice President Joe Biden Announce Appointment of Special Envoy for Middle East Peace George Mitchell," January 22, 2009 (www.state.gov/secretary/rm/2009a/01/115297.htm).

2. In the spring of 2009, polling showed a plurality of Arabs with a favorable view of Obama while a majority expressed optimism about the prospects for U.S. policy in the Middle East under his leadership. A year later, 61 percent of Arabs polled identified the Arab-Israeli conflict as the issue they are most disappointed about in Obama's foreign policy. Obama's approval rating declined from 40 percent to 20 percent. By 2011 it had declined even further to less than 10 percent. See Shibley Telhami, "Can Obama Please Both Arabs and Israelis?" *Foreign Policy,* August 25, 2010 (www.foreignpolicy.com/articles/2010/08/25/can_obama_please_both_arabs_and_israelis?page=0,0); Jim Lobe, "U.S. Standing Plunges Across the Arab World," *Al Jazeera,* July 14, 2011 (http://english.aljazeera.net/indepth/features/2011/07/2011714104413787827.html).

3. Ryan Lizza, "The Consequentialist," *New Yorker,* May 2, 2011.

4. The expression "leading from behind" came from an unnamed senior White House official, quoted in Ryan Lizza's *New Yorker* article, "The Consequentialist."

5. He declared in Sderot: "The first job of any nation state is to protect its citizens. And so I can assure you that if —I don't even care if I was a politician—if somebody was sending rockets into my house where my two daughters sleep at night, I'm going to do everything in my power to stop that. And I would expect Israelis to do the same thing." See "Obama's Speech in Sderot, Israel," July 23, 2008.

6. Ron Kampeas, "Democrats Launch Major Pro-Obama Pushback among Jews," June 7, 2011 (www.jta.org/news/article/2011/06/07/3088053/democrats-launch-major-pro-obama-pushback-among-jews).

7. "In Cleveland, Obama Speaks on Jewish Issues," *New York Sun,* February 25, 2008.

8. "Transcript: Obama's Speech at AIPAC," NPR, June 4, 2008.

9. Ron Kampeas, "At White House, U.S. Jews Offer Little Resistance to Obama Policy on Settlements," July 13, 2009 (www.jta.org/news/article/2009/07/13/1006510/obama-gets-jewish-support-on-peace-push-questions-about-style).

10. See Andrew J. Shapiro, "The Obama Administration's Approach to US-Israel Cooperation; Preserving Israel's Qualitative Military Edge," keynote speech at the Brookings Institution, July 16, 2010 (www.brookings.edu/~/media/Files/events/2010/0716_us_israel/20100716_us_israel.pdf); Hillary Clinton, "Remarks at the Brookings Institution's Saban Center for Middle East Policy Seventh Annual Forum," December 10, 2010 (www.state.gov/secretary/rm/2010/12/152664.htm); "Remarks by National Security Advisor Thomas E. Donilon," Washington Institute for Near East Policy 2011 Soref Symposium, May 12, 2011 (www.washington institute.org/html/pdf/DonilonRemarks20110512.pdf).

11. It was not until May 2011, in his second address to an AIPAC annual conference, that Obama identified himself with the Jewish narrative: "When I touched my hand against the Western Wall . . . I thought of all the centuries that the children of Israel had longed to return to their ancient homeland." White House, Office of the Press Secretary, "Remarks by the President at the AIPAC Policy Conference 2011," May 22, 2011 (www.whitehouse.gov/the-press-office/2011/05/22/remarks-president-aipac-policy-conference-2011).

12. White House, Office of the Press Secretary, "Remarks by the President on a New Beginning," Cairo University, June 4, 2009 (www.whitehouse.gov/the-press-office/remarks-president-cairo-university-6-04-09). The State Department offered highlights via text message in Urdu, Farsi, Arabic, and English, allowing people to receive the speech in real time and comment on it. The White House website carried it live, and transcripts were available in thirteen languages. The White House also sponsored links to the speech on social networking sites such as MySpace, Twitter, and Facebook, the last of which has 20 million users in Muslim countries alone.

13. "Obama Says Middle East Peace Deal Doable, but Will Be 'Wrenching,'" *CNN Politics,* July 08, 2010 (http://articles.cnn.com/2010-07-08/politics/obama.israel.interview_1_obama-and-netanyahu-peace-agreement-peace-process).

14. U.S. State Department, "Press Availability with Egyptian Foreign Minister Ahmed Ali Aboul Gheit," May 27, 2009 (www.state.gov/secretary/rm/2009a/05/124009.htm).

15. Jimmy Carter had labeled the settlements "illegal," but Ronald Reagan said they were "not illegal" but "ill-advised." George H. W. Bush referred to them as "an obstacle to peace." Bill Clinton and George W. Bush stuck with that language. No previous president had called them "illegitimate."

16. Whatever the Saudi ambassador in Washington might have led the White House to believe, Saudi spokesmen on the eve of the meeting were quite categorical with the media that it was up to Israel, not Saudi Arabia, to make gestures, since Saudi Arabia had already made its concessions in the Arab Peace Initiative and the

new Israeli government did not even accept the two-state solution. See Michael Slackman, "As Obama Begins Trip, Arabs Seek Israeli Gesture," *New York Times. com,* June 3, 2009.

17. The tradition started in the Clinton administration with Yitzhak Rabin, who used a back channel from Eitan Haber, the director of his office, to Martin Indyk at the NSC. Ehud Barak would call Clinton directly. During the Bush administration, Ariel Sharon used Dubby Weisglass, his office director, to communicate with Bush's NSC advisor Condoleezza Rice, and Ehud Olmert used Yoram Turbovich, his office director, to communicate with Elliott Abrams at the NSC.

18. "Palestinians Reject Israeli Offer," Aljazeera and Agencies, November 26, 2009 (http://english.aljazeera.net/news/middleeast/2009/11/2009112665926722643. html_).

19. Already in mid-July 2009, on a tour of the Arab capitals, Mitchell heard from Arab leaders that they would not reward a partial freeze of settlement activity with steps of normalization. For example, after meeting Mitchell in Cairo, Amre Moussa, the head of the Arab League, declared, "There will be no Arab steps before Israel stops its policy of settlement building." And after meeting with Secretary Clinton at the State Department on July 30, Saudi foreign minister Saud al-Faisal declared that incremental steps and confidence building measures would not bring peace. He noted that "Israel hasn't even responded to an American request to halt settlements, which President Obama described as illegitimate." See "Obama Envoy: Arab-Israeli Normalization Will Come," July 27, 2009 (www.ynetnews. com/articles/0,7340,L-3752981,00.html); "Saudi Arabia Rebuffs US on Ties to Israel," July 31, 2009 (www.ynetnews.com/articles/0,7340,L-3755188,00.html).

20. This is underscored in a remarkable exchange between George Mitchell and Palestinian chief negotiator Saeb Erakat in October 2009, which appeared in the leaked Palestine Papers. Mitchell: "I tell you there has never been a president on this issue like this one. You are denying him the opportunity to create the state that you want." Erakat: "How can I convince anyone if he could not even deliver a temporary settlement freeze? It's not up to me to decide your credibility in the Middle East. He has lost it throughout the region." See Al Jazeera Transparency Unit, "Meeting Minutes: Saeb Erekat and George Mitchell," October 21, 2009 (http://transparency.aljazeera.net/document/4899).

21. See President Obama's interview with Joe Klein, "Q&A: Obama on His First Year in Office," *TIME Politics,* January 21, 2010 (www.time.com/time/politics/ article/0,8599,1955072,00.html).

22. The press was told that Clinton demanded that Netanyahu reverse the housing plan, avoid further provocations in Jerusalem during the negotiations, and commit to substantive rather than procedural negotiations in the proximity talks. See Mark Landler, "Netanyahu Takes Hard Line on Jerusalem Housing," *New York Times,* March 22, 2010; Glenn Kessler, "Clinton Rebukes Israel over East Jerusalem Plans, Cites Damage to Bilateral Ties," *Washington Post,* March 13, 2010.

23. The president reportedly went off to eat dinner with his family while Netanyahu conferred with his aides. In reality, Obama ate dinner alone, as the White House later averred. But that fact only made matters worse for Israelis and their supporters in the United States who could not understand why the president would treat a democratically elected ally in that way.

24. White House, Office of the Press Secretary, "Remarks by the President in the Rose Garden after Bilateral Meetings with Prime Minister Netanyahu of Israel, President Mahmoud Abbas of the Palestinian Authority, His Majesty King Abdullah of Jordan and President Hosni Mubarak of Egypt," September 1, 2010 (www.whitehouse.gov/the-press-office/2010/09/01/remarks-president-rose-garden-after-bilateral-meetings).

25. White House, Office of the Press Secretary, "Press Conference by President Obama," September 10, 2010 (www.whitehouse.gov/the-press-office/2010/09/10/press-conference-president-obama).

26. Netanyahu publicly made a similar case, a day after his encounter with Abu Mazen, before a visiting delegation of the Conference of Presidents of Major American Jewish Organizations: "We have to ensure that we have solid security arrangements on the ground. We have to ensure that we can prevent the import of weapons from territories that we would vacate as part of a peace agreement with the Palestinians. And we have to make sure that we can address the potential threats to peace that will inevitably come. . . . These are the attempts . . . to smuggle a massive amount of weapons: rockets, missiles and other weapons from Iran to its proxies in the territories. And then there are other threats: the threats of the reemergence of a potential Eastern front or from an internal change in Palestinian politics. . . . What we need to understand is that a peace agreement by itself does not preserve the peace. We need to understand that the only peace that will hold in the Middle East is a peace that can be defended. I have made clear that in order to defend the peace we need a long-term Israeli presence on the eastern side of a Palestinian state—that is, in the Jordan Valley." "Remarks by Prime Minister Netanyahu to the Conference of Presidents of Major American Jewish Organizations," September 20, 2010 (www.conferenceofpresidents.org/media/user/images/netanyahu%20address_9-20-10.pdf).

27. White House, Office of the Press Secretary, "Remarks by President Obama to the United Nations General Assembly," September 23, 2010 (www.whitehouse.gov/the-press-office/2010/09/23/remarks-president-united-nations-general-assembly).

28. The United States had already committed to supply Israel with one squadron of twenty F35s; the addition of another squadron would ensure Israeli Air Force dominance of the region for another twenty years. For reporting on the original purchase, see Anshel Pfeffer, "Israel to Purchase 20 Lockheed Martin F-35 Fighter Jets," August 15, 2010 (www.haaretz.com/news/diplomacy-defense/israel-to-purchase-20-lockheed-martin-f-35-fighter-jets-1.308177). On the additional twenty, as part of an incentives package for settlement freeze extension, see Barak Ravid and Natasha Mozgovaya, "U.S. offers Israel Warplanes in Return for New Settlement Freeze," November 13, 2010 (www.haaretz.com/news/diplomacy-defense/u-s-offers-israel-warplanes-in-return-for-new-settlement-freeze-1.324496).

29. Klein, "Q&A: Obama on His First Year in Office."

30. See Clinton, "Remarks at the Brookings Institution's Saban Center."

31. The White House did not bother to announce his resignation until five weeks later, on a Friday afternoon to ensure minimum media coverage. See Steven Lee Myers, "Amid Impasse in Peace Negotiations, America's Chief Middle East Envoy Resigns," *New York Times,* May 13, 2011.

32. UN Security Council Draft Resolution S/2011/24, February 18, 2011 (http://daccess-dds-ny.un.org/doc/UNDOC/GEN/N11/239/87/PDF/N1123987.pdf?OpenElement).

33. See, for example, David Ignatius, "Obama Weighs New Peace Plan for the Middle East," *Washington Post*, April 7, 2010; Brent Scowcroft, "Obama Must Broker a New Mideast Peace," *Financial Times*, April 13, 2011; Zbigniew Brzezinski and Stephen Solarz, "To Achieve Mideast Peace, Obama Must Make a Bold Mideast Trip," *Washington Post*, April 1, 2010.

34. Hillary Clinton took the unusual step of announcing that the president would give this speech in remarks to the U.S.-Islamic World Forum. It had taken her personal intervention with Obama to get him finally to decide that he would do so, and she apparently wanted to lock it in before others could raise doubts again. See U.S. State Department, "Gala Dinner Celebrating the U.S.-Islamic World Forum. Remarks: Hillary Rodham Clinton," April 12, 2011 (www.state.gov/secretary/rm/2011/04/160642.htm).

35. White House, Office of the Press Secretary, "Remarks by President Obama on Middle East and North Africa," May 19, 2011 (www.whitehouse.gov/the-press-office/2011/05/19/remarks-president-middle-east-and-north-africa).

36. The Palestinians had long demanded and the Israelis had long resisted the proposition that the negotiations should be based on the 1967 lines, even though all previous substantive Arab-Israeli negotiations had ended up there. From Netanyahu's point of view, however, there was a difference between ending up there and starting there.

37. Netanyahu basically laid out his own parameter: "Israel cannot go back to the 1967 lines—because these lines are indefensible; because they don't take into account certain . . . demographic changes that have taken place over the last 44 years. Remember that, before 1967, Israel was all of nine miles wide. . . . And these were not the boundaries of peace; they were the boundaries of repeated wars. . . . So we can't go back to those indefensible lines, and we're going to have to have a long-term military presence along the Jordan." White House, Office of the Press Secretary, "Remarks by President Obama and Prime Minister Netanyahu after Bilateral Meeting," May 20, 2011 (www.whitehouse.gov/the-press-office/2011/05/20/remarks-president-obama-and-prime-minister-netanyahu-israel-after-bilate).

38. White House, "Remarks by the President at the AIPAC Policy Conference."

39. "Letter from President Bush to Prime Minister Sharon," April 14, 2004 (http://georgewbush-whitehouse.archives.gov/news/releases/2004/04/20040414-3.html).

40. Acting as if he was speaking truth to power, Obama told the heads of state and governments there assembled: "Let us be honest with ourselves: Israel is surrounded by neighbors that have waged repeated wars against it. Israel's citizens have been killed by rockets fired at their houses and suicide bombs on their buses. Israel's children come of age knowing that throughout the region, other children are taught to hate them. Israel, a small country of less than eight million people, looks out at a world where leaders of much larger nations threaten to wipe it off the map. The Jewish people carry the burden of centuries of exile and persecution, and fresh memories of knowing that six million people were killed simply because of who they are. Those are facts. They cannot be denied." See White House, Office of the Press

Secretary, "Remarks by President Obama in Address to the United Nations General Assembly," September 21, 2011 (www.whitehouse.gov/the-press-office/2011/09/21/remarks-president-obama-address-united-nations-general-assembly).

41. United Nations, "Quartet Statement," September 23, 2011 (www.un.org/News/dh/infocus/middle_east/quartet-23sep2011.htm).

42. Sharm el Sheikh Fact-Finding Committee, "Mitchell Report," April 30, 2001 (http://eeas.europa.eu/mepp/docs/mitchell_report_2001_en.pdf).

43. George W. Bush, "Rose Garden Speech on Israel-Palestine Two-State Solution," June 24, 2002 (www.americanrhetoric.com/speeches/gwbushtwostatesolution.htm).

44. Jackson Diehl, "Abbas's Waiting Game on Peace with Israel," *Washington Post,* May 29, 2009.

45. Barak Ravid and Chaim Levinson, "US Says It's Closer to Israeli-Palestinian Talks," *Haaretz,* August 24, 2009 (www.haaretz.com/print-edition/news/u-s-says-it-s-closer-to-israel-palestinian-talks-1.282544).

46. After a meeting in Washington with Secretary Clinton in July 2009, Saudi foreign minister Saud al-Faisal publicly dismissed the idea of any Arab gesture of normalization, declaring, "Temporary security, confidence-building measures will also not bring peace . . . we believe that making conditions right for a settlement is not by making gestures." U.S. State Department, "Remarks with Saudi Arabian Foreign Minister Prince Saud Al-Faisal," July 31, 2009 (www.state.gov/secretary/rm/2009a/july/126829.htm). In September Turki al-Faisal, Saud's brother and a former Saudi ambassador to the United States, elaborated in a *Washington Post* op-ed piece: "For Saudis to take steps toward diplomatic normalization before this land is returned to its rightful owners would undermine international law and turn a blind eye to immorality." He also explicitly rejected the idea of a Sadat-like visit by the Saudi king to Jerusalem, arguing, "Until Israel heeds President Obama's call for the removal of all settlements, the world must be under no illusion that Saudi Arabia will offer what the Israelis most desire—regional recognition. We are willing to embrace the hands of any partner in peace, but only after they have released their grip on Arab lands." Turki al-Faisal, "Land First, Then Peace," *Washington Post,* September 12, 2009.

47. In a *Jerusalem Post*–Smith Research poll taken after Obama's May 2011 AIPAC speech, 600 Israeli Jews were asked whether they saw Obama's administration as more pro-Israel, more pro-Palestinian, or neutral. Just 12 percent of Israeli Jews surveyed said more pro-Israel, while 40 percent said more pro-Palestinian; 34 percent said the administration was neutral, and 13 percent did not express an opinion. This compares with 6 percent who viewed him as pro-Israel after his June 2009 Cairo speech compared to 50 percent who saw him as more pro-Palestinian. See Gil Hoffman, "Poll: 12% of Israeli Jews Consider Obama to be Pro-Israel," *Jerusalem Post,* May 27, 2011.

Obama fared only a little better in a *Haaretz*-Dialog poll, which found that a quarter of the Israeli Jewish public considers him friendly to Israel, while 20 percent called him hostile, and 43 percent described him as "businesslike." However, after his September 2011 UN General Assembly speech in which he identified with Jewish suffering, his standing in Israel rose to 54 percent. Shibley Telhami, "2011 Poll of Jewish and Arab Citizens of Israel," Saban Center, Brookings (www.brookings.edu/reports/2011/1201_israel_poll_telhami.aspx).

NOTES TO CHAPTER 5

1. "Egypt's Unstable Regime," *Washington Post*, January 25, 2011.

2. Secretary of State Condoleezza Rice, remarks, American University in Cairo, June 20, 2005 (www.offnews.info/downloads/Document-458.pdf).

3. Joel Brinkley and David E. Sanger, "Lacking Details, U.S. Is Cautious on Egypt's Plan for Open Vote," *New York Times*, February 27, 2005.

4. White House, *National Security Strategy*, May 2010 (www.whitehouse.gov/sites/default/files/rss_viewer/national_security_strategy.pdf).

5. "Egypt Warns of 'Decisive Measures' Ahead of Protests," *RFI*, January 28, 2011 (www.english.rfi.fr/africa/20110128-egypt-warns-decisive-measures-ahead-further-protests).

6. President Obama, remarks on the situation in Egypt, January 28, 2011 (www.whitehouse.gov/the-press-office/2011/01/28/remarks-president-situation-egypt).

7. Robert Gibbs, press briefing, February 2, 2011. Gibbs would subsequently explain that both Secretary of Defense Gates and Chairman of the Joint Chiefs of Staff Admiral Mullen had spoken to their Egyptian counterparts.

8. Robert Gibbs, press briefing, January 28, 2011.

9. David D. Kilpatrick, "Mubarak's Grip on Power Is Shaken," *New York Times*, January 31, 2011.

10. President Obama, remarks on the situation in Egypt, February 1, 2011 (www.whitehouse.gov/the-press-office/2011/02/01/remarks-president-situation-egypt).

11. Mark Landler, Helene Cooper, and David D. Kirkpatrick, "Mubarak of Egypt Agrees Not to Run Again," *New York Times*, February 1, 2011.

12. President Obama, remarks on the situation in Egypt, February 1, 2011.

13. Obama said, "The passion and the dignity that has been demonstrated by the people of Egypt has been an inspiration to people around the world, including here in the United States, and to all those who believe in the inevitability of human freedom. To the people of Egypt, particularly the young people of Egypt, I want to be clear: We hear your voices."

14. Press Secretary Robert Gibbs, press briefing, February 2, 2011 (www.whitehouse.gov/the-press-office/2011/02/02/press-briefing-press-secretary-robert-gibbs-222011).

15. Mark Landler and Helene Cooper, "Allies Press U.S. to Go Slow on Egypt," *New York Times*, February 8, 2011.

16. Wisner compounded the disconnect between message and policy when he spoke by videoconference to the Munich Security Conference that weekend: "I therefore believe that President Mubarak's continued leadership is critical; it's his opportunity to write his own legacy." See Helene Cooper and Mark Landler, "In U.S. Signals to Egypt, Obama Straddled a Rift," *New York Times*, February 12, 2011; Robert Gibbs, press briefing, February 9, 2011; Ryan Lizza, "The Consequentialist: How the Arab Spring Remade Obama," *New Yorker*, May 20, 2011.

17. For example, on February 8 Suleiman raised doubts in a CNN interview about the readiness of the Egyptian people for democracy, while thugs were let into Tahrir Square to do violent battle with the peaceful demonstrators. Vice President Biden called Suleiman, and the White House then put out a statement reprising the conversation and issuing a list of demands for immediate action that the United States was insisting upon.

18. President Obama, statement on Egypt, February 10, 2011 (www.white house.gov/the-press-office/2011/02/10/statement-president-barack-obama-egypt).

19. President Obama, remarks on Egypt, February 11, 2011 (www.whitehouse.gov/the-press-office/2011/02/11/remarks-president-egypt).

20. President Obama, press conference, February 15, 2011 (www.whitehouse.gov/the-press-office/2011/02/15/press-conference-president).

21. "Obama Urges Bahrain's King to Show Restraint," Associated Press, February 19, 2011.

22. Saudi spare capacity is approximately three to three and a half million barrels a day, about 77 percent of OPEC spare capacity, and that amount is increasing, as OPEC spare capacity is projected to decline (www.theoildrum.com/files/OPEC_June2011_Graph_3.png).

23. Just how slow the king intended to move was evidenced by his October 2011 declaration that Saudi women would be enfranchised in time to vote in the next municipal elections, which are scheduled for 2015!

24. Within days of Mubarak's overthrow, revolts had broken out in Jordan, Yemen, Oman, and Bahrain, all of which border Saudi Arabia. The only neighboring country unaffected was Kuwait, but 40 percent of its people were Shias, who had become highly politicized in the aftermath of Saddam's invasion and the introduction of parliamentary elections as partial recompense for their liberation by the United States.

25. The demands of the demonstrators had been reinforced by the return to Bahrain of Hassan Mushaima, a long-time exiled leader of a banned Shia opposition party. He rejected any dialogue with the royal family.

26. See Elizabeth Bumiller, "Gates Tells Bahrain's King that 'Baby Steps' to Reform Aren't Enough," *New York Times*, March 12, 2011. Gates spoke to reporters after the meeting: "I expressed the view that we had no evidence that suggested that Iran started any of these popular revolutions or demonstrations across the region. But there is clear evidence—as the process is protracted, particularly in Bahrain—that the Iranians are looking for ways to exploit it and create problems."

27. Mark Landler, "Clinton Bluntly Presses Arab Leaders on Reform," *New York Times*, January 13, 2011.

28. Press Secretary Robert Gibbs, statement, March 13, 2011 (www.white house.gov/the-press-office/2011/03/13/statement-press-secretary-violence-yemen-and-bahrain).

29. Secretary of State Hillary Clinton, remarks, with Egyptian foreign minister, March 15, 2011 (www.state.gov/secretary/rm/2011/03/158404.htm).

30. Helene Cooper and Mark Landler, "Interests of Saudi Arabia and Iran Collide, with the U.S. in the Middle," *New York Times*, March 17, 2011.

31. Secretary of State Hillary Clinton, interview with Kim Ghattas, BBC, March 16, 2011 (www.state.gov/secretary/rm/2011/03/158444.htm).

32. In June 2011 the emergency decrees were lifted, and in August leaders of the opposition were released from jail along with other protesters. But the national dialogue has yet to be launched. Jenifer Fenton, "Bahrain Emergency Laws Lifted after Warning against Unrest," CNN, June 1, 2011.

33. President Obama, remarks on the Middle East and North Africa, March 19, 2011 (www.google.com/search?client=safari&rls=en&q=there+will

+be+times+when+our+short-term+interests+don't+align+perfectly+with+our+l
ong-term+vision+for+the+region&ie=UTF-8&oe=UTF-8).

34. Secretary of Defense Robert Gates, media availability, Riyadh, Saudi Arabia,
April 6, 2011 (www.defense.gov/transcripts/transcript.aspx?transcriptid=4806).

35. NSC spokesman Tony Vietor, statement on the national security adviser's
visit to Saudi Arabia and the UAE, April 13, 2011 (www.whitehouse.gov/the-
press-office/2011/04/13/statement-nsc-spokesman-tommy-vietor-national-security-
advisor-s-visit-s).

36. Rachel Donadio, " Italy Says Death Toll in Libya Is Likely over 1,000," *New
York Times,* February 23, 2011.

37. This was typically strange since Abdullah had done so much to persuade Bill
Clinton to take the first steps toward U.S. normalization with Qaddafi. However,
at an Arab League meeting in 2003, Qaddafi had blamed Abdullah for Bush's invasion of Iraq and called him a dwarf. Subsequently, he was implicated in a plot to
assassinate the Saudi regent.

38. President Obama, on the turmoil in Libya, February 23, 2011 (www.white
house.gov/blog/2011/02/23/president-obama-speaks-turmoil-libya-violence-must-stop).

39. Press Secretary Jay Carney, press briefing, February 25, 2011 (www.white
house.gov/the-press-office/2011/02/25/press-briefing-press-secretary-jay-carney-
2252011).

40. President Obama and President Calderon of Mexico, remarks, joint press
conference, March 3, 2011 (www.whitehouse.gov/the-press-office/2011/03/03/
remarks-president-obama-and-president-calder-n-mexico-joint-press-conference).

41. Defense Secretary Robert Gates, speech, West Point, February 25, 2011
(www.defense.gov/speeches/speech.aspx?speechid=1539).

42. Director of National Intelligence James R. Clapper Jr., remarks before the
Senate Armed Services Committee, *Hearing to Receive Testimony on the Current and
Future Worldwide Threats to the National Security of the United States,* March 10,
2011 (http://armed-services.senate.gov/Transcripts/2011/03%20March/11-11%20
-%203-10-11.pdf).

43. Steven Erlanger, "G-8 Ministers Fail to Agree on Libya No-Fly Zone," *New
York Times,* March 15, 2011.

44. Mark Landler and Dan Bilefsky, "As U.N. Backs Military Action in Libya,
U.S. Role Is Unclear," *New York Times,* March 17, 2011.

45. According to press reports, the main proponents of intervention were Susan
Rice and Samantha Powers, an NSC aide who had written a Pulitzer Prize–winning
book on genocide and the need for intervention. Hillary Clinton had been arguing
it both ways until she saw the humanitarian disaster unfolding, when she joined
with Rice and Powers. See Helene Cooper and Stephen Lee Meyers, "Obama Takes
Hard Line with Libya after Shift by Clinton," *New York Times,* March 18, 2011.

46. President Obama and President Funes of El Salvador, remarks, joint press
conference, March 22, 2011 (www.whitehouse.gov/the-press-office/2011/03/22/
remarks-president-obama-and-president-funes-el-salvador-joint-press-conf).

47. President Obama, remarks on the situation in Libya, March 18, 2011 (www.
whitehouse.gov/the-press-office/2011/03/18/remarks-president-situation-libya).

48. Gabriella Schwartz, "McCain: Obama Waited Too Long in Libya," CNN,
March 20, 2011.

49. Lizza, "The Consequentialist," p. 10.

50. For example, U.S. unwillingness to provide NATO combat helicopters delayed the provision of close air support to the rebels for some two months while Britain and France transported their own equipment to the theater.

51. Rod Nordland and Steven Lee Meyers, "Libya Could Become Stalemate, Top U.S. Military Officer Says," *New York Times,* April 22, 2011.

52. Cooper and Meyers, "Obama Takes Hard Line with Libya after Shift by Clinton."

53. President Obama, speech on Libya, March 28, 2011 (www.whitehouse.gov/photos-and-video/video/2011/03/28/president-obama-s-speech-libya#ranscript).

54. President Obama, remarks on the death of Muammar Qaddafi, October 20, 2011 (www.whitehouse.gov/the-press-office/2011/10/20/remarks-president-death-muammar-qaddafi).

55. Jason Ukman, "Libya War Costs for U.S.: $896 Million so Far," *Washington Post,* August 23, 2011.

56. The population of Syria is 74 percent Sunni Muslim, 12 percent Shia and Alawite Muslim, 10 percent Christian, and 3 percent Druze.

57. Henry Kissinger justified his many peacemaking shuttles between Damascus and Jerusalem by arguing that while there could be no regional war without Egypt, there could be no comprehensive peace without Syria. Similarly, Warren Christopher—as Bill Clinton's secretary of state in pursuit of an elusive Israeli-Syrian peace agreement that would have transformed the region—made sixteen trips to Damascus.

58. The partnership provided important economic benefits for Turkey, too, since it opened a neighboring Syrian market that had been closed. In 2008 it also enabled Erdogan to replace Washington as the go-between in indirect Israeli-Syrian negotiations between Assad and Israeli prime minister Ehud Olmert; these were aborted when Hamas provoked a conflict in Gaza just as Obama prepared to assume the presidency.

59. Jay Solomon, "U.S. Deploys Tech Firms to Win Syrian Allies," *Wall Street Journal,* June 15, 2010; George Baghdadi, "Syria Signals US School in Damascus May Reopen," *CBS News,* April 17, 2010.

60. "Interview with Syrian President Bashar al-Assad," *Wall Street Journal,* January 31, 2011.

61. The brutality of the crackdown was symbolized by the fate of Hamzi Ali al-Khateeb, a thirteen-year-old boy who was arrested in a protest near Dara'a at the end of April; a month later his mutilated body was handed back to his parents, who, despite warnings, allowed a video of their son to be posted on YouTube. As one account describes it, "Video posted online shows his battered, purple face. His skin is scrawled with cuts, gashes, deep burns and bullet wounds that probably have injured but not killed. His jaw and kneecaps are shattered, according to an unidentified narrator, and his penis chopped off." Liam Stack, "Video of Tortured Boy's Corpse Deepens Anger in Syria," *New York Times,* May 30, 2011.

62. Ahmadinejad told Fareed Zakaria in an interview on October 23, 2011: "We say that governments must be responsible for the requirements and desires of their own people, the security of the people and their rights. And this is general for Iran, for Libya, for Syria, for Europe, United States, Africa, everywhere. . . . And we are going to make greater efforts to encourage both the government of Syria and the other side, all parties, to reach an understanding." See also Nada Bakri, "Iran Calls on Syria to Recognize Citizens' Demands," *New York Times,* August 27, 2011.

63. Ambassador Robert Ford, interview with Christiane Amanpour of ABC's *This Week,* August 4, 2011.

64. Secretary of State Hillary Clinton, interview with Scott Pelley, *CBS Evening News,* August 22, 2011.

65. The full text of the presidential statement is contained in document S/PRST/2011/16 (http://daccess-dds-ny.un.org/doc/UNDOC/GEN/N11/442/75/PDF/N1144275.pdf?OpenElement).

66. President Obama, remarks on the Middle East and North Africa, May 19, 2011 (www.whitehouse.gov/the-press-office/2011/05/19/remarks-president-middle-east-and-north-africa).

67. President Obama, statement on the situation in Syria, August 18, 2011 (www.whitehouse.gov/the-press-office/2011/08/18/statement-president-obama-situation-syria).

68. Secretary Clinton, remarks on the situation in Syria, August 18, 2011 (www.state.gov/secretary/rm/2011/08/170673.htm).

69. Prime Minister Erdogan told a group of journalists, "[The Syrian opposition] will open an office in Turkey in one week's time. I told [Syrian President Bashar] al-Assad that we would let the Syrian opposition be organized in Turkey. I said that we were a democratic country and could not hamper [them]" (www.hurriyetdailynews.com/n.php?n=syrian-opposition-to-open-office-in-turkey-next-week-2011-09-26). In a sign of the increasing support Ankara is giving to anti-regime dissidents, the highest-ranking officer to defect from the Syrian military admitted he was in southern Turkey. Colonel Riad al-Asaad used the Turkish newspaper *Anatolia* to call on opposition forces inside Syria to close ranks and wait for the regime to collapse (www.guardian.co.uk/world/2011/oct/04/bashar-al-assad-syria).

70. "Cracks in the Army," *The Economist,* October 29, 2011.

71. Deborah Amos, "Russia Delivers Stern Warning to Ally Syria," *NPR News,* October 7, 2011; Sui-Lee Wee, "China Warns May Be Losing Patience with Syria," Reuters, October 11, 2011.

72. Helene Cooper, "For U.S., Risks in Pressing Egypt to Speed Civilian Rule," *New York Times,* November 25, 2011.

73. Under Saudi guidance, in March 2011 the GCC offered $20 billion to the king of Bahrain and the sultan of Oman to buy off their dissenters. In May the GCC offered the kings of Jordan and Morocco membership in this club of Arab monarchs, with the promise of similar subventions.

74. Prince Sultan, the heir to the Saudi throne, passed away in October 2011, while King Abdullah was in the hospital for yet another operation. The ascension of Prince Nayef to the position of crown prince strengthens this resistance since he is deeply conservative and a staunch promoter of the pact with the Wahhabi clerics.

NOTES TO CHAPTER 6

1. "Remarks by President Barack Obama, Prague, Czech Republic," April 5, 2009 (www.whitehouse.gov/the-press-office).

2. "Factbox: U.S., EU, and U.N. Sanctions against Iran," Reuters, January 20, 2011.

3. See Kenneth Pollack, *The Persian Puzzle: The Conflict between Iran and America* (New York: Random House, 2005).

4. See Shibley Telhami, "Arab Opinion Polls, 2010" (www.brookings.edu/~/media/Files/rc/reports/2010/08_arab_opinion_poll_telhami/08_arab_opinion_poll_telhami.pdf).

5. Translation of Ahmadinejad's letter, *Washington Post,* November 6, 2008.

6. Videotape, "Remarks by President Obama in Celebration of Nowruz," March 20, 2009 (www.whitehouse.gov/the_press_office/Videotaped-Remarks-by-The-President-in-Celebration-of-Nowruz/).

7. See Barbara Slavin, "Exclusive: U.S. Contacted Iran's Ayatollah before Elections," *Washington Times,* June 24, 2009.

8. President Obama, statement on Iran, June 20, 2009 (www.whitehouse.gov/the_press_office/Statement-from-the-President-on-Iran/).

9. President Obama, opening remarks on Iran, June 23, 2009 (www.whitehouse.gov/blog/The-Presidents-Opening-Remarks-on-Iran-with-Persian-Translation/).

10. President Obama and Israeli prime minister Netanyahu, remarks (www.whitehouse.gov/the_press_office/Remarks-by-President-Obama-and-Israeli-Prime-Minister-Netanyahu-in-press-availability/).

11. See Kim Zetter, "How Digital Detectives Deciphered Stuxnet, the Most Menacing Malware in History," *Wired,* June 11, 2011 (www.wired.com).

12. The new agreement capped the number of deployed long-range nuclear warheads on each side at 1,550, down from 2,200. It reduced the number of deployed nuclear-capable submarines, long-range missiles, and heavy bombers to a maximum of 700, with 100 more in reserve (the United States currently has about 850 deployed; Russia has an estimated 565). Finally, it would reestablish a system in which each of the nuclear giants monitors the other's arsenal. See Mary Beth Sheridan, "What Is New START," *Washington Post,* December 21, 2010.

13. See David E. Sanger, James Glanz, and Jo Becker, "Around the World, Distress over Iran," *New York Times,* November 28, 2010.

14. Subsequently, international inspectors who were granted access to the underground site in October 2009 found that the plant was about a year away from operation and that it was designed for 3,000 centrifuges—not enough to produce the large amounts of fuel needed for commercial reactors but sufficient for the stealthy production of highly enriched bomb fuel. By comparison, the Natanz plant, which is ostensibly for producing reactor fuel, is designed for 54,000 centrifuges. David E. Sanger and William J. Broad, "U.S. Sees an Opportunity to Press Iran on Nuclear Fuel," *New York Times,* January 3, 2010.

15. Lally Weymouth, interview with Iranian president Mahmoud Ahmadinejad, *Washington Post,* September 23, 2009.

16. As Hosein Naghavi-Hosseini, a member of Iran's Majlis Security Council, told Iran's state-run press, "The countries which were proposed to receive our 5 percent uranium were not countries that the Islamic republic trusts to trade with, because in the past these countries have not held up their side of trade agreements." Quoted in David E. Sanger, "Iran Said to Ignore Effort to Salvage Nuclear Deal," *New York Times,* November 9, 2009.

17. As his national security adviser, General James Jones, told the Washington Institute in April 2010, "President Obama has been very clear, and I want to repeat

it here: the United States is determined to prevent Iran from developing nuclear weapons." This prompted an intense debate within the administration about whether Iran's acquisition of a "breakout" capability would constitute "acquiring" nuclear weapons. Admiral Mullen issued guidance in December 2009 to prepare for military contingencies, and Secretary Gates wrote the president a memo expressing concern that the administration had not developed a strategy to back up the president's words. David E. Sanger, "Gates Says U.S. Lacks a Policy to Thwart Iran," *New York Times*, April 17, 2010.

18. As Obama noted in releasing the paper, "Those nations that fail to meet their obligations will therefore find themselves more isolated, and will recognize that the pursuit of nuclear weapons will not make them more secure." See statement by President Obama on the release of the Nuclear Posture Review, April 6, 2010 (www.whitehouse.gov/the-press-office/statement-president-barack-obama-release-nuclear-posture-review).

19. Israel had been particularly concerned about the S-300 sale; if Iran were able to protect its nuclear facilities with these systems, it would be much harder to strike them. Netanyahu reportedly told Putin and Medvedev that Israel might have to act militarily before the systems were deployed.

20. In rejecting the TRR offer in October 2009, the Iranian government had complained to the IAEA that the deal required Iran to ship out its stockpile of low-enriched uranium immediately but that it would have to wait a year for the TRR fuel rods to be delivered. This, Tehran argued, would give the United States a large window to renege on the deal after Iran had fulfilled its part of the bargain. Accordingly, in November 2009 the Obama administration responded by suggesting that the stockpile of Iranian LEU be shipped to Turkey and held in escrow there until the fuel for the Tehran reactor was delivered. Iran failed to respond directly to this offer, and Obama included it in his letter to Lula, outlining U.S. requirements as a way of illustrating American good intentions. Obama's letter to President Lula (www.politica externa.com/11023/brazil-iran-turkey-nuclear-negotiations-obamas-letter-to-lula).

21. For the text of the Brazil-Turkey-Iran "Tehran Declaration," see www.guardian.co.uk/world/julian-borger-global-security-blog/2010/may/17/iran-brazil-turkey-nuclear.

22. David E. Sanger and Mark Landler, "Major Powers Have Deal on Sanctions for Iran," *New York Times*, May 19, 2010.

23. The companies include Royal Dutch Shell, Total, ENI, Statoil, Repsol, Lukoil, Kia, Toyota, Daimler, Siemens, and foreign subsidiaries of GE, Honeywell, and Caterpillar.

24. In its February 2011 report, the IAEA lists seven outstanding questions about work that Iran had apparently conducted on nuclear warhead design. In its May 2011 report, the IAEA notes evidence that Iran had been working on detonators to trigger a nuclear explosion. It also notes that the pace of Iran's enrichment at Natanz had surpassed its pre-Stuxnet tempo. See David E. Sanger and William J. Broad, "Watchdog Finds Evidence that Iran Worked on Nuclear Triggers," *New York Times*, May 24, 2011.

25. For example, in October 2010 the United States and the EU reached agreement on a new offer to Iran that would require it to ship out 2,000 kilograms of its enriched uranium stockpile and halt all production of nuclear fuel to 20 percent

enrichment. See David E. Sanger, "Obama Set to Offer Stricter Nuclear Deal to Iran," *New York Times,* October 27, 2010.

26. Steven Erlanger, "Citing Options, Iran Rejects Uranium Deal, Diplomat Says," *New York Times,* January 24, 2011.

27. Mark Landler, "U.S. Says Sanctions Hurt Iran Nuclear Program," *New York Times,* January 10, 2011.

28. Isabel Kershner, "Israeli Ex-Spy Predicts Delay for Iran's Nuclear Ambitions," *New York Times,* January 7, 2011.

29. For example, Ayatollah Khamenei claimed, "Today's events in North of Africa, Egypt, Tunisia and certain other countries have . . . special meaning for the Iranian nation. This is the same as 'Islamic Awakening,' which is the result of the victory of the big revolution of the Iranian nation. . . . Today, the whole world admits Iran's influence and constantly speaks of Iran's presence in different arenas." Ayatollah Khamenei, Friday prayer at Tehran University, Office of the Supreme Leader, February 4, 2011 (www.leader.ir/langs/en/index.php?p=contentShow&id=7774).

30. The November 2011 IAEA report includes the following details about Iran's efforts to develop a nuclear explosive device: efforts to procure nuclear-related and dual use equipment and materials by military-related individuals and entities; efforts to develop undeclared pathways for the production of nuclear material; acquisition of nuclear weapons development information and documentation from a clandestine nuclear supply network; and work on the development of an indigenous design of a nuclear weapon, including the testing of components. The IAEA concludes, "The information indicates that prior to the end of 2003 the above activities took place under a structured programme. There are also indications that some activities relevant to the development of a nuclear explosive device continued after 2003, and that some may still be ongoing." See Report of the Director General, *Implementation of the NPT Safeguards Agreement and Relevant Provisions of Security Council Resolutions in the Islamic Republic of Iran,* November 8, 2011 (www.iaea.org/Publications/Documents/Board/2011/gov2011-65/pdf).

31. The breakout threshold is the point at which Iran has assembled the capabilities to build nuclear weapons, including a stockpile of highly enriched, weapons-grade uranium, such that it could throw out the IAEA inspectors and complete the process within a few months without being observed or prevented from doing so.

32. See Rick Gladstone, "Iran Admits Sanctions Are Inflicting Damage," *New York Times,* December 20, 2011; Rick Gladstone, "As Further Sanctions Loom, Plunge in Currency's Value Unsettles Iran," *New York Times,* December 20, 2011.

33. Jonathan Pollack, *No Exit: North Korea, Nuclear Weapons, and International Security* (London: Routledge, 2011).

34. U.S. Central Intelligence Agency, "CIA World Factbook: North Korea" (www.cia.gov/library/publications/the-world-factbook/geos/kn.html).

35. Anthony H. Cordesman, "The Korean Military Balance: Comparative Korean Forces and the Forces of Key Neighboring States," report (Washington: Center for Strategic and International Studies, May 2011), pp. 107–35 (http://csis.org/files/publication/110506_KoreaMilitaryBalanceMainRpt.pdf).

36. Glenn Kessler and Anthony Faiola, "In Pyongyang, Raising the Ante," *Washington Post,* February 11, 2005; Richard Bush, "North Korea's Nuclear Bargain," *Daily Beast,* May 26, 2009 (www.brookings.edu/opinions/2009/0526);

Kenneth Lieberthal, "The Folly of Forcing Regime Change," *Financial Times* (London), March 11, 2005.

37. Cordesman, "The Korean Military Balance."

38. Pollack, *No Exit*, provides ample evidence of this.

39. Andrew Ward, "N Korea Quits Nuclear Non-Proliferation Treaty," *Financial Times*, April 10, 2003.

40. "Khan 'Gave N Korea Centrifuges,'" BBC, August 24, 2005; Sharon A. Squassoni, "Weapons of Mass Destruction: Trade between North Korea and Pakistan," Congressional Research Service Report for Congress, March 11, 2004 (http://fpc.state.gov/documents/organization/30781.pdf).

41. Robin Wright and Joby Warrick, "Purchases Linked N. Korea to Syria," *Washington Post*, May 11, 2008.

42. David E. Sanger, "North Koreans Unveil New Plant for Nuclear Use," *New York Times*, November 20, 2010. Sanger estimates that North Korea has produced eight to twelve nuclear weapons. Siegfried Hecker estimates the plutonium arsenal at between four and eight weapons. Siegfried S. Hecker, "What I Found in North Korea," *Foreign Affairs*, December 9, 2010.

43. John Pomfret, "U.S. Alerts Asian Capitals to Possible North Korean Uranium Enrichment Program," *Washington Post*, November 21, 2010.

44. Chico Harlan, "U.N. Report Suggests N. Korea Has Secret Nuclear Sites," *Washington Post*, February 1, 2011.

45. Mark Fitzpatrick, ed., "North Korean Security Challenges: A Net Assessment," *Strategic Dossier* (Washington: International Institute for Strategic Studies, 2011); Kevin Sullivan and Mary Jordan, "Famine, Nuclear Threat Raise Stakes in Debate over North Korea," *Washington Post*, March 13, 1999; Joby Warrick, "On North Korean Freighter, a Hidden Missile Factory," *Washington Post*, August 14, 2003.

46. Bradley Roberts, deputy assistant secretary of defense for nuclear and missile defense policy, testimony before the Senate Armed Services Committee, April 13, 2011 (www.dod.gov/dodge/olc/docs/testRoberts04132011.pdf).

47. Blaine Harden, "Japan Prepares to Shoot down North Korean Missile in Case of Accident," *Washington Post*, March 28, 2009.

48. "Pyongyang's Cash Flow Problem," *The Economist*, January 11, 2007.

49. "Japanese Anger over North Korea Kidnaps," BBC, November 18, 2002; Mark E. Manyin, "Japan-North Korea Relations: Selected Issues," Congressional Research Service Report for Congress, November 26, 2003 (http://fpc.sgtate.gov/documents/organization/27531.pdf).

50. "Japan and North Korea: Not Yet Friends," *The Economist*, September 19, 2002.

51. This is based on Japan's having paid South Korea more than half a billion dollars in reparations when the two normalized relations in 1965. North Korea has demanded $10 billion in reparations for the Japanese occupation during 1910–45 (http://en.wikipedia.org/wiki/Japan%E2%80%93Korea_disputes#Japanese_compensation_to_Korea_for_colonial_rule). Korea was occupied and declared a Japanese protectorate in the 1905 Eulsa Treaty; it was officially annexed in 1910 through the annexation treaty (http://en.wikipedia.org/wiki/Korea_under_Japanese_rule).

52. The presidents were Kim Dae-jong and Roh Moo-hyun.

53. Sun Key-young, *South Korean Engagement Policies and North Korea: Identities, Norms and the Sunshine Policy* (New York: Routledge, 2006).

54. Aidan Foster-Carter, "Sunset for Korean Sunshine Policy?" BBC, March 28, 2008.

55. Charles Keyes, Laurie Ure, and Adam Levine, "China Key to Restraining North Korea, U.S. Officials Say," CNN, November 24, 2010.

56. Christopher P. Twomey, "China Policy towards North Korea and Its Implications for the United States: Balancing Competing Concerns," *Strategic Insights* 5, no. 7 (2006); Dick K. Nanto, Mark E. Manyin, and Kerry Dumbaugh, "China–North Korea Relations," Congressional Research Service Report for Congress, January 22, 2010 (http://fpc.state.gov/documents/organization/138774.pdf).

57. Twomey, "China Policy towards North Korea"; Nanto, Manyin, and Dumbaugh, "China–North Korea Relations"; Scott Shane and Andrew W. Lehren, "Leaked Cables Offer Raw Look at U.S. Diplomacy," *New York Times,* November 28, 2010.

58. Chris Buckley, "China Seen Nudging North Korea's Kim on Economic Reform," Reuters, May 26, 2011; Nanto, Manyin, and Dumbaugh, "China–North Korea Relations."

59. "Kim's Trip to China to Help N. Korea Learn Development Experience," Yonhap News Agency, May 22, 2011; Buckley, "China Seen Nudging North Korea's Kim on Economic Reform."

60. Pollack, *No Exit.*

61. Kenneth Lieberthal and Mikkal Herberg, *China's Search for Energy Security and Implications for US Policy* (Washington: National Bureau of Asian Research, 2006).

62. Glenn Kessler and Anthony Faiola, "In Pyongyang, Raising the Ante," *Washington Post,* February 11, 2005. In his second term, President Bush moved toward compromise to put North Korea on a path toward complete and irreversible destruction of its nuclear weapons capabilities: "Ending North Korea's Nuclear Program," *New York Times,* April 20, 2008; Tony Karon, "If North Korea, Why Not Iran," *Time,* October 4, 2007.

63. Kenneth Lieberthal, "The Folly of Forcing Regime Change," *Financial Times* (London), March 11, 2005.

64. Analogous concerns trouble analysts who focus on what regime collapse in Pakistan might herald. See Stephen P. Cohen, "Pakistan's Road to Disintegration," interview, Council on Foreign Relations, January 6, 2011 (www.cfr.org/pakistan/pakistans-road-disintegration/p23744); Anthony H. Cordesman and Varun Vira, "Pakistan: Violence vs. Stability," Center for Strategic and International Studies, June 2011 (http://csis.org/files/publication/110607_Stabilizing_Pakistan.pdf).

65. President Obama and President Lee Myung-bak of the Republic of Korea, remarks, joint press availability, White House, June 16, 2009 (www.whitehouse.gov/the-press-office/Remarks-by-President-Obama-and-President-Lee-of-the-Republic-of-Korea-in-Joint-Press-Availability/); Scott Snyder, "The Foreign Policy of the Obama Administration and Northeast Asia," remarks to the Tenth World Korean Forum, August 18, 2009 (http://asiafoundation.org/resources/pdfs/Snyder ObamaNEA090630.pdf).

66. President Obama and President Lee Myung-bak, remarks, June 16, 2009. The Obama administration's conditions for U.S. agreement to convening the

Six-Party Talks include having North Korea accept nuclear and missile test moratoriums, respect the 2005 joint statement and armistice, and agree to an internationally monitored freeze of its uranium enrichment program.

67. David Morgan and Jon Herskovitz, "U.S. Says North Korea Missile Launch Could Come April 4," Reuters, April 2, 2009.

68. Evan Ramstad, "Pyongyang Seeks Peace Pact ahead of Meeting," *Wall Street Journal,* July 28, 2011.

69. Some reports suggest that the second stage of the missile may have also failed. See William J. Broad, "Trackers Deem North Korea's Missile Flight a Failure," *New York Times,* April 5, 2009.

70. "Statement by the President of the Security Council," United Nations Security Council, April 13, 2009 (http://daccess-dds-ny.un.org/doc/UNDOC/GEN/N09/301/03/PDF/N0930103.pdf?OpenElement).

71. Jonathan D. Pollack, "Kim Jong-Il's Clenched Fist," *Washington Quarterly,* October 2009; Choe Sang-hun, "North Korea Claims to Conduct 2nd Nuclear Test," *New York Times,* May 24, 2009.

72. Michael D. Shear and Debbi Wilgoren, "Obama Discussed N. Korean Missile at G-20," *Washington Post,* April 2, 2009; President Obama and President Lee Myung-bak of the Republic of Korea, remarks, June 16, 2009.

73. "Deputy Secretary Steinberg: Travel to Asia, May 28–June 5, 2009," U.S. Department of State, June 5, 2009 (www.state.gov/s/d/travel/2009/124014.htm).

74. UNSC Resolution 1874, June 12, 2009.

75. Colum Lynch, "U.N. Security Council Sanctions North Korea Firms, Individuals," *Washington Post,* July 17, 2009; "Security Council, Acting Unanimously, Condemns in Strongest Terms People's Republic of Korea Nuclear Test, Toughens Sanctions" (www.un.org/News/Press/docs/2009/sc9679.doc.htm).

76. Kenneth Lieberthal, "The American Pivot to Asia: Why President Obama's Turn to the East Is Easier Said than Done," FP.com (December 21, 2011) (www.foreignpolicy.com/articles/2011/12/21/the_american_pivot_to_asia).

77. For details see Lee Dongmin, "North Korea's Power Transition: Rising Instability or Regime Resilience?" Commentary 188/2011 (Singapore: RSIS, December 2011) (rsis_publications@getresponse.com).

78. The Obama administration has no way to constrain what Republican candidates or any members of Congress have to say on the issue, but it should take care not to give gratuitous offense itself.

79. Pollack, *No Exit.*

80. During late 2011, Kim Jong-il sought in discussions with the United States to find a path back to the Six-Party Talks. At the time of this writing, it is too soon to tell whether Kim Jong-un and the key figures in the successor regime will soon pick up on this effort.

NOTES TO CHAPTER 7

1. Barack Obama, *The Audacity of Hope* (New York: Crown Publishers, 2006), pp. 271–323, especially pp. 314–15.

2. U.S. Department of State and U.S. Agency for International Development, *Leading through Civilian Power: The First Quadrennial Diplomacy and*

Development Review (2010), pp. 11–12 (www.state.gov/documents/organization/153108.pdf [June 8, 2011]).

3. White House, *National Security Strategy,* May 2010 (www.whitehouse.gov/sites/default/files/rss_viewer/national_security_strategy.pdf [June 8, 2011]).

4. See Michael A. Levi, "The Canadian Oil Sands: Energy Security versus Climate Change," Council Special Report No. 47 (New York: Council on Foreign Relations, May 2009), pp. 23–25.

5. Michael Greenstone and Adam Looney, "A Strategy for America's Energy Future: Illuminating Energy's Full Costs," Hamilton Project Strategy Paper (Brookings, May 2011), pp. 10–18 (www.brookings.edu/~/media/files/re/papers/2011/05_energy_greenstone_looney/05_energy-Greenstone_looney.pdf [May 10, 2011].

6. The burning of coal emits on average 0.99 metric tons of carbon dioxide per megawatt hour of electricity produced, oil emits 0.95 tons, and natural gas produces 0.44 tons. See Joseph E. Aldy, "Promoting Clean Energy in the American Power Sector," Hamilton Project Discussion Paper 2011-04 (Brookings, May 2011), p. 8 (www.brookings.edu/~/media/files/re/papers/2011/05_clean_energy_aldy/05_clean_energy_aldy_paper.pdf [May 20, 2011]).

7. To understand why oil still powers almost all vehicles, consider that a battery for an electric car, such as plug-in hybrid, costs about $8,000 today. See David Sandalow, *Freedom from Oil: How the Next President Can End the United States' Oil Addiction* (New York: McGraw Hill, 2008), p. 69. It is also important to note that new car sales in a year only constitute 7 percent of the vehicles on the road in the United States, so it would take many years to replace the current fleet even if electric vehicles became the nation's cars of choice. Sandalow, *Freedom from Oil,* p. 18.

8. See, for example, John S. Duffield, *Over a Barrel: The Costs of U.S. Foreign Oil Dependence* (Stanford University Press, 2008), pp. 16–55.

9. See U.S. Energy Information Administration, "China Country Page," 2011 (http://205.254.235.24/countries/cab.cfm?fips=CH [September 7, 2011]); "India Country Page," 2010 (http://205.254.135.24/countries/cab.cfm?fips=IN); "South Korea Country Page," 2010 (www.eia.gov/cabs/South_Korea/Full.html); "Japan Country Page," 2011(http://205.254.135.24/countries/cab.cfm?fips=JA).

10. This estimate is highly imprecise because there are few U.S. forces devoted exclusively and permanently to the Persian Gulf (or any other specific region of the world, for that matter).

11. See, for example, William W. Kaufmann, *Assessing the Base Force: How Much Is Too Much?* (Brookings, 1992), p. 3; Michael E. O'Hanlon, *The Science of War* (Princeton University Press, 2009), pp. 18–52.

12. Sandalow, *Freedom from Oil,* pp. 14–16.

13. U.S. Energy Information Administration, *International Energy Outlook 2011,* September 2011, p. 159 (www.eia.gov/forecasts/ieo/pdf/0484(2011).pdf).

14. For example, many regions, such as South America, saw increases in production led by hydroelectric and coal production. Others have seen natural gas and renewable energy increases outpace that of oil. U.S. Energy Information Administration, "World Energy Overview: 1996–2006" (www.eia.gov/iea/overview.html).

15. See "The Second Presidential Debate," *New York Times,* October 7, 2008.

16. Some propose even more restrictive goals—specifically, no more than a 1.5 degree Celsius increase, as argued by Christiana Figueres, executive secretary for the

UN Framework Convention on Climate Change. See "Climate Official Urges Limit on Warming," *Washington Post*, June 4, 2011, p. A5.

17. U.S. Energy Information Administration, *International Energy Outlook 2010*, July 2010, p. 1 (www.eia.doe.gov/oiaf/ieo/index.html [May 23, 2011]).

18. William Antholis and Strobe Talbott, *Fast Forward: Ethics and Politics in the Age of Global Warming* (Brookings, 2010), pp. 2–9.

19. See Brian Vastag and Ed O'Keefe, "A Storm Season on a Deadly Path," *Washington Post*, May 24, 2011, p. A1. Note that melting of ice at the North Pole would not increase sea levels because that ice already floats in the water and displaces a volume equivalent to the volume of water that would be released if the ice melted. The Antarctic ice is on land, but temperatures there are much farther below freezing; therefore catastrophic melting of Antarctic ice is unlikely to occur in the foreseeable future.

20. Antholis and Talbott, *Fast Forward*, p. 48.

21. Kenneth Lieberthal, "Challenges and Opportunities for U.S.-China Cooperation on Climate Change," testimony before the Senate Foreign Relations Committee, Washington, June 4, 2009 (www.brookings.edu/testimony/2009/0604_china_lieberthal.aspx [September 6, 2011]). China showed some flexibility on this issue for the first time at the 17th Conference of Parties that met in Durban, South Africa, in November-December 2011.

22. Jennifer Morgan, "Reflections from Copenhagen: The Accord and the Way Forward," December 29, 2009 (www.wri.org/stories/2009/12/reflections-copenhagen-accord-and-way-forward [May 4, 2011]).

23. Antholis and Talbott, *Fast Forward*, pp. 87–88.

24. Kenneth Lieberthal and David Sandalow, "Overcoming Obstacles to U.S.-China Cooperation on Climate Change," John L. Thornton China Center Monograph Series no. 1 (Brookings, January 2009), p. 28.

25. Antholis and Talbott, *Fast Forward*, pp. 29–45.

26. Ryan Lizza, "As the World Burns," *The New Yorker*, October 11, 2010.

27. John M. Broder, "'Cap and Trade' Loses Its Standing as Energy Policy of Choice," *New York Times*, March 25, 2011.

28. For example, FedEx presently operates an 81,000 square foot solar power facility providing nearly 1 megawatt of power (during a sunny day) at Oakland's airport. See U.S. Department of Energy, Office of Energy Efficiency and Renewable Energy, "Fedex Installs 904-Kilowatt Solar Power System," August 17, 2005 (www1.eere.energy.gov/solar/news_detail.html?news_id=9288 [May 25, 2011]). Today the United States has a peak electricity-generating capacity of about 1,000 gigawatts (see Aldy, "Promoting Clean Energy in the American Power Sector," p. 9). Assuming a future electricity need of roughly 1,000 gigawatts—more than one million times as much as FedEx produces in Oakland—implies a need for 3,000 square miles of generating surface. Assuming roughly 20 percent solar cell conversion efficiency, and allowing for transmission and storage inefficiencies as well, implies roughly 20,000 to 30,000 square miles of total land requirement in sunny areas. The total area of the United States is about 3.5 million square miles, so this would require just under 1 percent of total land area. As a reference point, the federal government owns about 30 percent of all U.S. land in the form of parks, forests, wildlife refuges, Native American reservations, and military bases, as well

as other assets. Similar theoretical potential exists with wind power. For example, in principle, wind power from just Kansas, North Dakota, and Texas alone could provide all the electricity the United States currently uses, and the overall national potential is ten times current total national electricity production from all energy sources. Biomass offers further big opportunities. There is debate about whether biomass might satisfy 5 percent or 50 percent of future global energy demands, or something in between, and thus about whether it might be able, in principle, to replace a small fraction of fossil fuel use or more than half of it. Even for critics of corn ethanol who worry about how it contributes to growth in global food prices, a huge untapped potential exists for biomass through use of other plant matter and therefore other areas than existing fertile farmland.

For data on wind power, see Cristina L. Archer and Mark Z. Jacobson, "Evaluation of Global Wind Power," *Journal of Geophysical Research* 110 (2005) (www.stanford.edu/group/efmh/winds/global_winds.html [May 25, 2011]); Worldwatch Institute and Center for American Progress, "American Energy: The Renewable Path to Energy Security," September 2006, p. 26 (http://images1.americanprogress.org/il80web20037/americanenergynow/AmericanEnergy.pdf [May 26, 2011]); and U.S. Department of Energy, National Renewable Energy Laboratory, "Estimates of Windy Land Area and Wind Energy Potential, by State," February 4, 2010 (www.windpoweringamerica.gov/docs/wind_potential_80m_30percent.xls [May 15, 2011]). For data on biomass, see Christopher B. Field, J. Elliott Campbell, and David B. Lobell, "Biomass Energy: The Scale of the Potential Resource," *Trends in Ecology and Evolution* 23, no. 2 (2007), pp. 65–72 (www.cas.muohio.edu/~stevenmh/Field%20et%20al%202008.pdf [May 15, 2011]); Svetlana Ladanai and Johan Vinterback, "Global Potential of Sustainable Biomass for Energy," Report 13 (Swedish University of Agricultural Sciences, 2009) (www.worldbioenergy.org/system/files/file/WBA_PP-1_100122final10.pdf [May 10, 2011]); and Lester R. Brown, "The New Geopolitics of Food," *Foreign Policy* (May-June 2011), p. 57.

29. Greenstone and Looney, "Strategy for America's Energy Future," p. 18.

30. See White House, Office of the Press Secretary, "Clean Air: An Investment in Health, the Environment, and the Economy," September 2, 2011(www.whitehouse.gov/the-press-office/2011/09/02/zichal-blog-post-cleaner-air-and-stronger-economy-record-success [September 7, 2011]).

31. John M. Deutch, "An Energy Technology Corporation Will Improve the Federal Government's Efforts to Accelerate Energy Innovation," Hamilton Project Discussion Paper 2011-05 (Brookings, May 2011), pp. 9-10 (www.brookings.edu/~/media/files/re/papers/2011/05_energy_corporation_deutch/05_energy_corporation_deutch_paper.pdf [May 10, 2011]).

32. Stephen M. Goldberg and Robert Rosner, *Nuclear Reactors: Generation to Generation* (Cambridge, Mass.: American Academy of Arts and Sciences, 2011), p. 22.

33. See Stephen Thomas, "The Credit Crunch and Nuclear Power," in *Nuclear Power's Global Expansion: Weighing Its Costs and Risks,* edited by Henry Sokolski (Carlisle, Pa.: U.S. Army War College, Strategic Studies Institute, 2010), pp. 125–48.

34. For a summary of such ideas, see, for example, Michael A. Levi and Michael E. O'Hanlon, *The Future of Arms Control* (Brookings, 2005), pp. 58–63.

35. Ellen Tauscher, "Addressing the Nuclear Fuel Cycle: Internationalizing Enrichment Services and Solving the Problem of Spent-Fuel Storage," in *Multinational Approaches to the Nuclear Fuel Cycle,* edited by Charles McCombie and others (Cambridge, Mass.: American Academy of Arts and Sciences, 2010), pp. 36–39; Gregory L. Schulte, "Strengthening the IAEA: How the Nuclear Watchdog Can Regain Its Bark," *Strategic Forum,* no. 253 (March 2010) (www.ndu.edu/inss/docuploaded/sf%20253_web.pdf).

36. Sharon Squassoni, "Mapping Nuclear Power's Future Spread," in *Nuclear Power's Global Expansion: Weighing Its Costs and Risks,* edited by Sokolski, p. 72. See also Fred McGoldrick, "The Road Ahead for Export Controls: Challenges for the Nuclear Suppliers Group," *Arms Control Today* 41, no. 1 (2011): 30–36; Daniel Horner, "India, U.S. Agree on Terms for Reprocessing," *Arms Control Today* 40, no. 4 (2010): 60–62.

37. This initiative was announced at the spring 2010 Washington summit that included forty-seven nations. See Friends Committee on National Legislation, "Success!: Nine Percent Increase in Nuclear Nonproliferation Funding," April 12, 2011 (http://fcnl.org/issues/nuclear/nine_percent_increase_in_nuclear_nonproliferation_funding/ [May 20, 2011]). The Washington summit has led to a number of useful nonproliferation steps, such as Chile sending all of its highly enriched uranium to the United States, Kazakhstan securing enough fissile materials to make several hundred warheads, and Russia ceasing production of plutonium. See Robert Golan-Vilella, Michelle Marchesano, and Sarah Williams, "The 2010 Nuclear Security Summit: A Status Update" (Washington: Arms Control Association, April 2011), p. 27 (www.armscontrol.org/system/files/Status_Report_April_11_2011_WEB.pdf [May 10, 2011]).

38. See, for example, "Pursuing the Prague Agenda: An Interview with White House Coordinator Gary Samore," *Arms Control Today* 41, no. 4 (2011): 8–14.

39. Doing more to encourage green energy with the stimulus bill, beyond what he did undertake, might not have been the best approach as it would have risked discrediting clean energy, given the unfavorable reaction to that spending package by many.

40. For a discussion of how the Environmental Protection Agency might use regulatory requirements to improve some particularly inefficient power plants, see Dallas Burtraw and others, "Opportunities for Flexibility and Cost Savings within EPA's Greenhouse Gas Rules," workshop summary (Washington: Resources for the Future, July 2011) (www.rff.org/RFF/Documents/RFF-Burtraw.etal_workshop%20summary.pdf [September 7, 2011]).

41. See Gareth Evans, *The Responsibility to Protect: Ending Mass Atrocity Crimes Once and For All* (Brookings, 2008). See also Anthony Lake, David Ochmanek, and Scott Vesel, "Richard Ullman and His Work: An Appreciation," in *The Real and the Ideal,* edited by Anthony Lake and David Ochmanek (New York: Rowman and Littlefield, 2001), pp. 1–23; Seyom Brown, *Higher Realism: A New Foreign Policy for the United States* (Boulder, Colo.: Paradigm Publishers, 2009).

42. See, for example, John D. Steinbruner, *Principles of Global Security* (Brookings, 2000); Bruce Jones, Carlos Pascual, and Stephen John Stedman, *Power and Responsibility: Building International Order in an Era of Transnational Threats*

(Brookings, 2009); Lael Brainard, ed., *Security by Other Means: Foreign Assistance, Global Poverty, and American Leadership* (Brookings, 2007).

43. Center on International Cooperation, New York University, *Annual Review of Global Peace Operations 2010* (Boulder, Colo.: Lynne Rienner Publishers, 2010), p. 2.

44. See Condoleezza Rice, "Promoting the National Interest," *Foreign Affairs,* January-February 2000, p. 53.

45. White House, *National Security Strategy;* U.S. Department of State and U.S. Agency for International Development, *Leading through Civilian Power.*

46. Barack Obama, "Remarks to the Chicago Council on Global Affairs," April 23, 2007 (https://my.barackobama.com/page/content/fpccga/).

47. See, for example, M. Ayhan Kose and Eswar S. Prasad, *Emerging Markets: Resilience and Growth amid Global Turmoil* (Brookings, 2010), pp. 29–33.

48. See, for example, Curt Tarnoff and Marian Leonardo Lawson, "Foreign Aid: An Introduction to U.S. Programs and Policy," Congressional Research Service Report for Congress, February 10, 2011, pp. 5, 14, 15, 18, 30–31 (www.fas.org/sgp/crs/row/R40213.pdf [May 31, 2011]); Stimson Center, "FY 2011 State and Foreign Assistance Budget," May 2011 (www.stimson.org/images/uploads/FY2011_State_and_Foreign_Assistance_Budget.pdf [May 31, 2011]).

49. Eckhard Deutscher, *Development Cooperation Report 2010* (Paris: Organization for Economic Co-operation and Development, 2010), pp. 172–88 (www.oecd-library.org/development/development_co-operation_report_2010_dcr_2010_en [May 26, 2011]).

50. See Joao Augusto de Castro Neves and Matias Spektor, "Obama and Brazil," in *Shifting the Balance: Obama and the Americas,* rev. ed., edited by Abraham F. Lowenthal, Theodore J. Piccone, and Laurence Whitehead (Brookings, 2011), pp. 43–54; Michael Shifter, "The United States and Colombia: Recalibrating the Relationship," in *Shifting the Balance,* edited by Lowenthal, Piccone, and Whitehead, pp. 55–68.

51. See, for example, Carlos Heredia and Andres Rozental, "Mexico and the United States: The Search for a Strategic Vision," in *Shifting the Balance,* edited by Lowenthal, Piccone, and Whitehead, pp. 29–42.

52. Center for Global Prosperity, "The Index of Global Philanthropy and Remittances" (Washington: Hudson Institute, 2011) p. 13; Steven Radelet, *Emerging Africa: How 17 Countries Are Leading the Way* (Washington: Center for Global Development, 2010), pp. 105–6.

53. Jones, Pascual, and Stedman, *Power and Responsibility,* p. 172; Center for Systemic Peace, "Global Conflict Trends" March 15, 2011 (www.systemicpeace.org/conflict.htm [June 3, 2011]).

54. For an interesting articulation of this concept, see Ivo H. Daalder and Robert Kagan, "America and the Use of Force: Sources of Legitimacy," in *Bridging the Foreign Policy Divide,* edited by Derek Chollet, Tod Lindberg, and David Shorr (New York: Routledge, 2008), pp. 16–20. For a criticism of such a league of democracies, see Theodore J. Piccone, "Democracies: In a League of Their Own?" Foreign Policy Paper no. 8 (Brookings, October 2008), pp. 8–13 (www.brookings.edu/papers/2008/10_democracy_piccone.aspx [June 4, 2011]).

55. Elizabeth G. Ferris, *The Politics of Protection: The Limits of Humanitarian Action* (Brookings, 2011), pp. 162–70; Evans, *Responsibility to Protect,* pp. 31–54.

56. See, for example, Jeffrey Gettleman, "Brinkmanship in Sudan as a Deadline Nears," *New York Times*, June 6, 2011.

57. Jeffrey Gettleman, "Sudan Attacks Disputed Border State," *New York Times*, September 2, 2011.

58. See Richard Williamson, "How Obama Betrayed Sudan," *Foreign Policy*, November 11, 2011 (www.foreignpolicy.com/articles/2010/11/11/how_obama_betrayed_sudan?page=0,2 [June 6, 2011]).

59. George Clooney and John Prendergast, "Dancing with a Dictator in Sudan," *Washington Post*, May 27, 2011; Douglas H. Johnson, "Sudan's Peaceful Partition, at Risk," *New York Times*, May 30, 2011; Christiane Amanpour, "Analysts Weigh Obama's Global Human Rights Policies: Interview with Tom Malinowski," CNN, October 14, 2009.

60. See Jackson Diehl, "South Sudan Shows What Obama Can Do When He Leads," *Washington Post*, July 3, 2011; Dan Bilefsky, "U.N. Approves Troop Deployment in Sudan," *New York Times*, June 27, 2011.

61. "DR Congo War Deaths 'Exaggerated,'" BBC News, January 20, 2010.

62. International Crisis Group, "Conflict in Congo" (Brussels, January 27, 2011) (www.crisisgroup.org/en/key-issues/conflict-in-congo.aspx [June 6, 2011]).

63. For a good description of what such an effort might have entailed, see Anthony W. Gambino, *Congo: Securing Peace, Sustaining Progress* (New York: Council on Foreign Relations, October 2008), pp. 28–37. For a more recent assessment of Congo's historical challenges and recent lack of progress, see Jason K. Stearns, *Dancing in the Glory of Monsters: The Collapse of the Congo and the Great War of Africa* (New York: Public Affairs, 2011), pp. 327–37.

64. See International Institute for Strategic Studies, *The Military Balance 2009* (Oxfordshire, England: Routledge, 2009), p. 430; International Institute for Strategic Studies, *The Military Balance 2011* (Oxfordshire, England: Routledge, 2011), p. 456; Center on International Cooperation, *Global Peace Operations 2010*, p. 233.

65. President Obama's annual aid levels for Congo, actual and proposed, have been approximately $210 million to $280 million; under President Bush, aid levels (for all purposes combined for Congo) were roughly $200 million to $300 million. See U.S. Department of State, "Foreign Assistance by Country, 2006–2012 Request" (www.foreignassistance.gov/CountryIntro.aspx [June 9, 2011]).

66. Mvemba Phezo Dizolele, "The Mirage of Democracy in the DRC," *Journal of Democracy* 21, no. 3 (July 2010): 156.

67. Jeffrey Gettleman, "U.N. Officials Say Famine Is Widening in Somalia," *New York Times*, September 5, 2011.

68. See Alex Thurston, "Withdrawals, Lack of Pay for African Union's Somalia Forces Could Thwart Progress," *Christian Science Monitor*, June 6, 2011.

69. Bush administration funding for 2008 and 2009 averaged about $300 million a year; funding under Obama has averaged about $100 million annually. See U.S. Department of State, "Foreign Assistance by Country."

70. Thurston, "Withdrawals, Lack of Pay for African Union's Somalia Forces."

71. See, for example, International Crisis Group, "Somalia: The Transitional Government on Life Support," Africa Report no. 170 (Brussels, February 2011) (www.crisisgroup.org/en/regions/Africa/horn-of-africa/Somalia/170-somalia-the-transitional-govenrment-on-life-support.aspx [June 5, 2011]).

72. International Crisis Group, "Somalia's Divided Islamists," Africa Policy Briefing no. 74 (Brussels, May 18, 2010) (www.crisisgroup.org/en/regions/africa/horn-of-africa/somalia/B074-somalias-divided-islamists.aspx [June 1, 2011]).

73. Ginger Thompson and Simon Romero, "Clinton Aims to Improve Ties with Latin America," *New York Times,* May 18, 2011.

74. International Bank for Reconstruction and Development, *World Development Report 2011* (Washington: World Bank, 2011), pp. 350–51 (http://wdr2011.world bank.org/sites/default/files/WDR2011_Indicators.pdf [June 9, 2011]).

75. Kevin Casas-Zamora, "Democracy in Latin America: Miles Traveled and Miles to Go," February 2, 2011 (www.brookings.edu/opinions/2011/0202_latin_america_casaszamora.aspx [June 9, 2011]); Riordan Roett, *The New Brazil* (Brookings, 2010).

76. Tom A. Peter, "Mexico Denies Hillary Clinton's 'Insurgency' Comparison," *Christian Science Monitor,* September 9, 2009.

77. About 70 percent of illicit guns seized in Mexico had American origins, according to recent estimates. See Mark Stevenson, "U.S. Report: 70 Percent of Arms Seized, Traced in Mexico Came from U.S.," *Winnipeg Free Press,* June 13, 2011 (www.winnipegfreepress.com/breakingnews/us-report-70-per-cent-of-arms-seized-traced-in-mexico-came-from-us.html [July 15, 2011]); Mary Beth Sheridan, "Treaty to Curb Gun Smuggling to Mexico Remains Stalled," *Washington Post,* October 22, 2010, p. A19.

78. Randal C. Archibold, "Mexican Police Arrest Leader of Crime Gang," *New York Times,* June 21, 2011.

79. Victor E. Renuart Jr. and Biff Baker, "U.S.-Mexico Homeland Defense: A Compatible Interface," *Strategic Forum,* no. 254 (February 2010): 2; Mauricio Cardenas, "Beyond the Crisis: Thinking Strategically about Mexico's Economic Future," remarks at Brookings Institution, Washington, June 25, 2010 (www.brookings.edu/~/media/Files/events/2010/0625_mexico_economy/20100625_mexico_economy.pdf [June 9, 2011]).

80. Heredia and Rozental, "Mexico and the United States,", pp. 29–42.

81. Binyamin Appelbaum, "U.S. and Mexico Sign Trucking Deal," *New York Times,* July 6, 2011.

82. U.S. Department of State, "Foreign Assistance by Country."

83. For an explanation of ink-spot strategy, see Vanda Felbab-Brown, "The Violent Drug Market in Mexico and Lessons from Colombia," Foreign Policy Paper no. 12 (Brookings, March 2009) (www.brookings.edu/~/media/Files/rc/papers/2009/03_mexico_drug_market_felbabbrown/03_mexico_drug_market_felbabbrown.pdf [June 8, 2011]); Felbab-Brown, *Shooting Up: Counterinsurgency and the War on Drugs* (Brookings, 2009).

84. Diana Villiers Negroponte, "Crisis in the U.S.-Mexican Relationship," March 2, 2011 (www.brookings.edu/opinions/2011/0302_calderon_negroponte.aspx [June 9, 2011]).

85. Shifter, "The United States and Colombia: Recalibrating the Relationship," pp. 55–56.

86. See, for example, James G. Stavridis, *Partnership for the Americas: Western Hemisphere Strategy and U.S. Southern Command* (National Defense University Press, 2010), p. 243.

87. International Crisis Group, "Colombia: President Santos's Conflict Resolution Opportunity," October 13, 2010 (www.crisisgroup.org/~/media/Files/latin-america/colombia/34%20Colombia%20-%20President%20Santoss%20Conflict%20Resolution%20Opportunity.ashx [June 9, 2011]).

88. Annual funding was over $500 million in the latter Bush years but has dropped below that, and the 2012 Obama administration request was $400 million. U.S. Department of State, "Foreign Assistance by Country."

89. For discussion of some of these concepts, see Jones, Pascual, and Stedman, *Power and Responsibility*, pp. 195–203. For a proposal to reorganize the new structures to create a more powerful agency to coordinate the efforts, see John C. Vara, "National Security and the Interagency Enterprise: A Critical Analysis," in *Preparing for an Era of Persistent Conflict*, edited by Tammy S. Schultz (Marine Corps University, 2011), pp. 25–40. The *Quadrennial Diplomacy and Development Review* proposed a departmental reorganization that would affect existing structures for these activities but without substantially elevating their bureaucratic clout. See U.S. Department of State and U.S. Agency for International Development, *Leading through Civilian Power*, p. 7.

90. See, for example, Michael E. O'Hanlon, *Budgeting for Hard Power: Defense and Security Spending under Barack Obama* (Brookings, 2009), pp. 61–75.

91. White House, *National Security Strategy*.

92. Nina M. Serafino, "Peacekeeping/Stabilization and Conflict Transitions: Background and Congressional Action on the Civilian Response/Reserve Corps and Other Civilian Stabilization and Reconstruction Capabilities," Congressional Research Service Report for Congress, March 4, 2011, pp. 16–21 (www.fas.org/sgp/crs/natsec/RL32862.pdf [June 1, 2011]).

93. See, for example, U.S. Department of State and U.S. Agency for International Development, *Leading through Civilian Power*, pp. 107–58.

94. Nancy Soderberg, "Enhancing U.S. Support for U.N. Peacekeeping," *Prism* 2, no. 2 (2011): 23 (www.ndu.edu/press/lib/images/prism2-2/Prism_15-28_Soderberg.pdf [June 7, 2011]); Marjorie Ann Browne, "U.N. System Funding: Congressional Issues," Congressional Research Service Report for Congress, January 14, 2011, pp. 1–22 (www.fas.org/sgp/crs/row/RL33611.pdf [June 7, 2011]).

NOTES TO CHAPTER 8

1. See Strobe Talbott, "Obama and the World: A Promise at Risk," Ditchley Foundation Lecture, Ditchley, England, July 10, 2010 (www.brookings.edu/speeches/2010/0710-obama-foreign-policy-talbott.aspx [October 6, 2011]).

2. Daniel W. Drezner, "Does Obama Have a Grand Strategy?" *Foreign Affairs* 90, no. 4 (July-August 2011): 57–68.

3. Fareed Zakaria, "Stop Searching for an Obama Doctrine," *Washington Post*, July 6, 2011.

4. For another reasonably positive interim assessment, see Robert Kagan, "America: Once Engaged, Now Ready to Lead," *Washington Post*, October 1, 2010, p. A19.

5. For a good discussion of some of these ideas and trends, see Eric S. Edelman, *Understanding America's Contested Primacy* (Washington: Center for Strategic and Budgetary Assessments, 2010); Bruce Jones, "Largest Minority Shareholder In

Global Order LLC: The Changing Balance of Influence and U.S. Strategy," Foreign Policy Paper no. 25 (Brookings, 2011).

6. See, for example, Frederick W. Kagan, *Finding the Target: The Transformation of American Military Policy* (New York: Encounter Books, 2006), pp. 180–97, 222–36, 281–86.

7. On the demands of the Iraq surge, for example, see Kimberly Kagan, *The Surge: A Military History* (New York: Encounter Books, 2009), pp. xix–xxxii.

8. Michael O'Hanlon, *Unfinished Business: U.S. Overseas Military Presence in the 21st Century* (Washington: Center for a New American Security, 2008), p. 37.

9. Vanda Felbab-Brown, "A Shared Responsibility: Counternarcotics and Citizens' Security in the Americas," testimony before the Subcommittee on the Western Hemisphere, Peace Corps, and Global Narcotics Affairs, Senate Foreign Relations Committee, March 31, 2011 (www.brookings.edu/testimony/2011/0331_counter narcotics_felbabbrown.aspx [April 1, 2011]).

10. On the trends, see Curt Tarnoff and Marian Leonardo Lawson, "Foreign Aid: An Introduction to U.S. Programs and Policy," Congressional Research Service, February 10, 2011, p. 31 (www.fas.org/sgp/crs/row/R40213.pdf [April 1, 2011]).

11. See, for example, Steven Radelet, *Emerging Africa: How 17 Countries Are Leading the Way* (Washington: Center for Global Development, 2010), pp. 54–60, 77–107; Wolfgang Fengler and Homi Kharas, "Overview: Delivering Aid Differently," in *Delivering Aid Differently: Lessons from the Field,* edited by Wolfgang Fengler and Homi Kharas (Brookings, 2010), pp. 1–41.

12. See Teresita C. Schaffer, "U.S.-India Strategic Dialogue: All-Star Cast, Playing Small Ball," Brookings Institution Blog, July 19, 2011 (www.brookings.edu/opinions/2011/0718_clinton_india_schaffer.aspx?p=1 [August 1, 2011]); Michael Green and Daniel Twining, "Why Aren't We Working with Japan and India?" *Washington Post,* July 18, 2011; Andrew H. Card and Thomas A. Daschle, chairs, *U.S. Trade and Investment Policy,* Independent Task Force Report no. 70 (New York: Council on Foreign Relations, 2011), p. 70 (http://i.cfr.org/content/publications/attachments/Trade_TFR67.pdf [January 7, 2011]).

13. For example, in the middle of the previous decade, a program was proposed to provide 50 percent compensation for lost wages for two years, up to a cap of $10,000 a year; it would have cost around $5 billion a year. See Lael Brainard, Robert E. Litan, and Nicholas Warren, "A Fairer Deal for America's Workers in a New Era of Offshoring," in *Brookings Trade Forum: Off-Shoring White Collar Work,* edited by Lael Brainard and Susan M. Collins (Brookings, 2005), pp. 427–56 (http://muse.jhu.edu/journals/brookings_trade_forum/v2005/2005.1brainard02.html [April 20, 2011]).

14. See, for example, Metropolitan Policy Program, *Metro Policy: Shaping a New Federal Partnership for a Metropolitan Nation* (Brookings, 2008); Rosanne Altshuler and Barry P. Bosworth, "Fiscal Consolidation in America: The Policy Options," December 7, 2010, p. 22 (www.brookings.edu/papers/2010/1207_fiscal_consolidation_altshuler_bosworth.aspx).

15. Klaus Schwab, "The Global Competitiveness Report 2011–2012," *World Economic Forum,* Fall 2011, p. 15 (www3.weforum.org/docs/WEF_GCR_Report_2011-12.pdf).

INDEX

Surnames starting with al- are alphabetized by the following part of the name.

331

INDEX

state, 17–18, 261; on Arab Spring, 141–42, 154, 156; Burma visit by, 60, 222; and Egypt's transition of power, 146–47, 149; and Iran, 202; and Iraq war, 74, 77; and Libya, 161, 165, 248; on Mexico's drug violence, 253; and Middle East peace process, 112, 121, 123, 129–30, 133, 138, 139; as presidential candidate, 2, 6; and Russia, 195; on soft security agenda, 231; and South China Sea territorial disputes, 48; and Syria, 169, 173; and U.S.–China Strategic and Economic Dialogue, 55
Coal, 233–34, 235
Cohen, William, 282
Coll, Steve, 104
Colombia, free trade agreement with, 247, 255
Communications issues, 88–89
Communist Party (China), 29
Comprehensive Iran Sanctions, Accountability, and Divestment Act of 2010 (U.S.), 203
Comprehensive national power, 28
Congressional Budget Office, 7
Containment policy, 275
Convention of the Law of the Sea (UN), 50
Copenhagen Conference (2009), 13, 29, 35, 36, 238–39, 262
Corruption, 97
Countercyclical tools, 8
Counterinsurgency operations, 87–88, 92, 281
Counterterrorism, 14–15, 99–110
Craig, Greg, 18–19
Criminal activity, 232
Crocker, Ryan, 89
Currency valuation, 39, 52, 266
Cybersecurity, 50–51

Dai Bingguo, 54, 55
Dalai Lama, 39, 40
Damascus Spring (2001), 167
Daughters of Iraq, 82

Davutoglu, Ahmet, 168, 177
Debt forgiveness and relief, 105, 247
Defense Cooperation Agreement (U.S.–Brazil), 252
Democratic Party of Japan (DPJ), 43, 46, 226
Democratic Republic of Congo, as failed or failing state, 233, 247, 250–51
Democratization: and Asian policy, 60–61; and China, 29, 60–61; in Middle East, 15, 143
Disarmament, 186
Domestic policy: and climate change, 238–41
Donilon, Tom, 20, 133, 157, 196
DPJ. *See* Democratic Party of Japan
Drone strikes, 71, 103, 106, 265
Drug trade, 245

East Asia Summit, 59
East China Sea territorial disputes, 39, 46–47
East Jerusalem: and Middle East peace process, 117, 130; settlements in, 120, 123–31, 138
Economic policy: and Asian policy, 59; and China, 51–53, 59
Edwards, John, 3, 74
EEZs. *See* Exclusive Economic Zones
Egypt: and Arab Spring, 113–14, 132, 142, 144–50, 180; and democratization, 272; Israel peace agreement with, 114, 142, 145, 180; military aid to, 145; and Syria's Arab Spring response, 177
Eikenberry, Karl, 87, 94, 96, 272
El Baradei, Mohammed, 243
Elections: in Democratic Republic of Congo, 251; in Egypt, 146; in Iran, 191; in Iraq, 76–77, 79, 85; in Palestine, 115, 188
Electricity, 80, 235
Emanuel, Rahm, 138, 140
Energy policy, 233–44; and alternative energy, 241–44; and China, 25; and international vs. domestic politics,

334